THE SÁMI PEOPLES OF THE NORTH

NEIL KENT

The Sámi Peoples of the North

A Social and Cultural History

HURST & COMPANY, LONDON

First published in the United Kingdom in 2018 by
C. Hurst & Co. (Publishers) Ltd.,
41 Great Russell Street, London, WC1B 3PL
This paperback edition published 2018
© Neil Kent, 2018
All rights reserved.
Printed in the United Kingdom

Distributed in the United States, Canada and Latin America by
Oxford University Press, 198 Madison Avenue, New York, NY 10016,
United States of America.

The right of Neil Kent to be identified as the author of
this publication is asserted by him in accordance with the
Copyright, Designs and Patents Act, 1988.

A Cataloguing-in-Publication data record for this book
is available from the British Library.

ISBN: 9781787380318

www.hurstpublishers.com

This book is printed on paper from registered sustainable
and managed sources.

CONTENTS

ACKNOWLEDGEMENTS

I would especially like to thank Professor Leif Rantala (formerly of the University of Lapland, Rovaniemi, Finland), and Dr Inga-Maria Mulk (formerly of the Ájtte Museum, Jokkmokk, Sweden), who expended many hours assisting me with this book. Others who enriched my research include Professor Tim Bayliss-Smith (University of Cambridge), Professor Knut Helskog (Tromsö Museum, Tromsö, Norway), Tarmo Jomppanen (director of the Sámi Museum, Ivalo, Finland), Jouni Laiti of the Sámi Council and Leena Jansson (University Library, Helsinki, Finland). Above all I am grateful to the Nordic Culture Fund, Copenhagen, which provided the resources to make my research and this book possible.

AUTHOR'S NOTE

This book is intended for both an academic as well as a more general audience. I endeavour to give a general overview of the Sámi throughout their history, whilst at the same time homing in on more detailed aspects of their life. While I am fluent in all the major Nordic languages and Russian, I have also endeavoured to acquire some knowledge of Northern Sámi, but am no professional linguist in this area. Most Sámi names have been provided in Northern Sámi but there are occasional inconsistences, in particular, when sources using other Sámi dialects have been included.

INTRODUCTION

What is Sápmi?

On 4 February 2009 an article appeared in the *Daily Telegraph* entitled 'Family Adventures in the Arctic Wilderness', about the visit of a British family to Swedish Lapland. The caption to the article's photograph boldly stated that 'Lapland is a largely unpeopled vastness that spans a northern swath of Sweden.'[1] The indigenous inhabitants—the Sámi people—were not even mentioned once: it was as if they did not exist. But is the Sámi homeland really a wilderness and is it really largely unpeopled? To some extent, both questions can be answered in the affirmative—the area known as Lapland is among the most sparsely populated in Europe, and its vast, often snow-covered landscape has long served to attract those enamoured by its natural, unspoiled beauty. Yet such sweeping assertions hardly do justice to the vitality of the Sámi homeland and the rich culture and history of the Sámi people, who have inhabited the region for thousands of years. Indeed, the oldest settlements in Finnmark, in the north of Norway, are Sarnes, near Magerøya, and on the Varangerfjord, both of which were already settled in the early Stone Age, the Sámi having migrated there from both the north and the south, according to their ancient sagas.[2]

If one is to rely on data relating to research on DNA, however, it seems more likely that the ancestors of the Sámi in fact came from Central Europe, even if their language came from the east, where the Finno-Ugric languages disseminated. In this latter context, the modern Sámi and Finnish languages have a common Finnic linguistic ancestor spoken by both the Sámi and the Finns at the beginning of the first millennium BC.[3]

1

What constitutes an indigenous people is of course a complicated issue, and even when this is resolved for those concerned, their rights remain a matter of considerable dispute. For those who consider the area in the Nordic countries and north-western Russia known as Sápmi to be their home, it is a subject of great import. After all, Sápmi extends over a territory almost 400,000 square kilometres in size, with a Sámi population, according to the Sámi Parliament of Finland (there is no official census), of more than 45,000 in Norway, 20,000 in Sweden, 8,000 in Finland and 2,000 in Russia—a total of between 75,000 and 100,000 people.[4]

To a certain degree, new peoples could be, were and continue to be absorbed into the Sámi nation, but when their presence became overwhelming this process often meant not the absorption of the newcomers into the Sámi, but that of the Sámi into the wider general population. It has thus been said that Sápmi, as it is today in the far north of Fenno-Scandia and the Kola Peninsula, is in fact the result of this negative process which began further south, when the Sámi still resided in those areas.[5]

Yet regardless of how they first became established in the region, the Sámi have long perceived Sápmi to be their homeland, one in which the intrusion of their southerly neighbours has been an unwelcome, and indeed overwhelming, experience. The Skolt Sámi of the east, for example, trace their history on the Kola Peninsula back for millennia, a concept of historical identity which is reflected in the modern writings of the Sámi there:

For a long, long time we have lived in the country of the North, where the sun did not shine. And the moon did not shine. It was a thoroughly dark country. Only the stars could be seen in the dark firmament ... And the people of this country did not know of fire. They lived on things from turf and twigs ... That is the way people lived in this land of darkness for thousands of years. And they will live there for thousands of years to come. And for a further thousand and yet another ...[6]

Although it has been said by some that the word 'Kola' derives from the Kildin Sámi word *koall*, signifying 'gold', in this context a golden river, it seems far more likely that it refers to 'fish' and that the signification is therefore 'Fisherman's River'.[7] In any case, it is clear that the Sámi have lived in the region for thousands of years despite the harshness of the climate and its extremely short growing season, which is only 120 days long in the north. They have been enabled to do so by the extraordinary warming effect of the Gulf Stream,[8] which has allowed dairy farming to be practised as far north as Utsjoki in northern Finnish Lapland.[9] Yet the warmth of the Gulf Stream during the summer months cannot be taken for granted because it snows in June in Sápmi almost every year.[10] As the entire region is also blanketed by snow throughout the winter, it is perhaps not surprising that the Sámi language is rich in words which describe different types of snow. For example, the word *čearga* (in North Sámi) is used to refer to hard-packed snow, while *seanas* signifies a type of dry, rough-grained snow, near ground level.[11]

Another highly specific northern physical characteristic of Sápmi is the presence of the Aurora Borealis, or Northern Lights. It was previously believed that there was an old Sámi legend according to which this natural phenomenon was caused by a fox which had stirred up a cloud of snowflakes by a flick of the tail, creating a dazzling reflection of the moonlight.[12] However, it is now commonly held that this is incorrect. Rather, the connection of the fox to the Northern Lights relates to the fact that they are called *revontulet* in Finnish (i.e. 'fires of the fox'). In Sámi the correct term for the Northern Lights, *guovssahasat*, has no connection to a fox.[13]

The Geography of Sápmi

The Sámi homeland stretches across a broad swathe of northern Fenno-Scandinavia, eastwards to the Kola Peninsula, in what is geographically known as the Arctic-Alpine zone. The high coastal mountains which skirt much of the region have a climate heavily influenced by the ocean and are cool and wet during the summers and cold and snowy during the winters. However, beyond them to the south and east, summers are typically of the continental type: drier and warmer than the coastal areas in summer but brutally cold in winter, with only four months during which the ground is free of snow cover. Its lakes are frozen for at least half the year.

A map of Lapland from 1594, which was the result of the surveying skills of an expedition led by the Dutch cartographer Jan Huyghen van Linschoten, is one of the earliest to show the geographical scope of the Sámi homeland.[14] Already by this time, the coastal areas as far east as Russia were important for Western European trading interests. Kildin, an island off the northern coast of the Kola Peninsula, was an important trading centre for the Europeans as well as the Sámi and it featured prominently in the atlas of van Linschoten, which appeared in 1601, accompanied by exotic but realistic illustrations of Sámi huts, smoke streaming upwards from their central, chimney-less hearths, along with images of European sailing ships and Sámi boats.[15] More widely disseminated was another map of Lapland, including the Kola Peninsula, published that same year by the Dutchman Simon van Salingen and entitled *Lappia par Norwegiæ*, which had been commissioned by the Danish king, Christian IV, two years before.

The map at the end of Johannes Schefferus's book *Lapponia*, first published in Latin in 1673, depicts Lapland as extending down the shores of both sides of the Gulf of Bothnia, well beyond Umeå and Nykarleby. The mountains of Sweden to the south-west, the Arctic Ocean to the north and the northern, western and southern shores of the White Sea are also included in this early printed work about the Sámi. Born in 1621 in Strasbourg, then part of the Holy Roman Empire, the author eventually emigrated to Sweden where he became a professor at Uppsala University in 1648. His book, which is richly illustrated with copperplate pictures and includes depictions of Sámi winter and summer clothing,[16] ultimately became much more widely known than Olaus Magnus's monumental work of the previous century.

Another important figure who conveyed information about the Sámi was Hans Hansen Lilienskiöld (c.1650–1703), who worked as a government official in Finnmark from 1685 to 1701. Towards the end of the seventeenth century he wrote and illustrated *Speculum Boreale* (The Northern Looking Glass), a book in which he describes the geography, history and economy of the region with colourful illustrations of Sámi dress,[17] among the most striking of which are perhaps his coloured illustration of Varanger reindeer herders.[18] Yet another noted figure in regard to disseminating knowledge of the Sámi was Knud Leem (1697–1774), a Lutheran missionary in Porsanger and Ávjovárri from 1724 to 1728. Later the rector of the parish of Alta from 1728 to 1734, he went on to produce *Beskrivelse over Finnmarkens lapper* (A Description of the Lapps of the Finnmark), which was published in 1767 and included 100 copperplate illustrations by Odvardt Helmoldt von Lode depicting the exotic qualities of Sámi dress.[19]

Yet for visitors to Sápmi in the modern period it was more the ardours of the climate than the inhabitants themselves which most impressed and repelled them. As the Italian diplomat and traveller

Giuseppe (Joseph in the English edition of his reminiscences) Acerbi (1773–1846), a native of Mantua, wrote after his visit there, 'The long continuance of the winter and its horrors; the oppressive multitude of tormenting insects in the summer, would, in the opinion of most men, counterbalance any advantages which the beauty of the situation, or the allurements of rural life, could present.'[20] Whatever these beauties might have been, the Italian anthropologist Paulo Mantegazza, writing in the late nineteenth century, was hardly impressed. He found the nature monotonous, declaring that, 'All the mountains of Lapland look the same ...'[21] And, like so many others before him, he lamented, 'I don't speak of the mosquitoes, which are the primary plague of a Lapland journey.'[22] The small settlements of the Sámi also filled him with scorn:

Kautokeino is, indeed, a great and beautiful city! Some twenty houses all of wood, 200 inhabitants composing 40 families, and, in the winter, 600 Lapp nomads, encamped in the metropolis from a radius of a hundred kilometres.[23]

Yet despite all that the Sámi could sometimes be perceived as a noble, albeit savage people, unspoilt by civilisation. As Acerbi put it, 'I have seen very few places where the people live in so easy and happy a simplicity as in the maritime districts of Lapland.'[24]And even Mantegazza later came to find aspects of the Sámi highly praiseworthy, noting that 'We have seen old people quite well preserved, without any infirmity, aged between 80 and 90.'[25]

Early Settlement of Fenno-Scandia

By the beginning of the nineteenth century there was thus a general awareness throughout Europe of the long-established existence and individuality of the Sámi people and their culture. However, few, even among the Sámi, were aware of how ancient and deep-rooted they were in the region, where human settlement had been established for millennia.

It was following the retreat of the ice towards the end of the Ice Age that diverse groups of people first arrived in Fenno-Scandia and today's far north-western Russia. Some came from the region of modern-day Denmark and the outlying areas now submerged under the North Sea. They mainly hunted wild reindeer, gradually moving northwards along the Norwegian littoral, first arriving on the Fisherman's Peninsula by about 9000 BC and creating settlements similar to the earliest Palaeolithic ones of Scania, in the south of the Scandinavian Peninsula. The settlement found at Slettnes, situated on the island of Sørøya in the north Norwegian province of Finnmark, has been dated to between 9200 and 8000 BC,[26] while ancient settlements in the Lule river valley at Stora Sjöfallet and at Killingholmen, by Lake Fatjats, date back to around 6000 BC.[27] By this time climate warming had occurred and the winters were in fact considerably milder than they are today, enabling rich mixed forests to thrive, full of alder, birch and pine, with plentiful game, including reindeer and elk, and lakes well stocked with fish, all of which these mesolithic peoples could exploit.[28]

However, it took over a millennium—until about 7900 BC—for these people from the Arctic coast of Norway to settle in the vicinities of what are now Inari and Utsjoki, in Finnish Lapland, with the remaining areas of Finnish Lapland and the Kola Peninsula becoming occupied by 7300 BC. Northern Sweden, on the other hand, took until around 7000 BC to be settled by people arriving from Norway.[29] Further settlements followed over the course of the next millennia, and between 2000 BC and the dawn of the Christian era Lákšjohka, in Tana, was settled. As the archaeologist Marianne Skandfer put it in the newspaper *Finnmark*, while carrying out excavations there on 24 August 2006, 'I cannot say the Sámi lived there, but I can say that we have found a settlement of the ancestors of the Sámi.'[30]

Actual Sámi hunters, though, were settled at Karlebotn in Varanger by 2000 BC, at a time when agriculture had already been implemented in the lowlands of the south of Norway. Indeed, archaeological remains have been uncovered of their rectangular dwellings, 4 by 9 metres in dimension, as well as such practical implements as knives, nails and harpoons.[31] Thus by the dawn of the Christian era the Sámi were firmly established not only in most of northern Norway and the northern half of the province of Norrland in Sweden, but in all of Finland, the Kola Peninsula and what is today Russian Karelia,[32] where local place names with reference to the Sámi can be found as far south as the town of Medvezhegorsk (or Karhumäki in Finnish).[33]

Early Sámi Petroglyphs (Stone Carvings) and the Rock Art Site of Badjelánnda

One area in which the aesthetic and religious aspirations of the Sámi found expression was petroglyphs (i.e. rock engravings) and in partic- ular the production of rock art—something in which the Sámi excelled—the remains of which are to be found throughout the Sámi homeland. The oldest of these date from a period around 6,200 years ago. These are now located some 25 metres above sea level, but those carved about two and a half millennia ago are only 8.5 metres above sea level. Of great international importance, those found at Hjemmeluft, in Alta, were placed on UNESCO's World Heritage List in 1985.[34]

More recently, Inga-Maria Mulk and Tim Bayliss-Smith have provided us with great insights with respect to early Sámi rock art from their research at Badjelánnda (formerly Padjelanta), which was only discovered in 1990. Among the most prominent are the anthropomorphic figures which are said to be stylised representations of the mother earth entity *Mattáráhkká*.[35] Also striking are recognisable elements of shipping, including sails, rigging, dinghies and anchors, which is not surprising since large sailing boats ploughed the seas off the northern coast of Norway as early as the eighth century. Such images as these were not mere decorations but were instead symbolic of the spiritual cosmology which informed much of Sámi life and was deemed to assist them—with the help of shamans—in their passage from this world to the next.[36]

The world in which the Sámi lived had its own inconstancies. By around 3000 BC the climate of the region became significantly cooler. In consequence, pine and spruce came to dominate, and in the Lule Valley fishing from lakes became increasingly difficult, encouraging settlements at higher altitudes, such as that at Lake Virihávrre from around 3000 BC, where the fish were found to be plentiful. The hunting pits from the vicinity of Lake Sállohávrre also date from this period.[37]

Further environmental changes, from about 2000 BC, obliged the inhabitants of the North Calotte to abandon their sedentary settlements in favour of a more migratory life in which their activities and movements varied according to the seasons. This new mode of living would be a pattern of life followed by the majority of the Sámi for almost 4,000 years: the establishment of sedentary winter settlements in forested areas with summers spent in migration by lakes and among the foothills of the mountains, which form a spine inland from the coast.[38]

A period of increasing warmth and bounty was followed by one that was once again cooler and less hospitable, so that by about 500 BC the tree line had receded and a climate like that of today had come into being. A lower tree line meant a reduction in the hunting resources available to the Sámi, but it also demanded a wider scope for their roaming, one which increasingly brought them into contact with other peoples to the south and east.[39]

Contacts with the Mediterranean World

It has long been maintained that the first, albeit sparse, mention of the Sámi is to be found in the Latin work *Germania* (AD 98) by the Roman senator and historian Publius Cornelius Tacitus (AD 56–117), who called them *fenni*. They were a people, he remarked, who travelled on skis. At this time the Sámi lived and ranged far to the south of their current homeland. Etymologists consider the root of the word *finn* to be of Germanic origin and such word was never used by the Sámi themselves. It therefore signifies a nomadic and hunting people, rather than a specific ethnic group.[40] Thereafter, it was the Byzantine historian Prokopios of Caesarea (c.490–c.562) who again wrote about them, calling them *skritiphinoi*, that is, *fenni* 'who propel themselves on skis' and reside in tent-like structures. Next is the eighth-century Lombard historian Paulus Diaconus, who noted the importance of reindeer in their lives, the first comment upon this animal with respect to the Sámi, whose presence since has been seen as inexorably intertwined with them. Yet it was only in about 1300 with the production of the famed *Hereford Mapa Mundi* that the first illustration of a Sámi man travelling on skis appeared, against the background of a map of Norway.[41]

Óttar's Chronicles

Norway, with its extensive coastline long sought out by traders, became the medium through which foreigners to the region increasingly experienced the Sámi, especially during the late Iron Age which took place during AD 750–1300.

Archaeological remains from this period are rich and include iron accoutrements for horses and blades found in the vicinity of Inari, in the far north of today's Finland.[42] Already in 871, the Sámi were written about, after the British king Alfred of Wessex, received the Norse warrior-chief Ottar, at his court. This occurred within the introduction to the abridged and translated historical chronicles originally written by Paulus Orosius in the early fifth century AD. Tradition has it that this was carried out by the king himself. However, modern scholarship largely rejects this. Crossing the North Sea to England from his northern Fenno-Scandinavian homeland, Ottar had presented the West Saxon king with no less than 600 reindeer, six special decoy reindeer and furs, as well as providing him with a great cultural, economic and political insight into the life of his people. Said to have been a late ninth-century princeling of Hålogaland on the northern coast of Norway opposite the Lofoten Islands, Ottar spoke in depth of the hunting of whales and walruses and the delivery of tribute tax in furs and skins by the Sámi to their local overlords. For example, he noted that the richest, probably representing their poorer brethren as well, delivered five marten pelts and five wild reindeer pelts, a bearskin, 10 tonnes of down, another pelt of either bear or otter, as well as two ropes made of either seal or whale skin that were suitable for ships.[43] In this context it was not without reason that the Sámi word for walrus, *morša*, was rapidly adopted at this time as a loanword in a wide range of European languages including Russian, French and English.[44] Ottar also left the first written record of his visit to the north of Norway and eastwards to the Kola Peninsula and the White Sea, encountering Sámi fishermen and hunters on the way. He himself was just one link, albeit an important one, in the mercantile web emanating from Western and Central Europe after 800.[45] Reindeer hides were a significant element of this trade and were to remain an important trading commodity for over 1,000 years, as the remains of an eighteenth-century Norwegian ship, the *Metta Catharina*, clearly demonstrate: when the wreck was found off the English coast in the 1970s, the remains of many reindeer hides were found on board.[46]

After 1000, the Norwegian king was himself able to seize control of Hålogaland and other northern centres of power to the detriment of local warrior-chiefs in the Sámi homeland. As a result, the Norwegian monarch was able to levy his own tribute tax, known as *finneskatten*. His heirs followed this aggrandisement of power and in 1114 the Norwegian king declared that the Sámi dwelling north of 'Umeyarsund' (i.e. Vennesund in Brønnøy) would henceforth be obliged to pay tax to him exclusively, thereby bringing the Sámi into conflict with the powerful Russian mercantile Republic of Novgorod, which also laid claim on Sámi tribute.[47]

This was obviously a profitable arrangement for the Norwegian king, as is clear from the Norse chronicle *Historia Norvegiæ* which was written in the second half of the twelfth century and describes the life of the Sámi and their reindeer hunting and fur-trading while underscoring just how much revenue thereby accrued to the monarch. Various features of Sámi life were also noted, including their ability to travel on skis and their special footwear, known as *ondrer*, as well as their domestic arrangements; in particular, it is discussed how they reside in huts of bark which they carry on their shoulders while migrating rather than living in houses.[48]

Speed and ease of migration were highly important to the Sámi during the Middle Ages for means of escape as much as for hunting and fishing. The Chuds, probably a Finnic-speaking people who lived in Russian Karelia, south of the White Sea, infringed aggressively upon the Sámi and were themselves spurred on by an increasingly aggressive Republic of Novgorod, which was jealous of Norway and frequently attacked both the Chuds and the Sámi, seizing their furs and skins. Archaeological remains of the Sámi from this period, including artefacts made of reindeer horn and bronze, such as a ladle, pegs and other practical items attesting to the high level of their civilisation,[49] have been uncovered at Vestvatn, Skjerstad in Salten, and are now exhibited in the Tromsø Museum in Norway.

The Sámi and Later Chronicles

In the eleventh century a German ecclesiastical chronicler, Adam of Bremen, considered the Sámi in his four-volume Latin work, *Gesta Hammaburgensis ecclesiae pontificum*. Yet it was the Danish historian Saxo Grammaticus who through allusions elevated the Sámi to concrete historical figures for a wider public in his famed Norse lyric poem *Völundarkviða* and the epic *Egils* saga. In particular, he focuses upon the value of the tribute they provided the Norse magnates in terms of fur, down and other commodities and for which, in return, they received iron tools, grain and other items. In another saga, *Heimskringla*, it is even reported that the late ninth- and early tenth-century Norse king Harald Fairhair had married a Sámi woman. Here, for one of the first times in European literature, the Sámi are linked to sorcery and witchcraft: in the *Sagas of the Kings*, the monarch's son, Erik, is reported to have met a woman who was said to have learnt witchcraft while residing among the Sámi.

Various chronicles of the following centuries also mention the Sámi: in Saxo Grammaticus's *Danmarks krønike*, written in about 1200, the term '*lapp*' is used, taken from the contemporary Swedish term for the Sámi. However, in the first half of the thirteenth century, the Icelandic *Vatnsdæla* saga appears to 'speak' of the Sámi using the term *semsveinar*.[50]

As for the word 'Lapp', some have maintained that the origin of the term is to be found in the Karelian word *Loppi* and the Finnish word *Lappi*, each of which signify the 'end' or 'limits', possibly referring to their location on at the far reaches of the known world, on its edge. This view enjoys a general consensus today, even if there are some dissenting opinions on the matter. The Finn Toivo I. Itkonen, for example, took a slightly differing view, maintaining that in Finnish the root of the word *Lape* or *Lappea* means 'side', while his brother Erkki Itkonen saw the word as deriving from the Swedish word *Lapp*, or 'place'.[51] This latter view, which has been shown to be erroneous, is based upon the confusion of Soviet linguists of the early 1980s who used a mistranslation of the Finnish equivalent *paikka*, sometimes meaning 'place' but in this instance signifying 'patch'.[52]

Whatever the origins, however, it should be noted that today the word is widely felt to have derogative connotations. Indeed, the Sámi Liitto (The Sámi Association) had begun to discourage its usage as far back as the end of the Second World War, while in 1930 a policy had already been initiated by Professor N.N. Poppe and S.E. Chernyakov in the Soviet Kola Peninsula to use the Finnish term 'Sámi', rather than 'Lopar' (Lapp), in reference to this population.[53]

Growth of Norwegian Colonisation

Increasingly, and especially from the middle of the thirteenth century, Norwegian colonists had made inroads into Sámi territory in the north of Norway. By 1300 not only the Norwegians had settled in the environs of Varanger, but also some Danes, Germans, Dutch, Scots and Faroese, all drawn there by the rich bounty of the fishing grounds. While the Sámi may have resented their presence, the prosperous merchants of Novgorod actually fiercely contested them, using their Karelian allies and henchmen to carry out raids against them. In response, Norway turned its far eastern outpost of Vardø into a powerful fortress, a major administrative centre and a bulwark against the encroachments of Russian Novgorod.[54]

Meanwhile, to the south, the Peace of Nöteborg which was signed in 1323 with Novgorod confirmed Swedish sovereignty over Finland.

Norway then followed suit in 1326, making a treaty with the Republic of Novgorod which not only established peace but confirmed its trade and taxation rights over the Sámi in a territory stretching from the White Sea north to Malangen, thereby encompassing effectively the whole of the Kola Peninsula. However, the peace proved lasting only on paper: both the Sámi and the colonising Nordic settlers continued to suffer the brunt of attacks from Novgorod well into the 1400s, a situation which only ended when that city itself fell victim to Russia's Ivan III and his increasingly aggressive approach to extending the political and economic power of the Grand Duchy of Moscow, which had also gained control of the former Grand Principality of Vladimir and Suzdal in 1389.[55]

Transport

In an area as large as the Sámi homeland, with its arduous climatic and geographical conditions, transport was an important issue. During the Middle Ages, in the inland regions of Sápmi, it was the Sámi themselves who provided transport for visitors, even official ones, to the region. This largely consisted of draft reindeer. Documents issued by the Piteå General Assembly in northern Sweden from 1424 confirm this as an obligation which would seem to date back at least to the beginning of the fourteenth century.[56] The Hansa, the great mercantile German trading 'empire', also exerted an increasingly powerful influence in the region, especially in the north of Norway during the fourteenth century. But this declined in the sixteenth century, and by the end of the Kalmar War in 1613 its economic tentacles had shrunk into virtual oblivion beyond the Baltic. By then, fish, formerly a highly important component of northern European trade during the Catholic period when abstinence from meat was *de rigueur* for long periods, had lost its importance in the north in the post-Reformation period. Thus trade along the Arctic coast ceased to have the international importance which it had formerly had. Many early Norwegian settlers therefore moved south during this period, governmental disapproval of their emigration notwithstanding, their settled places now increasingly taken over by the Sámi, albeit as individuals rather than by the *siida* (community) as such. That said, the authorities did take means to mitigate this emigration, and in about 1650 tax privileges were introduced according to which new settlers to Norwegian Finnmark were to be granted the first six years tax free. Another regulation of 1681 encouraged the transportation of convicted male criminals from Copenhagen, not only to the fishing stations of Finnmark, but to work in the mines of the regions where the southern Sámi resided. Some local administrators took a highly pragmatic, if dubious, moral approach: one local government official in Finnmark wrote to the authorities in Denmark that female criminals, even those guilty of prostitution, should also be allowed to migrate to the far north in the interests of increasing the population. This indeed happened to at least some degree, and such transportation continued—as in Australia— until the middle of the nineteenth century.[57]

Olaus Magnus

By the Reformation period Sápmi was beginning to enter the wider European consciousness, owing not least to new published material on the subject in this early age of print. One of the most important figures to write about the Sámi was the Swede Olaus Magnus (1490–1557). Ordained a Roman Catholic priest in 1521, he later served as a diplomatic emissary to the popes until his resignation and retirement to Rome during the course of the Reformation in Sweden. Well travelled, he had himself journeyed as far north as Torneå[58] and his writings emphasise the long, dark days of a seemingly endless winter amongst the Sámi people.[59] The snow and mosquitoes appalled him, and yet the cornucopia of fish and game amazed him. In fact, for him, Lapland was an icy wonderland of marvels with heroes carrying out exploits in which reality and fantasy mingle.[60] Indeed, much of Olaus Magnus's texts are rich in exotic imagery and his illustrations include the first artistic depictions of the Sámi, albeit hardly in realistic terms.[61] True, Olaus Magnus depicted the Sámi milking reindeer in 1555, but he illustrated European, rather than Sámi, methods of milking, since the latter did not use milking stools at that time, and the *náhppi*, a traditional Sámi milk container, was not included.[62] Interestingly, according to Olaus Magnus's *Carta Marina*, which was printed in Venice in 1539, the term *Lappia* is reserved as a name only for the region situated across the river to the west of Torneå. *Finnarchia* is the name given to the region north-east of *Lappia*, with *Scricfinia* to the north and the Kola region is listed as *Biarmia*. Some local northern landmarks are also included, such as the churches of Hålogaland and Trondenes.[63]

Some characteristic activities of the Sámi are also presented. In an illustration depicting a battle between the Norwegians and the Russians and Karelians from 1555, for example, the Sámi are shown as fighting and shooting their arrows whilst swiftly moving on skis. Ever more aggressive Russian claims over the Kola Peninsula led to Norwegian–Danish protests in response. As a result, and in an effort to resolve this issue, in 1573 emissaries of the tsar were sent to the region who proceeded to establish the border at the village of Pavikelva, enabling another village, Paesz-Reka, on the other side of the border, to be returned to Norwegian sovereignty. However, in order to strengthen Russian interests a few years later, a Russian administrator was sent to Kola on a more permanent basis.[64] Yet Kola was by no means the only important trading centre: Torneå, too, along with sites at other river mouths, became an important trading centre for Russians as it was there that the Swedish *birkarler* (colonial settlers), Norwegians and Sámi all came together, if Olaus Magnus is to be believed.

These *birkarler* were Swedes who first appear in 1328 as emissaries of the king sent forth to Sámi *siida*, first in Kemi Lappmark, Torne Lappmark, Lule Lappmark and Pite Lappmark, but later in Ume Lappmark as well. Establishing themselves at coastal sites ranging from Tysfjord to Varanger, they enjoyed a monopoly of trade for over two centuries until 1553 when Gustaf Vasa, Sweden's first hereditary monarch, appropriated these rights himself, in consequence of which he appointed his own officials to collect them in his stead. Henceforth, every taxable Sámi man was obliged to pay the Crown three reindeer skins or martin pelts, or six reindeer carcasses.

Twenty-four reindeer skins and six carcasses accrued to the Crown from Kautokeino, while ten and a half reindeer skins and three and a half reindeer carcasses went to the royal bailiff. Fifteen reindeer skins and four reindeer carcasses went to the Crown from Tana, and six reindeer skins but no carcasses to his bailiff.[65] The Sámi had thus become highly lucrative subjects of the Swedish Crown.

Meanwhile, Rovaniemi, today the capital of Finnish Lapland, was established, its name first recorded from 1453; in reality it was a cluster of villages that formed a frontier focus of trade between Karelia to the south and east and the growing settlement of western Finns.[66] Yet it remained small. Indeed, by 1543 there were a total of only fifteen houses.[67] Only thereafter did it begin to grow, before being claimed by Sweden in 1595 when it subsumed all of Norrbotten into the kingdom,[68] and incorporated as a town in 1631.[69]

Later European Impressions of Lapland

During the later seventeenth and eighteenth centuries, as the Enlightenment took roots and blossomed, there was a growing preoccupation among many European intellectuals with 'natural man' unfettered by the demands of civilisation or any social contract. So it was that in reference to Lapland, Europe's last remaining 'great wilderness', attention was drawn to the Sámi. One of the first to arrive in Lapland was the French dramatist Jean-François Renard, who was enamoured of its exoticism. He was followed in 1701 by Olof Rudbeck the Younger (1660–1740), whose lyrical ode *Lapponia* achieved wide recognition. Yet rather than being based on any significant scientific research, it looked back to the *History of the Northern Peoples* (1555) composed by Olaus Magnus, whose work, as we have seen, was infused with fantastical conceptions of the Sámi people and was more a reflection of the European imagination than of Sámi culture and lifestyle.[70]

The eccentric Swedish confidence man Nicolaus Örn, who visited Versailles in 1706, purporting, in outlandish garb, to be the prince of Lapland, also attracted considerable attention among the jaded aristocrats of the French court, and a fashionable interest in Sámi life and culture subsequently caught hold.[71] However, only with the arrival of the Swedish botanist and explorer Carl von Linné (1707–78) in 1732 did a more truly scientific scrutiny commence with respect to the Sámi. This is despite the fact that von Linné himself was famously portrayed in Sámi attire in a work by the artist Martin Hoffman carried out in Holland in 1737, accoutred in the garb he wore in Paris where he lectured about his visit to Lapland in 1738, accompanied by a 'typical' Sámi drum decorated with mystical symbols. More important, though, were his researches which had genuine scientific significance: his botanical studies in the Sámi homeland were published in his rightly famed *Flora Lapponica* (1737), winning him a Europe-wide audience. Yet for him, too, the Sámi remained 'noble savages', a nomadic community unsullied by the corruptions of European civilisation.

In Linné's wake came the French academician and astronomer Pierre-Louis Moreau de Maupertuis. His scientific expedition to Lapland took place in 1736–7, with the express purpose of measuring the length of a degree along the meridian, a task which he successfully completed. A fellow Frenchman, Reginaud Outhier, arrived shortly thereafter in Lapland, going on to publish his travel diary *Journal d'un*

Voyage au Nord, en 1736 & 1737. This work appeared in Paris in 1744 and was accompanied by the exotic illustration *Renne attelé au petit Traineau* (Reindeer Pulling a Lapp Sleigh), thereby linking the Sámi people to domestic reindeer herding in a way which has made this activity synonymous with their identity itself. Thus by the time the Swedish artist Pehr Hilleström the Elder (1732–1816) painted his noted late eighteenth-century painting *Lapps in Front of their Summer Tents*, one of three ethnic works which included images of Dalecarlians and Karelians, the Sámi had long since entered deep into the mainstream cultural cognisance of Europeans.[72]

In the early nineteenth century, Acerbi, who left so many rich impressions of the Sámi, nonetheless also found his emotions tempered by the negative. Indeed, the elation which he first felt on arriving at the North Cape was quickly soured:

Alas! The moment of entrancement quickly evaporated! Melancholy and a deep sadness overcame the noble enthusiasm of our triumph; the naked rocks, the earth without vegetation, the sites without inhabitants seemed to us to be filled with an air of timelessness, labours, cares and anxieties, that it was as if we had been led to the very tomb of nature itself.[73]

Even in Denmark, far removed from Lapland, albeit in the period prior to the Congress of Vienna when it exercised hegemony over the Norwegian part of Lapland, the Sámi remained a source of exotic fascination, as is apparent in works such as A *Reindeer Herd on the Drive* (1875) by the Dane Carl Bøgh (1827–93) which depicts the Sámi on the move in the mountainous passes of Trøndelag in the north of Norway. Indeed, for many in the highly pragmatic scientific world of the late nineteenth century Sápmi remained a land and people apart. As the Russian N.N. Kharuzin wrote of the ancient Sámi in 1890, in words which many of his contemporaries felt still applied:

The ancient tribes were like wild beasts, living in impassable wastelands, dwelling in stone crevices, having neither temples nor the other things which are the necessities of human life, but eating animals, wild beasts, birds and the fish of the sea ... Sometimes they kill wild beasts with stones and stones they worship ...[74]

Why should it be surprising then that Lapland still retains exotic connotations and remains, in the international imagination, a world where fantasy and reality merge? It has been said that the association of Santa Claus with Rovaniemi—a subject unrelated to Sámi life and culture—really began in 1950, when Eleanor Roosevelt, widow of

President Franklin D. Roosevelt, visited the city and, in anticipation of her visit, a small cabin was constructed as Santa Claus's home.[75] However, today—for adults as well as children—Sápmi and the Sámi people remain a legendary people, poorly understood but a source of fascination, an ethnos whose culture and history deserve a far more thorough examination than legends and fairy tales provide.

1

ETHNICITIES, THE LAW, REPRESSIONS AND WAR

When the pioneering Sámi reindeer-herder and author Johan Turi, born in Kautokeino, Norway (1854–1936), but later living in Swedish Lapland, was asked from where the Sámi came he replied, 'One hasn't heard that they came from anywhere.'[1] This quip characterises the Sámi sense of their indigenous, multifaceted identity in Sápmi, the Sámi homeland now subsumed into four nation states: Norway, Sweden, Finland and Russia. For many people around the globe, reindeer and skis also seemed (and continue to seem) to characterise the Sámi people, with the humanist Johannes Schefferus being one of the first to provide illustrations of the Sámi on skis.[2] Yet for others, like the seventeenth-century French traveller François Bernier, they were a people apart, at least from his vantage point on the other side of Eurasia, in India, where he was court physician to Aurangzeb, the great Mughal emperor. In his writings on the races of mankind he concluded that the Sámi (he used the term Lapps as almost all non-Sámi people did until about 1980) formed their own fourth race, separate from the other three, the white Europeans, the black Africans and the yellow Asians. But the Sámi people were far more complex and ancient than any of these writers realised, and so their history deserves close examination in a multifaceted context.

Linguistic Links

One major aspect of Sámi culture and continuity is their language. A consensus of modern linguistic research today confirms that the ances-

19

tors of the present-day Sámi once spoke a single unified language. Indeed, the ethnonym *sámá* > *sámi* originates from an early proto-Finnish word from which the Finnish word *häme*, now the name of a province in south-central Finland, also derives.[3] While the indigenous nature of the Sámi in the region and their ancient presence to the south and east is little debated, their ethnic and linguistic roots are more difficult to discern and a study of their genetic make-up has only been conducted very recently. Certainly, by their language they have long stood in especially close relationship to a number of other peoples of central and northern Europe speaking one of the Finno-Ugric languages. Among these should be mentioned Finnish and Estonian, among the Finnic languages, and Hungarian among the Ugric ones. There are also some ten other related languages spoken elsewhere in Russia. However, most of these, like Komi (called Izhemtsy by the Sámi), Hanti and Mansi are spoken by people living considerable, sometimes even vast, distances away from the Sámi. During the 1990s some attempts were made to analyse their genetic make-up and their links to Finns, Norwegians, Swedes, Russians, Karelians and other neighbouring peoples. So far, the results seem to indicate that not only are there considerable differences between the Sámi and their neighbours, but that there are also great distinctions even among the various Sámi groups themselves. In any case, such 'racial' issues did not interest many Sámi themselves. Indeed, most Sámi today have concluded that it is their linguistic heritage, culture and way of life that most unite them, rather than their racial make-up. Yet though they are relatively isolated among themselves and from their neighbours, a multiplicity of connections between them has always been present, and consequently the genetic links between the Sámi and their Nordic and Russian neighbours are considerable.

Even more important in terms of their influence on Sámi life, however, are the cultural, social and economic links which have tied them together for centuries, military incursions and violence notwithstanding. This is hardly surprising since Norwegians, Swedes, Finns, Russians and Karelians have been a presence there in one way or another for centuries. One can thus speak more appropriately of a symbiosis of peoples and their cultures which has permeated the entire region throughout historical times. But this symbiosis did not always work for the benefit of the Sámi, as their social life and culture often suffered; this was especially the case during the course of the nineteenth century when increasing political and other restrictions were imposed upon them by central governments. Forced into a defensive position, many Sámi became self-consciously aware of their unique identity, which soon came to encourage a sense of political identity as well.

The Early Sámi

The oldest presence of human settlements in the Sámi homeland dates back to 9000 BC.[4] To what degree these had links to the Sámi inhabitants of Sápmi is not known, but already by the first millennium BC it is clear that a Sámi people with a distinctive ethnic identity and commonality of language becomes recognisable, speaking a Finnic language with close etymological links to Finnish, from which it probably diverged at about the same time. Individual Sámi families, generally related to one another, tended to settle together in a so-called 'siida' (a Sámi community or village) in groups of eight or twelve. Aligned with one another, these *siida* were in turn organised into a '*vuobme*' (a regional network of settlements). In the second millennium AD these formed the basis for the establishment of Kemi, Torne, Lule and Pite '*jälldet*' (i.e. Lapp areas), the former two in Finland (under Swedish sovereignty until 1809) and the latter two in Sweden. That of the Lule River was composed of four *siida*, specifically Tuorpon, Sirkas, Jokkmokk and Suokkjokk.[5]

It has been said that among the proto-Sámi's proto-Germanic peasant neighbours, the term 'Finni' was used to signify those with whom they traded. As such, these ancestors of the Sámi were integrated into a wide network of trade which had spread across Eastern Europe by the sixth century BC, when iron had become an important commodity throughout this region.[6] Although this trade continued for centuries, the end of this proto-Sámi period seems to have occurred rather abruptly, as from about AD 300 the archaeological record confirms that the production of ceramics and iron suddenly diminished dramatically. A transitional period ensued thereafter, which by the eighth century saw the Sámi living in a wide swathe above the 62nd parallel and the Finns to the south. This new era among the Sámi is characterised by the construction of rectangular hearth dwellings and the artefacts, often of iron, found within them. It is quite clear that trade was enjoying a major revival during this period, in particular owing to the demand for furs.[7]

Taking one typical example, the Sámi had originally settled all of the eastern and southern shores of the Tysfjord. However, first the Norse and then the Norwegians shared the north-western coast and the head of a small peninsula jutting out from the opposite shore.[8] Fishing and wild reindeer hunting were the main livelihoods of the Lule Sámi of Tysfjord: while the vital activity of reindeer hunting was originally carried out using specially constructed traps, these were no longer employed by the end of the thirteenth century as cod fishing around the Lofoten Islands, under the supervision of merchants from Hanseatic Bergen, had superseded hunting as the economic mainstay of the region. This is clearly indicated in Olaus Magnus's illustration of boats fishing in the Lofoten Islands (1555),[9] from a period when the Coastal Sámi had come to be settled at Ofoten and Salangen. Boat-building and the sale of boats were thus highly significant for the livelihood of the local Sámi. Indeed, it is said that the Norwegian heir to the throne Sigurd Slembe had local Sámi from Iinnasuolu Hinnøya build two ships for him, which were long famed for their remarkable speed.[10]

Interaction with the Norse

It seems that the heyday of interaction between the Norse and Sámi inhabitants of the coastal areas of Helgeland, in northern Norway, was between AD 300 and 600. This is evinced by archaeological remains in the Lofoten-Vesterålen coastal region of the country.[11] Norse settlement spread widely in this region as agriculture and the establishment of farming were possible and trade convenient and profitable.[12] As for the indigenous Coastal Sámi, they remained in or retreated to the inner fjords, and particularly the smaller ones near Tysfjord.[13] This increasingly close proximity of the Sámi with the Norse facilitated a growing symbiosis, so that each absorbed elements of the other's culture and language. Nonetheless, by contrast with the Norse, the Sámi continued to be 'fishers and bird-catchers and hunters' as *Ottar's Chronicles* put it, from about 880–90.[14] Still, the Norse skills in boat-making and sailing had a great influence on the Coastal Sámi; indeed, many Sámi words relating to boats are borrowed from the Norse.[15]

The Coastal Sámi, in turn, served as intermediaries between the Norse population and the Mountain Sámi of the interior, with some of whom they intermarried.[16] One further important source of ethnic interaction was the fur trade, which led to considerable cultural interchange by the end of the first millennium AD.

Influences from the Far Abroad

Many Sámi relics evince forms, designs and ornamentation derived not only from other Nordic societies and cultures, but from as far afield as Ireland, as the designs on horn combs dating from the 800s found in Birka in central Sweden illustrate. These clearly influenced not only such everyday artefacts as Sámi spoons, but also the rims that decorated the openings of Sámi leather bags which would be produced for over 1,000 years.[17]

The Birkarlar

The Sámi were in the majority in Lapland until the early twelfth century.[18] However, this situation changed forever with the arrival of the first newcomers to settle in the Sámi homeland, the so-called *birkarlar*, who started to establish themselves as peasant farmers in the vicinity of the Torne, Lule and Pite river valleys from the twelfth century onwards. The *birkarlar* were granted special taxation rights over the Sámi, but they also traded with them and frequently provided the Sámi with material assistance in difficult times. The imposition of two important twelfth-century Norse legal codes on the Sámi, the Eidsivathingslag and the Borgarthingslag, laid down the legal relationship of the Sámi to their now Norwegian overlords in those areas controlled by the latter.

Records of these relationships were first recorded in 1328, at a time when the traders and government representatives of the Republic of Novgorod were becoming a growing presence in the region, leading to heightened confrontation between the Catholic Nordics and the Orthodox Russians.[19]

Nordic–Russian Conflict

By the fifteenth century virtually the whole of the Kola Peninsula had come under the control of Novgorod. However, with the collapse of that city's independence during the 1470s, Moscow assumed hegemony in its place and attempted to assert its growing authority over the following century. A settlement was already established at Lovozero by 1574, along the shores of the lake whose name it signifies, the second largest lake in the whole of the Kola Peninsula.[20] Yet this state of affairs did not go unchallenged, and in the course of the sixteenth century conflict over the area heightened between Russia and Denmark, soon to incorporate Norway into the Danish state in 1536. Towards the end of the century and at the beginning of the next, the Danish king Christian IV attempted to assert his authority through diplomatic channels, but to little avail,[21] ultimately leading to an escalation of this conflict which smouldered with occasional eruptions throughout the later 1500s at the expense of the Sámi, who were caught in between. The conflict also had religious and cultural elements, for Russia had been successful in spreading the influence of the Russian Orthodox Church—and therefore Russian political influence as well—throughout the peninsula. This had also led Russia into confrontation with Sweden (Finland being a part of the Swedish Kingdom), which had its own territorial claims on the region. In consequence, on Christmas Eve 1589 the Finnish 'guerrilla' leader Juho Vesainen and his men surprised and then destroyed the Russian Orthodox monastery at Pechenga (in Russian; Petsamo, in Finnish). Nonetheless, despite the desecration and brutality, the area remained staunchly Orthodox and the church and monastery were eventually rebuilt, leaving Russian hegemony there increasingly secure.

Under King Karl IX, Swedish immigration to the contested region was encouraged and the establishment of a necklace of Lutheran churches decreed, but few benefits ensued. Rather, matters were temporarily resolved by the Peace of Teusina in 1595, whereby Russia was obliged to relinquish its taxation rights over the Sámi to Sweden along the Arctic coast from Varanger to Tysfjord.

Yet those to the east of Varanger continued to be subject to Russia. All this, of course, aroused the ire of Denmark–Norway which resorted to political propaganda by commissioning and funding the research and publication of the map *Lappia par Norwegiæ* by the German Simon von Salingen in 1601, hoping that this would bolster its territorial claims not only over the Arctic coast, but over the whole of the Kola Peninsula as well.[22]

In response to these issues and to force back the Swedes, the great Danish–Norwegian warrior king Christian IV (1577–1648) himself travelled in 1599 to Varanger, in Finnmark, and the northern shores of the Kola Peninsula. The Sámi in Russia now found themselves the object of aggression from both sides of this Nordic conflict, forbidden by the Danish–Norwegians from paying their taxes to the Swedes and by the Swedes from paying their taxes to the Danish–Norwegian authorities. This situation became acute when open war broke out between the two states in 1611, the so-called Kalmar War, which continued until 1613. The victory of Denmark–Norway over Sweden ultimately resolved the tax issue with respect to the Sea Sámi: henceforth, they were the undisputed taxable subjects of the former. But this was not the case for the Mountain Sámi of the interior in Utsjoki, Tana, Ávjovárri and Kautokeino, who remained subject to the taxation of both states. Yet after 1612 the Sámi of the Kola Peninsula were now in practice freed from the burden of Danish–Norwegian taxation, which was rapidly retaken by Russia, the *de jure* claims of Denmark–Norway notwithstanding. Nonetheless, actual double taxation in the interior of the Kola Peninsula persisted until 1751. In fact, these *pro forma*, if practically empty, claims to levy taxation in the Kola Peninsula were maintained until 1813. By then official Norwegian visits to Kola (or Malmis, as it was known long ago in Norway) once every three years, around the New Year—rather than yearly as had been the case in the early seventeenth century—had become occasions of diplomatic cordiality and festivity, rather than brutal oppression as had originally been the case.[23] By this time the Sámi were living almost exclusively on the Kola Peninsula extending westwards. However, documentary evidence confirms that the Sámi still had settlements to the north of Lake Onegin and along the Karelian coast of the White Sea in the middle of the sixteenth century.[24] Other documents from around 1670 also demonstrate that some Sámi lived in the vicinity of Olonets.[25] They had thus often lived in the vicinity of Chudi and Vepsian peoples, with whom they frequently engaged in armed conflict.[26]

Colonisation of the Sámi homeland in Swedish territory began in earnest after the Kalmar Lappmarksplakat (Lappmark Placard) of Karl XI in 1673 exhorted Swedish subjects to settle in 'unused land' in Lapland. (The first recorded use of the term *Lappmark* was in a letter of the Norwegian king, Magnus Eriksson, from 1340, and the area encompassing the north Norwegian *Lappmarker* was and remains known as Finnmark.)[27] Many, both Swedes and Finns, heeded this call and arrived as colonists, encouraged by a proclamation in 1695 which granted them freedom from taxation and conscription for up to fifteen years. As a result, in a very short period of time up to 700 settlers arrived in the Finnish part alone, bringing the total population there to some 2,200 people. These numbers increased significantly after the second Lapland Placard was issued. By no means were all of these new settlers colonists from the south, for some Sámi people themselves now came to adopt a sedentary lifestyle hardly distinguishable from that of their new neighbours. In this way, the *siida* of Kitka, Maanselkä and Keminkylä were absorbed into the mainstream Finnish population and culture.[28] According to Pentti Virrankoski, the population of Finnish Lapland at the end of the seventeenth century was between 2,100 and 2,200 people, 600 to 700 of whom were Finnish settlers.[29]

Many Sámi from Oulu province had been assimilated into the wider Finnish population as early as the eighteenth century,[30] and a significant number of these Sámi in Finland who took to a settled farming life also adopted Finnish names.[31] Surnames were first adopted in the fifteenth century, but many of these remain limited to the Sámi community. Today there are at most about sixty Sámi family names which are still in common use on the Kola Peninsula, although some have maintained that even this number is too high.[32]

Intermarriage between the Sámi and their neighbours was another path of assimilation, despite the Italian Giuseppe Acerbi's bold statement that 'It rarely happens that the natives of Norway intermarry with the Laplanders.'[33] The assimilation that took place could occur in both directions: by the early nineteenth century, reverse assimilation was not infrequent, with the children of public servants who married Sámi often themselves becoming Sámi.[34]

More usual, however, was the assimilation which occurred through domestic employment. During the eighteenth century, many Varanger Sámi became household servants among the Norwegians who had settled the region, later being absorbed into their community. The displacement of wild reindeer hunting and fishing in favour of domestic reindeer husbandry also encouraged assimilation, at least to the degree that it undermined the social and political structure of the *siida*, while at the same time increasing competition for limited resources. For example, conflict over pasture for the other domestic animals tended by the Norwegians created hostility between the increasingly settled Sámi and Norwegians. At sea, competition for whales also created problems between the Sea Sámi and the Norwegians. A legal settlement was eventually enacted to reduce this source of economic friction at the beginning of the seventeenth century, by determining that whales obtained off the interior coast of Hvalbukta were to be Sámi property, while those from the exterior shore were to be allocated to the Norwegian settlers. Such juridical arrangements as these were to have lasting social as well as economic consequences, since even today that old dividing line forms the border between the Norwegian-settled Vadsø and the Sámi village Unjárga (Nesseby, in Norwegian). Yet despite these occasional sources of conflict, the distinctions between the Sámi and Norwegian settler lifestyles and livelihoods gradually diminished over the course of time. Many Norwegians acquired reindeer herds at Vadsø towards the end of the seventeenth century, with the actual herding carried out by Sámi hired for the purpose, and most servants and hired help at Vadsø at this time were also Sámi.[35] But this is not to say that the Sámi were always relegated to an inferior position. Indeed, some were able to acquire considerable property and resources that enabled them to make their way in the wider world, with one even becoming governor of Västerbotten in the north of Sweden.[36] Yet each ethnic community generally maintained its own internal legal structures. Thus by contrast with the rest of the Nordic region, Sámi inheritance rights, with the youngest inheriting the bulk of an estate, took precedence over the customary Scandinavian primogeniture.[37]

The Great Northern War (1700–21) between Russia and Sweden encouraged the arrival in the Sámi areas of a multitude of Finnish refugees accompanied by their domestic animals who were fleeing the war zone and its upheavals. A large number of those who fled north were absorbed into the surrounding communities of the Sámi. Borders remained fluid and contested. Although the Great Northern War ended in 1721, it was only in 1734 that an agreement was finally reached to demarcate the northern border between Denmark–Norway and Sweden–Finland. At the border conference, the former, represented by Major Peter Schnitler, claimed Kautokeino, Ávjovárri, Tana and Utsjok. Schnittler came to the region in 1742–5 in order to investigate how the demarcation should best be determined and came to the conclusion that the way the land was utilised should figure into the equation. Therefore, the Lapp Codicil of 1751 appended the old border treaty between Norway and Sweden, confirming a number of traditional Sámi rights: their right to move back and forth across their respective nationalities, as well as cross-border fishing rights and political neutrality in times of war. Some Sámi law courts were also established and given precedence over national ones in many circumstances where the two came into conflict. This was an arrangement which proved relatively durable, surviving until 1852 when the border between Finland (since 1809 an autonomous grand duchy, with the Russian tsar as grand duke) and Norway finally ceased to be permeable for the Sámi.[38] In consequence of its clauses, Sámi living in Utsjoki and Inari were granted freedom of trade in Norway, while the Sámi on both sides of the border were granted rights to hunt and fish, subject to certain charges.[39] In 1886 the Italian botanist and traveller Stephen Sommier (1848–1922) noted of Inari that: 'this major northern Finnish town consists merely of a church and just one house, that of the priest and his dependents, 10 people altogether, including children'.[40] All the rest, almost exclusively Sámi, lived scattered in the surrounding area 200 by 160 kilometres; indeed, so few people attended church that the priest only held a service every couple of weeks.[41] Sommier left copious writings on his visit to the Sámi, which he carried out together with another Italian, Professor Paolo Mantegazza, who returned earlier than Sommier to Italy. Mantegazza cited statistics which suggested that there were fewer than 30,000 Sámi scattered in an area of 10,000 square Norwegian miles. According to Professor Friis in Christiania (modern-day Oslo), these included 17,178 Norwegians of pure Sámi blood, 1,900 of mixed, 7,238 Swedish Sámi, 1,200 Finnish Sámi and 2,000 Russian Sámi.[42]

But Sommier's impressions were hardly accurate in other respects and he could only summarise his visit to the Sámi homeland by declaring that 'The Lapps are of a sweet and infantile character.'[43] As for the region itself, the comparison which came to mind seems slightly self-satisfied: 'The deserts of Lapland are similar to the tundra of Siberia and I have experienced them in all their squalor.'[44]

In the Russian part of Sápmi a condominium was maintained by Russia and Norway over the north-west corner of the Kola Peninsula until 1826. According to the Codicil:

In so far as the Lapps need the land of both states, they shall, in accordance with their ancient customs, be permitted, in autumn and spring, to migrate with their reindeer herds over the borders and into each of the states. And thereafter, just as is the case with other subjects of the state, with the exception of those few places specified herein, make usufruct of land and shore to maintain their animals and themselves, to be received with friendliness, protected and helped to succeed ...[45]

At this time, most of the Skolt Sámi settled in Norway became Norwegian citizens and were subject to its constitution. However, in Russia, civil life remained subject to the tsarist autocracy where notions of the good life were at variance with those of Sámi culture. According to one traditional tale of Sámi life there, the tsar determined to reward one of his faithful Sámi subjects who had rendered him heroic service in a military campaign. However, the Sámi man declined his offer of a mansion in another part of Russia, among other forms of largesse, explaining:

There is no disagreement; your mansion is fine, full of light and beautiful, but Lapland is even better. Our mountains are bigger than your palaces, our skies are higher than your roofs, our sun, moon, stars and northern lights are brighter than your lamps. How can I exchange my Lapland for that ...?[46]

In Norway, the population of Norwegian settlers dominated in Finnmark from at least the mid-sixteenth century until the second quarter of the eighteenth. Thereafter, the Sámi were in the majority until the middle of the nineteenth century. In 1567 about 4,000 Norwegians had been recorded, but under 2,000 Sámi. In 1747, the number of Norwegians and Sámi briefly achieved parity.[47] Although the Kvens—Finnish-speaking fishermen and farmers who first arrived in Norway in the 1740s—had become a significant ethnic group in the region in the 1840s, it was the Norwegians who surpassed the Sámi in number by the 1850s. By 1910, there were about 24,000 Norwegians, just over 10,000 Sámi and just over 5,000 Kvens. By contrast, in 1815 there had been just over 5,000 Sámi and under 3,000 Norwegians, while the Kvener—who were only recorded from 1845—numbered just over 2,000.

With respect to Finland, by 1758 some Finns had settled at Inari where they established farms, but they remained few in number over the following half century. Indeed, in 1810 there were only twenty Finns living in the vicinity of Inari compared to some 412 Sámi, many of whom were by now practising farming. Moreover, at Utsjoki, the twenty-five Sámi households who had lived there in the middle of the eighteenth century had grown to twenty-nine by the beginning of the nineteenth century. Enontekiö, home to 102 Sámi families in 1756, suffered a setback later in the century because of a burgeoning migration to Norway, leading to a decline in this number to only eighty-five. However, by 1803 their numbers had increased once more to 103. Yet what had earlier been a trickle of Finnish settlers now became a flood, with no fewer than 402 such families establishing themselves in the area, totally dominating the indigenous population. This was also the case in Inari, where, despite a doubling in the number of Sámi from about 400 to 850 due to the thriving state of the reindeer husbandry which the area supported, the growth of the settler population was even stronger: whereas there had been only twenty settlers in 1810, there were over 600 by the turn of the following century. Thus at the turn of the twentieth century only Utsjoki could boast of a Sámi majority population, their numbers having increased from 250 to 470, and even here there were as many as fifty-seven settler farms, while at Enontekiö the Sámi population had actually declined by this time from 130 to only ninety-five.[48]

Inter-Sámi Competition

As competition for land and woodland increased, inter-Sámi friction also grew. The Forest Sámi of northern Kemi Lapland, for example, encountered friction due to the immigration of western reindeer-herding Sámi into the area in the late 1800s and the burning of forests in order to bring land into cultivation. This meant that large-scale reindeer herding came to dominate the region, which in turn led to a dramatic decline in the remaining wild reindeer population. It also led to a circumstance—unlike that in the rest of the Nordic Sámi homeland— of those who were not of Sámi ethnicity taking up reindeer herding. Far from being an empty wilderness, therefore, the Sámi homeland was suffering from growing competition for land and resources. And it was the Sámi who often came out the worst in this struggle, finding themselves obliged to move out of the way of Finnish settlers, with some Sámi families from the southernmost *siidas* moving to the northern ones, in whose parish registers they now appear.

Impressions of Lapland and the Sámi

By the middle of the seventeenth century the Sámi were beginning to attract the interest of a growing coterie of European intellectuals. Among the first was the Frenchman Pierre Martin de la Martinière who travelled to the northern coast of Russian Lapland in 1653 in the company of a Danish expedition. He eventually published his impressions, illustrated by scenes of the Sámi hunting with bows and arrows upon skis, in *Voyage des pais septentrionaux* (Voyage in northern countries), published in Paris in 1671.[49] But there was also a Christian religious dimension, for by the end of the seventeenth century Pechenga, with its newly rebuilt Russian Orthodox monastery, had some eighty Sámi inhabitants. However, Ponoi, in the east of the Kola

Peninsula, was much more significant in demographic terms, with at least 250 Sámi residents at that time. Russian settlers were still quite rare and those who were there had only a seasonal presence. The Sámi community was by no means monolithic, formed, as it was, by three principal ethnic groups, including the Ter Sámi who were the largest, some 660 in number, with the smallest being the Lesh (Forest) Sámi, who numbered 100, each using their highly distinct dialects.[50]

Despite the localised regional conflict, none of the Sámi communities were considered warlike. Rather than finding war a virtue, the Swedish Lutheran priest and missionary Samuel Rheen (d. 1680), who arrived in Jokkmokk to preach to the Sámi—he served from 1666 to 1671—complained that 'The Lapps are a people who, for the major part, are thoroughly unsuited to waging war, for they lack manly courage ...'[51] Of *birkarlar* family origins, he was, nonetheless, fluent in Lule Sámi, which helped him to gather considerable information about their lives and customs. Indeed, his reputation for insights into their lives came to the attention of Johannes Schefferus, for whose work *Lapponia*, published in Frankfurt in 1673, he provided much information.[52] *Lapponia*, as we have seen, provided a thorough linguistic, social and cultural history of the Sámi people and was accompanied by splendid illustrations focusing upon the exotic aspects of Sámi life and culture. One of the most interesting depicts a Sámi altar on which reindeer antlers are displayed and the role of Sámi *noaidi*, or shamans, is considered at length, though not without negative moral judgements. In some these mediators of Sámi spiritual life are seen as diabolical and malicious, in others as powerful and a force to be harnessed for practical benefits because of their mastery of the magical arts, though again, their reluctance to take to arms is perceived as a moral failing, proving them to be 'cowards' and 'shiftless idlers'.[53] Other more neutral aspects of Sámi culture are also examined, including Schefferus's concept of Lapland as a republic (at this time, only oligarchical Venice and Genoa provided contemporary examples of this type of political system),[54] and its laws and language, including a comparative study of vocabulary and grammar.[55] Further insight into the life of the Sámi in the seventeenth century was provided by two Swedish professors of medicine at Uppsala University, Olof Rudbeck the Elder (1630–1702) and his son Olof Rudbeck the Younger (1660–1740). Both placed a particular stress on Sámi linguistics which they used to gain insight into Sámi life and culture.[56] In the last century and today, the Rudbecks have been criticised for holding a plethora of false views concerning the Sámi, but they were only two of many who have been held to account for presenting a wide range of ethnic prejudices. The world-renowned botanist Carl von Linné and the philosopher Pierre-Louis Moreau de Maupertuis, for example, were also guilty of entertaining European conceptions and misconceptions of the Sámi in the early and mid-eighteenth century, as was the lesser known Nicolaus Hackzell's work, *Dissertatio Historica de Urbe Lula* (Historical Dissertation on the Town of Luleå), published in Latin in Uppsala in 1731, which focused upon the Lule Sámi.[57] Even in the more enlightened age of the later nineteenth century, such a towering man of letters as the Swedish-speaking Finn Zachris Topelius (1818–98) found detractors who lamented his failure to appreciate Fenno-Ugrian culture.[58] Yet it was precisely these scholars, with all their flaws, who first attracted the interest and then the respect of many people throughout Europe to the uniqueness and value of Sámi life and culture.

Some visitors to Sápmi, however, arrived at conclusions about the Sámi which could hardly withstand even a superficial scrutiny. For example, at the end of the eighteenth century, Acerbi came to the conclusion with regard to the Sámi that:

Four out of the six men had black hair; from whence I conclude this to be the prevailing colour amongst the Laplanders, distinguishing them from the Finlanders, amongst whom, during the whole of my journey, I did not remark one who had hair of that colour.[59]

However, there were positive elements in his commentary, for although the Sámi (at least those who lived by the coast of Norway) were perceived to have a unique lifestyle, Acerbi was also convinced that they were an integral part of European society. He wrote:

Each Laplander is the proprietor of the territory around his little mansion, to the extend of a Norwegian mile, or eight English, in every direction. They have some cows which furnish them with excellent milk, and meadow land which yields hay for their fodder in winter. They have every one a store of fish dried in the sun, not only for their own use, but wherewithal to purchase luxuries; that is, salt, oatmeal, and some woollen clothes. Their houses are constructed in the form of tents: a hole in the middle, which gives them light, serves also as an aperture for letting out the smoke of the fire, which is always placed in the centre of the cabin; around which they sleep quite close to one another. In winter, besides the heat of the fire, they have the benefit of the animal warmth of the cows, with whom they share the shelter of their roof, as the inhabitants of Scotland do in the highlands and the northern isles. The doors of their houses in summer are always open; and although in that season there is no night, they are accustomed to sleep at the same time as other Europeans ...'[60]

Acerbi also came to the conclusion that the inland Sámi were really one people with the coastal ones, noting that 'They slept as the maritime Laplanders do in general, with their clothes on ...'[61]

Others, such as Paulo Mantegazza, left a mixed picture. Thus while he considered the Sámi to be a deceitful and cunning people,[62] Mantegazza also found that 'The Lapps are of a sweet character and benevolent and the generosity of their hospitality is one of their chief virtues.'[63] This had also been the conclusion of Johannis Tornæ in the late seventeenth century, who wrote, 'All the Lapps are great Hosts and hospitable towards strangers. Whether or not one arrives home to someone unknown or known, one is given whatever food they have.'[64]

Meanwhile, in faraway Hungary, the Jesuit priest János Sajnovics (1733–85), who was also a keen linguist, postulated a missing link between the Sámi language and the Magyar tongue of his native country. This he did at a time when Latin remained the only official language of administration there, and where German and Slavic continued to dominate in spoken language. Indeed, his copious research, published in 1770, confirmed a linguistic relationship between Magyar and Sámi. Far from being far-fetched, his work laid the foundations for an understanding of the Finno-Ugric family of languages, a grouping still linked together to this day, including Sámi in the former and Hungarian in the latter branches. However, back in Hungary at that time, the proposition caused a minor outrage: a 'kinship smelling of oily fish,' as it was decried, did not fit the illustrious linguistic forebears most Hungarian scholars, among whom nationalism was taking root, would have liked to have associated themselves. Rather, they preferred to see a link with the ancient Scythians, a warrior tribe glorified by the ancient Greeks, despite the spuriousness of the connection in linguistic terms.[65]

With respect to Lule Lappmark, the Sámi continued to comprise the overwhelming majority of the population well into the eighteenth century, even if colonists, the so-called 'new builders', had first settled in small numbers by the end of the 1600s. Thus at the turn of the eighteenth century, out of a total population of about 1,500 people in Lule Lappmark, only 2 per cent of them were not Sámi. But this situation began to change dramatically after 1750.[66] Indeed, by the early decades of the nineteenth century some villages of the Sámi homeland had become almost cosmopolitan, attracting traders from far and wide, while even the Sámi peoples who resided there spoke and dressed in ways which sharply distinguished them from one another. In the 1820s, for example, at Pielpajärvi, 8 kilometres from Inari—where, incidentally, virtually no one lived permanently—Pastor Fellman noted that there was:

a court-house, a parsonage and a bailiff's house, 70 to 80 church huts, and four private merchant's shops. The Christmas market is attended by all the Lapps as well as many merchants from Tornio and Norway looking for profit. … All the languages of the European polar region are spoken there, in addition to several Lapp dialects, which differ so much from each other that the Lapps have difficulty understanding each other. Judging by their clothing, one might indeed not consider them as belonging to one people.[67]

This had not been the impression picked up in the late seventeenth century by Johan Schefferus, one of the first to provide illustrations of Sámi clothing which he saw as indicative of their common ethnicity and culture.[68]

During the second half of the nineteenth century the region even began to attract pensioners. In the late 1860s there was apparently an elderly Prussian general who had taken up residence in Hammerfest, which he used as a base to explore the Norwegian and Russian Arctic coasts, and to whom funds could be sent on regular basis for his support at a branch of the Bank of Christiania that had been established there.[69]

Coastal areas adjacent to the Sámi homeland now had communities with a wide social mix. Thus on the Swedish coast of the upper Gulf of Bothnia, where a Swedish social order had long been established, out of the 7,453 inhabitants residing in the district of Neder Luleå in the late nineteenth century, sixteen people were from the aristocracy, twenty-three were clergymen and 131 were burghers. Further down the social scale there were an additional 4,959 soldiers, craftsmen, peasant farmers and farm labourers.[70] The Sámi, however, had long since ceased to reside in the vicinity. Such coastal communities were now completely Swedish in ethnicity and language, attracting a growing population from elsewhere in the country.

Even Russian Lapland was attracting people from far and wide. In the late nineteenth century, for instance, a Japanese student from Yale University came to stay at Kola.[71] Yet aside from such exotic visitors, the Russian authorities encouraged the immigration to the region of other peoples from both within and without the Russian Empire. Not only Russians and Karelians, but also Finns and Norwegians, were

invited to settle. Indeed, in order to encourage this, in 1868 all new settlers were granted exemption from the onerous burdens of taxation
and military service. Others came for economic reasons. This was the
case with reindeer-herding communities from the east, starting with the
arrival of the Komi in the 1880s, and later the Nenets. Their advent in
Sápmi would have serious long-term consequences for the economic
life and well-being of the indigenous Sámi, since all of these peoples
depended to an overwhelming degree on reindeer herding for their livelihood and vied for the same pastures.[72]

There was also an academic and research dimension to the presence
of many new arrivals, for the Kola Peninsula, in particular, attracted
research expeditions from a variety of countries, but especially from
Finland, which had been ceded to the Russian Empire as an autonomous grand duchy in 1809. The first of these *savants* was Jacob
Fellman, a priest from neighbouring Utsjoki, who visited in 1820. For
almost a century, until the advent of the 1917 Revolution, no less than
seventy-three Finnish researchers arrived to carry out a wide range of
fieldwork, both scientific and ethnological.[73]

Some noted the various problems confronting the Sámi given that
they were increasingly living amid a non-Sámi population. The Russian
geologist Wilhelm Böhtlingk (1807–51), who visited the region in
1839, noted that the Russian Sámi who resided within the vicinity of
Pasvik, despite its proximity to a Russian monastery, had great difficulties since they generally lived as an enclave among the settlers
around them and were prohibited from fishing in the Pasvikfjord,
unless they gave a portion of their catch to the Norwegians.[74] Not surprisingly, then, many Sámi found themselves obliged to reside and
work in areas that were less satisfactory and more constrained than
those dominated by their new neighbours. Indeed, one Russian imperial government official reported that in the Kola Peninsula they could
take up residence in the most circumscribed of locations, expressing
astonishment at the locations where the Sámi could live, for other than
they 'Only a cock and three hens could live in those places.'[75] Yet if the
Kola Sámi tended to be more disadvantaged than the Nordic Sámi,
they still felt a sense of common identity and their outward appearance
seemed to confirm this fact to visitors such as the ethnologist Nikolai
Kharuzin, who wrote that the dress of the Sámi of the Kola Peninsula
was hardly to be distinguished from that of the Nordic countries.[76]

Some visitors noted the importance, not of French, but of English as
the *lingua franca* in the region, the status of which has not diminished

to this day. When the French Count Goblet d'Alviella arrived at Haparanda in 1868 at the start of his visit to Lapland, he noted that 'Our party was made up of Belgians, Germans, Norwegians and Swedes ... However, it was a fifth language which was our *lingua franca*; all of our companions understood and spoke English, a knowledge of which is of great service in the north.'[77] Apparently, it was quite a cosmopolitan group of visitors, for one of Stockholm's most famous singers, Luisa Michaeli, was a fellow traveller, journeying there in preparation for a northern musical tour.[78] The Frenchman also gave his demographic impression of Kautokeino, commenting that as many as 4,000 to 5,000 Lapps set up temporary winter residence there. He additionally noted that 'There was also a small quantity of *Quènes* (Kväner, in Swedish). They were said to be Finns from the east, who dressed like the Lapps. The local Norwegians are said to fear them as a Trojan horse, encouraged by the Russians to move westwards, in preparation for a Russian conquest of the area. They were also criticised for refusing to learn Norwegian.'[79]

Be that as it may, Norwegian Lapland was, in the early modern period, that part of Sápmi with the largest preponderance of Sámi. In 1599 there were twenty-two households at Kautokeino, twenty-eight at Ávjovárri, ten at Tana and nine at Utsjoki. In 1699 there were five at Kautokeino, sixteen at Ávjovárri, five at Tana and twenty-four at Utsjoki. In 1750 there were fifty-eight at Kautokeino, twenty-nine at Ávjovárri, four at Tana and fifty-four at Utsjoki.[80]

One notable date in Sámi–Norwegian relations occurred in 1733 when King Christian VI visited his Sámi dominions and determined to import 'specimens' of the Sámi to Copenhagen to intrigue the court:

Application was made to numbers of individuals among the Lapland youth to go to court, where they would be kindly received and taken care of by the king—but in vain. At length, however, a young man called Peter Nicolas Korfnæs, was prevailed on to suffer himself to be taken on board of ship to Copenhagen, though not without great difficulty. This Nicolas had nothing remarkable to recommend him, either in his stature or figure....

When the young Laplander arrived at Copenhagen, he was treated with all possible attention and kindness, being handsomely dressed, and well entertained; all which things Mr. Leem describes minutely: but in the autumn he was taken ill, and languished till the end of the year, when he died. ... The body of the youth was interred in a very solemn and honourable manner, and the fine clothes in which he had been attired by his majesty, were sent for some small consolation to his sorrowful parents.

At the same time that Nicolas was sent to Copenhagen, another Lapland boy, called Peter Jonas, who lived as a domestic with Mr. Leems, was induced by the promise of many good things ... to go with Admiral Rosenpalm, with the intention of becoming one of his seamen. As the lad did not want capacity, the admiral had him instructed in writing and arithmetic, and sent him on board a Danish East Indiaman, that he might learn the art of navigation. He made one voyage to India, but died soon after his return to Copenhagen.[81]

Swedish Lapland

Sweden's drive into Lapland and on to the Arctic Ocean was launched by King Gustaf Vasa (1496–1560), who established a hereditary dynasty and introduced the Reformation. This expansion reached its peak under the reign of King Karl IX (1550–1611) during the second half of the sixteenth century.

Although this brought some benefits for the Sámi, who were supplied with considerable quantities of butter and flour by the state—albeit comestibles not traditionally eaten by them—they were in turn obliged to provide large quantities of furs in the form of taxation. A tax revision at the beginning of the seventeenth century also included dried fish and reindeer among the goods to be provided by the Sámi as a form of taxation. This new intrusion upon the Sámi proved more onerous insofar as it intruded upon their own food resources, which contributed to a major crisis during the 1610s. The fur trade also increasingly suffered as the quantity of prey was dramatically reduced, in part by overhunting and in part as a result of unusually severe winters. Moreover, the very structure and organisation of Sámi hunting and reindeer herding was itself being affected, especially as the Swedish government began to acquire large reindeer herds tended by the Sámi herders. These consisted mainly of male reindeer which had been paid as tax by the Sámi. As a result, Sámi herds had an increasing predominance of females, which tended to alter their focus to breeding, rather than for other usages.[82] Of course, mercantile trade with the Sámi continued apace, with Sámi boots, reindeer horn, textiles and skins as the main commodities during the seventeenth century at Varanger and other Sámi trading centres.[83] However, a collapse in the availability of resources necessary to continue hunting, fishing and gathering could not be avoided and this led to the establishment of nomadic reindeer herding as a mono-culture, as the Swedish historian Lennart Lundmark has demonstrated.[84] Moreover, the increasing colonisation of the region created further upheavals for the Sámi. The pace of this colonisation was further increased after a new regulation came into effect in 1749 which gave the governor the right to grant permission to new settlers to establish new farms, despite other previous regulations limiting them.[85] This severely damaged the community structures in which the Sámi traditionally lived—the *siida*.

The Siidas

The *siidas* were the geographical building blocks of Sámi life. Each taxable Sámi 'owned' about 410 square kilometres of land on average, yet life was nomadic; for example, with respect to the Suonikylä *siida*, the winter village was moved every twenty to forty years because of the scarcity of lichen and firewood.[86] Some *siidas*, like those at Pielinen and Lieksa, both in Karelia, straddled both sides of the Finnish and Russian borders.[87] However, these disappeared centuries ago.

The *siida* was also a unit of administrative jurisdiction and, in the east of the Sámi homeland, the *siida* convocation made judicial decisions, the so-called *lapprätt* (Lappish right). In the west, on the other hand, historical documents show that a different system was used. Documents from the 1753 Jokkmokk court session in the Lule Sámi region, for example, confirm that conflicts in these areas were resolved by straightforward parish meetings or sent to the courts.[88]

The establishment of firm borders in the midst of the Sámi homeland also had repercussions. In 1826 the border between Norway and Russia was drawn right through the middle of the Paatsjoki *siida*, while a part of the Näätämö *siida* was incorporated into Finland. In the late nineteenth century governmental bodies with their own agenda also became involved. For example, in 1879, documents concerning settlement were transferred to the state forestry administration and the Forest Act of 1886 favoured this industry over the rights of the Sámi and, in particular, those of the *siida*, since the rights of municipalities in Finland now took precedence. This enabled the state to claim ownership of all land not specifically registered as belonging to an individual or judicially registered organisation. The state was thereby given the right to grant some of this land for the establishment of farming homesteads. Municipalism won out and, to take one case, the lands formerly belonging to the Inari *siida* became the municipality of Inari.[89] Here, in an area by the old Russian border with Finland—the boundary stone on Kaamassaari Island in Lake Inari is said to have delineated it as confirmed by the 1595 Peace of Teusina[90]—the Sámi had immemorially lived from fishing and hunting, in particular for wild reindeer in the uplands. In consequence, over time their land and livelihood became increasingly constrained.

The Kemi Sámi

Kemi Lapland was one major historic area of Sámi settlement which suffered growing colonial intrusion. While the population of Kemi Lapland fluctuated between 100 and 200 households between the fifteenth and the eighteenth century, it climbed dramatically after 1750 to 295 households, in possession of some 3,620 reindeer in total. To the east and south, in Kuusamo, they herded around 2,000 reindeer, while to the north, in Inari, they herded about 500, making its *siida*, with its thirty to fifty taxpayers, the largest. Assuming that each household had about half a dozen members, the population may have actually varied between 600 and 1,300 people.[91] Yet by the late nineteenth century the Sámi had been effectively evicted from many parts of the region, the last of the Kemi Sámi having come to reside at Sompio. The rest had either been assimilated into the rest of the population or left. As for the Sámi from Kautokeino, in the 1890s they, too, had come to be displaced, moving into the border area of the current-day Sámi homeland, taking their reindeer herds with them.[92]

The Inari Sámi

The Inari Sámi were and remain another important Sámi people. As a distinct ethnic group they are first mentioned in documents from 1517, when the Russia tsar issued a decree in relation to the collection of tax in northern Lapland. Russia was particularly keen to impose the so-called 'crossbow tax' on hunting. By then the Norwegian government was already making its own tax claims on Inari, and the Swedes eventually followed suit in 1551, laying claim not only to Inari but Utsjoki as well, thereby earning the Inari region the dubious nickname of 'the Land of Three Kings'.[93]

In Inari there were some sixty-three Sámi in 1751, but only forty-eight by 1780.[94] In the former year, the border between the kingdoms of Denmark–Norway and Sweden–Finland were firmly delineated according to the Strömstad Border Treaty of 1751. Nonetheless, the spring and autumn migratory rights of the Sámi across this border were confirmed by virtue of its *Lappkodicill* (Lapp Codicil).[95]

Despite this provision, there were still frequent conflicts with colonists from the south, which led to increasing confrontation, especially in the later eighteenth century. A police chief was consequently appointed to Inari to help resolve these issues. He himself was a local Sámi, Juhana Morottaja from Lake Ukonjärvi, and in 1798 he was called to the headwaters of the Ivalo River to resolve a conflict relating to beaver hunting, involving new settlers from Kittilä accused of poaching. Although Morottaja caught them in the act and confiscated their catch, the poachers put up considerable resistance, regaining the poached items and murdering him in the process.[96] In this manner, whatever the legal structures enacted by the government for their protection, the Sámi increasingly found their life and livelihood encroached upon and illicitly exploited. It is thus not surprising that some travellers to the region thought that there was neither a militia nor a police force in Lapland.[97]

Criminality

In the eighteenth century each Sámi village in the Nordic countries had its own court of justice. Appeals made above its jurisdiction were also largely heard by their fellow Sámi, who enjoyed local government administrative authority.[98] If government protection was limited or non-existent, the *siida* administration could itself even impose its authority when capital punishment was applicable in serious criminal cases. One such case in Kautokeino involved Nils Andersson, a hired hand who had murdered five members of a single family for whom he had worked.[99] Much if not most of the violence erupted through the aggravation of alcoholic drinks, plentiful at the annual fairs or feast day celebrations where ethnic tensions among Sámi, Swedes, Finns and Norwegians sometimes led to riots and murders. Family disputes and altercations among young men also occasionally had a violent outcome when drink was involved. With respect to the role of alcohol and crime committed by the Sámi, the teetotal religious revival movement initiated by the priest Lars Levi Læstadius (see Chapter 2) in the 1840s dampened its usage, leading to a major reduction in crimes committed under the influence of such beverages. On other occasions, though, crimes were purely economic in motivation. Burglary and theft were relatively infrequent, but smuggling was a common practice, even involving priests, especially where the smuggling of spirits was concerned. While the penalties were high for burglary and theft, commonly punished by penal servitude through hard labour, smuggling incurred the death penalty. Nonetheless, the crime thrived, and the gallows remained a common site on major traffic crossroads well into the nineteenth century, not only in Lapland but throughout the Nordic region.[100] In the Russian part of Sápmi, Sámi courts only dealt with administrative matters; serious crimes, such as murder, were referred to Russian courts for judgement.[101]

The Skolt Sámi

The Skolt Sámi provide a particularly instructive microcosm of Sámi life, having preserved their traditional lifestyle to a greater degree than most of the other groups which make up the Sámi people, based on hunting and fishing, as well as reindeer herding. The Skolt Sámi homeland traditionally extends from Näätämö (Neiden, in Norwegian) to Pechenga and the Tuuloma region, much of it historically under the control of Russia.[102] Today significant insight into their lives from half a millennium ago is provided by the Skolt Sámi Archive, an extraordinary document preserved in a wooden box in the Finnish National Archives in Helsinki, which contains the roll of the decrees and permits granted to the Skolt Sámi by the tsars since the 1600s.[103] At the turn of the nineteenth century, some have maintained that there were at least 800 to 900 Skolt Sámi living in their homeland. According to them, up to 200 lived in the large *siida* of Suonikylä and Paatsjoki, while in Nuortijärvi alone there were about 200. In each of the other *siidas* there were said to be at most 100, but often far fewer. Except for the Hirvas and Suonikylä *siida*, moreover, they were not exclusively Sámi. Leif Rantala, however, is of the opinion that there was a maximum of 300 Skolts in Suonikylä, 200 in Notozero, about fifty in Paatsjoki and another fifty in Hirvasjärvi, altogether 500 to 600 Skolts at that time.[104]

The Russian Sámi often enjoyed privileges the Scandinavian and Finnish Sámi did not, at least until later in the nineteenth century. For example, after the border between Russia and Norway was closed in 1852, the Russian Sámi continued to enjoy the rights of migration, at least until the late 1880s when they were compelled to settle, leaving their reindeer to graze on the same pastures throughout the year—an ecological disaster. Even worse followed when, at the beginning of the twentieth century, the Skolt Sámi of Neiden, the Norwegian part of a *siida* straddling the border with Finland, lost their reindeer herds and herding rights to the Northern Sámi reindeer herders already there. This meant the end of the Norwegian part of that *siida* on the Norwegian side of the border and the forced assimilation of its inhabitants into the wider population.[105] By contrast, on the Finnish side, known as Näätämö, the Sámi retained their herds and related rights.[106]

The Skolt Sámi migrated according to the spawning seasons of the fish, and by the early 1900s they were based in settlements of small log or sod houses. Conical tents provided them with temporary accommodation while on the move, especially at the end of April when they migrated to the lands of their clan in the interior. In the spring the reindeer calves were earmarked. Then, in June, the Skolts would move to the grazing pastures of the uplands. Along with fishing, they sheared and processed the reindeer and sheepskins. In August or September, the inland Skolt Sámi migrated to their autumn homes, from which they fished, hunted and tended their reindeer. Their round-up would then begin and continued throughout the autumn. When they were all collected, those found to belong to other families would be brought to special places of collection. Finally, towards the end of autumn, at the latest by the second half of December, they returned to their winter villages to tend their herds, collect firewood and conduct trade, until spring arrived at the end of April.[107] Traditionally, the Skolt Sámi used the occasion of a village meeting (*siidsobbar* or *norraz*) during this period to choose their village elder, a time which continues to be customarily set aside as an occasion for community discussions even today.[108]

The outbreak of the Russian Revolution in 1917, however, was to intrude dramatically not only upon their lifestyle, but also upon their very existence, as its poisonous fruits ripened over the following years. In addition, the annexation of what had for centuries been Russian territory—an act which had already been anticipated in 1864 when Tsar Alexander II had promised to give Finland an Arctic harbour in exchange for a piece of land in the south of Finland upon which a munitions factory had been built—finally became a reality.[109] Thus, between 1917 and 1940, many Skolt Sámi acquired Finnish citizenship by default.

In 1920, according to the Treaty of Tartu, Finland—still recovering from a vicious civil war lasting from January to May 1918 in which the anti-Bolshevik Whites were victorious—received the region around Pechenga, which the Finns called Petsamo, from the Soviet Union, finally providing it with a port on the Arctic Ocean. The new border fell between one-quarter of the Suonikylä *siida*, on the Soviet side, and the remainder of that *siida*, as well as the Notozero *siida*, on the Finnish side. Of the Sámi population resident there, some 95 per cent remained on their respective traditional territories.[110] As a result, in 1921 and 1922 all the Skolt Sámi residing in Petsamo (now Pechenga) became Finnish citizens, with the exception of thirty-five people from Suonikylä who were said to have opted for Soviet nationality, although others have put this figure as no more than five or six.[111] Moreover, a small number of people from the Muotka *siida* moved to the Petsamo *siida*, becoming Finnish citizens. Finland also sold the rights to the western parts of the Paatsjoki *siida* to Norway, but the Skolt Sámi who lived there received little personal compensation, the bulk of the money instead going directly into the Finnish state coffers.[112] Much of this money, however, eventually filtered back in the form of government-funded projects, as a variety of initiatives was undertaken in the newly Finnish Petsamo region to develop its life and infrastructure. With the old winter village, Potklasjoki, subsumed within the Soviet Union, a new winter village for the Skolts was constructed in 1930 at Suonikylä, by Lake Marnjärvi, funded by the Finnish state. Reindeer herding and trade continued to be the main livelihoods. Those Sámi based at Suonikylä were also granted summer fishing rights off the Petsamo coast. This was significant since fishing had long taken priority among the Skolt Sámi as a means of employment and even reindeer herding sometimes took second place to accommodate it.[113]

The concluding phase of the Second World War (discussed in depth later) devastated Lapland, leaving traumatic scars on a plethora of levels and forcing massive migration. In the aftermath of the Lapland War between Finland and Nazi Germany, the transfer to the Soviet Union of Petsamo (Pechenga, in Russian) and the concentration of reindeer herding to the Kola Peninsula, virtually all of the Skolt Sámi in the USSR fled to Finland or were evacuated there; all too aware as they were of Stalin's repression elsewhere in Russia and, in particular, on the Kola Peninsula. A few of the elderly went to reside in Ylä Tuuloma and Upper Tuloma, in the former lands of the Nuortijärvi and Hirvas *siida*. On the Finnish side, the Inari Sámi (numbering 900 at most in 1995)[114] were long established on their traditional lands and were a group with whom they had been in contact for centuries, so that many Skolts today live cheek by jowl with them in the vicinity of Lake Sulkusjärvi.[115] While the three Skolt Sámi villages in the Petsamo (Pechenga) region were subject to immediate evacuation to central Finland in 1944, they were later encouraged to resettle themselves in the vicinity of Inari when enough housing was built after 1948. The Sámi of Suonikylä were transported to near Sevettijärvi and Näätämö, to the north of Lake Inari. Others from the Petsamo *siida* moved to Nellim, Tsarmijärvi and Mustola, to the south-east, and the Sámi of the Paatsjoki *siida* settled at Keväjärvi.[116] All benefited from generous land grants, which gave them existing buildings, timber rights and the usufruct of state-owned land and water sources. Local amenities including a school, dormitory, health clinic, church and general store were also provided.[117] However, a growing competition for resources led to local conflict—in particular over issues relating to the regulation of local water levels in Lake Inari—which drove a growing Sámi diaspora away from the region altogether in these early post-war years before the matter was fully resolved.[118]

The Skolt Sámi Act, enacted by the government of Finland in 1955, which was the first 'Sámi' law of its kind, granted the newly resettled Sámi a wide range of special rights: to fish, to herd reindeer on land owned by the state and to gather local wood for household use. Free housing was also provided, but only on condition that any future transfer could only occur with the permission of the Ministry of Agriculture and that such ownership would be restricted exclusively to the Skolt Sámi.[119]

These measures notwithstanding, the Skolt Sámi were increasingly assimilated into the wider Finnish population and culture, not only in the Paatsjoki and Petsamo *siida*, but in those of Nellim and Keväjärvi as well. Even at Sevettijärvi, virtually a Skolt Sámi enclave where Skolt Sámi continued to be spoken, almost everyone also acquired the Finnish language.[120] By the turn of the twenty-first century, Skolt Sámi was still spoken in Sevettijärvi and Nellim, although in total there were no more than 200 Skolt Sámi speakers. On the Russian side of the border, at Notozero, only twenty to thirty such speakers remained, and as for Neiden, on the Norwegian side of the border, speakers of Skolt Sámi, although not their descendants,[121] had disappeared towards the end of the previous century. As for Kildin Sámi speakers, by contrast, there were 707 in 1994, but just six people spoke Ter Sámi and only seven Akkala Sámi (the term is said to derive from the ancient Finnish word for woman, *akka*). By 2000, only one native Akkala speaker remained.[122] This had occurred despite the fact that the Akkala Sámi had retained many more ancient traditions than their fellow Sámi in the west. For example, they continued to maintain both winter and summer *siidas*, from which they sent out their reindeer herds in search of lichen, and gathered firewood. Common land had, moreover, sometimes been held on behalf of two *siidas*. Moreover, despite the introduction of reindeer herding in the seventeenth century, wild reindeer hunting had continued to prevail to varying degrees until the Russian Revolution, even if a semi-nomadic way of life had long ceased under Russian governmental pressure.[123]

By 1992, 545 Skolt Sámi were living in the Inari region of Finnish Lapland, but their community was beset by economic difficulties. As the end of the second millennium approached, unemployment among them was extremely high—some 40 per cent of the adult working population had no jobs in the relatively isolated Sevettijärvi area, and even in areas closer to Ivalo unemployment was high. Many Skolt Sámi consequently moved away, often to places outside Sápmi where work was available.[124] There were also local issues of dispute which encouraged a growing Sámi diaspora: the regulation of the water level of Lake Inari was a particularly serious source of local contention, with important ecological implications for those living in the area. The establishment of the Näätämö reindeer-herding cooperative also created difficulties for Muddusjärvi which thereby lost a number of its summer pastures to the newcomers. Many Sámi of various cooperatives have also been affected by the establishment of the Utsjoki Common Forest, a form of National Park set aside for public enjoyment, which intrudes upon complex property rights and which remains an issue not yet fully resolved.[125]

Social Exchanges among the Non-Sámi

The relations of the Sámi with their neighbours often had complex dimensions, with gifts playing a significant role in smoothing over misunderstandings and in demonstrating respect. As Acerbi wrote:

It is usual with them, as in the East, never to wait on a superior without a present. If a Laplander has occasion to attend a magistrate, or his clergyman, he brings with him either a cheese, a hare, partridge, tea or river fish, a lamb, some venison, a reindeer's tongue, butter, a quantity of down feathers, or something of the like kind. In return for his present, he never goes back empty, but receives either some tobacco, or a bottle of mead, a keg of beer, some ginger and spices, or, in short, whatever is at hand which may be supposed acceptable. The same custom prevails amongst the Muscovites.[126]

For the academic Matti Enbuska, who has carried out research on Sámi conflicts with colonial settlers, the conflict between the two has been overstated. He writes:

The life of farmers in Ostrobothnia's northern districts was hardly distinguishable from the way of life of the Sámi in the southern districts of Kemi Lappmark. Since families had heavily intermixed with one another, ethnic differences were hardly pronounced.

According to available information, the Lappmark borders remained intact, but the farmers owned a lot of fishing waters. There were often disputes on their exploitation, but the farmers disputed these rights to an even greater degree with their farming neighbours. It was a different matter in the districts around Kuusamo, where the farmers, who had a different system of exploiting their resources, arrived in great numbers. In these areas the Sámi suffered considerably. … With respect to the developments in Kemi Lappmark one cannot agree with Tegengren's conclusions that the Finnish colonisation should have been the most destructive factor with respect to Sámi culture. One must also disagree that the Finnish and Sámi way of living was sharply differentiated one from another. The situation was quite the opposite.[127]

In any case, it should be remembered that Ostrobothnia, as a result of the Great Northern War (1700–21) and the War of the Hats (1741–3), in both of which Sweden fought Russia, suffered a particularly brutal Russian occupation, with many Finns carried off into serfdom or military service, leaving those who remained with a common sense of defensive identity.

The distinction between the Sámi land and the land of the colonists became blurred by the early nineteenth century, and this did not make for ethnic harmony between the two peoples who were competing for limited resources, especially woodlands. Indeed, the land belonging to Forest Sámi tended to be subject to far more scrutiny from the authorities than that of the Mountain Sámi. These matters quite naturally exacerbated ethnic tensions.[128]

Colonial immigration was obviously very strong, but within the colonists' communities it was highly democratic in nature as, by contrast with the south-west of Finland where aristocrats made up 14 per cent of the population in 1805, in Lapland there were virtually none in the settler population.[129] Yet in many ways this was the continuation of a demographic change within all of Finnish society, a result of Russian occupation in the early eighteenth century when many Finns were carried off into serfdom or military service by the Russians, never to return. Many others had fled to Sweden, where the establishment of new farmsteads obviated the attractiveness of returning once peace was made. In consequence, many abandoned farms in Finland were taken into possession by new settlers in quest of land, who, if successful in establishing themselves there, were granted new patents of ownership; even so, many farmsteads throughout Finland remained unoccupied long after the upheavals of war and plagues had abated.[130] Therefore, the pressure to colonise land in the far north remained less than might have been expected: during the early 1830s, at the Swedish internal border of the Sámi homeland between Degerfors and Lycksele, a three-column post was erected by the road, with a painting affixed depicting a Swede and a Sámi man shaking hands with one another as a sign of peace and friendship.[131] Yet the frontiers were not delineated strictly according to national linguistic groups. Thus while Sámi life in nineteenth-century Finland was centred around Inari, Utsjoki and Enontekiö, when the Peace Treaty of Hamina with Russia fixed the Torne River as the border between Sweden and Finland in 1809, a large Finnish-speaking population belonged henceforth to Sweden itself. In consequence, until about 1870 all the teaching in Swedish Tornedalen, the valley of Torne River, was conducted in Finnish. However, a policy of Swedification was introduced later in the century and by around 1920 teaching activities in the Torne Valley were carried out exclusively in Swedish.[132]

Taxation

Taxation had for centuries been imposed as a serious burden upon the Sámi, who, until the later modern period, derived few benefits from its imposition. Its application was relatively straightforward. The taxable land was divided among the Sámi as they themselves saw fit, provided the taxes were paid.[133] However, by the late seventeenth century there was a general consensus in Sweden that a Sámi village, along with its land, should be seen as a single taxable unit.[134] Indeed, the taxable land of the Sámi increasingly began to be seen by the government as land belonging to the Crown, and the rights of the Sámi to their land became subject to what the governmental authorities considered the most 'fruitful' use of the land. Many who lost their reindeer herds also lost their land. Others, when the land began to be deemed more useful for cultivation, lost their land even with reindeer herds.[135]

A provincial governor, priest or important farmer often gained the 'right' to purchase former Sámi land, now confiscated by the state as 'Crown land'. Figures such as Petrus Læstadius wrote in the 1830s that this type of abuse was forbidden, but that it happened nonetheless. His exhortations to return to the traditional division of land as the Sámi saw fit, however, went largely unheeded,[136] especially in Pite och Lule Lappmark. Indeed, an administrative initiative with respect to Lule encouraged the complete abolition of Sámi taxable land. The Sámi were increasingly removed from land considered more suitable for agriculture or other activities and resettled elsewhere.[137]

Finally, in 1867 a compromise was reached which delineated Sámi taxable lands from land elsewhere. Two further meetings between Sámi leaders and the government were held in 1868 and 1869. However, the increasing influence of the forestry industry had a deleterious effect. Henceforth, taxable Sámi land came to signify areas where Sámi reindeer herding was carried out, even if the concept—taxable Sámi land—remained.[138]

By the mid-1880s, taxable Sámi land could only be found in Arjeplog and Arvidsjaur in Norrbotten and in the whole of Västerbotten. 'The Lapp should be a Lapp' was the political motto in Sweden of those keen to encourage this trend.[139] Yet the 1886 law provided no definition of who was a Lapp.[140] Moreover, new settlements which had been illegally established in Sámi taxable lands after 1867 were legalised in 1909–15. In consequence, and despite new laws enacted in 1886 and 1898 which were intended to protect them, many Sámi also lost hunting and fishing resources. These tendencies, which were perceived as pernicious by many Sámi, continued into the 1920s.[141]

The Sámi, moreover, continued to be categorised as a nomadic people and their permanent settlement discouraged. In the early part of the twentieth century, for example, many bureaucratic obstacles were put in place to dissuade them from constructing turf-covered wooden huts which seemed likely to be used as fixed homes, as the minister for justice, Bernt Hasselrot, expressed it. Only with respect to the Sámi in Jämtland was he disposed to allow all of them to settle as farmers. This paternalistic approach extended to the elderly and infirm among the

Sámi, who were to be given homes 'in settlement areas provided by the governmental authorities, where they could continue their lives in the manner of their traditions and according to their needs'.[142]

An era came to an end in 1928 when Sámi taxable land, as a legal and economic concept, was finally abolished, even if the term continued to be used 'inappropriately' on occasion in land registries until 1951.[143] Yet while their former colonial status was finally dissolved, this period also coincided with a highly ambiguous attitude to the nature of the 'Lapp race'. On the one hand, during the 1920s and 1930s, the Sámi were perceived by the other Nordic peoples as belonging to a somewhat Asiatic race, while many Germans, on the other hand, and Hitler and the Nazis in particular, considered them favourably as a virile offshoot of the Aryan peoples and later, during the Lapland War, they were treated more considerately than virtually any people caught up in the hostilities of the eastern front.[144]

Language Shifts among the Sámi

One particularly notable characteristic of the Sámi is their highly distinct languages, and language shifts have often mirrored the fate of the Sámi people themselves over their long history. The Finnish linguist Mikko Korhonen has provided considerable insight into the history, changing structure and use of the Sámi languages in his work *Johdatus lapin kielen historiaan* (Introduction to the History of the Lapp Language), published by the Finnish Literature Society in Helsinki in 1981. He has demonstrated that the proto-Sámi language (*kantaSámi*; its pronunciation is still a matter of dispute between Finnish and Hungarian philologists) was spoken in the first millennium around the Gulf of Finland, the interior of mainland Finland and Finnish Lapland, from which he concludes that it spread both westwards into Sweden and eastwards into the Kola Peninsula. Indeed, he stresses that such Sámi settlements in which the proto-Sámi language were used still flourished in in the south-west of Finland around AD 500 and, indeed, even in parts of the extreme south as late as 1000. He has also produced evidence to show that small Sámi pockets of settlements still existed in south-central Finland from the thirteenth to as late as the seventeenth century.[145]

Yet at no time has the use of the Sámi language undergone more enormous shifts and changes than over the previous century, as confirmed by the study of Marjut Aikio in 1988. This sociolinguistic study focuses on the cycle of language shift among the Sámi in five reindeer Sámi villages from 1910 to 1980. As she put it:

Language shift was more rapid from one generation to the next than within a single generation, in fact far more rapid than previously assumed. The actual crux as far as language change is concerned occurred between 1930 and 1950. Language shift took place in the family, the domain most important to language survival ... The Sámi language was retained longest among men.

Dense, protected contact networks as well as the remoteness of the community protected the language from shift.[146]

A detailed study of many aspects of eastern Sámi philology, as well as a monumental four-volume Inari Sámi dictionary, was provided by Erkki Esaias Itkonen (1913–92), professor of Finno-Ugric Linguistics at the University of Helsinki and the son of a priest who served in Inari. His brother was the ethnographer Toivo Immanuel Itkonen (1891–1968), who also produced a number of works on Skolt Sámi dialects spoken in Finland, Norway and Russia, including a two-volume dictionary of Skolt Sámi that was published in 1958.[147] Reference works such as these were just some of the attempts, many emanating from the Nordic countries, to increase the teaching of the indigenous languages, which with respect to the north-west of Russia encompasses not only the Sámi but the Komi, Nenets and other ethno-linguistic groups as well.[148] In 1990, the Komi folklore ensemble Izhma was established under the direction of S.V. Filipchenko. There were by now more Komi (1,246) than Sámi (948) in Lovozero and its vicinity.[149] Nonetheless, by 2003, along with Skolt Sámi, the westernmost of the Sámi languages spoken in Russia, three others still remained in use, albeit spoken by an ever declining number.

In Finland, the Inari Sámi Language Association or Anarâškielâ Servi was established in 1986 and soon had some 200 members. The association provided the means to publish the Inari Sámi newspaper *Anarâš*, while also encouraging the publication of other material in Inari Sámi.[150] Spurred on by the UN 'Year of Indigenous Peoples', Finland also undertook financial assistance for a language project which provided for the instruction of thirteen Skolt Sámi children from Sevettijärvi and Nellim.[151]

One important innovation with respect to Sámi language preservation was the introduction of the so-called 'language nest'. This approach was based on the method initiated by the Maori of New

Zealand in the late 1980s. It facilitates learning by pre-school children within families who do not use the indigenous tongue, by providing outside cultural and entertainment activities in the indigenous language. This method was especially successful among the Inari and Skolt Sámi in Finnish Lapland, financed by a joint initiative between the municipality of Inari and the European Union that was launched in 1997.[152]

The Sámi of the Kola Peninsula

With respect to the Skolt Sámi, on the Russian side of the border of the Kola Peninsula they had settled into a peaceful period of relative tranquillity in the later part of the eighteenth century, with Lovozero, the principal Sámi settlement there, having a total population of ninety-four, fifty-two men and forty-two women, composing altogether some fifteen families in 1785. All male adults knew Russian, but only one of the women did.[153] However, this period of peace eventually came to an end with the advent of war in the region during the nineteenth century, when British warships arrived in bellicose circumstances during the Crimean War in 1854. The British aimed to take control of the town of Kola, which had always been an *ostrog* (i.e. a fortified town). When two British sailors who had gone ashore in quest of water were shot, the British commander ordered the inhabitants to evacuate the town within twenty-four hours and to remove whatever personal chattels they could. The British gunboat *Miranda* then initiated a bombardment which destroyed most of the buildings, including almost 100 houses, the old battery, two churches and the government store of corn and salt.[154] The Sámi, moreover, were not only affected by the British on this front. A number of Sámi young men, in particular, those from Panoi, were recruited to fight in the Crimea itself against them, some of whom never returned.[155]

By this time the legal and military infrastructure of Russian Lapland was well established. Already, in 1838, Tsar Nicholas I had created the Jurisdictional District of Lapland, and in 1847 he also established the Circuit Court of Lapland, to include Inari. The village of Kittilä then became the administrative centre of all of northern Russian Lapland, soon to be assisted by a bailiff based at Kittilä's wooden prison which had been built in 1855.[156]

The arrival of the Komi, a semi-nomadic reindeer-herding people, occurred in the autumn of 1883 as a flight from the devastation of a reindeer epidemic in their homelands to the east, as well as from their overgrazed pastures which had helped to cause it. By the spring of 1884, four families had crossed the frozen Kanda River with some 9,000 head of reindeer, having made their way through Karelia in caravans of draught sledges.[157] These were pulled by reindeer rather than dogs because the reindeer could survive on lichen while dogs needed precious meat, and hence the latter were not normally used as draught animals by the Sámi and the Komi in this eastern part of the Sámi homeland.[158]

These herders came from their native Komi villages of Bakur, Dijur, Kolomitskoe, Njazja, Ust-Tzjemskoe and Ust-Cilma, among others, on the Pechora River, across the White Sea to the east, in the province of Arkhangelsk. Soon they settled near Lovozero, opposite the Sámi, on the Virma River, before establishing new Komi villages at Krasnoshelje, Kanevka and Ivanovka.[159]

The Russian language had by now come to dominate in the region, with the overwhelming majority of Sámi on the Kola Peninsula knowing the Russian language by the late 1870s. As Nemirovich-Danchenko put it, 'They not only spoke Russian well, thought in it, as well, but used the Russian expressions, which were current amongst our Murmansk and Kola people. Only a few women, living in far-flung corners, could not understand Russian.'[160] By this time Lovozero was a multi-ethnic settlement, at least as far as northern peoples were concerned, for 117 Komi resided there, alongside twenty-five Nenets people. In 1899 the settlement was provided with an administration, the first mayor of which was Nikolai Shmakov.[161] Although by the beginning of the twentieth century about eighty-five Sámi households resided in permanent settlements on the Kola Peninsula,[162] even by 1905 Lovozero only consisted of ten houses and thirty-two cabins.[163]

That year was a significant one for the Sámi to the west in Scandinavia, since it was in 1905, following Norway's unilateral declaration of independence from Sweden, that the authorisation of Sámi seasonal migrations through the Lapp Codicil of 1751 was abrogated, and cross-border seasonal migrations were prohibited. Many Northern Sámi were consequently resettled in traditionally South Sámi areas. For example, some seventy-five families, encompassing 279 individuals and 16,500 animals, were resettled around Jokkmokk, Arjeplog and Tärna in Swedish Lapland. As a result, conflict between the two Sámi communities—which had formerly been separated and had different social customs and even languages—grew, a situation aggravated by the fact that the Læstadian religious tradition had come to dominate in some Sámi communities, a non-ecstatic one in others. Even today, this divergence in attitude has been maintained despite the fact that both encourage teetotalism.[164]

By 1897 there were 1,736 Sámi in the Kola Peninsula, comprising 20 per cent of the total population. Of these, Russians numbered 5,276, or 60.8 per cent of the total.[165] During the First World War Lovozero's population increased dramatically to 690 inhabitants by 1915, and by 1917 Lovozero and its environs had a population of 707, including 167 Sámi, 493 Komi and forty-seven people of diverse ethnicity. By now the Bolshevik Revolution had taken hold and a local Soviet was rapidly established under Rochev Semyon Mkarovich (1875–1945), a Komi reindeer herder and farm labourer. This was followed in 1920 by the first sitting of the district Soviet.[166]

Now it seemed as if the Sámi, at least in the Soviet Union, would take their place among the community of nations, and even in neighbouring Finland a new focus was given to the Sámi, as Petsamo and its Arctic corridor became a part of the newly independent country. It was in this context that Samuli Paulaharju (1875–1944) published his notable book *Kolttain mailta* (The Land of the Skolt Sámi) in 1921 (a second edition was republished in Helsinki in 2009).[167] Paulaharju had first visited the region in the pre-war years, carrying out research in Lapland in 1910, before returning again in 1914 and in 1920.[168] By this time, as we have seen, there were also other ethnic communities now settled there, in particular the Komi, who laid the foundations of their own villages, Krasnoshelje and Kanevka, in 1921 and 1923 respectively.[169] The Finnish anthropologist Väinö Tanner also visited the region and in 1929 published an important book on the Skolt Sámi in Swedish, which disseminated much information on the Sámi to a wider international readership.[170]

Revolution and Civil War in Russian Lapland

Support existed for the Bolsheviks in the Kola Peninsula even before the outbreak of the October Revolution. Already in early 1917 meetings and marches in their support were organised and held by sawmill workers at Kandalaksha and at Knyazhaya Guba, on the north-western corner of the White Sea coast.[171] However, Murmansk, a new city in which the British were a major presence, had been further filled during the course of the First World War with Allied forces sent to support their Russian allies in the war against Germany. When the revolution broke out in Petrograd and later during the Civil War, Murmansk thus became an important base for the Western powers. Not only Britain, the United States and France, but also Italy, Serbia and Canada took part in this military intervention, with fresh troops arriving at Murmansk and Arkhangelsk. Bolshevik prisoners who fell into Allied hands were sent to a camp by the estuary of the Yokanga River, where some 150 were held in transit at any one time. Conditions, as always in the Russian far north even at the best of times, were brutal and hundreds died. Of the 1,200 prisoners concentrated there, 700 died.[172] Yet the situation was highly complex. For one thing, both the Allies and the Bolsheviks still feared Germany even more than each other, even though the latter had just signed the Treaty of Brest-Litovsk. Indeed, some 55,000 Germans and 50,000 Finns, from their now independent nation state in which a Bolshevik revolution had just been crushed with the former's aid, loomed threateningly to the west, commanded by the able German general Count Rüdiger von der Goltz. A highly unstable oral accord was eventually reached, sanctioned on the Russian side by Leon Trotsky, at that time the commissar for war, according to which the Allied Command and Murmansk Soviet would together defend the northern ports against any possible German assault, along with the newly built railway which ran from Murmansk to Petrograd, close to the Finnish border. However, on 8 June 1918, Vladimir Lenin himself ordered the Allies to evacuate, despite the opposition of the Murmansk Soviet. This order was ignored and a 2,000-strong multinational interventionist force—one of the first of modern times—composed of British, French, Italian, Serbian, American and Canadian troops led by the British general, Sir Charles Clarkson Maynard, arrived. Altogether the anti-Bolshevist forces soon totalled some 48,000 men, 28,000 of whom were foreign, the rest White Russian. Since the general population by now, along with Russians and Sámi, included Poles, Letts, Chinese and Koreans, the Bolshevik base in the Russian north-west was highly insecure. Nonetheless, the Allied interventionists were defeated: in June 1919, those stationed near the White Sea departed and on 10 September 1919 the last British ship withdrew from the rest of the region. The last stationed on the Kola Peninsula finally left on 12 October 1919. Over the following four months many

White Russians on the Kola Peninsula and in Karelia fought on under General V.S. Skobeltsin. To the east, White Russian General Evgeny Miller and his army carried on until 19 February 1920 when an ice-breaker took Miller, some of his leading officers and what remained of the old administrative and mercantile elite abroad into permanent emigration and the 154th Red Army marched into Arkhangelsk. Finally, on 21 February 1920, following a Bolshevik uprising on behalf of seamen, port workers and railwaymen, Murmansk itself surrendered, an event commemorated by a plaque at Five Corners Square.[173]

As we have already seen, when the new borders of Soviet Russia and Finland were firmly established in 1920, there were serious consequences for the Sámi with most of the Skolts of the Petsamo region becoming Finnish, as they and their descendants have remained until today. Petsamo would be returned to the Soviet Union (and known as Pechenga) after the Second World War, when virtually all the Sámi who resided there emigrated to Finland.[174]

Early Soviet Initiatives towards the Sámi

The Soviet authorities had established firm control of the Kola Peninsula by 1920.[175] This was to have an immense effect on the Sámi residing there, not merely because of collectivisation and the GULAG, as we shall see, but also because of its demographic implications. Thus whereas there were 1,554 Sámi living in the Kola Peninsula in 1920, comprising 8.4 per cent of the population, with Russians numbering 12,234 or 71.9 per cent, by 1933 the number of Sámi living there had only risen to 1,932. Over the same period, the number of Russians had increased to 141,136, and, this meant that the Sámi now comprised a mere 1.3 per cent of the population, with the Russians constituting 94.2 per cent.[176]

One of the most important figures dealing with Sámi affairs relating to the Kola Peninsula was Vasilii V. Alymov (1883–1938). A native of Rutii, near Novgorod, he was one of the most important activists on behalf of the Sámi during the early Soviet period, and underscored the problem of Sámi assimilation.[177] As Alymov put it in the early Soviet period, this problem was the principal reason that the Sámi population failed to achieve a notable demographic increase.[178] Alymov was appointed the chairman of the Northern Committee a few months after it was set up in May 1927 under the administration of the regional presidium (soon to be incorporated into the Leningrad region). Then, in

October 1930, the Advisory Board of the People's Commissars appointed him the committee's ombudsman, a position he held for three years.[179]

Alymov wrote to Professor Wiklund:

For our Lapps one has built a large hospital, excellent boarding schools and there is also a veterinary-zootechnical station for reindeer; 10 young Lapps are studying in Leningrad at the special 'Nordic Faculty'. All Lapps, except for the very rich (those who have more than 500 reindeer), are exempt from all taxes. The Central Executive Council Committee (VCIK) in Moscow, has established a special committee to help the small people who live in the north culturally, politically and economically.[180]

The Sámi were just one such people, among twenty-nine others, living in the Soviet north.[181]

Interestingly, Alymov felt that the Kildin dialect of the Kola Peninsula was the most appropriate to foster.[182] But there were other pressing issues as well, for local ethnic conflict was abrading local relationships: the Sámi and Komi communities were highly suspicious of one another and even on the scientific expeditions in which they were involved their mutual hostility created numerous difficulties, as Vladimir V. Tsharnolusky, one of the participants, noted in a letter to Alymov in October 1929. Friction also occurred with other ethnic groups in the region.[183]

Later, as the attitude towards non-Russian indigenous peoples turned increasingly sour in the Soviet Union, such organisations as the Northern Committee which fostered their interests were shut down. Alymov was then transferred to the Ethnographic Museum in Murmansk, where he was appointed director until his arrest during the repression of the 1930s.[184]

Solovetsky Monastery and Burgeoning of Soviet Repressions

The infamous history of the use of Solovetsky Monastery as a Soviet political prison began when it was requisitioned from the Orthodox monks by the Bolsheviks. By September 1923, 3,049 were being held prisoners there, in what, on 13 October 1923, had officially become the Solovetsky Special Purpose Camp (SLON), set up by order of the USSR Council of People's Commissars.[185] Soon, under the leadership of Commissar Alexandr Nogtev, prisoners were being transferred there from other northern cities, such as Arkhangelsk, Kholomogry and Petrominsk.[186] By 1924 there were some 4,100 prisoners and, by 1925, 6,800.[187] Indeed, during the period 1923–9 there were over 840,000 prisoners concentrated at various times in one or the other of the different prison camps set up in and around the former Solovetsky Monastery.[188]

The death rate for prisoners, which was high from the very beginning, increased incrementally over this period. In a twelve-month period from 1926 to 1927 some 728 prisoners died, at a time when there were about 12,700 prisoners in the camp altogether. Interestingly, it was in 1927–8 that the propaganda film *Solovki* was produced by a SOVKINO film crew, presenting the camps as a collective institution where anti-Soviet behaviour was 'corrected' and where the culprits were 're-socialised' in the appropriate forms of behaviour and attitude required by the new Soviet order. It obviously failed in this mission, for, in 1928, there were no less than 13,366 prisoners in the camps, collectively commanded by the secret police officer Fyodor Eikhmans, and, during an eight-month period during 1929–30, no less than 979 'criminals' died at the Golgotha sub-camp alone, out of a total prison population in 1929 of 21,900 prisoners, after A.P. Nogtev (1892–1947) had again been appointed commandant.

Altogether it is thought that about 15,000 died at the camps where the ethnic origins of the victims seem to have played little role: along with native Russians and some Sámi, many Germans, Italians, Albanians, Greeks, Chinese and Koreans were also incarcerated. Amazingly, few among the Soviet intelligentsia found anything amiss, even when they actually toured the camps there. Indeed, during his visit to the camps between 20 and 23 June 1929 Maxim Gorky found them to be a worthy corrective to anti-Soviet behaviour and went on to publish his notorious article 'Solovki', which lauded its goals, as expressed in its motto of 'education through work'.[189]

By 1930, the camps, under the leadership of A.A. Ivanchenko, contained some 65,000 prisoners on average. As part of a wider reorganisation of prison administration, it was transferred from the OGPU and subsumed within the infamous GULAG, an acronym for *Glavnoye upravlyeniye ispravityel'no-trudovih lagyeryey i koloniy*, that is, the Chief Administration of Corrective Labour Camps and Colonies. Arbitrary abuse was common but occasionally the government clamped down, and around this time sixty administrators and others in positions of authority were convicted of abuse and shot.[190]

Nonetheless, the camps continued to grow in size with 71,800 people being held in them by 1 January 1931. That year E.I. Sienkiewicz was appointed overall commandant. He ensured that many prisoners were sent to the mainland to work on the White Sea Canal Project, the apple of Stalin's eye during this period, linking the White Sea to Lake Ladoga, to the north of Leningrad (by which time St Petersburg/Petrograd had once again been renamed). As a result, by 1932 the number of prisoners had dropped dramatically to only 15,130, though their number increased to 19,280 in the following year. SLON now became known as the Solovetsky Sub-Camp for the White Sea-Baltic Corrective Labour Camp (BELBALTLAG). Data on the number of prisoners that were held in the camp during the later 1930s are scarce. It is known, however, that the camps underwent yet another reorganisation on 28 November 1936 when the Solovetsky Special Purpose Prison (*Solovetskaia Tiurma Osobovogo Naznachenya* or *STON*) was established, subject to the authority of the NKVD's Chief Administration of Security. Solovetsky consequently assumed a new importance during the Great Purge—no less than 1,825 prisoners were shot there in 1937 and 1938. STON was finally shut down in the following year, and all of its 4,500 prisoners were transferred elsewhere. Solovetsky's infamous period now came to an end: in 1940 it became a naval base, in which function it continued to serve until 1973 when the Solovetsky State Historical and Architectural Museum and Nature Reserve was set up and the former key monastery buildings began to undergo some restoration. However, it was only with the collapse of the Soviet Union that it became a memorial museum to the Solovetsky Special Purpose Camps, 1923–9, under the auspices of both the Memorial Society and the Solovetsky Museum. It became prominent worldwide and, in 1993, Alexander Solzhenitsyn, famed author of *The Gulag Archipelago* in which such camps are described, himself provided the funding for a motor yacht, *Monastyrsky*, which enabled the Solovetsky Monastery to establish regular communication with the mainland during the months when the White Sea was not frozen.[191]

Meanwhile, in 1938, in the Sámi heartland of the Kola Peninsula, repression by the NKVD became intense even in Lovozero, with thirty-four Sámi people arrested, fifteen of whom were shot.[192] These were not the first of such persecutions, for already other figures, like the Russian A.G. Endukovsky—author of a variety of linguistic works, as well as a noted early twentieth-century Sámi primer—had fallen victim to the purges in 1937. By this time the Sámi language itself had become highly suspect, and was only spoken at special events and in the home from the end of the 1930s to the 1950s.[193]

The fates of a number of prominent Sámi cultural and political figures who disappeared are also now known. Arrests had begun among the Sámi in 1930 in order to crush resistance to the collectivisation of reindeer herding, which was extremely unpopular. However, it was in 1937 that massive repression in the Kola Peninsula was undertaken. In October of that year the NKVD arrived in force in the Sámi coastal village of Ozerko in order to carry out a series of arrests. Seaman Egor Andreevitj Snaul, who came under suspicion because of his Lutheran faith and birth in Norway, was the first to be arrested, followed by his five sons, all of whom were eventually shot.[194] Some of those arrested were not sent away but ended up in the thirty camps actually on the Kola Peninsula.[195] According to A.A. Kiselev in 1933, in the Kola Lapp Region, as it was now known, there were some 800 Sámi people altogether: in Lovozero 599 Sámi resided there, in Ponoi 300 and in Polyarnoi 185, but between 1931 and 1940 many Sámi, and particularly those from Semiostrov, Jokanda, Kamensk, Kildin and Babino (Akkala), were obliged to leave—the latter group going to Kovdor where even today there are now 120 Sámi, mostly elderly women.[196]

It is also now known that the scientist Vasilii Alymov, one of the Sámi's greatest Russian champions, was arrested in Murmansk in February 1938 shortly after his wife Sofia, a hospital worker, had been executed for espionage and terrorism. Alymov was accused of a conspiracy to support the creation of an independent Sámi state in league with Finland against the Soviet Union. Altogether some thirty-four people were convicted in the 'plot', of whom fifteen, including Alymov, were executed in October 1938 at the Levasjovsky Forest on the outskirts of Leningrad. Many of the co-condemned had worked at the Ethnography Museum.[197]

Ivan Andreyevitch Osipov, the first Sámi student to study at the Northern Peoples' Institute, was investigated by the security authorities along with Alymov. Correspondence with relatives in Finland had brought him under suspicion and he is thought to have died during the war. Matrechina Anastasia Lukinitina, the first female student and teacher, was also investigated at the same time. However, she avoided conviction and lived until the 1980s. Adrian Ionovitch Gerasimov (1907–38?) was less fortunate: he was condemned to ten years' imprisonment in the GULAG and was never seen again.[198] They were just a few of the many who suffered repression at this time. For, indeed, no Sámi village escaped throughout the Kola Peninsula and the grounds for arrest were various: an injudicious comment, a conversation at some point in one's life with a Scandinavian or Finn, contact with another accused—all might lead to imprisonment or even death, although the latter was only meted out to the Sámi and their Komi neighbours from 1937. The execution in September of that year of the Sámi fisherman Andrei Romanovitch Galkin from Ozerko for 'traitorous behaviour against the Motherland' was merely the first of such actions. On just one day, 15 October 1938, a trial held in Leningrad condemned to death seven Sámi, five Komi and three Russians from the region, with eight Sámi, three Komi and two Nenets given thirteen-year prison sentences, none of whom ever returned. Thus, altogether, fifty-five people, thirty-seven Sámi and eighteen Komi, were executed, condemned by Paragraph 58 of the Soviet Criminal Code of 1926. Only the Nenets escaped this fate.[199]

Chilling as such mass executions undoubtedly were, they were just some of many carried out in this north-western corner of Russia: some 1,111 people alone were shipped at the time from the Solevetsky Islands to a forest near Medvezhegorsk (Karhumäki, in Finnish) in Russian Karelia, where even those actually sentenced to only a few years in the GULAG were in reality shot.[200] Today a monument there commemorates the massacre.

The arrests began to diminish as the outbreak of the Second World War approached, and they had largely petered out altogether by 1941. Thereafter, between 1942 and 1945, there were no political arrests, nor did they resume after the war was brought to an end. Yet by then many Sámi had moved elsewhere to Hiipinä, Umba and other fishing posts on the White Sea coast where they worked in the fishing or sawmill industries, or led hunting expeditions for government officials.[201]

Leif Rantala collected information about the number of Sámi who were arrested during the period from about 1930 to 1940. He concludes that around 120 Sámi, five of whom were women, were arrested out of total of about 1,500 Russian Sámi at that time. Nine of these were eventually released, but forty-nine were executed. A further fifty-two were sent to the GULAG; only four of these survived. Three people are known to have been killed while imprisoned. The destinies of a further three Sámi are not known, while two were exiled. Rantala has also pointed out that while political arrests as such thereafter ceased, Sámi prisoners of war who had been in Germany, Finland and other enemy countries incurred severe punishments after they were 'repatriated' to the Soviet Union: indeed, many were shot.[202]

Wartime Evacuation

The arrival of the Second World War also had a traumatising effect on the Sámi of the Kola Peninsula. Among the first people to be affected by wartime evacuation were the Sámi of Petsamo. On 30 November 1939 the Soviet Union had attacked Finland, beginning a war which was to last 105 days and which the country was obliged to fight on its own. The inhabitants of the Petsamo area, both Sámi and Finnish, were evacuated. Soviet troops subsequently occupied the entire Petsamo region, by which time all the remaining inhabitants had fled to either Norway or Finland, or had become prisoners of war. After the conclusion of the Winter War, the former inhabitants of the Petsamo region, excluding those from mined areas in the eastern parts of the Suonikylä *siida*, were granted leave in April 1940 to return home—if homes they still had, for the Skolt Sámi villages on the Paatsjoki and Petsamojoki rivers, with the exception of the Suonikylä *siida*, had been wiped out. As for Petsamo, except for its heights, it was briefly returned to Finland. However, the Continuation War which followed, in which the country felt itself obliged to avail itself of help from Nazi Germany in order to regain the territories lost in the Winter War where formerly some 400,000 Finns had made their home, forced renewed evacuation. The Skolt Sámi were once again obliged to flee, and from 1941 to 1944 Suonikylä, with its environs, became a war zone. Yet this military confrontation was characterised not by trench warfare but by a mobile war, in which patrols sought the enemy in the forests and windswept hills that characterised the region. In consequence, the Skolt Sámi living in Suonikylä and most of those living in Paatsjoki were evacuated to Tervola, in southern Lapland. However, those from the winter villages of the Petsamo *siida*, at Moskova and Puska in Petsamo *siida*, whom the Finnish authorities could not reach quickly enough, were deported by the arriving Soviets to the Pullijärvi *kolkhoz* (Soviet farming cooperative) on the Kola Peninsula. Still others, from the Paatsjoki *siida*, were evacuated to Narvik, in Norway.[203]

The war also intruded upon the Sámi in another way, much as it did upon all the Russian people. In 1941, at least 200 soldiers were sent to the Western front from Lovozero and its environs, a figure rising to 800 over the war years. A quarter of these never returned.[204]

Flight of the Sámi from the Petsamo Region

During the brief respite that followed the outbreak of the Continuation War, all remaining Skolt Sámi from the Petsamo area, which had been ceded to Finland just after the First World War, were forced to evacuate. Many were taken to Lake Inari and to Tsuolisjärvi, from which they could continue their reindeer herding.[205] Others were transferred to central Ostrobothnia, although the overwhelming majority of them only remained until 1946.

The area first settled by the Skolt Sámi in this post-war period was on land situated between the Luttojoki River and the village of Nellim. However, the land proved to be too small for the more than 100 families brought there, and so in the summer of 1947 representatives of the Suonikylä *siida* took the initiative to consider the acquisition of land with good autumn fishing and winter reindeer pastures (formerly used by the Näätämö *siida*, from the Norwegian side of the border), in the Näätämö area, close to Lake Sevettijärvi.[206] This proved successful and the Skolt Sámi from Suonikylä Skolt moved to their current homeland in 1949–52. Thus, they joined the Inari Sámi reindeer herders and fishermen who, together with some Finns, were the local inhabitants. Far more numerous than the former, they soon dominated the whole of Sevettijärvi, as the area was called, which stretched some 50 kilometres from lakes Nitsijärvi to Kirakkajärvi and had become home to a total Sámi population of some 267 people by the 1950s, despite the absence of any roads. These were not seasonal homesteads, as old Suonikylä had been, but formed a permanent settlement, even if small huts by the lakes also came to be built for use while fishing. So popular did these seasonal dwellings become that no less than two out of three families had them by 1974 and 12 per cent of the entire Sámi population even had two.[207]

The evacuation effected during the Lapland War when Finland turned against Germany, its erstwhile ally, was among the greatest challenges to the identity of the Sámi. The war erupted in the autumn of 1944 when Stalin ordered Finland to expel all German troops: while Finland publicly demanded the withdrawal of German forces, the latter refused to depart immediately. After a few weeks direct military confrontation had broken out between the two former allies.

It was at about this time that the Inari Sámi founded the Sámi Liitto, the first association of Finnish Sámi, during their evacuation in 1945.[208] Niilo Aikio, himself a Sámi evacuee of that time, has carefully studied the upheavals this caused in a work from 2000: he noted that many of those uprooted, in particular children, never returned to their homeland. Instead, they coped as best they could in the regions of Sweden, Norway or south of Finland to which they had been removed or had fled, not least because of their low immunity to diseases then plaguing these areas. His book on the subject, *Lieekejä pakoon: Saamelaiset evakossa 1944–1945 (Flight from the Flames: the Sámi evacuated 1944–1945)* is thus unique in shedding light on the hardships they endured during and after the war.[209]

An opposite evacuation had earlier taken place on the Soviet side of the border. In January 1940, while the Molotov Pact with Nazi Germany still held, the Germans began to carry out their plan to construct a harbour on the coast of the Barents Sea, by the mouth of the West Litsa River. In consequence, an evacuation of predominantly women and children took place from there to Ristikenttä, in Kola Commune. The Molotov Pact was, of course, broken by Germany through its invasion of the Soviet Union. However, from 1941 to 1944 this coastal tract remained occupied by the Germans,[210] and in this scenario the Sámi suffered severely.

The Lapland War

The Lapland War, although relatively small in scope, was one of the most vicious but least known fronts of the Second World War. Some 774 Finns were killed during the war, and around 1,000 Germans.[211] As Jukka Pennanen has put it, when the Skolt Sámi were evacuated to Finland after the cession of Petsamo, 'the last ancient winter village of Europe, the Suonikylä siida, vanished'.[212]

In the final resolution of border issues the upper course of the Paatsjoki River was given to the Soviet Union in 1947.[213] Yet while borders were resolved, the damage to Sámi infrastructure and society was immense. In Norway, the majority of buildings in Finnmark and Northern Troms had been destroyed so as to hinder the advance and occupation of the Soviet troops. Thus much Sámi history was obliterated in one go, and that which was rebuilt followed contemporary Norwegian practices rather than the traditional Sámi. Only the semi-nomadic lifestyle of reindeer herders remained as an obvious example of Sámi life and culture, surviving all the vagaries of war in war-torn Sápmi.[214]

Prisoner of War Dislocation and the post-War Period

Many Sámi men fighting for the belligerents also met the troubled fate of millions of others in their situation when they became prisoners of war. The fate of one Sámi soldier, Maksim Antonov, fighting on the Soviet side, is indicative of the degree to which the Second World War could be dislocating to Sámi prisoners of war. He never saw his relatives again; they were told by the authorities that he had died in September 1941. Having been taken a prisoner of war by either the Finns or the Germans during the Continuation War between the Soviet Union and Finland (just one of over 50,000 prisoners at that time), he took advantage of the option of joining a newly formed battalion of prisoners of war who had been formed to assist Finland. Antonov joined the battalion sometime before November 1942. It was during this period that he was first interviewed by linguists. Then, in the aftermath of the Second World War, he left Finland, settling in Sweden in 1947 where he became a subject of interest for researchers in Finno-Ugric linguistics. He died in Eskilstuna in Sweden in 1983.[215]

As we have seen, in consequence of the 1920 Treaty of Tartu between Finland and the Soviet Union, a number of Sámi villages in the Petsamo region had been transferred to Finland, but after the Winter and Continuation Wars these territories were returned to Russia, though virtually all of the inhabitants emigrated to Finland.[216]

During the 1960s many Sámi villages on the Kola Peninsula were razed in the interest of collectivisation and social concentration. Most of their inhabitants were sent to Lovozero where they remain to this day.[217] In any case, by the 1970s the cultures of the Komi and Nenets became increasingly dominant, even if that of wider Soviet society—food, clothing and transport—played an even more important role in the life of the reindeer-herding areas of the Kola Peninsula.[218] Indeed, an increasingly uniform Arctic culture was coming into being in the region, although one in which the Komi community was the most dominant and cohesive. Moreover, where the Komi and even the Nenets who were vastly fewer in number and employed in a more subordinate role to them tended to maintain a strong sense of identity—

for example, the children of only one parent who was Komi or Nenets (even though they no longer spoke their own language as the Sámi often did) tended to assume that ethnic identity—the Sámi were less inclined to do so.[219]

Finally, in 1976 the boarding school at Lovozero was granted permission to resume the teaching of Sámi, although Russian still tended to be spoken in the home.[220]

After the fall of the Soviet Union, life for the Sámi people of the Kola Peninsula changed significantly, and in some respects for the better. The Kola Peninsula remained closed to researchers from 1920 to 1990. The first research project in the region thus took place between 1991 and 1994, when joint Finnish–Russian research teams undertook six expeditions to various reindeer herding sites. In particular, they focused upon not only the Sámi, but Komi and Nenets herders and their families, whose ancestors had moved to the Kola Peninsula as far back as the 1880s.[221]

By the early 1990s Lovozero—the only village accessible by road— itself had a population of some 3,000 inhabitants. However, the largest ethnic group were the Komi—about 1,000—with the Sámi numbering about 800. There were also a few dozen Nenets. The village of Krasnoshelye had 350 Komi, ninety-two Sámi and sixty-two Nenets, making a total of 750 inhabitants. The remotest of the villages, Kanevka, had only 112 inhabitants: sixty-six Komi, thirteen Sami and two Nenets. The population and its distribution were similar in the northern coastal village of Sosnovka. The villages of the Sámi homeland on the Kola Peninsula were thus composed of a variety of ethnic groups, with Russian the principal medium of communication even if the majority of reindeer herders there spoke Komi as their mother tongue. No longer were the Sámi the principal community leaders, even if the Minorities Act of the 1980s had attempted to put the different ethnic groups on a more equal footing. This is perhaps unsurprising, bearing in mind that the Komi, unlike the Nenets, were not granted this status.[222]

However, the situation began to improve over the course of the 1990s. New Sámi commercial companies were founded in the 1990s which combined modern business methods with traditional techniques and ways of life. The establishment of a Sámi museum in Lovozero has also boosted their sense of identity. More important, however, has been the encouragement from the Nordic countries, both in cultural and financial terms, in strengthening the Sámi ethnic identity.[223] Those living in Lovozero, Kola and Kovdor, for example, were granted fishing rights in specific waters, including the use of nets, either free or at reduced rates, and they have also been granted special privileges with respect to reindeer herding. They have also been allowed to engage in the sale of reindeer meat and are permitted to chop down up to 50 cubic metres of wood annually at the reindeer markets.[224] Thus the Sámi have been able to stabilise themselves, and even to thrive. In fact, in Lovozero there were 940 Sámi, and in the mountain village of Revda a further 150 in 1995. The remainder of the Sámi were living at Murmansk, Apatity, Olenegorsk, Loparskaya, Gremikha, Tuloma, Teriberka, Pushnoy, as well as Umba on the Ter coast. Indeed, on 1 January 2002 there was a total of 1,820 Sámi living in Murmansk Oblast, in which all of the aforementioned places are situated.[225]

Three of the Kola Sámi dialects—and it should be remembered that less than half of the Kola Sámi actually speak a Sámi tongue—continue to be spoken today, using the Cyrillic alphabet. Kildin, which is the most frequently spoken of these, serves as the mother tongue of some 600 people, most of whom live in Lovozero, forming a third of the town's population. Although few Kildin Sámi texts have been printed in Russia, some have been printed in Norway, often with a Northern Sámi translation. Although the next most important in terms of the number of speakers, the Notozero dialect is actually the tongue of only about twenty-five people, virtually all of whom reside in the Kola area, and it has no written literature. Ter Sámi, the third dialect, is spoken today by only a dozen people, living on the north-eastern Arctic coast. Sadly, a fourth dialect, Akkala Sámi, died out with the demise of its last native speaker in 2003.[226] Even a short while before, it was limited to the villages of Babino and Yokostrov, by Lake Imandra, just north of Kandalaksha, in Russian Lapland. It had many affinities with Skolt Sámi, despite the influence of Russian and Karelian, while its archaic use of nasal consonants was unique.[227]

Urban Sámi

Today approximately 7,000 Finnish Sámi, that is, one-third of the country's total, live outside the Sámi homeland. Many of these live in urban areas throughout the Nordic region. In Finland one major centre is Helsinki, where a Sámi association was founded in the 1970s.

While it only survived for a short period of time, another association that was established in 1988 has since become one of the most active and important in Finland, culturally, socially and, to some degree, politically. The Sámi and Finnish languages are both used not only within the Sámi community in Helsinki but abroad with other Sámi people in Scandinavia and Russia.[228] However, individuals tend to use one or the other predominantly as their native tongue, since most such Helsinki Sámi used either Sámi or Finnish, almost exclusively, in their childhood.[229]

The Scandinavian Sámi in the Later Twentieth Century

Per Gustav Park (1886–1968), a Sámi priest from Arjeplog, played a key role during the 1950s and 1960s in furthering the interests of the Swedish Sámi, and was the leading figure in the establishment of the National Union of Swedish Sámi in 1950, as well serving as its first chairman. As editor-in-chief of *Samefolks Egen-Tidning* (renamed *Samefolket* in 1960), a Swedish-language newspaper dedicated to furthering Sámi interests, he was also able to use this medium in defence of Sámi interests.[230]

However, in 1970s Sweden there were only about 2,500 people who were officially listed as Sámi, roughly the number of people and their dependants active in reindeer herding. Yet today, with a much broader self-imposed definition of Sámi ethnicity, some 20,000 people in Sweden are said to consider themselves Sámi.[231]

The Alta River Protest

In Norway, during the 1970s the Sámi passed through one of their most significant crises, at least in a political sense. For one of the most significant events in the formation of the modern Sámi ethnic identity was the damming of the Alta River, in the heart of the Sámi homeland, the result of a decision first made by the Norwegian energy company NVE in 1968, but then temporarily aborted in 1973. This was not the first of such ventures. The Skolt Sámi who had formerly resided in Russia along the banks of the Nota River, near Lake Girvas, had suffered from the flooding brought about by the construction of the Tuloma Reservoir in the 1930s. They had not only lost their villages (Sámi village, Masi, was submerged) and ancestral lands but had been removed altogether, for political as well as geographical reasons: their villages had been situated near the country's western border.[232] Nonetheless, the Norwegian government eventually reinitiated the scheme, leading to the construction of a hydroelectric power station there in 1978. Protests were almost immediately organised by both the Sámi themselves and environmentalist organisations at Stilla, on the Altafjord. Seven young Sámi went as far as to go on hunger strike, prominently photographed in a *lávvu* (traditional Sámi herding tent) which they set up outside the Norwegian Parliament in Oslo. Tension increased when some 600 policemen were called in to remove the Sámi and the environmentalists, some 1,100 in number, who were blocking the road to the construction site. This situation was then aggravated by the fact that fourteen Sámi women in Oslo, many of whom were relatives of the protestors, occupied the office of Gro Harlem Brundtland, then prime minister of Norway (she would later become the chairman of the UNESCO World Commission on Environment and Development), before being removed by the police. The protests failed with respect to the dam, which was ultimately built. However, in the sense that it proved to be a crucible forging Sámi political and ethnic identity for the rest of the century, the protest should be viewed as a success. Moreover, both the government and wider Norwegian public opinion now began to encourage Sámi cultural and environmental initiatives. It was as a direct result of these that the Sámi Act was promulgated in 1987, which led not only to the recognition of the Sámi people as indigenous to the region but also to the establishment of a Sámi parliament in Norway in 1987.[233] It also led to the strengthening of the Sámi interest organisation Norgga Sámiid Riikkasearvi (The Norwegian Sámi Association), which had been founded in 1968 and was directed by Johan M. Klemetsen. Its ability to drum up support for the Sámi in the Alta dispute, as well as the successful passing of the Sámi Act in parliament, showed that it was a force to be reasoned with in respect of Sámi interests across the board.

The Sámi Flag

The Alta River protests also served as the occasion for the creation of a three-colour Sámi flag, designed in 1977 by Synnøve Persen, a Coastal Sámi from Porsanger in Norway. Although this was clearly an important development for the Sámi, and indeed the wider world, on the Sámi road to 'nationhood', the flag failed to find wide acceptance; as a result, in the 1980s the Nordic Sámi Council organised a competition to decide on the best design for an official Sámi flag. The Sámi artist Astrid Båhl, from Skibotn in Norway, was successful in the competition: her four-colour flag was adopted and flown officially at the XIII Sámi Conference held in 1986 in Åre in Sweden, and has been internationally renowned as the flag of the Sámi nation ever since. According to the artist, the motif of the flag was influenced by the South Sámi Anders Fjellner's (1795–1876) poem *Páiven párneh* (The Sons of the Sun), in which the poet declares the Sámi to be the sons and daughters of the sun. The imagery of the Sámi magic drum, traditionally used for shamanistic purposes, also played a role. Some have stated that the two-coloured circle in the centre of the flag is designed to symbolise the sun (the red part) and the moon (the blue part).[234] Others maintain that the yellow line on the flag represents the heavens, with the red colour symbolising the earth.[235]

The official days on which the Sámi flag is flown are outlined in Table 1.1.

Table 1.1: National days and festivals when the Sámi flag is flown.[236]

Date	Event	Description
6 February	National Day	Commemorates the first pan-Sámi conference, held in Trondheim in 1917
Variable	Annunciation Day (Lady Day, variable in March) and Midsummer Day (variable in June)	
Traditional Sámi festivals		
9 August	UN International Day of Indigenous Peoples	A worldwide event observed in order to recognise the contributions and achievements of indigenous peoples
15 August	Sámi Flag Day	Celebrates the adoption of the Sámi

		flag and the birthday of Isak Saba (1875–1921), the first Sámi member of parliament
18 August	Founding Day of the Sámi Council	Recognises the founding of the Nordic Sámi Council in 1956
26 August	Founding Day of Sweden's Sámi Parliament	Recognises the founding of the Swedish Sámi Parliament in 1993
9 October	Founding Day of Norway's Sámi Parliament	Recognises the founding of the Norwegian Sámi Parliament in 1989
9 November	Founding Day of the Finnish Sámi Parliament	Recognises the founding of the Finnish Sámi Parliament in 1976

One further important development for the Sámi was the appointment of the linguist, and president of the Norwegian Sámi Parliament, Professor Ole Henrik Magga (born 1947) as chairman of the first meeting of the Permanent Forum, composed of sixteen members and organised by the United Nations at its headquarters in New York in May 2002. Eight of its members were nominated by the UN member states and eight by the UN Economic and Social Council. Their role was to advise and negotiate over a plethora of issues relating to the 'indigenous peoples' of the world.[237]

SIIDA

The foundation of the first Sámi Museum at Inari in 1959, which opened to the public in 1962 as an open air museum with nearby buildings to house relevant artefacts, was a significant date for the fostering of Sámi culture. Its administration was given over to the Sámi Liitto (Sámi Association), which maintained and developed it until 1986. Thereafter, the Sámi Museum Foundation was established to carry on its administration and it was eventually re-established as SIIDA, the Sámi Museum and Northern Lapland Nature Centre, officially opening on 27 March 1998. In the following year the Finnish Ministry of Education granted it coveted 'special museum' status. Today the museum produces up to eight temporary exhibitions each year, focusing on Sámi culture and nature as well as that of other indigenous peoples throughout the world. With more than 50,000 visitors annually, over 40 per cent of whom are foreign, it is one of the most important to be found in the Sámi homeland. In consequence, Inari itself has become one of the most important cultural centres of the Sámi homeland, a status further reinforced by the fact that it is also now the seat of the Sámi Parliament, the Sámi Radio, the Sámi Educational Centre the Sámi handicraft association Sámi Duodji (Sámi Crafts), and the Friends of Sámi Art Association, whose members come from far and wide.[238] Yet in the part of Sweden where the Lule Sámi live, the annual meetings of Sámi villages are usually held in Swedish.[239] As for the four dialects of Pite Sámi, they are now only spoken by a small number of people in the vicinity of Arjeplog, in northern Sweden, since in nearby parts of Norway they have died out altogether. Other Sámi-language groups in Sweden include Ume Sámi, spoken by a small number to the south (previously it was spoken around Arjeplog). With a vowel system evincing metaphonic characteristics, labial harmony and umlaut sounds, it stands aloof from the other northern and eastern Sámi languages.[240] Today there is also a boarding school at Lovozero, in which pupils have the option of being taught using the Kildin Sámi language during the first four years. This learning process is supported with some thirty Sámi-language books.[241]

The Sámi on the International Stage

Today, as Joann Conrad has noted, the more global and international the perspective of the Sámi, the more their ethnic identity becomes articulated and anchored in the Sámi core area.[242] Many people today complain that the Sámi youth suffer criticism—from both the Sámi themselves and others—that they are failing to act and live in a 'traditionally correct' way.[243] Yet with some 2,000 Sámi said to be living in Stockholm, it is hard to see how this could be otherwise.[244] The political and cultural rights of the Sámi have now been seen to have a broader and more pragmatic base than before, at least by the Sámi themselves. In 1996 the Sámi philosopher Nils Oskal stated that the

Samerettsutvalg (Sámi Rights Commission) did not base its proposal about particular Sámi rights on the necessity of making a foundation for equal political rights inside Norway. Rather its aim was to protect Sámi culture as such, in a similar way to those politicians who are more interested in getting finance for Sámi museums than in granting greater political rights.[245] Yet as Mikael Svonni, professor of Sámi at the University of Tromsø, has observed, 'With few exceptions, such as Kautokeino and Karasjok in Norway, and Utsjoki in Finland, public domains are dominated by the majority language.'[246] With respect to schools he has found that:

In Karesuando, which is the northernmost situated school, Sámi is the dominant conversation language for nearly all children (94%). On the other hand,
in Tärnaby, the southernmost of the schools, Swedish is the dominant conver-
sational language at home for all children. According to the study, the use of
Sámi within the family decreases the further south one goes: in Kiruna, Sámi
the dominant language among 70% of the children; in Gällivare, among 33%
of the children, and in Jokkmokk, among only 17%.[247]

A museum of history and culture of the Sámi of the Kola Peninsula was opened in Lovozero as far back as 1962 by P.P. Uryev, attached to the boarding school. Most aspects of Sámi life are covered with thou-sands of objects on display and in the reserve collection. A subsidiary of the museum later opened in 1968 in the province of Murmansk. The museum was run by Galina Alexandrovna Kulinchenko, who had stud-ied at the Pedagogical Institute in Murmansk.[248]

Meanwhile, the demographics of the Sámi on the Kola Peninsula were changing negatively. In 1959 the number of Sámi living there had declined to only 0.3 per cent of the population, that is, some 1,703. By contrast, ethnic Russians numbered 484,224 or 85.3 per cent of the population. Yet the situation subsequently worsened still further: although the Sámi population had grown to 1,715 by 1970, it now formed only 0.2 per cent of the population. The Russian population, on the other hand, had grown dramatically to some 676,319, or 64.6 per cent of the total. In the decade which followed, however, the demo-graphic statistics remained fairly constant: while in 1979 there were 1,565 Sámi (0.2 per cent of the population) and 819,492 Russians (83.8 per cent of the total), these figures had changed only slightly by 1989—thus whereas the Sámi now numbered 1,615, and continued to constitute 0.2 per cent of the population, the number of Russians had risen to 965,727, or 82.9 per cent of the total.[249]

During the 1990s the population of the Kola Peninsula declined even further. Indeed, from 1995 to 1998, it fell from 1,067,100 to 1,016,600. Only 0.2 per cent of these were Sámi, that is, 1,600 from a total of 1,800 living in Russia altogether. The situation has since improved slightly and, as of 2005, there were about 1,820 Sámi in Russian Lapland.[250] Of these, only one group of about twenty, by virtue of their language, could still be called Skolt Sámi.[251] In Finland, at about this time, there were also some 400 to 500, but in Norway no more than thirty.[252]

Yet while the number of ethnic Sámi living in Russia has effectively remained static since 1989, this was not the case for Sámi cultural associations, the number of which increased dramatically in the final years of the Soviet Union and in the post-Soviet period. The first of these was the Murmansk-based Association of Kola Sámi, which was founded in 1989 and had 653 members, with Vasilii Pavlovich Selivanov (1989–91) elected as its first president. This was followed in 1998 by the establishment in Lovozero of another group, the Sámi Public Organisation in the Murmansk Region, with 453 members under the direction of Alexandr Kobelev.[253] A Committee for Indigenous Peoples was also created within the Murmansk provincial administration. This had beneficial cultural consequences because Seitajärvi, a lake traditionally sacred to the Sámi, became an officially 'protected area'. Moreover, the political role of the Sámi in the region grew in scope from the time, during the 1980s, when there had only been three Sámi, out of fifty-two members, on the Municipal Council of Lovozero. Indeed, one municipal officer was created expressly to deal with Sámi affairs. *Sáráhkka*, a Sámi women's group, was established in 1993 and a youth organisation known as *Saam nuras* was established the following year. But despite these new organisations and the opportunities for political cooperation that they provided, many issues relating to the use of land and water resources still remained highly controversial.[254]

The National Cultural Centre, directed by Avdeyeva Larisa Pavlovna, opened its doors in Lovozero in 1994 with the assistance of a Swedish company, AO AMU-Gruppen.[255] With a focus on Sámi folk culture and lore, the centre was established at a time when the population of Lovozero was experiencing a period of growth, reaching 3,498 by 1996—including 1,117 Komi, 190 Nenets and 927 Sámi— and has helped enable the Sámi to achieve a significant improvement in their cultural profile in the region.[256] The centre moved to new purpose-built premises in 2003.

Another important development was the new stress given to the *Prasnik Severa* (Festival of the North), a regular event first instituted by the Soviet authorities in the 1930s when *kolkhoz* (collective farms) and *sovkhoz* (state farms) competed with one another in a fraternal spirit, which served to encourage ethnic harmony. The festival remains a feature of life on the Kola Peninsula today, and continues to provide an event where all of the people of the region can come together to celebrate their respective cultures. Among the activities which form a part of this festive occasion are poetry recitals, singing, dancing, reindeer races and skiing competitions, all of which are held either at Murmansk or in Lovozero. Many Sámi also participate, and since the 1990s the Sámi flag—also representing those who come from the Scandinavian countries—flies prominently together with the flag of the Russian Federation.[257]

Other Sámi organisations of note include Rodovaya Obshchina 'Kil'din' (The Kin of the Kildin Community), under the leadership of Yelena Semenovna, which has both cultural and ecological dimensions. Early on it received financial assistance for its ecological activities from the Marja and Mikk Sarv Foundation, based in Estonia. In the late summer of 2002 an international festival of ecology, 'The Earth and its Peoples', was held at Lovozero. The event received considerable media coverage and an appeal was made to Russian President Vladimir Putin, in the presence of M.M. Kasyanov, the governor of Murmansk, to heed ecological issues confronting the Sámi of the Kola Peninsula, an area which is notorious for having suffered many ecological disasters, not least at Monchegorsk. Piras (The Family) is yet another organisation which focuses on ecological issues, especially those relating to reindeer herding, under the direction of Andrei Yulin. It plays an especially important role in such reindeer-herding centres as Krasnoshelje, Kanevki and Sosnovki.[258]

A Recapitulation of the Development of Sámi Unity

As we have seen, it was in the later nineteenth century that the concept of Sámi unity and political identity began to come to the fore, following as a latecomer in the national political movements which drew their inspiration from the philosophical writings of Fichte and other figures of the German nationalist awakening, as well as from revolutionary political movements born in Frankfurt in the early nineteenth century and then in the revolutionary upheavals of 1848 elsewhere in Central Europe. In this Sámi women took a highly prominent role. One important figure in the early development of Sámi political unity was the South Sámi activist Elsa Laula Renberg (1877–1931). She not only helped to establish the first Sámi women's organisation, the Norwegian-based *Brurskanken Sámiske Kvindeforening* (Brurskanken Sámi Women's Association), but also assisted in the foundation of the Sámi National Assembly in Trondheim in 1917.[259]

Thus Sámi political and cultural awareness was clearly in the ascendant by the early twentieth century. Isak Saba, from Nesseby near Varanger in Norway, became the first Sámi to sit in Stortinget (the Norwegian Parliament) from 1906 to 1911. As a teacher, writer and editor, he took a keen interest in supporting Sámi culture. His collection of Sámi artefacts and such musical text accompaniments as *Samefolkets sang* (Song of the Sámi People)[260] are also of considerable importance.

Partly as a reaction to conflict with their Nordic neighbours but also for more positive reasons, a movement arose in the early twentieth century to give an organisational arena to the Sámi peoples and—in comparison with the demands of other ethnic and national groups throughout Europe—their modest aspirations. On 6 February 1917 the first pan-national Sámi conference, bringing together Sámi from Norway and Sweden, was held in Trondheim to foster Sámi unity and political interests. Today this occasion is still celebrated as the National Day of the Sámi.[261] The following year, the first Swedish Sámi national conference took place in Östersund, which, in turn, fostered a growing sense of political solidarity among the Sámi in Sweden.

Although many Sámi in Russia died during the First World War, as we have seen, the neutral Scandinavian countries were relatively little affected, especially in the Sámi areas. However, the situation was radically different with respect to both Norway and Finland in the Second World War. This conflagration had an enormous effect on Sámi life and culture, as it did on virtually all peoples in Europe, but, in particular, in the belligerent countries Norway, Finland and the Soviet Union, leaving only neutral Sweden unscathed. Although countless Sámi lost their homesteads in the war-torn areas, a feeling of solidarity was fostered which led to the creation of a new organisation in Central Ostrobothnia in Finland, the Sámi Liitto (Sámi Association). This new association supplemented the Lapin Sivistysseura (Lapland Education Society), established in 1932 by the general population of Finland for the promotion of Sámi culture. In the aftermath of the war and a return to the normality of peacetime, in 1953 the first of the Sámi conferences was held at Jokkmokk, in Sweden, in which representatives from all the Nordic countries participated. This was followed in 1956 by the establishment of the Sámiráđđi (Nordic Sámi Council), which focused, in particular, on issues relating to reindeer herding. A Confederation of Swedish Sámi was also set up in 1971. After the collapse of the Soviet Union this was expanded to include Russian representation and the confederation was renamed the Sámi Council in 1992.

Meanwhile, in 1976 the Sámi Conference joined the World Council of Indigenous Peoples. A second sitting took place in Kiruna in Sweden, and others followed. It was on the occasion of the Fifteenth Sámi Conference, held in Helsinki in 1992, that the Sámi established their own National Day along with the official establishment of other festive Sámi holidays. A focus was also given to current cultural, social and economic issues. That same year, the Sámiráđđi was granted the status of an NGO by the United Nations. This was followed by the election of a 'Sámi parliament' in Sweden in 1993, an event which was of great importance for the political life of the Sámi. The political fate of the Sámi in Russia, on the hand, seemed less rosy. Not only was their political clout extremely limited, but they also remained separated on a wide range of levels from their fellow Sámi living in the Nordic countries. Matters have since improved dramatically, and the Russian Sámi are now involved in the Arctic Council, as well as the Inuit Circumpolar Conference and RAIPON, the organisation of indigenous peoples in the Russian Federation.[262] Rubbing noses, a traditional form of greeting among the Skolt Sámi, also found among the Inuit of North America and Greenland,[263] is now just one more symbol, linking the two nations of peoples separated by enormous geographical distances but linked by lifestyles that share much in common.

By the 1960s, many of the functions of the Sámi umbrella political organisation, the Sámi Liitto—which had initially been founded to provide support for Sámi refugees seeking a safe haven in the Finnish province of Ostrobothnia—began to be assumed by other Sámi organisations. This was especially the case with regard to Sámi culture. Consequently, when the Sámi Museum Foundation was set up to oversee the Sámi Museum in Inari (discussed in Chapter 4) in 1986, which had previously been one of the association's principal responsibilities, the Sámi Liitto was dissolved.[264]

In Finland, one of the most important Sámi campaigners was Johan Erkki Jomppanen (1918–87), who was chairman of the Sámi Liitto for some thirty years from 1957. He was also prominent on the Sámi Council, as well as being a permanent member of the Committee on Sámi Affairs from 1960. Perhaps of equal importance, though, was his work as a member of the Programme Council of Sámi Radio from 1973 to 1979, which helped stir up support for the establishment of *SIIDA*, the foundation which became the basis of the Sámi Museum in Inari.[265]

By now the Sámi as a nation had come to conclude that strength was to be found in numbers, and they therefore joined forces on a variety of levels—political, cultural and economic—with other indigenous groups from around the globe. This dovetailed well with the high profile increasingly given to indigenous peoples by the United Nations. In a UN study conducted in 1971–84, its special reporter, José R. Martínez Cobo, concluded:

The Indigenous communities, people and nations are those which, having a historical continuity with pre-invasion and pre-colonial societies that developed on their territories, consider themselves distinct from other sectors of the societies now prevailing in those territories, or in parts of them. They form at present non-dominant sectors of society and are determined to preserve, develop and transmit to future generations their ancestral territories, and their ethnic identity, as the basis of their continued existence as people, in accordance with their own cultural patterns, social, institutions and legal systems.[266]

In 1993 the rising profile accorded to the world's indigenous peoples led the United Nations to decree an International Decade of the World's Indigenous People, to begin in 1995. Although its Declaration of the Rights of Indigenous Peoples ultimately failed to be ratified, the less ambitious establishment of a Permanent Forum for Indigenous Peoples was successful.[267]

The Arctic Council was another important organisation in which the Sámi were able to take a major role. Founded in Ottawa in 1996, it is composed of some eight member states, including Canada, Denmark, Finland, Iceland, Sweden, the Russian Federation and the United States. As such it was based on an earlier Arctic conference held in Rovaniemi in 1989, which had also included representatives from these countries. The purpose of this earlier meeting had been environmental in scope, but it also served as an arena in which indigenous peoples could assert their legal and cultural rights.[268]

The Council of Europe's Framework Convention for the Protection of National Minorities, which was drawn up in 1995, has also proved an important milestone for the Sámi insofar as it has served to help guarantee the rights of minorities and to protect their cultural heritage. Finland ratified it first, in 1997, followed by Russia in 1998, Norway in 1999 and Sweden in 2000.[269]

With the exception of those in the Russian Federation, all of the Sámi now have their own parliaments, one for each of the Nordic countries, established in Finland in 1973, in Norway in 1989 and in Sweden in 1993. The Finnish Parliament strove for a greater profile of autonomy by passing a law which replaced the previous representative body, the Sámi Delegation. It considered the Sámi legal claim to land against the background of Nordic law, with the new Sámi Parliament, under the leadership of a president, based on research carried out by Kaisa Korpijaako during the 1970s. This initiative was further bolstered by Samuli Aikio's history of the Sámi, *Olbmot ovdal min: Sámiid historjá 1700-logu rádjái* (People before us: the history of the Sámi until the 18th century), the first book of its kind to be written by a Sámi himself.[270]

Today the Sámi, their small numbers notwithstanding, have taken their place in the roll-call of nations, a proud people whose unique social, cultural and economic identity is of considerable import for not only other indigenous peoples worldwide but for everyone concerned with the globe's ecology.

2

RELIGION

Prehistoric Sámi Religious Practice

The old Sámi religion was animistic in its essence in that it was based on the belief that a form of pantheism infused the natural animate and inanimate world which made up the Sámi cosmos. The influences which emanated from this pantheistic world could be benevolent or malevolent with respect to mankind. Although this framework never formed a unified system—and was increasingly undermined by the advent of Christianity from the fourteenth century—there was a tendency for the cosmos to be envisioned as being composed of three distinct levels: the upper, the middle—earth—and the lower, all held in order by a world-tree or pillar, fixed to the North Star.[1] Various geographical phenomena were considered to have spiritual implications. Thus, along with channels to the other levels provided by caves, ravines and rapids, a landlocked lake—known as *sájvva* (in Lule Sámi)—was deemed to have beds containing openings which led to the netherworld. Bubbling springs—*ája*—were also perceived as the gateways to this other level. Animals such as bears and wolves were often personified as spirits from the other realms which, in consequence, informed the rituals associated with hunting and killing these animals that featured so prominently in the life of the Sámi.[2] The late eighteenth-century Italian visitor Giuseppe Acerbi translated one such invocation:

> Accursed wolf! far hence away!
> Make in these woods no longer stay:

Fly hence! And seek earth's utmost bounds,
Or perish by the hunter's wounds.[3]

The goal of this invocation for the Sámi shaman was to influence the behaviour of the natural world, in this instance the wolf, which was to be kept at bay. Although the bear also played a role in the Sámi spiritual pantheon, as it did among other Finno-Ugric peoples, it was not of primary importance; that place was taken by the reindeer, the animal more central to the Sámi way of life and therefore the principal focus within the Sámi religious pantheon.[4] One of the most important myths in this respect is that of the 'holy white reindeer', *Myandash*—the significance of the name itself is still unclear—with his golden horns, the tales of which derive from the Russian Kola Peninsula, and in particular from Imandra in the west, Lovozero in the centre and Kamensk in the east.[5] Although these myths were first recorded in 1873, long before the Bolshevik Revolution, it was the Soviet ethnographer Vladimir Tjarnolusky in 1927 who publicised their importance as the possible remnants of an ancient Sámi epic, which would have been sung or recited at clan gatherings. Indeed, he noted that sacrifices to *Myandash*—his mother was the Goddess of the Earth and Childbirth *Máttaráhkká*—were still carried out in his time there by the shores of Lake Akkajaur. Piles of stones of various sizes formed the nuclei of these sacrificial sites which were surrounded by offerings of reindeer antlers, some of which were decorated with red cloth and shells. Devotees of this cult hoped to ensure good hunting by carrying out this ritual.[6]

Similar ceremonials were also carried out in what is today Finnmark, in northern Norway. At Murggiidbaste, on the north side of the Varangerfjord, the remains of a sacrificial site have been uncovered where ceremonies to encourage success in fishing and hunting took place by an outcrop of stone resembling the profile of a man.[7]

Wild reindeer had a central place in the spiritual beliefs and religious ceremonies of the ancient Sámi (domestic reindeer herding was a phenomenon which only really came to dominate Sámi life in the seventeenth century). This can be seen at the famous rock art site uncovered by Alta, in Norway (to be discussed at length later), which can be dated from 4200 to 3600 BC.[8]

Pantheon of Gods

A pantheon of gods played a major role in the Sámi understanding of life, the natural world and their place in it. One of the most important of the traditional Sámi gods was *Veralden-radien* (the ruler of the world), the provider of fertility and sustainer of life whom the Sámi would ceremonially sacrifice male reindeer to each autumn. On the one hand, he provided *Máttaráhkká* with the human soul and on the other, on death, he repossessed it, bearing the soul back to the Sámi Hades, or *jápmináibmu*, the abode of the dead. For this reason the Sámi incorporated a cult of the dead into various aspects of their everyday life, for which it had crucial significance.[9]

The Wind God, *Bieggalmmái*, also had an important place in the Sámi pantheon, particularly for those Sámi who herded reindeer, since the wind, it was felt, greatly influenced the direction in which they moved.[10] Yet the Wind God was just one of many gods linked to natural phenomena or *sieidi* (e.g. an unusually formed stone, a pile of stones or a strangely shaped tree), which were honoured among the Sámi as sacred places. Reindeer herders and fishermen had their own, sometimes local, private deities, worshipped in the autumn and spring, when they left for or returned from their summer migrations. Homage was carried out by means of offerings such as reindeer antlers, heads, leg bones or even whole animal carcasses, often decorated with special bandings. Customarily, they would smear their offerings with reindeer tallow or fish oil, kneeling down in ceremonial fashion while proffering prayers, on occasion even offering money, spirits or jewellery as well.[11]

Afruvvá was, for the Sea Sámi, a mermaid, who tended to act in an admonitory fashion, giving warnings and, to some degree, protection in time of storms. However, she could also show a malicious side if the goddess decided to assail mariners by the very storms they sought to solicit her protection against. The Sámi were therefore keen to propitiate this ominous side, capable of wrecking their boats and drowning their sailors through the action of the winds and waves.[12]

There was also *Jábmiidáhkka*, a venomous female deity of the underworld who could afflict people with diseases and other torments.[13] Three spirits, in particular, considered to be brothers, were considered by the Sámi to personify the epidemic diseases themselves. The eldest, for example, the inflictor of smallpox, was *stuora namma* (great name), which the Sámi were particularly at pains to avoid calling by his right name, as that action was felt likely to bring on the disease itself to the namer.[14]

Yet it was the sun, *Beaivi*, which was the most important of the Sámi gods, and which in some South Sámi areas was conceived as a goddess rather than a god,[15] for it brought warmth and light, its annual arrival in the spring heralding the yearn for the return of life, growth and a revival of the natural resources on which the very existence of the Sámi depended. Among the western Sámi, the *Ailekis Olmak* spirits were important because they served to spread the sun's beneficial influence in the spring and summer. As such they were possessed of wings, decorated with the skins of Sámi drums, instruments played by shamans who served as intermediates in Sámi spiritual and temporal life. As the Norwegian anthropologist Erich Jessen has written, *Sodna-peiwe-ailek*, the god of Sunday, had primary importance among such gods since Sunday was the most efficacious day of the week for the performance of shamanistic ceremonies. Then there was the somewhat less powerful *Lawa-Ailek*, god of Saturday, and further down the scale of potency, *Frid-Ailek*, the god of Friday, albeit an important day for the purposes of divination. All three had strong associations with particular mountain locations, and notably the northern Finnish fells near today's Utsjoki, which are known to the Sámi as *Áiligas*.[16]

Some gods looked over the family: namely, the grandfather god *Immel-aiya*, the father god *Radien-adje*, the mother goddess *Radien-aka*, the son god *Radien-kidte* and the daughter goddess *Rana-nieta*. We have already encountered the sun god; others relating to the heavenly bodies included the thunder god *Grom*, the moon god *Mann*, the full moon *Mannpell* and the full moon's daughter *Atyis-yedne*. The chief of the Northern Lights was *Nainas*, his assistant god, *Kuvkas*.

Then there are the gods of the earth, the daughters of these gods, the spirits of the mountains, those which are to be found around human habitations and those associated with the hearth and fire, among others. There are also divinities and spirits associated with bodies of water and rivers. Some have animal characteristics, such as the reindeer man and those associated with bears, wolves and dogs. Yet other divinities and spirits are associated with the underworld.

Among the most legendary shamans serving as intermediaries between the spirit world and man was Akmeeli, said to have fallen into a trance from the beat of his drum. Since his wife was reported to have previously been told by him the words that could release him from this stupor, he should have been awoken by her almost immediately. However, she was purported to have forgotten these words for some thirty years before remembering them, after which he was finally awakened. But, alas, too much time had elapsed; his corpse had decomposed, and so he was obliged to return to the netherworld, never to return.[17] There Yamma-akka-aibmo, the 'mother who watches over the dead', reigned.[18]

Among the lesser entities were the *Juovlagázzi*, peaceful beings who carried out a wide range of more or less benevolent activities during the dark months of winter, while the *Kaddz*, among the Skolt Sámi at least, were guardian spirits who appeared in the guise of various animals. While generally helpful to people, they could also harm them if offended, and so it was important to appease them.[19] *Myandash*, too, as we have seen, was another mythical Sámi being, sometimes appearing as a wild reindeer in the open, sometimes in the guise of a man, and in Ter and Kildin Sámi culture, it is he who traditionally imparts hunting skills to the Sámi.[20] Sámi mythology and ancient religion were closely linked to those of the pre-Christian Finns.[21] However, despite the fact that all these Sámi spiritual beings may have receded to a greater or lesser degree as Christianity, first Catholic, then Orthodox and Protestant, made inroads in Sápmi, in the twentieth century they were to assume new vigour not in religious terms, but in literary endeavours. Edgar Reuterskiöld (1872–1932), Professor of the History of Religion at Uppsala University from 1916 and Bishop of Växsjö from 1928, has shed considerable light on this subject. The works which he edited, *Källskrifter till lapparnas mytologi* (Sources for the Mythology of the Lapps, 1910), and *De nordiska lapparnas religion* (The Religion of the Nordic Lapps, 1912) provided insights into the subject for decades.[22] The Swedish–Finnish ethnographer Erik Therman (1906–48) later brought this pantheon to the attention of a wider public through his seminal work *Bland noider och nomader* (Among Shamans and Nomads), which was published in 1940. Not only did the latter explore various aspects of shamanism among the Sámi culture at that time, it also inspired him to edit his controversial Swedish-language novel *Renhandlarna* (The Reindeer Merchants), which focuses upon ancient Sámi spirituality.[23] This, as we shall see subsequently, would inspire many others in the later twentieth and early twenty-first century.

Sacred Sites

Sacred sites, locations of important ceremonial ritual, were of great significance for the Sámi. Indeed, the importance of invocations at such sites for the purposes of hunting is plainly evident at one noted mountainous location in the north of Sweden, Áhusjgårsså, where an image etched into a boulder by a metal implement illustrates a humanoid figure crowned by antlers and with a bow in one arm, which is possibly *Juoksáhká*, the Sámi goddess of hunting.[24]

Many sites evincing archaeological remains were from prehistoric times, but considerable archaeological evidence from such sites as Badjelánnda and Voujatädno near the outfall of Lake Sállohávrre confirms the theory that the use of sacred sites and their associated settlements increased during the eleventh and twelfth centuries AD. With respect to the former, the archaeologists Inga-Maria Mulk and Tim Bayliss-Smith have concluded that anthropomorphs should be interpreted as depictions of *Máttaráhkká*:

She is the cosmic power that is represented on drums in the image of her three daughters, and, following Eidlitz Kuoljok (1993), we suggest that the same Earth Mother figure appears in the Alta rock art and, in mythical form, as the mother of *Myandash*. She also features as a source of help in stories about the Sun's Son, who in some respects resembles *Myandash*. There are two strands to support this argument: iconographic resemblance, and ritual context.[25]

The latter site contains at least thirty sacred *siedidi* (i.e. in North Sámi stones and the remnants of sacrifices carried out between the early Iron Age and the medieval period). Ancient coins have also been found, as have the remains of antlers and reindeer bones which radiocarbon dating confirms as belonging to the period 1450–1650.[26] Others are to be found on Ukonsaari Island in the middle of Lake Inari in Finland, close to the Sámi Museum 'Siida', which is about 10 kilometres from the village of Inari. In a nearby cave the remains of offerings have been uncovered, including the bones of bear, reindeer and birds. Another site was uncovered by Lake Somasjärvi, in the northwestern corner of Finnish Lapland, containing *siedi*, an enormous block of stone some 25 cubic metres in size, at the bases of which offerings of antlers and coins have been discovered. Such *siedi* have also been excavated in Russian Lapland, of which the most noted is to be found in the environs of Lake Seitozero on the Kola Peninsula.[27]

Acerbi gave us considerable insight into the sacred sites of the Sámi during his late eighteenth-century visit:

Several mountains and a number of rocks were esteemed by the Laplanders as sacred, and held in great veneration. They are distinguished by the general name of *passe-warek*, which means *holy places*, and were formerly places of sacrifice and religious worship.

The veneration for these *passe-warek* has not yet entirely disappeared: some Laplanders visit them yearly in their best clothes, and though they offer no fresh sacrifices, they are careful to leave the bones of former offerings untouched. On no account will they pitch their tents in the neighbourhood of these sacred spots, lest they should disturb the deities with the cries of their children, or other noises. When they pass them, they conduct themselves with the utmost reverence: they would not attack a fox, a bear, or any other animal, near these places; and if a woman be in their company, she is under the necessity of turning her head aside, and covering her face with her hands.[28]

Such animals might, indeed, be transmogrifications of the Sámi themselves. As the anthropologist Stein R. Mathisen has written:

it was a common belief that some of the Sámi who were versed in witchcraft could change themselves into wild and harmful animals, like bears and wolves. In this disguise they would hurt or kill the domestic animals of the Norwegian farmers. The cause for this would typically be that a poor Sámi begging for meat was refused, and this way made his revenge on the domestic animals.[29]

A wide range of metamorphoses were possible according to shamanist beliefs, but especially that of people into bears and wolves, among the most important animals in the cultures of Europe and Asia's indigenous northern peoples.[30]

Christianisation of the Sámi in Norway

Already during the period from the eleventh to the fourteenth centuries, it seems that Sámi sacrificial rituals reflected the adoption of religious symbols from outside peoples, in particular Catholic Christians, which was probably the result of their growing contact with a wider world through the ever more intensive fur trade.[31] According to the *Håkon Saga*, composed in Iceland in the 1260s, King Håkon Håkonsson (1217–63) had the first church built in the Troms region around 1250, at about the time that the inhabitants were obliged by him to accept Catholic Christianity. Certainly, a stone church was constructed in this period in the area and a missionary church was also built for the Sámi in Ofoten.[32] Later, in the fourteenth century, the Norwegian King Håkon V ordered the construction of a fortress and a church at Vardø, on the Arctic Sea, where a royal proclamation of 1313 exhorted the Sámi to accept Christianity. Much later, during the sixteenth century, numerous chapels came to be constructed throughout the coastal regions of the Norwegian north, on both the islands and the mainland coasts into Finnmark. In fact, there were some thirty-six Norwegian churches built along the northern coast of Norway before 1589. But Orthodoxy from the east was also making inroads at this time and there were four Russian Orthodox churches on or near the Arctic coast in territory over which the Russian government claimed hegemony. Eight additional Norwegian churches were built further inland, albeit on waterways, between 1700 and 1750. In Sweden, too, there was a spate of church-building, with some twenty-three churches constructed not only in the far north of Sweden proper and Swedish Finland but into the areas of what is today Norwegian Finnmark, to the north of the Finnish border.[33]

In Norway, it was King Christian IV who took the initiative to propagate Lutheran Christianity among the Sámi after visiting the north of the country in 1599. In 1602 he gave the royal consent for the construction of a chapel at Tysfjord, where the Sámi were to be taught in their own language. Anders Arrebo, Bishop of Trondheim from 1618 to 1622, also took a keen interest in the Sámi, albeit in a literary sense. He composed the epic *Hexameron* in which the Sámi and their reindeer featured prominently.[34] In 1635 an itinerant clergyman was appointed to the Sámi in Trøndelag, and in 1641 the parish priest of Snåsa was made responsible for a wider mission to the Sámi. Erik Bredal (1607–72), bishop of Trondheim from 1643 to 1672, also took considerable initiatives in undertaking missionary activities to the Sámi, infused with Norwegian political undertones, for the Lutheran Swedish were also making inroads in the area. When Sweden temporarily occupied Trondheim in 1658, Bredal fled to Trondenes in the company of some of his older students from the Cathedral school and so he used the occasion to utilise them on his own missions to the Sámi. However, they were sometimes violently received by those Sámi who remained 'pagan'—on occasion even being killed by them—and so a new initiative was taken to use Sámi converts themselves as missionaries. Sometimes, as in the case of one Skole-Nils, said to have been the bishop's best Sámi pupil, the missionary himself reverted to ancient Sámi 'wizardry' to the great consternation of the churchman and his Christian flock. The Christianisation of the Sámi nevertheless proceeded apace, and Bredal's successor on the episcopal throne from 1673 to 1678, Bishop Erik Pontoppidan, translated Luther's own catechism into Sámi. The manuscript was never printed, and no copy appears to be extant, but it would seem that the two principal initiatives stemming directly from the established Lutheran Church in

Norway proved increasingly successful. Yet it was only under the Norwegian Pietist Thomas von Westen (1682–1727), who himself wore a traditional Sámi garment, the *gákti* (or *kofte* in Norwegian), that the missions which set forth to convert the Sámi actually achieved substantial success. This was accomplished primarily through his outdoor preaching. A keen promoter of Sámi education as a means to further their conversion to Lutheran Christianity, he has been called Norway's 'Apostle to the Sámi'. Those of the coast were the easiest for the missionaries to bring into the fold since they had long ceased to be nomadic and so came much more frequently into contact with other Norwegians and their cultural and spiritual values.[35]

Westen ensured the availability of the next generation of missionaries to the Sámi by establishing his famed Seminarium Domesticum, in Trondheim in central Norway, serving as its rector from 1716 to 1727, and he also made two lengthy visits to the Sápmi, the first to the province of Finnmark and the second to Nordland, Helgeland and Troms. Not content merely to preach, he took a deep interest in acquiring in-depth knowledge of Sámi life and culture. This resulted in his so-called 'confession books' that dealt with 'pagan' views of the Sámi as he perceived them. Alas, they were consumed in a fire in the Danish (and then Norwegian) capital Copenhagen in 1793, but by then they had been read by many scholars as well as by scores of missionaries of the generations which followed him.[36]

Under the leadership of Westen, the ecclesiastical authorities provided considerable financial resources to assist in the conversion of the Sámi. A misjonkollegium (missionary institute), also known by its official Latin name as the Seminarium scholasticum, was established in Copenhagen in 1714, and was given a wide remit to carry out a mission to the Sámi in 1716. The Danish king Frederik IV himself took over its supervision, for its dimensions were political as well as religious. During these bitter years of the Great Northern War, with Denmark and its ally Russia pitted against Sweden–Finland, the mission was intended to hinder Swedish inroads in the north, in whatever guise it might take. Although Westen was based at the Cathedral school in Trondheim, he was keen to carry out his mission through the medium of the Sámi language. However, the church hierarchy, and in particular Bishop Peder Krogh (1654–1731), preferred to use Danish (the administrative language of Denmark–Norway at this time). In fact, he was determined to carry out not only the Christianisation of the Sámi, but also their Norwegianisation, in sharp opposition to Westen's approach.[37]

Westen travelled throughout the Sámi regions in 1716 and then for longer periods in 1718–19 and 1722–3. Wearing the Sámi *kofte*, he famously preached out of doors, attracting large audiences.[38] Isaac Olsen, a missionary in Varanger who helped in translations into Sámi and in teaching in that language, assisted this mission. He, in turn, was helped by two young Sámi converts, Ivar Paulsen and Sivert Henriksen. As a result of these activities many Sámi in Varanger and Porsanger were converted to the Lutheran faith. Westen also used his itinerant mission among the Sámi to collect their drums—viewed by some of the missionaries as vicious relics of paganism, but by others as fascinating artefacts—which were sent on to Copenhagen, and many of which were later destroyed in an accidental fire. Westen went on to found some thirteen mission circles in a region which spanned a vast area from Trøndelag in south-central Norway to Varanger in the far north. Through his initiative churches were built at Nesseby, Tana, Lebesby, Masi and the *Finne Capell* at Kålfjord. Associated schools were also established. By 1724, this Norwegian mission had no less than twenty-six assembly rooms and eleven schools at their disposal, as a result of which Sámi children came to be provided with a basic educational system well before the wider population of Norway–Denmark itself were given such benefits in 1739. A catechism translated by Morten Lund also appeared in 1728, with texts in both Sámi and Danish. ABCs and other teaching materials, though originally intended to be published, did not appear. It was this catechism which came to be utilised by Knud Leem (c.1696–1774), a former pupil of Westen and Olsen. He himself had served as a missionary in Porsanger in 1725–8, and, in that latter year, was appointed parish priest at Talvik and Alta in Vest-Finnmark.

After Westen's death, Bishop Krogh closed the school and focused instead on missions using the Danish language, after which the use of Lund's catechism was prohibited, although the missionary Johan Falch continued to use Sámi in his mission at Alta in Finnmark from 1728. His position was strengthened after his appointment as priest at Alta in 1735 and at Talvik (the church was completed in 1737), where he began to use Bishop Erik Pontoppidan's popular religious work *Sandhed ti Gudfrygtighed* (*Truth onto Godliness*) to assist those preparing for Confirmation. He eventually began to translate it into Sámi, and although the project was never completed, the manuscript did provide considerable assistance for the Sámi teachers at Alta. Yet with the advent of a new bishop, Ludvig Harboe (1709–83), who ascended the episcopal throne in 1743, Westen's approach subsequently came back into favour with the Norwegian ecclesiastical authorities. Missionaries and teachers were once again encouraged to learn and use Sámi. True, the Danish missionary and priest Hans Frugaard (1716–92) continued to follow the late Bishop Krogh's approach, eschewing Sámi as a medium of instruction while serving as parish priest at Kjøllefjord from 1751, and then as dean of Alta in 1757. But others, like the Norwegian theologian Frederik Nannestad (1693–1774), who succeeded Harboe as bishop of Trondheim, continued to favour Sámi. Indeed, in 1752 he established a new seminary, the Seminarium Lapponicum (Lapp Seminary), under the leadership of Knud Leem, which was modelled on that first established by Westen.[39]

The Danish king Frederik VI took an especially keen interest in the Sámi, fascinated by their exotic qualities. Indeed, during his visitation to Ålesund, which was part of a wider progress through Norway as far north as Trondheim, he met Leem, who was in the town celebrating his marriage. The monarch took advantage of the occasion to request that a Sámi youth be sent to Copenhagen to join his court, and after great difficulties in securing one because of the reluctance of Sámi parents to sacrifice a child for such a purpose, the Sámi boy Niels Pedersen, from Kornes, was finally secured for the purpose. Sent to the Danish capital in the autumn, he was warmly received as a budding and exotic courtier, only to die of illness during the ensuing winter, his courtly clothes being later sent to his parents to honour his memory. A similar misfortune met another young Sámi man, Peder Jonsen, who had been invited to join the Royal Danish Navy as an officer by Admiral Rosenpalm, and who also succumbed to an illness, in this instance on an extended journey to the Far East on a ship of the Royal Danish East India Company.[40]

More propitiously, further endeavours were being undertaken at this time to bring the Sámi more fully into the Christian fold. The first of these was the translation of the New Testament into South Sámi at the beginning of the eighteenth century by the Sámi priest Lars Rangius, based at Piteå, although only sections of it were published.[41] Pehr Fjellström (1697–1764) subsequently translated the entire New Testament into Northern Sámi in a work which appeared in 1755.

Fjellström also attempted to transcribe a uniform South Sámi script, utilising the Ume, Pite and Lule Sámi dialects (from Sweden). A catechism, grammar and glossary appeared using this script in 1738. However, Henrik Ganander, the parish priest at Enontekiö, objected to this use of these South Sámi dialects and instead advocated the use of North Sámi as a uniform written language. He therefore produced his own North Sámi grammar in 1744. Knud Leem further assisted in the project to make North Sámi the medium of local instruction by collaborating with the Sámi theologian Biret-Ánde (Anders) Porsanger (1735–80), from Olderfjorden in Porsanger, to compile a dictionary in North Sámi which proved to be a considerable success; its first part was published in 1768 and the second, posthumously, in 1781. Porsanger himself had been a pupil in Trondheim at the Latin school and took his examinations as a theologian in Copenhagen in 1761, before becoming a missionary in Varanger. Later, in 1764, after he had returned to Trondheim, he became a chaplain of the hospital there, prior to his appointment as a priest specifically to serve the Sámi at Varanger in 1772. From 1764 he was also connected to the Seminarium Lapponicum. A highly learned scholar of considerable breadth, Porsanger considered the use of Hungarian orthography when devising a script for Sámi. He also translated large portions of the Bible, produced a grammar and made formulations for a Sámi script. Nonetheless, the bishop of Trondheim rejected him as a candidate for the professorship at the seminary, preferring to send him as parish priest back to the Sámi in East Finnmark. Tragically, he and his family drowned in a shipwreck off the Norwegian coast by Risør, during a journey to Copenhagen from Vadsø.[42]

Christianisation and Development of the Early Church in Swedish Lapland

With respect to Sweden, some trace the conversion of the Sámi to Christianity to as early as the 1300s, at least in the vicinity of Tornio.[43] Certainly, in 1345, Sámi people were baptised in Tornio during a famous visitation there by the Swedish primate and archbishop of Uppsala. Tradition has it that in 1389 a Sámi woman named Margareta entreated her namesake, the Danish queen of the Scandinavian Union, to send missionaries to the far north to convert the Sámi to Christianity. However, the reaction was slow and only in 1419 was a certain Toste sent as a missionary to the Sámi, among whom he built several chapels. Yet it was only in the early seventeenth century, after the Lutheran Church had become formally established under the Swedish king Karl IX, that an ecclesiastical infrastructure was finally organised among them.[44]

The earliest churches, which were actually small chapels, had been built in Pite and Lule Lappmarks in the late sixteenth century. After the turn of the century, though, they tended to be built at their *Dálvadis* (winter camps), located at Lycksele, Hetta and Jukkasjärvi. A church was also built at Nasafjället after the opening of the local silver mine, as well as at Arvidsjaur, Arjeplog and Silbojokk. Although the local clergy did not always reside in their parishes, the new church infrastructure reflected the fact that Karl IX was preoccupied with having his authority asserted over the Sámi, whose king he had specifically declared himself to be. Therefore, in 1606, through the initiative of his emissary Daniel Hjort, sixteen Sámi men were sent to Uppsala University in order to train for the priesthood. However, the initiative proved largely unsuccessful since the majority absconded during the journey, and although six of the young men actually reached the archiepiscopal seat, none of them ultimately entered the priesthood. Therefore, in the following years it was arranged for training for the priesthood to be carried out in Sámi areas and to this end Johan Skytte's school was, in part, established in 1632. Its headmaster was Olaus Stephani Grann, a priest of Sámi ancestry. Sámi pupils were admitted *gratis* and the school itself continued to function in Lycksele over the following two centuries, after which it was relocated to the north.[45] One of the first native Sámi Lutheran priests to benefit from this education was Nicolaus Lundius (1656–1726), a native of Nasafjäll, in Pite Lappmark, noted for its silver mine (active from 1635–59), who became a student at the Skytte school in Ume Lapland. While rejecting traditional Sámi religious belief and customs, he nonetheless collected a large quantity of information on shamanism, as well as other aspects of Sámi life. Much of this he had expected to provide a basis for Johannes Schefferus's great work *Lapponia*, but it was never used.[46]

Some Sámi even made their way into the highest levels of Swedish society. The Sámi Johannes Grann, the son of Gerhardus Jonæ, a native of Umeå-Lappmark who had been raised in the household of a Lutheran clergyman in Piteå, was the first to become a priest. As well as theology he also studied philosophy, and eventually he became a doctor of jurisprudence. He was later appointed high court judge in 1642 and was elevated to the nobility in 1645, possibly the only Sámi to have achieved this status. In 1653 he was appointed governor for the far north of Sweden.[47]

One of the first Sámi missionaries in Swedish-governed Finland during this period was Olaus Sirma (c.1655–1719), a native of Kemi Lappmark in the vicinity of what is today Sodankylä. Having attended a Finnish school, in 1672 he went to Uppsala University, which was the seat of Sweden's archiepiscopal primate, where he became closely acquainted with Schefferus. He also visited Stockholm during this period. The nickname he was given, *Čearbmá-Ovllá*, the first word of which signifies 'reindeer calf',[48] is indicative of the impression he made in the archiepiscopal seat. In 1675 he was consecrated a priest at Enontekiö and appointed to a parish at Márkan, about ten kilometres from Karesuando, the church of which was built in 1728. He served his parish—and indeed much of Lapland as far as the Arctic coast—until his death in 1719. In contrast to other priests in the region he used Sámi rather than Finnish and was keen to establish a Sámi school in Torne Lappmark. The prayer book which he composed, *Máná buoremus dávvir* (The Child's Best Helper), however, failed to receive the financial support needed for its publication. Moreover, it proved difficult to win over his flock from their ancient Sámi beliefs. Indeed, some even said that Sirma himself continued to practise rituals of the ancient religion and made many compromises between the two. Yet despite these problems he was greatly revered, and after his death the village of Sirma, in the Tana Valley, was founded and named after him.[49]

One element in the new ecclesiastical initiative in the Nordic Sámi homeland which facilitated church-building was the introduction of wooden churches. The newly constructed churches in these northern territories of Sweden were no longer built mainly of stone, as had previously been the case, but of wood, a much cheaper and more accessible material, albeit one that is vulnerable to fire. This was a usage which persisted well into the eighteenth century. Karl IX himself ordered the construction of five new wooden churches in Swedish (and Finnish) Lapland, sending out his emissary Daniel Hjort to scout for appropriate locations in 1605. Four of these were erected in the Sámi heartland at Lycksele, Arvidsjaur, Jokkmokk and Jukkasjärvi, on the Swedish side of the Torne River, and one at Enontekiö, on the Finnish side. While a principal motivation was religious, another was political, not only to assert Swedish royal political authority over the Sámi and to hinder Norwegian incursions, but also to serve as points of thrust to make good Swedish claims over adjacent Norwegian Finnmark.[50] This aggressive stance proved only partially successful, however, for while Finnish Lapland did become firmly embedded in the Swedish royal dominions, the Treaty of Knäred (1613) obliged Sweden to abandon all territorial claims to Norwegian Lapland.[51]

With foreign threats now minimised, the process of thorough Christianisation could proceed apace. One of the most important missionaries among the Sámi at this time was the Swede Johannes Tornaeus (c.1600–81), who served as rector of the parish of Alatornio from 1640 to 1681 and enjoyed the support of Baron Gabriel Oxenstierna, a highly prominent figure at the Swedish court. Among Tornaeus's many missionary ancillary activities was a translation into Sámi of the Lutheran Church service book, *Manuale lapponicum* (Lapp Manual), which was published in 1648. He also produced a great work for the Swedish College of Antiquities in which he describes, in highly fanciful terms, the life of the Sámi in Torne Lappmark. This, in turn, provided not only the basis for the scholar Johannes Schefferus's renowned tome *Lapponia*, but also for two other works on the same subject which became the authoritative works on the Sámi for the following 200 years, even though they were highly dependent, in part, on a previous description of the region and its indigenous inhabitants by Samuel Rheen.[52]

As we have seen, the Lule, Pite and South Sámi (the latter from Jokkmokk-Salten and further south) were the first to be Christianised. Instrumental in this was the publication of the first book using Lule-Pite Sámi, as written by the missionary Nicolao Andreæ. This ABC book, *på lappesko tungomål* (in the Lappish Language), was printed in Stockholm in 1619 and includes the 'Our Father', 'Nicene Creed', 'Ten Commandments' and 'Order of Baptism', among other prayers.[53] Missionary activities were also encouraged by a wide range of administrative changes: Kautokeino was made subject to the ministry of a Swedish priest, who also had Utsjoki under his purview, while Karasjok, Tana and Utsjoki were separated from Torne Lappmark. New churches were then built at Kautokeino and Utsjoki in 1701, by the shores of Lake Mantojárvi, the latter on the site of the present church which opened its doors to worshippers in 1654 with a prayer house constructed that year at Karasjok. Johannes Nicolai Tornberg, who served from 1675 to 1682, was the first priest appointed there, followed by his brother Anders Nicolai Tornensis (1682–1705) as the second.

However, the incumbency of the latter, together with his wife Aile, was highly troubled. Land and fishing rights were a source of legal and social strife, while the rectory itself became a subject of scandal, in particular during Aile Tornberg's widowhood, when it was said to be more frequently favoured as a tavern and haunt of thieves than as a house of worship.[54] Despite these accusations, in 1723 the Swedish government decided to continue to focus upon strengthening Christianity among the Sámi and to this end decided to establish a so-called *lappskola* (Lapp School), to whom a schoolmaster was assigned, connected to the region's principal church. Instruction was to be carried out in the Sámi language. After a debate about whether or not it should be located at Kautokeino or Utsjoki, the latter was eventually decided upon, with the construction of the school being completed in 1728. Its first pupils, including some from Kautokeino, only arrived in 1743, the year in which instruction commenced. Strangely, although the catechisms were provided gratis, they made use of Lule and Southern Sámi rather than the locally spoken Northern Sámi. With such a misapplied linguistic infrastructure it is not surprising that the school closed its doors in 1750.

Meanwhile, in 1747 Utsjoki was established as a parish with its own pastoral administration, associated with Inari as a so-called parish annex. Its first priest was Anders Hellander (1718–57), who had already been the schoolmaster at the associated school since 1743, and he was also provided with a Sámi assistant. Yet international politics ultimately intruded on this endeavour. When Hellander began to accompany the Sámi on their migrations to Lower Tana, political waves became to roll against the background of a wider border conflict between Sweden and Denmark–Norway. The Danish–Norwegian government took umbrage, sending a missive to the governor of Västerbotten in 1746 accusing the Swedish priest of holding religious services at Gullholmen, on Norwegian territory, during the period 1743–4 and again in 1745, in the Tana chapel which he had opened at his own behest.[55] Although political tensions continued to be high in the region with its disputed national borders, new churches continued to be built, including the parish church of Jokkmokk in 1753 which was curiously designed with eight corners.

Sometimes it was not the Sámi who came under Christian missionary influence, but the descendants of the missionaries who increasingly imbibed Sámi spiritual beliefs and values. The Lutheran priest and missionary Solomon Tornberg settled during the eighteenth century in a new parish close to Karesuando, as a missionary to the Sámi herders and their families who formed some 64 per cent of the population. However, his son, a constable and farmer at Naimakka in Finnish Lapland, near the Norwegian border, married a local Sámi and took up reindeer herding himself. His descendants, in turn, became fully integrated into Sámi society and culture, even adhering to many Sámi spiritual beliefs and values.[56]

The Sámi Conversion to Russian Orthodoxy

In the Russian areas, Orthodoxy was introduced at an early date in the second millennium AD and this aroused far less conflict with the local Sámi than the introduction of Catholicism or Lutheranism. This was in part because of the tolerance of the Eastern Church in absorbing Sámi mythology and religious ceremonies, whereby the natural gods of the Sámi were subsumed into a cult of Christian saints.[57] One of the first Orthodox missionaries in the far north was the monk Lazar Muromsky (1286–1391). Sent forth from the rich Republic of Novgorod, he went as a missionary to convert the Sámi, first along the shores of Lake Onega and then much further to the north. Along with conversion there came the establishment of monastic life, in particular the foundation of the Muromsky Monastery in the vicinity of Pudozh in Karelia, and Vytegra, in the Vologda region, where he eventually died.[58]

The first Sámi in Russian Lapland to convert to Christianity were those living along the banks of Kandalaksha Bay. Chronicles of the period confirm that they were baptised in 1526. Those living in the interior of the Kola Peninsula, however, proved less amenable to conversion and, in any case, their contact at the time with Russians was limited, the heightened missionary activity of the time notwithstanding. It remained a region apart: indeed, unusually at this time for the rest of Europe, but following a custom until the late sixteenth century in Russian Lapland, the year began on 29 August and was based on a lunar calendar. There were thirteen months in this lunar year, which varied from twenty to forty days in length.[59]

During the 1540s the Russian monk Feodorit Kolsky was active in the Kola Peninsula. He came from the Solovetsky Monastery, first built in the 1430s, which was by then an important mercantile trading centre. While this was the main base of missionary activity, a secondary one was eventually established at Kandalaksha which became a centre for Orthodox Sámi missionary activity.[60] Kolsky began his activities among the Sámi at the mouth of the Kola River, where he founded the Kola Monastery and the nearby Holy Trinity Church. He had begun learning Sámi already at the Solovetsky Monastery and was the first to translate a number of prayers into the language using the Cyrillic alphabet—it is said that he baptised more than 2,000 Sámi converts over a period of two decades.[61] His somewhat hagiographical biography was written by his contemporary Prince A.M. Kurbsky (1528–83) and achieved considerable acclaim in clerical circles. A monumental Orthodox cross to his memory was erected in Kola on 30 August 1996 when the Russian Orthodox Church began to enjoy its post-Soviet revival. In 2002 he was declared a saint of the Russian Orthodox Church and his saint's day is celebrated on 17 August. His personal charisma notwithstanding, however, the relationship of the Sámi to the monks of his time and the following century was often troubled. In 1673, for example, they wrote an entreaty to Patriarch Piterim of Krutitsy in Moscow which asked him to intervene on their behalf in a local conflict of economic interests.[62]

Of equal importance was the missionary monk Trifon (1495–1583, called Riffan by the Sámi), originally from a location near Novgorod, who devoted himself for some twenty years to the conversion of the Skolt Sámi along the Pechenga River (called Petsamo under Finnish sovereignty in the years between the two world wars). Having become a monk in 1533 he oversaw the building of the Sacred Trinity Church in the area during that same decade and went on to found the monastery of Pechenga (restored in the post-Soviet period as a place of monastic pilgrimage) in 1565. He built the Church of Saints Boris and Gleb that same year by the Pasvik River (Paatsjoki, in Finnish) at Borisoglebsk, which is today the site of a Russian customs station by the Norwegian border but was originally a village named after the two saints Boris and Gleb who had been the younger sons of Vladimir Svyatoslavovich, the prince of Kievan Rus' who had first accepted Orthodoxy in his realms. They would eventually be martyred by their eldest brother, Svyatopolk, known as 'the Cursed', in 1015. Situated on the banks of the Paatsjoki River, the site was deliberately located adjacent to the Danish–Norwegian frontier as a bulwark against territorial and religious aggrandisement by Denmark–Norway, which had recently undergone the Reformation and an enforced conversion under the leadership of its monarch from Catholicism to Lutheranism. As a consequence, the Sea Sámi of the Norwegian coast had been converted to Lutheranism, while the Skolt Sámi of the Kola coast and the Kola interior had converted to Russian Orthodoxy.[63] As previously mentioned, elements of the old Sámi religion continued to persist in the latter. For example, St Nikolai Chudotvorec became a patron saint of Sámi fishermen, a figure in whom elements of the old Sámi god *Kiose-Olma*, a protector of fishermen, came to be blended. St Evstafii Plakida, in turn, became the patron saint of reindeer herding. He merged together with ancient Sámi cult figures connected with reindeer herding, such as *Luot-emenyt* and *Rassy-aike*.[64]

Christian symbols and elements also became integrated with the social customs of the Sámi. Acerbi sympathised with the Sámi, who he felt often failed to experience exclusive Christian practice as providing for their needs, both spiritual and physical:

But as the God of the Christians seemed to them only to have provided for their happiness hereafter; and was, moreover, too mild and gracious to afflict them with diseases, they still considered it to be their interest, occasionally to continue their sacrifices to the gods of their fore-fathers, in order to relieve themselves from sickness and the evils of their present fate ...[65]

The Russian academic Nikolai Kharuzin also noted how Christian and pagan elements merged in Sámi practice, writing:

Two Lapps frequently exchange crosses, having which they consider themselves brothers. In Lovozero and Notozero, this custom is carried out with the exchange of presents. The Lapps do not only take one another as brothers in this way but sometimes, indeed, Russians. ... This making of brothers among the Lapps does not create any obstacle to marriage. One 'cross' brother is allowed to marry the sister or daughter of another.[66]

Still, Pechenga, the spiritual centre of Orthodox life on the Kola Peninsula, thrived, not only as a religious centre, but as an economic one as well. For that reason, the Dutch also became an economic presence there.[67]

As for Trifon, at first his work at the monastery was assisted by twenty monks and thirty laymen. However, within a few decades there were at least fifty monks and 200 laymen helping him in his work. Trifon also founded chapels by the Sámi summer camps, one dedicated to Boris Gleb at Keeuŋes, by the mouth of the Pasvikelva River, and another at Neiden. Indeed, it was at a pool by the latter that Trifon first baptised the Sámi; later, in the nineteenth century, a chapel dedicated to St George would be constructed nearby.[68]

But the monastery was dangerously situated on the contested frontier with Sweden–Finland and an attack on the monastery by Swedish–Finnish forces in 1589 resulted in the massacre of almost all the monks and laymen, including thirty-five Sámi from the local *siida*. The monastery was also plundered and then burnt by the Finnish 'guerrilla' leader Juho Vesainen and his band, obliging the remaining monks to seek refuge at the Kola Fortress and, although the monastery was refounded in 1591, it was burnt down again in 1619. Once again, though, it was rebuilt, with privileges extended and the benefits of imperial largesse bestowed. This not only included a wide range of land allotted to the monks, but increased water and fishing rights and—most importantly and notoriously—the right to tax the local Sámi and to employ some of them as slaves. The monastery consequently thrived in material terms until it was despoiled of large tracts of land before finally being closed by imperial decree in 1764.[69]

Trifon was eventually canonised by the Russian Orthodox Church at the beginning of the seventeenth century and his biography as a missionary was published to great acclaim during the early eighteenth century. A special liturgy dedicated to him as a miracle worker was introduced into the Russian Orthodox service. Also canonised was an important, albeit lesser-known Orthodox spiritual figure, the monk Feognost, who worked in the late sixteenth century on the Kola Peninsula among the Ter Sámi.[70]

Altogether at least ten Orthodox churches were established in the Kola Peninsula by the end of the sixteenth century. After the Church of Boris and Gleb, that of Saint Peter and Saint Paul was built in the 1570s on the shores of the Ter coast near the mouth of the Ponoi River in the far east of the Kola Peninsula. Feognost was instrumental in its establishment and Tsar Ivan the Terrible himself endowed it with icons, books and other items deemed useful for effecting the conversion of the Sámi.[71] Yet these came at a cost: an *ukas* (Russian royal proclamation) from the final years of the sixteenth century compelled the Ter Sámi residing by the Pyönne River to give tithes to the latter's priests, or what amounted to more than a tithe, namely half of their catch of fish. This led to enormous resentment, and ultimately liturgical services ceased to be provided. Missionary activity slowed down to such a degree that by the seventeenth century there remained unbaptised 'wild' Sámi throughout the east of the Kola Peninsula. To rectify this situation, during the 1670s another *ukas* decreed that money should be paid to every baptised Sámi and an exemption from paying taxes accorded for two years. In consequence, by the 1720s the Yokanga Sámi of this eastern region had all been baptised. Indeed, by the 1750s virtually all the Sámi of the Kola Peninsula had become Orthodox Christians, at least in name.[72] The religious settlement of Kamensk was established around the turn of the eighteenth century and in 1716 the Resurrection Monastery was founded, which was supported by the service of at least twenty-three serfs by 1748–9.[73]

One of the most interesting of the ancient Orthodox churches still existing today in the region is the Church of the Assumption of the Blessed Virgin at the village of Varzuga, which straddles the Varzuga River near its mouth on the Terskaya Embankment on the southern shore of the Kola Peninsula, overlooking the White Sea. Completed in 1674, it was commissioned by a prosperous Pomor merchant called Kliment. Constructed of wood around a square base with four transepts, and surrounded by outbuildings and a small chapel, its lofty octagonal steeple rises to a height of 34 metres, surmounting its pegged tent-like roof typical of the Karelian architecture of the period.[74] Not surprisingly, therefore, it was further made famous by Elias Lönnrot, the author and compiler of the Finnish epic *Kalevala* in the first half of the nineteenth century.

Several hundred kilometres to the west, at Kandalaksha, was the settlement of the Old Believers, a religious community still living there today which broke with Patriarchal Orthodoxy because of the reforms promulgated by Patriarch Nikon during the 1650s.[75]

Over the border in Finland, the first church in the Finnish Sámi area was built in 1607 in the parish of Márkan, near Enontekiö, using local wood. Along with fulfilling the spiritual needs of the Sámi, it was part of a political programme initiated by Karl IX, the future king, in order to bolster dominance in Swedish Lapland, and supplement an alternative to the wooden church of the Rounala *siida* in Sweden—long disappeared—which was built in the 1560s. Located at the confluence of the Lätäseno and Könkämäeno Rivers, it also served as an important marketplace, particularly during Candlemas, in the beginning of February, which lasted about ten days. It was a regional administrative seat as well, serving as the site of court sessions and tax collection. That said, many of the Sámi were not happy with the foundation of the church there—they did not want to support it financially, nor to be forced to travel the long distances from their *siidas* that were required to reach it. To resolve these issues and encourage Sámi collaboration, the Swedish king himself provided the materials needed for its construction. Some seventy church cottages were also built to facilitate the accommodation of the Sámi on their visits. These were the first of many local developments over the following years: a new wooden church on the same site was built in 1661, and a third reconstruction in wood took place in 1728. When, in 1809, the market was moved slightly to the south, to the village of Palojoensuu, it was decided that the church would follow suit and, in 1826, a new wooden one opened its doors to parishioners.[76]

Rovaniemi (today the principal city of Finnish Lapland and seat of the Sámi Conference, held every fourth year since 1953) was founded in 1632.[77] Yet its priest long had to support himself by means other than the tithe. Typical was Esaias Fellman, the rector from 1785 to 1819, who not only preached, but farmed in order to support himself.[78] The rectory as it is today was built in 1812, the church in 1817 and the vicarage in 1894.[79]

Due to its geographical location in the south of the Sámi homeland, and just south of the Arctic Circle, Rovaniemi was one of the earliest areas in which Christianisation was completed. Yet by the middle of the eighteenth century the southern parts of Kemi Lapland were also thoroughly Christianised and many had abandoned their traditional lifestyle in its wake: documents confirm that, in 1754, the practising Christian Sámi of the area, all of whom had taken to speaking Finnish, had given up the nomadic life and taken up farming. Thus traditional Sámi economic, cultural and religious life had all vanished, leaving few relics.[80]

This was no sudden revolution, however, but instead marked the end of a long evolution. Acerbi, visiting the area in the late eighteenth century, saw the roots of this Christian conversion of the Sámi, with all the other changes it brought about, as stretching back well into the early Middle Ages. He wrote of:

Christianity ... it is certain that the truths of this religion had been preached amongst them as early as the middle of the ninth century, there being still extant a rescript of the Emperor Ludovicius Pius, who lived at that time, for this purpose, wherein the Laplanders are expressly mentioned by the name of Skrit Finni.[81]

Acerbi also observed wryly that:

When the kings of the North, animated by a spirit of religion and piety, send missionaries into those forlorn regions to preach the Gospel and propagate the

Christian religion, the missionaries did not only make the poor natives pay the expenses of their journey, but also gave them to understand that they were to be remunerated for their trouble.[82]

With further acerbic wit he lamented that:

The poor ignorant Laplanders paid with tolerable patience the contributions required by the Missionaries, who promised them happiness in another world, which probably, according to their limited conceptions, would consist in drinking brandy from morning to night.[83]

Ultimately, he found them a people with little taste for the spiritual. Indeed, he expounded, 'During the whole of our intercourse with these people, we could never discover among them the smallest sign of any sentiment of religion or devotion.'[84] As Karin Granqvist-Nutti has suggested, however, perhaps this was because 'Sámi society to a greater or lesser degree probably saw the attempts to convert them as a threat against their way of life in a plethora of ways.'[85]

Not surprisingly, the infrastructure of the Church of Sweden in the Sámi homeland remained highly fragile. When King Gustaf Adolf was obliged by the Peace of Knäred in 1613 to retract claims on the area between Tysfjord and Varanger, the activities of the church in the region crumbled. The taxes which supported them diminished dramatically through the loss of many Sámi taxpayers now under Danish–Norwegian sovereignty, and many others still living in Swedish-controlled territory who fled to avoid the added tax burden that now fell on them like an avalanche. Their ability to exploit the fish and game in the areas, in any case, was in decline, and this also exacerbated the situation since their overall income was reduced. That said, the growth of mining of malm in the region soon led to an economic revival and this facilitated the establishment of a new ecclesiastical infrastructure. In consequence, by the third-quarter of the seventeenth century, the local governor Johan Graan had succeeded in effecting a complete re-establishment of the state church's authority and financial structure. To further strengthen the spiritual image of the church among the Sámi, the Church Reform Act of 1673 obliged those priests ministering to the Sámi to also serve the newly arrived colonists, as well as those already settled along the coasts.[86]

There was also an ancient church at Inari, which, after a fire destroyed it, was reconstructed in 1914.[87] But the Inari Sámi around Pielpajärvi already had had their own church by 1640.[88] Most of the year it was hardly used, since religious services were concentrated in a small period of the church calendar, from Christmas to Candlemas. This arrangement was not in place for theological reasons, but because the Sámi and those who traded with them were concentrated in towns and villages where the winter markets took place only for brief periods when the herding migrations were in suspension.[89]

By the later eighteenth century in Finnish Lapland, firmly integrated into the Swedish kingdom, a formal church infrastructure was fully established. Acerbi noted that in Kautokeino, Swedish by virtue of the border delineated in 1751, the local priest, based at his church there, looked after the village's four resident families, as well as those in the very extensive surrounding countryside.[90] Most of these were nomadic. He wrote:

In the whole of the district or parish of Kautokeino, which is twenty-five Norwegian miles in Length and twelve in breadth [A Norwegian mile is about eight English miles], there are but two places occupied by settled Laplanders, which amount together to no more than twelve families. The rest are all of the shepherd, or vagrant kind ... In 1756 they reckoned ninety distinct families; but it is possible that some of these families may also have been counted among those of other districts.[91]

Nonetheless, even at this late date the persistence of Sámi 'paganism' continued to trouble the local priest when Acerbi visited in the final years of the eighteenth century:

He informs us that the wandering Laplanders still preserve among them some remains of paganism. It happens here and there in the deserts, that a stone is seen bearing some resemblance of the human form. The Laplanders, when they chance in the course of their movements from place to place with their herds, to pass by any of these stones, offer their sacrifices to the idol. There is always found near them a number of rein-deer's horns.[92]

Today the *värromuorra* (wooden idols) of the old Sámi themselves are a rarity, only a few having survived at their original sites. The idol uncovered in a cave at Marsfjället near Vilhelmina, Åsele Lappmark, is now exhibited in the Nordiska Museum in Stockholm.[93] But pagan traditions lingered longer in the more remote Sámi areas where the Skolt lived, persisting well into the late nineteenth century and beyond, where Christian and pagan elements were integrated into the same rituals. As was noted at the time:

If a Lapp takes Holy Communion at church, before making his confession in church, he also confesses to his Lapp gods; this practice is performed either at home or at the first site of any water which he might encounter on his way to church. For this purpose, he takes a piece of meat, cheese and bread; falling to his knees, he prays to Sarakka, Saivo, Aike and the other gods, not excluding the dark powers of the underworld, like Fudno and the spirit Tshappes'-Olmai; he begs them to remove all his sins as well as those which he intends to commit, going to church, in order to take, against his will 'Christian communion'. He only does this in order not to create a disturbance. Then he takes the bits of meat, cheese and bread and, blessing them, says: this is the body of Sarakka, the bread of Saivo, the body of Garagallessa (Aike).[94]

The Noaidi

A key element of the Sámi religion was the trance into which the *noaide* (shaman) entered while performing his prayers and sacrifices as a means of gaining access to the extraterrestrial spiritual world. The *noaidi* (modern female shamans have been called *noaidegálgu*)[95] were central to the practice of Sámi religion for millennia and play a prominent role in epic tales with a spiritual dimension. They were believed to have the ability to change their appearance, sometimes into animal form, as well as to travel in these guises or as natural phenomena such as gusts of wind. Conflict with the forces of nature is central to these tales, which invariably involve reindeer and fish, the core ingredients of the Sámi diet.[96]

Acerbi noted that 'they knew how to separate and divide the different parts of the animal, according to the nature of the sacrifice, and the deity it was intended for. Upon these occasions they constantly wore a particular habit.'[97]

According to Acerbi, the *noaidi* also used invocations even to recover stolen goods.[98] Thus, useful in such a plethora of ways, their status in the Sámi community was high and even their ancestors were accorded special honour, in particular on those sacred mountains in which they were considered to dwell.[99] To this the ancestor cult of *Myanntasha* was linked, long said to be of particular importance among the Skolt Sámi of the Kola Peninsula.[100] On some occasions, Sámi drums were decorated with images of the three daughters of *Máttaráhkká*, the Earth Mother and mother of the holy white reindeer *Myandash* (*Mjandas,* in Swedish).[101]

The Sámi Drum

The Sámi drum was and remains the musical instrument most important for traditional Sámi religious ritual. The eleventh-century *Historia*

Norvegiae (History of Norway) is the first document to describe such a shamanistic ritual and to comment upon a Sámi drum which was decorated with depictions of whales, harnessed reindeer, skis and a boat with oars. Among the most ancient Sámi drums still extant are two drums from Kemi Lapland, one now in Stockholm, the other in Leipzig. They appear to have been taken from the Sámi in the 1670s by the Finnish priest Gabriel Tuderus (1638–1705), who has gone down in history as the missionary who converted the Kemi Sámi to Lutheran Christianity. Having studied theology at the Åbo Academy in Turku (Åbo, in Swedish) in south-western Finland he became convinced that shamanism and its accoutrements were devilish, and he therefore zealously scoured the region for drums and other material elements of Sámi religious practice. These he immediately had removed, while endeavouring to suppress all other non-Christian religious practices which he encountered among the Sámi. At the same time, devoted to the material and Christian spiritual well-being of his flock, he took a keen interest in other aspects of Sámi life and culture, leaving accounts which give considerable insight into Sámi society of that time. Moreover, he was able to use his position as the rector of Alatornio from 1684 to defend the political and economic interests of the Sámi to whom he ministered, thereby hindering the increasing intrusions of colonists who were interested in obtaining Sámi lands.[102]

Although Christian symbols were used to decorate Sámi drums by as early as 1600, traditional ones including reindeer and boats were also still employed.[103] Indeed, they frequently continued to predominate, for the stylised image of the sun remained the central focus, generally situated in the centre of the drumhead in the form of a circle or quadrangle. The circle tends to be characteristic of northern drums, while the quadrangle is more typical of southern ones. Yet if the sun was central to Sámi worship, in particular in the late winter and spring when its absence was felt, so the moon also occupied an important place in the Sámi spirituality and the pantheon of their gods, in particular at the time of the New Year, most especially in February.[104]

Acerbi made the following remarks with regard to the imagery of their drums:

They are decorated in such a manner that the outer skin of the drums are divided into three parts, the uppermost representing heaven, the middle, temporal life and the lowermost, the abode of the dead. The gaps in the lines which distinguish these different levels represent those points of passage which allow communication between the three worlds.[105]

104

He also shed light on the way in which they were used:

Before a Laplander sets out upon a journey, or undertakes any matter of moment, he consults his drum, which he does in the following manner. He places a ring, which is used for this purpose only, upon the drum, and then striking upon it a smart stroke with a small hammer made from a deer's horn, the ring is shaken or driven over the surface from side to side, which, as it touches certain figures of good or bad omen, he conceives the better or worse opinion of his success in what he is about to undertake. As for example, if the ring moves according to the course of the sun, he pronounces that he shall succeed; if contrarily to the sun's course, that he shall fail in his enterprise, whatever it be, of hunting, fishing, or the like.[106]

Today only seventy-one historic Sámi drums are still documented to be in existence—the majority, forty-three, are in Sweden, with the rest elsewhere in the other Nordic countries and around Europe. This state of affairs has led to vociferous calls for such ancient 'booty' to be returned to the Sámi but, so far, such Sámi demands for their 'repatriation' have not been accepted by the governments, museums or foundations in whose possession they remain.[107] Thus the Nordic Museum in Stockholm continues to be one of the greatest treasure houses of Sámi artefacts. As such, it is an *ansvarsmuseum*, that is, a museum with official responsibility for preserving the Sámi material heritage in its collections.[108]

The circumstances that led to its leading role in this regard are to a considerable degree the result of the work and efforts of the Swedish ethnographer Ernst Manker (1893–1972). Appointed curator of the Lapp Department of the Nordiska Museet (Nordic Museum) in Stockholm in 1939, he carried on in this capacity until 1961 when he was appointed director, a position he held until his death in 1972. He was also the key figure in taking the initiative to establish *Acta Lapponica* (Lapp Journal), of which he was editor from 1938 to 1961. His most important research contribution with respect to the Sámi was his two-volume German-language work *Die lappische Zaubertrommel* (The Lapp Magic Drum), published in two editions in 1938 and 1950. Also of note in this regard is his German-language compilation *Lapparnas heliga ställen* (The Holy Places of the Lapps), published in 1975.[109]

Christian Reaction to Sámi Witchcraft and Sorcery

Because of the notoriety of Sámi shamanism and the sorcery said to be evoked by their drums, occasionally veritable pogroms were directed at their shamans with the aim of suppressing Sámi sorcery. In Norway, after 1600 the provincial administrator was obliged to live in Finnmark by order of Christian IV, in part for this purpose. Stringent measures were taken, and in 1609 capital punishment was decreed by royal proclamation for sorcery, which especially focused upon Sámi *noaidi-vuohta* (shamanism). Sorcery had, of course, been condemned throughout Europe by all Christian churches, both Protestant and Catholic, for many centuries. Indeed, even before the Reformation, Pope Innocent VIII had issued a bull in 1484 prohibiting all such practices.[110] But the upheavals of the Reformation and the social developments of the sixteenth and seventeenth century led to an increase in the prosecution of those accused of sorcery, not only in the Nordic world, but also in the rest of continental Europe and the British Isles.

During the Thirty Years War imperial propaganda was used on placards to vilify Swedish King Gustaf Adolf (1594–1632), a deeply committed Lutheran, for his purported use of Sámi sorcerers amongst his troops.[111] For others, they were simply practitioners of the devil's work. One seventeenth-century Sámi shaman, Anders Nilsson, a native of Sädvajaur in the parish of Arjeplog in Sweden, reacted to the confiscation of his drums and those of other local Sámi shamans by attacking a Lutheran priest and then repossessing him. Judicially condemned as a male witch, he was eventually burnt at the stake.[112]

Other Sámi shamans suffered a similar fate. Anders Poulsen, a Sámi shaman, was arrested in Unjárga, Norway in December 1691 and condemned to death at the court at Vadsø on 9 February 1692 as punishment for 'godless sorcery'. The drum said to be utilised in his ritual was confiscated and removed to Copenhagen. Decorated with a mixture of traditional Sámi and Christian images, it was finally returned to the Norwegian Sámi homeland in 1979 and is now on view at the *Sámiid Vuorkádávvirat* (The Sámi Collections) at Karasjok.[113]

Along with sorcerers, witches also faced persecution, for the witches of Lapland were considered especially diabolical and their notoriety gave the region ill fame as a citadel of witchcraft.[114] According to the historian Rune Blix Hagen, over 40 per cent of capital punishments for sorcery in Norway were carried out in the north of the country. Many of the condemned were Norwegian women from the coast who claimed that they had learnt the black arts from Sámi women. Similar claims were also made in Sweden by those accused of being witches. In the north of Norway twenty-seven Sámi were accused of sorcery in Finnmark between 1593 and 1695. Of the Sámi women, eleven were accused and eight were convicted, the executions taking place in Nordland (eleven), Troms (two) and Finnmark (five). Of the Smi men, twenty-six were accused and twenty were convicted (two in Nordland, five in Troms and thirteen in Finnmark). Of the Norwegian women, 120 were accused and eighty-seven were convicted (seven in Nordland, seven in Troms and seventy-three in Finnmark). Of the Norwegian men, fourteen were accused and five were convicted (three in Nordland, one in Troms and one in Finnmark). A further six convicted were of unknown origins. Thus in total 177 were accused and 126 convicted, just under 20 per cent of whom were Sámi. Most were women but some were male. One case of a Sámi condemned to death for the practice of witchcraft was that of the *noaide* Guivi (Kvive) Baardsen, from the vicinity of Alta. Brought to court in 1627, he was accused of having fomented a storm to sink a Norwegian fishing boat, causing the drowning of its crew. The accused denied this while nonetheless admitting his magical skills, but claimed his intentions were to help, rather than hurt, the Norwegians on board; he was eventually condemned to death and burnt at the stake for black magic, as was another Sámi, Guivi Baardsen, who was executed at Hasvik. Some, however, escaped execution. A woman could prove her innocence judicially if she sank after being thrown into water bound hand and foot. However, if she floated on such an occasion she was duly found guilty and executed.[115]

Sámi Yoiks

The Sámi *yoiks* (*juoiggus/juoige*, in the Sámi language), or chanted songs, were central to the Sámi's expression of their place in the universe and their relationship to one another and the rest of the natural world, even if few Sámi can now actually sing them. While the words were important, the rhythm was of greater significance, dominating the monotonic melody, all accompanied by the beating of the Sámi drum. The symbols with which it was decorated, as we have seen, played a role in invoking the spirits of nature and ancestors so important to the Sámi in their everyday life, dwelling, as they did, in the mountains, hills and other natural features among which the Sámi lived and migrated. These domains were male specific, and women were forbidden from intruding upon them.[116] There were also considerable regional variations. For example, while in the east *yoiks* consisted of long epic texts, in the west they were composed of a limited number of words, chanted in repetition. Musical accompaniment to them, whether by instruments or choir, was not a Sámi tradition and has only been introduced in recent years when the traditional Christian hostility to the *yoik* as a pagan chant has gradually been overcome.[117]

Acerbi was a particularly attentive witness to the performing of the Sámi *yoik* and noted:

The *juoige*, or song of incantation, is used by the Noaaid whilst in the exercise of his magical function. To say it is sung, is to give an imperfect idea of the magician's manner of delivering it, which he does in the most hideous kind of yelling that can be conceived. It is also frequently employed by those who are not professed magicians; for the juoige is supposed to have the power to drive away the wolf, and is considered as a protection for the herd.[118]

It was also thought not only in the Sámi homeland but abroad as far back as the twelfth century that Sámi *noaidi* could control the weather, in particular the letting loose and calming of storms. For this reason, Norwegian sailors sometimes 'bought' wind from the Sámi, despite the condemnation of others, as late as the sixteenth and seventeenth centuries, which they used to exert an '"impious" and "un-natural" control of the elements of nature'.[119]

Organisation of the Seasons and Festive Occasions

Another curious aspect of ancient Sámi ritual noted by Acerbi was that 'The Laplanders formerly made use of a stick called *priimstave*, by way of almanack, on which were marked the several festivals and principal days of the year.'[120] As for the present, though, he was convinced that 'The Laplanders do not observe Christmas as a festival; nor have they any similar days that they particularly distinguish.'[121] On the other hand, pagan sacrifices continued to be observed: 'The ordinary season, with the Laplander for offering up sacrifices, was about the close of the autumn, when they were killing their fat cattle for the winter's store; beside these, they showed their devotion upon extraordinary occasions, and as necessity required.'[122]

Later Missionary Activities

From the late sixteenth century to well into the second half of the nineteenth century, Roman Catholicism and the presence of Roman Catholic missionaries in Sápmi were forbidden, condemned as capital crimes in all of the Nordic countries and Russia. However, the situation changed in the late nineteenth century with the introduction of laws in the Nordic countries—albeit not Russia—tolerating the old religion. The Italian academic Paulo Mantegazza noted that there was a Catholic mission among the Sámi in the environs of Kautokeino when he visited during the 1880s.[123] Yet despite the inroads made by Catholicism, it was predominantly the established Lutheran Church and, to a growing degree, the now tolerated Free Church movements, which were most active and effective in carrying out missionary activities.

The Role of the Lutheran Pastor in Sámi Society

By the late eighteenth century the role of the Lutheran pastor had become quite central in Sámi life. According to Acerbi, 'The pastor, or parson of the place, is for the most part godfather to all the children of his parish; besides which, he does the duties of parish schoolmaster and churchwarden.'[124]

Not only did Lutheran pastors preach the Word of God there and elsewhere in Sweden, they also used their pulpits after 1766 to promulgate royal proclamations, which had previously been read out in parish halls or other public buildings. The pulpit thus became the voice of the Crown, as well as that of God.[125] This was also the case in Swedish Finland, but the situation changed there under Russian sovereignty, especially in the late nineteenth century, when the temporal activities that had been delegated for centuries to the Lutheran Church, including teaching, relief for the poor and parish meetings, were allocated to secular officials.[126]

The Shouters

One of the first of the evangelical movements to affect the Sámi during the eighteenth century was the Vilund Movement of the Lutheran Church which encouraged the spiritual renewal of the individual. This was later superseded by the Čuorvut (Shouters) movement which sprouted in the vicinity of Kautokeino during the 1760s and 1770s. The Čuorvut movement focused on ecstatic religious expression by means of which its adherents had visions, fainted or fell into convulsions. As such it had links not only with Christianity but with the old shamanistic Sámi tradition as well. Not surprisingly, this incurred the ire of more than a few non-Sámi Lutheran clergymen. Most of its preachers were, therefore, laymen who took advantage of local markets where multitudes assembled to preach.[127]

Church Villages

The establishment of church villages (i.e. villages which were characterised by having a church to which people from the surrounding region could come to worship) also helped to bring and keep Sámi Christians into the fold. Thus when the Sámi took up a settled life during the winter months they often did so in these so-called church villages, not unlike those church towns common in the coastal regions of northern Sweden. These winter Sámi parishioners frequently attended Lutheran church services on Sundays and other holy days—not under the legal obligation which constrained the non-Sámi population to attend church, at various frequencies, according to their residential proximity to the church, but through their own choice.[128]

Lars Levi Laestadius and his Followers

Lars Levi Læstadius (1800–61), a native of Arjeplog, was one of the most important religious revival leaders in the north of Finland and Scandinavia during the early nineteenth century. His mother was a South Sámi and his wife Brita Kajsa Alstadius also had Sámi ancestry. Writing and publishing in Sámi, his brother Petrus Læstadius (1802–41) also worked as a missionary among the Sámi. Lars Læstadius carried out his ministry as vicar in Karesuando on the Muonio River by the Finnish–Swedish border from 1826 to 1846, infusing a spiritual 'enthusiasm' or emotional intensity and expression—he called it ecstasy—which sometimes seemed to reflect that of a Sámi shamanist in his spiritual trances. This was a vision which emphasised not only the forgiveness of sin but also an abhorrence of alcohol, a substance which created many social problems among the Sámi. The life which he himself led was austere, and the primitive cabin in which he resided had few amenities, although it was large enough to accommodate prayer meetings focused around readings from the Bible and stirring hymns.[129] His diaries, which were first published later in the century, are among the richest of the period for the insight they give into Sámi life and culture, both spiritual and social. In 1832 he became the first church inspector appointed to Lapland, and he also facilitated the initiation of various educational reforms.[130] He had himself, in turn, come under the influence of a Sámi woman, Milla Clemensdotter, popularly known as Mary of Lapland because of her great Christian spirituality, whom he had heard preach at Åsele in 1844. Indeed, she helped inspire him to undergo a major process of spiritual regeneration, an indirect product of her own spirituality which had strengthened after she had joined the *Läsare* (Readers), a Moravian Pietist movement within the Swedish Church.[131] His movement went on to inspire numerous others whose influence has lasted to this day.

One important such follower of Læstadian was the Sámi preacher Per Anderson Vasara, commonly called Ies-Pieti (Orphan Pieti, 1815–96), a native of the vicinity of Karesuando. His sermons were so remarkable that the bishop of Tromsø employed him as his veritable representative in the Sámi regions of north Norway.[132] Another was Per Anders Nutt (1825–98), who had been his catechist in 1845. He served as the movement's missionary to Norway three years later, carrying out his work for half a century along the coast of Finnmark, as well as in the interior of the Sámi homeland, especially in Karesuando and Enontekiö.[133]

There was also the Swedish Sámi Heikki Niilonpoika Unga (1819–98). Born near Karesuando and popularly known as Posti-Heikki (Heikki the Postman), this itinerant preacher drew considerable inspiration from Læstadius, but adopted a far more aggressive approach that was frowned upon by the secular authorities.[134] Extremists in these movements sometimes went as far as to encourage or foment violence.

The Kautokeino Rebellion

The most violent event to occur in the Sámi homeland with respect to religion was the so-called Kautokeino Rebellion which broke out in 1852 and involved religious revivalists from Kautokeino, and was directed against local government officials. Extremely violent, it was swiftly crushed and its leaders Mats Somby and Aslak Hætta were convicted and executed by due process of law at the village of Bossekop. In line with the spirit of the age with respect to the physiological causes of criminality, their skulls were sent to the Anatomical Institute in Oslo to be studied.[135]

Count Goblet d'Alviella, who visited the town towards the end of the following decade, left his own purple description of the 'rebellion' with a mistaken comment as to how the 'culprits' were executed (they were in fact decapitated with an axe):[136]

Two Lapps were hanged at Alta and others condemned to heavy labour after a violent fracas at Kautokeino which involved the local Lutheran priest, a pastor Hvoslev, later Bishop of Tromsö, and a Lapp woman under arrest in the autumn of 1852. The culprits had been covered in animal skins and were said to be 'more akin to animals than humans', as Hooslef later wrote.[137]

In reality, the reason for the rebellion was far more complex than simple hooliganism. Prior to the event, the then fairly recent closing of the border between Norway and Finland, which prevented the customary migrations of Sámi reindeer herders, had already created animosity between some of them and the wider Norwegian and Finnish authorities, and there was also a religious dimension to the hostilities. After the murder of two people in the uproar—one a Norwegian trader, the other a local chief of police—some saw the Læstadian Movement, with its Finnish (Russian) base, as having stirred up the offenders who were quickly brought before the courts. Four people were initially condemned to death, but, in the end, just two, Somby and Hætta, were executed. Only in the new millennium were their remains given a proper burial, in line with similar circumstances and events elsewhere in the Western world. The other two were given imprisonment for life at the penitentiary at Christiania (now Oslo), where they wrote memoirs recounting how they themselves had come under the influence of the Čuorvut Movement among the Sámi, which anticipated Læstadianism.[138]

Later in the century some Sámi turned to other millenarian movements that continued to be followed well into the early twentieth century. In Finland, the Korpela Movement, centred in the Upper Torne Valley, established by Toivo Korpela, was among the most prominent of such movements. It was deeply embedded in local workers' movements of the time. But as Lundmark has put it, its contacts with political realities were limited:

The screaming mobs belonged to the Korpela movement and they waited for God, in a short time, to lead them to Palestine in a heavenly ark and then to establish his kingdom on earth. When the prophet failed to arrive the movement took on overtones of drunkenness and sexual excesses.[139]

The Church in the Late Nineteenth and Early Twentieth Centuries

Many Sámi, however, remained true to the core of the Lutheran Church. Indeed, Stephen Sommier was struck by the zealous Lutheranism of the Sámi when visiting the north of Norway in the 1880s.[140] The Lutheran Church also attempted to assert itself more strongly in Swedish Lapland, but it was in Finland that it exerted its greatest authority in practical terms.

During the second half of the nineteenth century, the ecclesiastical administration of the Church of Finland began to assume a more strident role, in part by encouraging education in a Sámi context. In 1861, for example, it supported the establishment in Finnish Lapland of a Sámi school. However, a local vicar in Lapland rejected the idea, maintaining that the Sámi population was too small to make it cost-effective. Nonetheless, a catechist (itinerant teacher) began to be employed to teach Sámi children on an ad hoc basis for the Ivalo School District in 1892, the Muddusjärvi District in 1893, the Paatsjoki District in 1906 and the Western Inari District in 1911. But after the development of the wider Finnish public educational system in 1920, the number of catechists began to decline, until the whole system was finally abolished altogether in 1954.[141]

In Swedish Lapland, Kiruna had become the most important town as a result of it being a centre of the mining industry. Thus the construction of its local parish church—for both Swedes and the local Sámi—was a matter of considerable importance, as is reflected in the fact that the famous Swedish architect Gustaf Wickman was commissioned to design it. Its belfry was completed in 1907 and the church itself was consecrated in 1912. Its interior is decorated with the murals of Prince Eugene, the highly accomplished Swedish artist and brother of King Gustav V, and as such is a *chef d'oeuvre* of Swedish National Romanticism, but it can hardly be said to have any reference to Sámi culture or cultural values. However, the fact that Kiruna was a town composed almost exclusively of Swedish immigrants from the south makes that unsurprising.[142] Yet elsewhere in the depths of Lapland there were, of course, many Sámi, and in these parts a minor boom in church-building was also taking place, but principally, it must be noted as well, to serve the need of new non-Sámi settlers. Some older churches, with origins in the Middle Ages, were rebuilt or moved to the areas where various industries and concomitant settlement was increasing. This was nothing new since churches in the region were rebuilt repeatedly, in response to rapid changes in local needs, tastes and resources for centuries. In the ancient Sámi village of Arvidsjaur, for example, no less than five churches had been constructed since the seventeenth century, each one replacing a former structure considered to be in need of more modern adaptations. The situation was similar in other areas. For example, the neo-classical church at Risbäck, in the south-west of Swedish Lapland, was constructed in 1858 to replace a much smaller chapel and to provide a local house of worship for parishioners who had formerly been obliged to travel to the parish church of the town of Dorotea (originally named Bergvattnet but renamed in 1799 after Swedish Queen Frederica Dorothea Wilhelmina). This church had, in turn, been built in the early nineteenth century to serve those who had previously attended the parish church of Åsele, whose parishioners had belonged to the church of Anundsjö. This development did not result from any needs of the Sámi themselves, but instead followed a population thrust of Swedish settlers expanding both westwards and northwards.[143]

The Orthodox Mission in Russian Lapland in the Late Imperial Period

The Skolt Sámi of the Kola Peninsula over the last several centuries have tended to be highly devout adherents of Russian Orthodoxy, and icons were and continue to be kept in a sacred corner in Skolt Sámi homes, in line with Russian Orthodox tradition. (During the Soviet period, government officials tried to enforce the replacement of icons by the hanging of red flags with pictures in these corners.)[144] The Russian Orthodox church, which had long been established at Lovozero, was among the more prominent churches, and had a bell-tower constructed nearby during the 1840s. The new Epiphany Church there was consecrated in 1862. The church itself, with its adjacent schoolhouse, burned down one night in late March 1896, but was rapidly rebuilt the following year with funds provided by the Holy Synod in St Petersburg. Its new bell-tower boasted seven bells. It thrived, and during the early years of the twentieth century, in 1910, Mikhail Ivanovich Rasputin (1881 to the mid- to late 1930s), having previously trained at the Arkhangelsk Seminary, was appointed parish priest to both the Sámi and the Komi.[145] Another Russian Orthodox priest, based at his parsonage in the vicinity of Kolttaköngäs, faithfully served the Skolt Sámi of the Paatsjoki *siida* until late 1917 when the Bolsheviks put a brutal end to his ministry. The Sámi were thus well endowed with houses of worship. There was another church and parsonage at the winter village which served the Nuortijärvi *siida*, while the Suonikylä *siida* had its own chapel and, in winter, a building which served as a primary school. There was also a makeshift building which served as both church and school in the last winter village of the Paatsjoki Skolt Sámi, on the Suonenjoki River.[146]

As for the Pechenga Monastery, closed by order of Empress Catherine the Great in 1764, it was reopened under the pious Tsar, Alexander III in 1888. Thereafter it became a bulwark active in support of both Sámi and Russian education in the region, a role it continued to play even after Pechenga, through the 1920 Tartu Peace Treaty, was transferred to Finnish sovereignty. With the loss of that region in 1944 and the destruction of the monastery, the monks of Pechenga were transferred to the New Valamo Monastery at Heinävesi, near Kuopio in Finland, and its function ceased. However, after the collapse of the Soviet Union, reconstruction began in 1997 and today it is a thriving site of pilgrimage for Orthodox Christians and a major publisher in the region of religious books and tracts.[147]

Soviet Religious Repressions

The February Revolution of Kerensky in Petrograd had little effect on religious affairs in Russian Lapland. However, the Bolshevik October Revolution and its after-effects devastated the Russian Orthodox Church even in this remote region, leading to the physical destruction not only of churches and their ancillary property but their clergy and parishioners as well. As early as 1918, when corn was requisitioned from the Solovetsky Monastery by the Red Army for use by troops at Arkhangelsk, it became clear to many that the monastery's centuries-old use as a centre of monastic spirituality were numbered.[148] On 25 May 1920, the monastery itself was requisitioned by the Archangelsk Executive Committee of the Russian Communist Party. In its place, the Solovetsky *sovkhoz* was set up to administer its agricultural land. In tandem with this, a military prison camp was established under the leadership of Commissar S.A. Abakumov, in which were interned some 300 White Army prisoners.[149]

In the autumn of 1923, under the leadership of Commissar Alexandr Nogtev, the commandant, the monastery was set on fire, severely damaging many of its historic buildings, and was otherwise desecrated.[150] In particular, the tombs of saints Zosima, Savvaty and Herman were opened and torn asunder and their remains unceremoniously exhumed. These were then put on display, at first in the prison camp itself and then in the Museum of Atheism, which was later established in the Kazansky Cathedral in Leningrad, now, with historic irony, functioning as the spiritual centre of the Orthodox Church in St Petersburg.[151]

By 1926 the Solovetsky Camp contained at least 9,300 prisoners, many of whom were clergymen, some invested with the highest offices of the church. Of the latter, twenty-three archbishops and bishops appealed from their incarceration to the national government in an open letter proclaiming that religious freedom had been guaranteed by the Soviet Constitution; however, this was to no avail.[152]

Even common parish priests who served the poor were shown no mercy, their churches desecrated and either abandoned or given over to secular use. The parish church of Lovozero met such a fate: it was turned into a workers' club. Its cupola and bell-tower were removed and its bells melted down. Furthermore, between 1932 and 1936, measures were taken to compel people to remove icons from the walls of their homes. As for its former parish priest, who had faithfully served his flock since 1910, he was exiled to the Solovetsky camp in 1932 like so many of his religious brethren, and was later shot.[153] Further details of the camp over the following decades are considered in Chapter 1.

Finally, however, in 1990, as the Soviet Union was collapsing, some buildings of the former prison camp monastery were returned to the Orthodox Church and it reopened its doors. The first monks began to re-establish themselves in the only partially restored monastery and major rebuilding took on a new impetus, work which continues to this day. Highly symbolic of its rise from the ashes was the return of the remains of saints Savvaty, Zosima and Herman from the former Museum of Atheism in St Petersburg in 1992. They were re-interred in a high-profile ceremony in which the late Alexei II, Patriarch of All the Russias, took part. Today the thriving monastery is included in the UNESCO World Heritage List.[154] As for Lovozero, a new church was constructed there in the 1990s to replace the former one, which had been demolished after it ceased to be useful as a workers' club.[155]

The Church in Lapland during the Second World War

On 4 February 1940, during the height of the Winter War between Finland and the Soviet Union, the old church of Inari was destroyed by Russian bombing.[156] Many other churches were also destroyed in the north of Norway and in the war zone during the Lapland War. However, in post-war Norway and Finland, the rebuilding of ecclesiastical property commenced rapidly. An Orthodox community and church were established after the war in 1950 for refugees from Petsamo (known as Pechenga by that time), with 1,038 members, the majority of whom lived in the Inari area.[157] A new and somewhat modernist church was also built at Ivalo in 1966.[158]

Reconciling Shamanism and Christianity in the
Late Twentieth Century

Although it was startling for some, in the pragmatic years of rebuilding during the 1950s there was a revival of interest in old Sámi religious beliefs and their relevance for the modern world. Arvi Järventaus, in *Risti ja noitarumpu* (*The Cross and the Magic Drum*) (1916), had dealt with the conflicts between Christianity and Shamanism and Annikki Kariniemi, in *Poro-Kristiina* (*Reindeer Kristina*) (1952), took up similar themes. Yet it was really during the 1990s that the conflict between the two came to a head beyond the world of academia, when some clergymen of the Finnish Church expressed their strong disapproval of the Sámi artist Merja Aletta Ranttila's work, and in particular the art exhibited at the Tornio Shamanic Summer Festival in Finland in 1993. Ranttila explicitly stated that this had been created and exhibited as an attempt to undermine the strict Laestadianism still in vogue with many Sámi, which she felt had blighted her childhood. This art also has other dimensions, including the crises of the modern world and the female distress within it, matters considered in greater detail in Chapter 3.[159]

Christianity and Yoiks

Despite the thorough acceptance today of the Sámi *yoik* as an integral part of Sámi culture and one that should be preserved, its relationship to Christianity and shamanism remains unresolved. When Norway

117

hosted the Winter Olympics in 1994, an event with a strong focus on Sámi culture, *yoiks* were included. Yet many Sámi themselves resented this inclusion. Indeed, on 24 February 1993 it was reported in *Nordlys* (*Norway's newspaper, Northern Lights*) that one Christian lay preacher from Karasjok had condemned the *yoik* as a 'parasite in Sámi culture', claiming further that it was born of drunkenness and heathen beliefs. Shortly thereafter, in *Altaposten* (9–11 November 1994), another incident was reported, according to which a member of a Pentecostal congregation had made a *yoik* to Jesus at Kautokeino, at a meeting in which some Maoris, representing New Zealand's aboriginal peoples, were present. Yet others in the congregation objected, accusing the man who had composed the *yoik* of having started his own congregation for the inappropriate purpose of using heathen *yoiks* as a form of preaching to the Russian Sámi on the Kola Peninsula in order to convert them. Indeed, Magga, the former president of the Norwegian Sámi Parliament, stated to the press that, following his local Sámi traditions, *yoiks* should not be part of religious services. As he put it succinctly in *Nordlys* (24 February 1993), 'even if both reindeer meat and cloudberries are delicious food, you do not mix them in the same dish'.[160]

The Church in the Sámi Homeland Today

Such conflicts notwithstanding, the Sámi people remain among the most faithful adherents of Christianity in the Nordic countries and Russia. In Finnish Lapland, Orthodox pilgrimages are still organised in honour of St Triphon at the end of August in Nellim, Sevettijärvi and Neiden. One focus of pilgrimage is the old St Georgios Chapel, but another pilgrimage is also regularly held that leads to the old Skolt Sámi cemetery at Svanvik in Norway. There, incidentally, birds symbolising the soul decorate the tops of the ancient crosses. Other festive occasions are also popular. On 1 February celebrations are held at the wooden Church of the Holy Trinity and St Triphon of Pechenga (Petsamo), in Nellim, commemorating the day the saint took monastic vows. Another is held on 15 December at Sevettijärvi in remembrance of the date of his death and ascent into heaven.[161]

Sámi religious literature has also enjoyed a revival. In Finland, for example, the Skolt Sámi prayer book, *Ristoummi mo'lidvake'rj*, first appeared in 1983, followed by a translation of the Gospel according to St John (1988) and a Russian Orthodox handbook which appeared in 1999.[162]

In the Russian Sámi homeland, a wide-ranging religious regeneration has also taken place. Not only did the Russian Orthodox Church begin to blossom in the region, but a variety of Russian and foreign evangelical Protestant churches and sects also made inroads, sensing a spiritual and cultural vacuum waiting to be filled, especially among the young. They tended to establish themselves in the Murmansk region, often, but not exclusively, from bases in the neighbouring and predominantly Lutheran Nordic countries and Germany. These included not only the German Protestant Mission and the Evangelical Lutheran Mission, but the Evangelical Lutheran Church of Ingria as well, which was attached to the International Lutheran Council. This intrusion frequently alienated the Russian Orthodox Church which perceived it as a threat to its own centuries-old religious tradition, historically embedded in Russian society and culture. In consequence, in September 1997 a new federal law was enacted with respect to religions and religious sects in the Russian Federation, as a result of which many foreign missionary societies and sects found themselves marginalised and sometimes even forbidden from operating. Others, however, often endowed with considerable funding from the Nordic countries, not only were tolerated but thrived. They included the *Norges Samemisjon* (Norwegian Sámi Mission), under the auspices of the Evangelical Lutheran Church of Ingria, which focused its missionary activities upon the Sámi of the Kola Peninsula. Establishing its seat at Lovozero in 1999, it extended its influence not only in the religious sphere, but in the economic and cultural as well. With respect to the latter, for instance, it has provided a variety of courses in the local Kildin dialect of Sámi, in which—along with Russian—it has also published newspapers with evangelical Christian content.[163] In 1999, a new church dedicated to the Epiphany was built there, and a nearby old wooden bridge which provided access was replaced by a metal one. Shortly thereafter, a conference on the Sámi language was held, followed in 2000 by a highly important conference focusing on the Sámi relationship to Russian Orthodoxy.[164] Aspects of shamanism were also considered, for, as the Russian Sámi Nadezhda Bolshakova has put it, 'Totemism is very characteristic of the Sámi.'[165]

The Norwegian and Swedish churches also continue to dominate in their Sámi communities. Many services are held in Jokkmokk in Sweden, for example, including funerals which are held using the medium of Lule Sámi.[166]

Burials

The transition of the Sámi from the material world to the realms of the dead was central to both the ancient Sámi religion and cosmos, and Christian Sámi today, of whatever domination. But the ceremonial context has changed dramatically. In ancient days, it would seem, sledges played an important role in burials throughout the Sámi home-land before the arrival of Christianity. They appear to have first been used along the Varangerfjord, in northern Norway, from about 400 BC, and were adopted elsewhere throughout Sápmi between AD 900 and the 1600s.[167] Among the Skolt Sámi, boats also played an impor-tant role in burials, and coffins were frequently made in the shape of sledges or boats by those who built boats.[168] Traditionally, in pre-Christian times, the Sámi buried their dead in or around the location in which they died and so, since the ground was frozen for most of the year, corpses were generally placed above ground, within the crevices of rocks, under a pile of stones or only just below the surface of the soil.[169] Ancient graves contained hewn out coffins, in which the corpse was covered by slivers of birch bark sewn together by gut string. In Varanger, graves have been uncovered containing personal objects of horn, boon, wood, metal and stone. The first Christian burial grounds in the interior of Finnmark were established by the missionary Tornæus in the 1640s. However, the woods and mountains remained favoured by the Sámi themselves.[170] Indeed, open grave chambers have been found at Mortensnes in Øst-Finnmark, while stone-covered mounds seem to have been the favoured form of graves found by the holy waters of Sávja at Nesseby. Here there are some 200 graves in a scree which appear to span over one and a half millennia, from the dawn of the Christian era to the seventeenth or eighteenth centuries.[171]

Burials also traditionally took place on small islands, dedicated to such purposes, and given the name *Jábbmek* or *Galmmesuoloj* which signified their role. It is possible that these sites were chosen to keep the spirits of the dead at one remove from the living and thereby lessen their influence, since it was commonly held that such spirits were unable to cross running water.[172] Out of some 220 recorded Sámi burial places, ninety-eight are located on small islands, frequently in rivers. From about 1800 onwards, after Christianisation had been completed, these islands or sometimes peninsulas were used for sum-mer graves, with the corpses exhumed and carried to consecrated Christian churchyards during the winter.[173]

Acerbi, who has shed so much life on Sámi life and culture in the late eighteenth century, closely observed the funeral rites of the Sámi he visited:

The funerals are conducted with little ceremony. The body, slightly wrapped up in a coarse cloth, is borne to the grave, attended by a small convoy of the family and friends of the deceased; for whose entertainment a slight repast is prepared ... It was an ancient custom with the Laplanders to bury those who excelled in shooting with the bow, or with fire-arms, in the ground consecrated to the rites performed in honour of their deities. The sepulchre is no other than an old sledge, which is turned bottom upwards over the spot where the body lies buried. It was likewise usual formerly to raise a heap of stones over the dead body; but that practice is now laid aside, and the sledge is at present the only monument. Another circumstance prevailed amongst the Laplanders before their entire conversion to Christianity, namely, that they placed an axe with a tinder-box by the side of the corpse, if that of a man; and if a woman's, her scissors and needle; supposing these implements might be of use to them in the other world. They likewise put up a quantity of provision with the dead body, and immediately after burial of one of the family, they removed their habitation to another spot. For the first three years after the decease of a friend or relation, they were accustomed, from time to time, to dig holes by the side of the grave therein to deposit either a small quantity of tobacco, or something that the deceased was fondest of when living.[174]

Sámi burial rites sometimes led to conflicts with the local authorities. According to Swedish juridical records, many Sámi were brought to court and convicted of burying their dead in the forest rather than in sanctified churchyards.[175] In some graves, such as that discovered at Kautokeino in 1917, the dead were buried in sleighs.[176] Today, a more relaxed attitude has come to dominate Sámi burials, with a wide range of forms and rituals tolerated. This reflects trends in wider Western society, where forest burials have become quite popular, especially in the United States and Canada. In the world of the Sámi today, religion, both in its daily practice and in its concept of the meaning of life until death, is as much a part of the marketplace as anywhere else: the individual, whatever his or her ethnicity, is largely free to pick and choose his or her own personal combination of ethnic, social, cultural and ecological elements, a mix in which religious elements may either merge or disappear altogether.

Prominent today among researchers on various aspects of Sámi religious, cultural and musical life is Elena Sergeyevna Porsanger (born 1967) who became a leading Sámi personality by the late 1990s after studying at the University of Tartu, in Estonia, and then at Helsinki, in

Finland. Her main area of academic focus, after she took up a position at the University of Tromsø in Norway, was the history of religion among the eastern Sámi peoples, in particular, that of the Russian Orthodox Church.[177] As such, she is one of a small number of culturally engaged Sámi who seek to redefine the Sámi practice of Christianity within their historical and cultural context.

3

HEALTH, FAMILY, SEXUALITY AND EDUCATION

Health and Hygiene—The Historical Perspective

In pre-modern times the Sámi believed that disease was caused by demons, and in particular one known as *Ruto* who resided in the hellish domains of *Rotáibmu*. He has frequently been represented as a horse on the Sámi drum (the use of which is so central to Sámi shamanistic ritual). However, since horses were a rarity in the Sámi homeland—the first horses were said to have come to Utsjoki in the 1870s—it is doubtful that the sacrifice of a horse was a traditional means for appeasing the spirits that caused ill-health.[1] Perhaps the figure of a horse on the Sámi drum therefore symbolised the ailment itself, with the speed of the animal serving as a metaphor for the swiftness through which epidemics overtook mankind when they struck.[2]

Giuseppe Acerbi has given us his perceptions of the general levels of health and hygiene of the Sámi, but in terms which seem contradictory and unlikely to correspond to reality. On the one hand he wrote:

The persons and dress of these Laplanders, taken together were the most filthy and disagreeable that it is possible to conceive. They held the fish they were eating in their hands, and the oil that distilled from it ran down their arms, and into the sleeves of their coats, which might be scented at the distance of some yards. The girl had rather more cleanliness in her person, and some portion of that decency which is so peculiar to her sex.[3]

And on the other that:

Disease and sickness are extremely rare among these people; there have been instances of peasants in this parish, who have lived to the age of one hundred

123

and ten years: and the only disorder that proves fatal to the inhabitants, is a kind of inflammatory fever.[4]

However, this seems highly implausible as an accurate perception. As Leif Rantala has pointed out:[5]

Professional medical services by trained doctors was extremely sparse. For, by the 1830s, as the Swedish medical doctor J. Engström noted at the time, 'There was a doctor recently stationed at Lycksele ... but this is hardly of any benefit for the Lappmark, since the whole place has a Swedish appearance, and there is not even one tax registered Lapp.'[6]

Indeed, despite a modest expansion of health services in Lapland—in 1797, for example, the district doctor of Tornio had begun to visit the Sámi as far afield as Inari[7]—medical doctors continued to be a rarity in Lapland even in the later nineteenth century. As French Count Goblet d'Alviella noted after a visit in 1868, he encountered only one doctor between Haparanda and the Arctic Ocean, and that was in Kengisbruk.[8] This was, moreover, at a time of one of Finland's greatest famines, that of 1866–8, a plight which so weakened the immunity of the population that epidemic diseases carried thousands off throughout the grand-duchy: the typhus epidemic alone killed some 7.6 per 1,000 inhabitants in the parish of Inari.[9]

Coping with Insects

The Sámi were spared malaria, a disease which afflicted parts of the south of Sweden until the 1930s but did not affect the Nordic and Russian far north despite the presence of mosquitoes and other insects that tormented the Sámi and their animals in equal measure. The Italian Giuseppi Acerbi observed some of the practical measures taken by the Sámi to cope with them:

When we arrived on the borders of the lake, we fell in with two Lapland fishermen, who had returned from their day's fishing, and were preparing to pass the night there. ... On approaching them we found that they had besmeared their faces with tar, and covered their heads and shoulder with a cloth to protect themselves from the mosquitoes.[10] [The Sámi in fact used a type of balaclava in which only their eyes were uncovered.[11]]

Acerbi was also impressed by the other methods they employed for keeping the insects at bay:

In the summer season the mountain Laplander, being greatly infested with gnats, or mosquitoes, has a contrivance to defend himself from their stings whilst in bed, and at the same time not suffer from being too closely covered. In order to effect this, he fixes a thong of leather to the poles of his tent over his bed, which raises his canvas quilt to a proper height, but so that the sides or edges of it touch the ground: under this covering he creeps and passes the night securely.[12]

Although the use of this mosquito tent was very effective in coping with the insects, teamwork was sometimes also needed to keep the troublesome insects away:

Smoke is found to keep the insects at a distance; therefore, while one Laplander is milking, another holds a firebrand over him, which prevents the gnats from approaching, and accordingly the beast remains untormented and quiet. The pleasure which is expected to be enjoyed during the summer, after a tedious winter that lasts from Michaelmas to July, as the good missionary observes, entirely marred by these troublesome flies.[13]

Mosquitoes were a problem for the reindeer as well as for people, and so the Sámi used smoke to protect their flocks during the height of the summer when the insects were at their worst.[14] It was also for this reason that the reindeer were led to the coast, where the sea breezes helped to keep the mosquitoes at bay. For those who remained inland, placement in the middle of roads offered a modicum of relief, since they were more likely to benefit from at least some wind.[15]

A Russian author who visited the Kola Peninsula in the summer of 1907 noted in flowery prose that:

The mosquitoes are not singing now, as they usually do, treacherously plain-tive, but battle on, like legions of evil spirits. My little Virgil, with his twisted legs, with twisted shoes, does not walk, but jumps. All of his neck is covered in blood. We run, pursued by the devils of Dante's *Inferno*.[16]

Smallpox

While plagues of insects were a major annoyance, the infectious diseases which periodically ravaged Sápmi were of an entirely different order because they carried off people in droves. The first epidemic of smallpox was recorded in the Sámi homeland in Jokkmokk in 1732, although it is hardly likely that this would have been its first appearance there. It was the great natural scientist Carl von Linné who noted that although smallpox rarely broke out among the Sámi, when it did the mortality rate was enormous, especially among children and the elderly over seventy years of age. (This differs from later observations according to which the disease among the Sámi carried off mainly adults, in contrast to the rest of Sweden where 95 per cent of those who died were under the age of ten.)[17] Unlike the general population of Sweden who cared for those who had fallen ill with the disease, von Linné also claimed that the Sámi often took to flight upon an outbreak, even abandoning relatives to avoid the contagion.[18]

While another outbreak subsequently occurred in 1747, according to the local priest in Gällivare, no more than six people fell ill with the disease. However, the epidemic of 1750 that afflicted both Jokkmokk and Gällivare was extremely severe: the mortality rate from the disease climbed to 70 per cent in some places. Nonetheless, when the traveller Abraham Hulphers visited the region in the 1780s and noted a variety of ailments afflicting the Sámi in a number of districts, he formed the opinion that smallpox was very rare. This seems to have been true, since from 1750 until 1820 there were only sixteen deaths from small-pox in Jokkmokk, fifteen in Gällivare and eleven in Enonetkis, the latter of which, at least until 1757, seems to have avoided the disease altogether—although it did eventually break out there some four times, after 1780 no further smallpox epidemics as such were recorded.[19]

Acerbi similarly found that 'The small-pox has at times proved very fatal in Lapland, but has not made its appearance there for many years.'[20] He was of the opinion that unhygienic pagan practices encouraged epidemics of smallpox and other diseases:

Those acts of worship, occasioning a great reduction of their stock of cattle, often brought the Laplanders to a situation of misery and want: as the mountain Laplanders, when attacked by the small-pox or the measles, with difficulty got over these disorders, owing to the pores of their skins being rendered impervious by the dirt and smoke in which they lived, they made numerous sacrifices of rein-deer during their illness, sometimes to the number of twelve rein-deer to one person.[21]

Inoculation against smallpox—first introduced into western and northern Europe by Mary Wortley Montagu, wife of the British ambassador to the Porte of the Ottoman Empire in Constantinople where she had seen it practised to good effect—was also introduced into Sweden, Finland and Russia, but it does not seem to have played a major role in the containment of the disease. A Piteå newspaper reported in 1770 that a settler had inoculated his two Sámi children, and that a Sámi woman had also availed herself of the procedure. However, by 1781 there was only one doctor appointed to carry out inoculation for the whole of Swedish Lapland, including all of Västerbotten and Norrbotten. Thus only a small number of Sámi in Jokkmokk and Gällivare were ultimately inoculated, and even this was done half-heartedly. With regard to the Sámi of the Gällivare district, for example, the doctor appointed to carry out the inoculations in 1783, Dr Daniel Naezeen, felt that there were few practical reasons for their inoculation and that the risks were considerable. According to communion book records, it was only much later, in 1793, that the region's first organised attempt at mass inoculation took place, with vaccinations of Sámi in the local rectory in Jokkmokk.[22] Further efforts were made after the outbreak of the Enontekis epidemic in 1798 through the initiative of the Swedish clergyman Eric Grape: some forty, predominantly Sámi people over the age of thirty took part, and all survived. Thereafter the disease struck rarely in the Sámi homeland: from 1800 onwards, less than 1 per cent of the population in Gällivare and Enontekis died from the disease.

By the early nineteenth century infection and mortality from smallpox had begun to diminish throughout Europe. Whereas some 41,000 died of smallpox in Sweden in the 1790s, the total percentage of deaths from the disease fell dramatically over the following two decades. One reason for this dramatic decline might have been the fact that three-quarters of all children had been vaccinated by the 1820s (the clergy were obliged by law to record such statistics). However, owing to the difficulties in obtaining and transporting the vaccine, vaccination against smallpox—first developed by the British doctor Edward Jenner—was only introduced into Swedish Lapland in the 1820s, over a decade after it had been compulsorily implemented elsewhere in the country. Yet despite the comparatively late introduction of the vaccinations, the Swedish Sámi (who were far more receptive to the procedure than the general population, according to the local priests who oversaw the process in Gällivare) similarly experienced a dramatic decline in mortality rates over the same decade. It might simply be the case, therefore, that the virulence of the disease had of itself diminished or that a less virulent strain had supplanted it.[23]

The risk of contagion was undoubtedly greatest at the annual winter markets in February or March when the Sámi came together to trade, pay taxes, attend church and otherwise mingle. Documents confirm that almost all cases of death by smallpox in Lule Lappmark occurred about two weeks after these markets, in either late February or the first half of March.[24]

In Finland, severe epidemics of smallpox ravaged the population in 1754, 1763 and 1771. Vaccination was subsequently introduced in 1802, and by 1820, with the country now under imperial Russian hegemony, it could boast of the highest percentage of vaccinated inhabitants in the world, unlike Russia itself where vaccination was largely restricted to the imperial family and the nobility.[25] A special vaccinator who travelled around the province of Finnish Lapland was introduced to the Inari Sámi in 1826. However, the vaccinations he provided were not very effectively or efficiently carried out and in 1837 Stenbäck, the local Lutheran pastor, started carrying out this task himself among the Sámi of Utsjoki and Inari.[26]

Other Infectious Diseases

Typhoid was another epidemic disease which took its toll in times of famine, and with even more serious consequences in the prison camps of the region in the first half of the twentieth century when large numbers of people were concentrated together, as in the camps of the former Solovetsky Monastery where hundreds died of the illness in the late 1920s.

Tuberculosis was another major health issue. During the winter months the inhabitants of the Nordic and Russian far north, including the Sámi, tended to live in restricted spaces with poor ventilation, circumstances which encouraged the spread of TB among family members. Hans Ragnar Mathisen was just one noted Sámi artist who suffered from tuberculosis for many years, spending eleven of them as a patient in a sanatorium in Tromsø in Norway.[27]

Although rare, venereal diseases were also known to afflict the Sámi. In 1783, for example, Dr Naezeen, from Västerbotten, reported that he had been sent to Gällivare in that year to treat venereal infections,[28] but he found that the pathology was unevenly spread in the region. In the third quarter of the nineteenth century syphilis was also said to be relatively uncommon among the Sámi in contrast to the ethnic Russians on the Kola Peninsula.[29] The Sámi were, however, severely affected by other diseases, such as scabies, which was transmitted by close physical contact and infected laundry. This was among the most widespread of the illnesses afflicting the Sámi in the later 1920s, and often led to furunculosis. Hepatitis, on the other hand, was virtually unknown.[30]

Scarlet fever also seriously afflicted the Sámi homeland. In 1901 a large number of Sámi children suffered an epidemic of scarlet fever, and measles was also an issue. Traditionally, frogs, boiled or compressed, were a popular Sámi remedy, especially for measles.[31] Leif Rantala relates that one Sámi woman lost three sisters to the disease in just one day during the 1920s.[32] Measles raged with especial virulence after the First World War and during the late 1920s, along with recurring epidemics of scarlet fever and whooping cough and, most serious of all, influenza.[33]

As elsewhere in the world, the Spanish strain of influenza afflicted those between the ages of twenty and forty most severely. The first wave broke out in the autumn of 1918, afflicted Muonio and Enontekis especially, and lasted over the winter. The second occurred in the autumn of the following year and again lasted throughout the winter, well into 1920. The local doctor in Inari noted that 1,800 out of 2,000 people contracted the contagion, which had an incredibly high mortality rate: eighty-five victims died in January 1919 and 102 in February, a disproportionate majority of whom were women, although in the following March only one succumbed. Altogether the mortality rate was about 10 per cent of those who fell ill, that is, 9.5 per cent of the whole population, an even higher mortality than in the famine years of 1866–8. The parish of Arjeplog was also badly affected with eighty-seven people dying out of a population of 3,225, or around 3 per cent of the population. In consequence, many Sámi children were orphaned and some 120 Sámi orphans in and around Enare were left to the care of the community, which built an orphanage at Toivoniemi to accommodate them.[34]

Medicaments

The Sámi had their own ancient means of treating a plethora of illnesses before the advent of Western medicines. Acerbi observed, for example, that the Sámi made use of juices drained from fir trees, from which they made an ointment for dressing their wounds.[35] They also had a wide range of methods to deal with other illnesses, some of which Acerbi viewed with scepticism:

Inward complaints they pretend to cure by swallowing the blood of the seal and rein-deer as warm as possible. … Their method of cure for a disease of the eyes, called the *pin and web*, which is an imperfect stage of a cataract, is singular and curious, and hence is recommended by the missionary to the Danish faculty of physicians: it is effected by the introduction of the *pediculus huma-*

nus (common louse) within the eyelids, which, by its irritation upon the ball of the eye, they believe sufficient to rub off the membrane, and remove the cause of the complaint.

The sinew of the fore legs of the rein-deer is applied as a remedy for sprained ankles, or other strains of the legs, by binding it round the part aggrieved: but a particular restriction is to be observed in this method of cure, namely, that the buck's sinews only are to be applied to the legs of the female Laplander, and those of the doe to the male.[36]

The Sámi also used tinder, a soft material derived from a fungus, which was hosted on a birch tree in order to cure various painful conditions. The process involved the placing of a cone-shaped piece on the afflicted part, which was fixed in place by a metal ring or twig until it was absorbed.[37] Even today many Sámi attempt to use home-made cures for ailments such as pneumonia, while the gallbladder of a bear is still deemed the best medicament to treat burns.[38]

As for the state of dental care among the Sámi, Acerbi was saddened to find that: 'It is remarkable that the teeth of the Laplanders are often corroded by worms, and that in a manner unknown to the inhabitants of other climates.'[39]

Reindeer Epidemics

Epidemics occasionally decimated not only the Sámi but their reindeer herds as well, and this had major consequences as Johan Turi wrote in his book *Muitalus sámiid birra* (1910). When one such epidemic wiped out some two-thirds of the herds of the most westerly *siidas* of Torne Lappmark in 1760 it wrought havoc with Sámi life and the economy which supported it. A significant part of the Sámi population was thus obliged to emigrate to the Norwegian Arctic coast, abandoning seasonal reindeer herding in favour of year-round fishing. For those who remained, with the loss of considerable numbers of reindeer, their tax-paying ability declined dramatically: of seventy-seven who paid tax in the Rounala *siida* in 1760, only thirty-four were taxable in 1770. In Diggevárri *siida* and Siggevárri *siida* the decline was even more dramatic with the number of taxpayers falling from 124 to thirty-four in both, thereby creating a huge financial burden for those who remained.[40]

Reindeer herding suffered a major setback in 1911 when thousands of reindeer succumbed to a wide range of serious pathologies. Many herders lost their entire flock, putting not only independent herders but entire cooperatives in a disastrous situation from which it would take decades to recover.[41]

Diet

Visitors to the Sámi homeland began to take an interest in the diet and food preparation of the Sámi as early as the seventeenth century when European visitors to the region recorded that chopped birch bark, mixed with meat and fish, was an important component of the Sámi diet,[42] with others noting that the Sámi in the Kola Peninsula squatted down to eat.[43] This interest in the Sámi diet continued to be a prevalent feature in work about the Sámi in the following century, with Acerbi, for example, stating that 'The Lapland fashion of broiling, is by fixing a fish on a stick, and then holding it to the fire.'[44] Yet other European observers, such as the British Arctic explorer Edward Rae, were preoccupied with their dietary deficiencies. Writing in the late nineteenth century, Rae noted that, 'The Skolte Lapps or Bald Lapps are called such because of their former propensity to contract scurvy, a disease caused by a deficiency in Vitamin C.'[45] As the word for 'bald' in Norwegian is 'skallet', this may indeed be the origin of the word.

Jakob Fellman, a Finnish vicar who mainly served in Utsjoki during the years 1819–32, noted the more ingenious aspects of the Sámi diet, and in particular the importance of gathering pine bark for the local population, which became a major business since the cambium layer of the bark was quite nutritious.[46]

The Skolt Sámi, with their eastern links both in trade and culture, also enjoyed the custom of drinking tea, yet only the very wealthy among them (at most five or six families in the entire Kola Peninsula) used a samovar, which was ubiquitous among prosperous Russians.[47] The Western Sámi of the Nordic countries, on the other hand, were more exposed to coffee, which they drank strong and frequently in the typically Nordic way. Among the Skolt Sámi, however, coffee drinking was only introduced in the 1960s, and even today tea remains the favoured drink in Russian Lapland, with coffee a rarity.

Pine had always been a component of diet in Sápmi. While the Sámi there did not use it for bread-making as was done elsewhere, they did use it as a supplement to their fish soup.[48] In the summer, the Sámi ate dried- or salt-cured meat and lots of fresh and smoked fish. In Russian Lapland, however, where salt was expensive and difficult to obtain, the preservation of fish was a problem and, in former days, fish was buried in the ground to ferment and preserve it, much as was done in Iceland or Sweden. Fish salted in this way continued to be eaten in the late nineteenth and early twentieth centuries, as it is today in parts of Sweden on festive occasions, particularly around Christmas. However, with Western European eating habits, Sámi fondness for this delicacy has diminished.

In the autumn meat and fish were consumed in quantities relative to what was available. In the winter, the Sámi customarily ate fish, usually salted, as well as reindeer and partridge, but not hares, which they exploited only for their fur. In the spring they ate goose, duck and wild duck eggs, which were to be found along the shores of lakes and rivers. Green onions were collected from shorelines and various grasses were important components in Sámi meals. Potatoes were eaten by a minority, after their introduction in the late eighteenth century. The Sámi did not traditionally eat mushrooms, despite their ubiquity, tending to regard them as food for the reindeer. For this reason, there has been a traditional saying among the Sámi: 'We do not eat mushroom; the reindeer eat mushroom and we eat the reindeer.' In more recent times, however, mushrooms have become increasingly popular. Berries, and particularly cowberries, cloudberries and bilberries, were and continue to be a staple of the Sámi diet, as is the case with sugar, flour, oatmeal and barley meal. Flatcakes and similar items took the place of bread,[49] the latter of which was not a traditional staple, even if there were some thirty-two granaries in Lovozero alone by 1905.[50] The Sámi also drank *kvas*, a malted drink similar to beer but with a very low alcohol content, common in Finland and Russia even today. Rich Sámi enjoyed eating *yavv* (*yann*), a thick soup made of reindeer.[51] Reindeer brains were also highly esteemed in the past,[52] as was bear, a delicacy which required careful preparation to eliminate parasites and other threats to health.[53] Reindeer milk, traditionally stored in the pouch of the animal's stomach, was previously drunk, but reindeer milking had completely fallen out of fashion in the period before the Second World War.[54] Today, cow's milk has come to takes its place, as elsewhere in the Western world, and is now a principal staple of consumption.

Unlike in the Nordic countries, by the 1970s the diet among reindeer herders and their families on the Kola Peninsula, whether Sámi, Komi or Nenets, remained much as it had been for centuries, though this began to change thereafter.[55] Yet it was the Kola Sámi who were taller, rather than their Nordic counterparts. According to Zakhray Efimovich Chernyakov's account, in 1931 the average height of Kola Sámi men and women was 155 cm and 144 cm respectively, while those in the Scandinavian countries were slightly smaller, 152.3 cm for the former and 142 cm for the latter.[56] Yet today, at the beginning of the second decade of the twenty-first century, all of the Sámi have tended to increase in height, much as is happening in the rest of the world, which is perhaps due to more nutritional diets.

Regional hospitals started to be established in the nineteenth and twentieth centuries. A variety of hospitals were available in the north of Norway and Sweden in the late nineteenth century; in 1911 the first hospital was built in the municipality of Inari in Finland,[57] while a medical station opened its doors on the Soviet side of the border, at Lovozero, in 1922.[58] Curiously, however, despite the provision of modern medical infrastructure, certain herbs, like angelica, that the Sámi have used for many hundreds of years to treat various illnesses continue to be taken for a wide range of ailments.[59]

The Role of Alcohol in Sámi Society

One pathological condition which has long plagued Sámi society in all of the Nordic countries and Russia was and remains alcoholism. The affliction permeates all corners of society, even the church. Indeed, many priests were notorious for drinking and some even sold brandy. As the Sámi Olaus Sirma commented in Finnish Lapland some 300 years ago:

Which of us is the greater sinner? I or the priest at Čohkkiras (Jukkasjärvi)? The priest at Čohkkiras sells brandy for his own benefit, but thereby ruins others. I drink the brandy myself and thereby only ruin myself, whilst still serving others.[60]

Yet when Acerbi visited the Sámi in the late eighteenth century, he was as mistaken about the Sámi's attitude towards alcohol as he was about their musical culture:

The people are extremely sober, they never drink spirituous liquors, except on marriage days, when they indulge, not to excess, in mirth and gaiety. The ceremony of marriage is followed by a dinner in their style, and afterwards by a dance, but without music of any kind, except their cries and the snapping of their fingers. They have no relish for beer ... The parson assured us in the most pathetic accents, that there was not a single glass of brandy to be had in the whole two hundred square miles of his parish; he told us likewise, that drunkenness is regarded by the people as the most scandalous vice to which a man can be subject: and we could not help suspecting that this was one of the causes of his being so little revered and esteemed by his flock.[61]

Alcohol consumption, which was a major problem in the vicinity of Inari during the nineteenth century, obliged the convening of the Inari court in 1827 (the first time it had been summoned since 1812) to deal with a specific incident in response to popular pressure. The case concerned the murder of Juhan Morottaja, a local chief of police, whose son had subsequently assumed his father's position. Morottaja's son stood accused of abetting the Sámi who were migrating back from the Norwegian coast, from which they smuggled into Finland vast quantities of spirits. This had led to widespread discontent among the wider teetotal population who condemned the 'flow of alcohol around the church of Inari'. Eventually, Paul Christian Ekdahl, a police official from outside the community, was appointed as both police chief and teacher in Inari. However, he too proved to be addicted to drink and not only socialised with the Sámi but facilitated the distillation of spirits on the far shore of Lake Iijärvi. In consequence, Ekdahl was discharged from teaching in 1836 and removed from his position as chief of police in the following year. Only after the arrival of the new incumbent chief of police, Adiel Durchman, were 'the liquor taps finally turned off'. Henceforth, from 1842 no liquor was permitted to be sold or drunk at the Inari market, a prohibition which Durchman, from his office in the courthouse by Lake Pielpajärvi (built that same year), proved himself capable of enforcing.[62]

The clergyman Lars Levi Læstadius became the most outspoken supporter of those who took aim at the 'demonic' power of alcohol, and especially of those who sold it. 'The Devil's urine' or 'the worm's urine', as he called it, brought ruin upon those who fell under its sway, but it was not only the liquid itself which was diabolical. Læstadius believed that the Sámi religious and musical tradition of singing *yoiks* was in itself vicious: un-Christian in its spiritual essence and a further incentive to drunkenness, since, he was convinced, the *noaidi* (Sámi shamans) made use of it to encourage their communion with Sámi spirits, in particular those of the netherworld.[63]

Such a view has persisted to this day among many devout Christian teetotallers in the Sámi homeland, who still consider the *yoik* to be a song that is only sung when the singer is inebriated. Moreover, since the *yoik* was often used to insult, threaten or even curse others, these aspects also, they feel, make it untenable for the expression of Christian worship.[64] In this regard, the attitude of pious Sámi Christians was no different from that prevalent among their non-Sámi Christian brethren in the south of Norway where drinking, dancing and music were deemed to be inextricably woven together and therefore to be rejected.[65]

Beginning in the 1930s, and becoming particularly severe in the 1960s and 1970s, alcoholism also became a problem for the Sámi of the Kola Peninsula owing in part to the social, cultural and economic dislocation they suffered during the Soviet period.[66] For example, in the late 1930s, when it was common for some sixteen people, from several families, to live in a house with two rooms and a kitchen in Lovozero, drunkenness was a serious problem. Indeed, it was 2.7 times greater there than in the wider population elsewhere in the region, with half of all deaths attributed to the effects of alcohol. Suicide rates, which are often related to alcoholism, were also phenomenally high— up to 30 per cent of the population ended their lives in this way at various points during the Soviet era. In the 1960s, the 'liquidations' of the small Sámi villages on the Kola Peninsula accelerated at a ferocious pace, obliging people to leave their home villages and move to Lovozero where alcohol increasingly provided the only consolation for their lost homes and way of life. This was just part and parcel of the mass 'liquidations' which occurred in tens of thousands of Soviet villages deemed by the authorities to be 'without economic perspective'. As a result, half of all Russian Sámi who reached the age of forty had no families.[67] Tobacco use, which had remained a rarity in Sámi communities such as those in the vicinity of Murmansk until well into the twentieth century, also increased.[68] (The Ter Sámi, conversely, had long been renowned as being especially fond of this unhealthy habit.)

The Institution of Marriage

Although the family, much as it was in the rest of the Eurasian land mass, was the central social institution of the Sámi, they also had their own distinct marriage customs. In the late nineteenth century the British Arctic explorer Edward Rae maintained that 'In taking a wife, a Skolte Lapp to this day prefers to steal his bride from a stranger or enemy.' This followed the tradition among the ancient Sámi—predominantly hunters—who had long contracted marriages exogenous to the

135

siida, but endogenous within the *vuobme* (wider general community). However, with the advent of reindeer pastoralism in the sixteenth century, these customs began to change, and by the mid-seventeenth century, at least in the Lule river valley, a radical reorganisation of both *siida* and *vuobme* had occurred which, despite the retention of the old names, had led to a change of customs, with more marriages taking place among local people.[69]

One of the earliest literary depictions of Sámi marriages was provided by Olaus Magnus in the sixteenth century. With considerable literary licence he wrote:

as regards the costumes of the said Lapps, one must add this, that while celebrating the wedding with a ceremonial fire, the bride is dressed in ermine, sable or reindeer ... accompanied by a great multitude of people, positioned according to their station and the greatness of the relatives, accompanied by the sounds of different instruments both at home or in her husband's pavilion, praying for good health and fertility. And her husband, dressed in wolfskin, deerskin, or marten fur, as if he were a Venetian gentleman, the value of which attire is greater than much land, whilst adorning his person with silk and chains of gold.[70]

Yet the greatest impression was made by the fact that, although the Sámi smiled stoically at the approach of death, they wailed without reticence at marriages and births.[71] According to Acerbi:

When a Laplander has an inclination to marry a young female of his nation, he communicates his wish to his own family, who then repair in a body to the dwelling the parents of the girl, taking with them a quantity of brandy to drink upon the occasion, and a slight present for the young woman; for instance, a girdle ornamented with silver, a ring, or something of the like kind. When they come to the door of the hut in which she lives, the principal spokesman enters first, followed by the rest of the kindred, the suitor waiting without until he shall be invited to enter. As soon as they are come in, the orator fills out a bumper of brandy, which he offers to the girl's father, who, if he accepts of it, shows thereby that he approves of the match about to be moved for. ...

As soon as the parties are betrothed, the young man is allowed to visit the intended bride ... On the day of the nuptials the bride appears dressed in her gala habit; with this difference, that whereas her head is commonly close covered at other times, upon this occasion her hair is left to flow loose upon her shoulders.; and she wears a bandeau of different coloured stuffs, and sometimes a fillet. The marriage ceremony over, the nuptials are celebrated in a frugal manner and without show. Such of the guests as are invited, and are of sufficient ability to do it, make the bride a present of money, rein-deer, or something towards a stock.

In some parts of Lapland it is the custom, a few days after the marriage, for the relations and friends of the newly married couple, to meet and partake of an entertainment, which is but an homely one, as it consists of messes of soup, or broth, with a little roast mutton, and some metheglin ...

The bridegroom generally remains with the parents of his bride during the space of one year after marriage, and at the expiration of that period he takes his departure, with a view of settling himself in the world; for this purpose he receives from them what by their circumstances they are enabled to give him towards an establishment, such as a few sheep, a kettle, with some other articles ...[72]

It was also noted that the bridegroom, by residing with his parents-in-law, was in a practical position to assist them with his own labour, as well as a form of dowry-service.[73]

According to Magnus, a flint was used to throw a burst of fire over the young couple, providing a sort of blessing. During a visitation to the region, another prominent archbishop, Erik Valkendorf (?–1522), sent a missive to the pope in Rome noting that, during his sojourn at Vardø in Norway, near the Russian border, the Sámi appeared to hold marriage in contempt. In the 1670s Nicolaus Lundius (born c.1655), priest in Ume and Lule Lappmark, reinforced this view, adding that the Sámi 'give themselves over to whoring, especially when they are drunk or visit the fairs'. Yet Olaus Niurenius (1580–1645), a priest in Ume Lappmark, praised the Sámi for their faithfulness in marriage,[74] and only a few decades later Johannes Schefferus provided the European literary world with illustrations of their wedding ceremonies, with copious explanations.[75]

One aspect was clear with respect to Sámi marriages, namely, that as with Old Testament marriages, the prospective pair might have to be patient for years for the proposed marriage to be celebrated—until the material aspects of the contract were deemed satisfactory. In the 1690s Gabriel Tuderus, a priest in Kemi Lappmark, lamented that one of his flock was obliged to wait more than six years to marry his fiancée because his future parents-in-law continued to demand more and more gifts over that period.[76]

The Norwegian missionary Knud Leem noted that if a marriage did not come to fruition after an engagement, *gihlit* (gifts) and other expenses which had been given or incurred during that period had to be returned. When Nils Pålsson, a father of one prospective bride, for instance, rescinded his consent to Per Nilsson, from Ávjovárri, as the future groom, he was obliged to pay him compensation for half the brandy consumed during the period of their engagement.[77]

Marriage matches almost invariably had a strong material context and the age differences between bride and groom—as elsewhere in Europe—could be considerable, to say the least. To take just one example, in the 1830s, in Karasjok, in the north of Norway, a bride of twenty married a rich groom of ninety.[78]

Parental matches were the rule in Russian Lapland as elsewhere. According to A.Y. Efimenko, writing at the end of the nineteenth century, the Sámi at Varsuga married according to the wishes of their parents, the choice usually being made for materialistic reasons. Thus an eighteen- to twenty-year-old man might be married to a sixty-year-old woman, or a young girl to an old man. But if a girl remained unwilling to marry, she was generally not forced to do so. At the end of the late nineteenth and beginning of the twentieth century, the average age of Sámi marriage was twenty-one–twenty-two for men and seventeen–eighteen for women. The eligible men and women generally became acquainted with each other in the winter villages.[79]

As the twentieth century progressed, however—and in accordance with the trend elsewhere in Europe—the Sámi began to choose their own partners.[80] Often these were made with non-Sámi from regions in which the economic prospects were better than in the Sámi homeland itself.[81] This increasingly led to a drain of Sámi women southwards, which had accelerated by the 1970s when the subordinate role of Sámi men in their communities fostered the tendency of many Sámi women to marry men from other ethnic backgrounds, even men from abroad.[82]

In the seventeenth and eighteenth centuries, a newly married couple generally resided with the family of the bride for a year, the groom assisting his father-in-law. Only after a year was the dowry actually paid, generally speaking, enabling the couple only then to set up their own household. By the twentieth century, however, dowries were no longer provided and this custom was no longer practised.[83] In the late twentieth century, 80 per cent of Sámi who had reached the age of fifty had married.[84]

Child-bearing

The child-bearing practice of the Sámi also aroused the interest of some early visitors, with Acerbi noting that 'The midwife's office, throughout Lapland, is generally performed by the husband.'[85] He also observed that the future material well-being of the child was a matter of considerable concern that required the earliest preparations:

> It is a rule with Laplanders, on the birth of a child, to assign a female rein-deer, with all her future offspring, as a provision when the boy or girl shall be grown up, which he or she becomes entitled to, however the estate may be disposed at the decease of the parents. By this provision, the child sometimes becomes the owner of a considerable herd.[86]

According to the Swedish priest Samuel Rheen (c.1615–80), who provided Schefferus with much information, the Sámi would read the moon and the stars to predict the sex of a baby and its chances in early life before it was born:

> If they see a star hanging in the sky just above the moon, they take it for a sign that the child will be a boy. Should the star hang just below the moon, it will be a girl. If the star stands just before the moon, they see it as a sign that the child will thrive and will be born without any disabilities. If it stand just after, they take it to mean that the child will have a disability or die just after birth ...[87]

Yet according to his perceptions Sámi children were poorly trained. Indeed, he lamented:

> the Laplanders took no more notice of their children's behaviour, than if they had not existed. They saw all their motions; they suffered all the mischief they did with the most perfect indifference. They cared for nothing. The children seemed to be the sovereigns of the place. The Laplanders never said so much as one word to them of any kind. They never observed that it was not well done to throw water on the shoes of strangers, or gave them any lessons respecting good manners and propriety of conduct. These, indeed, are terms and ideas with which the Laplanders are wholly unacquainted; and their only mode of training up their children is not to train them at all.[88]

Incest was a taboo, as in all European societies, and those who offended could suffer the death penalty after strict legal prohibitions were introduced in Lapland in the first half of the seventeenth century. When the Sámi Hans Pedersen was convicted of raping his fifteen-year-old daughter Ingeri Hansdatter (born in 1684) during a wild reindeer hunting expedition to the Varanger Peninsula, he committed suicide and his corpse was publicly hanged and burnt. Yet the daughter was not exonerated; a petition to the Norwegian king himself, by the presiding judge in the case, requesting a pardon for the violated daughter was refused on the grounds that the Faculty of Theology in Christiania had considered her (along with a cousin who had also been raped) nonetheless culpable of incest and so she too was executed. Fornication, although also a crime, was far less grievous and punishment for it was a fine 'payable to the king' or corporal punishment, as well as a written condemnation of the offender in church. Conviction for living as a 'whore' could lead to confiscation of personal property and, in the case of re-offending, capital punishment could even be applied.[89]

Infanticide was also considered a serious crime of deliberate murder, but one late nineteenth-century visitor noted that it was nonetheless frequently committed.[90]

Childhood Mortality

Rates of childhood mortality were high among the Sámi until modern times. This was especially the case among the Skolt Sámi of the Kola Peninsula. Out of the 141 children born in the parish of Petsamo between 1855 and 1873, for example, a total of sixty-five died. A similar picture emerges from the Lovozero region in the period from 1875 to 1919—of the 505 babies that were born (266 of which were male and 239 female), no less than eighty-five died during their first year (fifty boys and thirty-five girls): that is, a mortality rate of 16.8 per cent. In contrast with general trends elsewhere in Europe, this mortality rate even increased during the following century, at least in the post-revolutionary period. According to statistics from 1924, for example, out of 119 births in various Sámi villages in the region, twenty-two babies died in their first year—a startling 18.5 per cent of the total. Yet even before the start of the First World War, mortality rates in Russia generally were among Europe's worst: in St Petersburg during the years 1909–13, childhood mortality during the first year after birth was on average 24.2 per cent, in 1914–15 24.8 per cent and in 1916 a whopping 27 per cent.[91] Hygiene was also poor in Russian Lapland, despite the fact that there were six Russian baths at Lovozero in 1905.[92] Russian activists, working on behalf of the Sámi, tried to ameliorate these and other health problems in the region, with the Russian Vasilii V. Alymov, for example, succeeding in acquiring funds to build a hospital at Lovozero in a difficult period.[93] But little was achieved: childhood mortality has remained high, and is part and parcel of the poor life expectancy in the region; even today adult life expectancy for men on the Kola Peninsula is one of the worst in

Europe, about forty-four for men, as compared to fifty-eight for Russia as a whole. However, life expectancy for women is significantly higher, in line with that in Russia.[94]

Early Educational Initiatives

The first Sámi school exclusively for boys opened in Piteå in 1619. However, of greater long-term significance was the Skytte Lapp School, established in Lycksele in 1632, through the efforts of the privy councillor John Skytte. Its purpose was to educate young Sámi men in preparation for joining the clergy—four of whom were eventually enabled to attend Uppsala University—and it continued to provide this service until the mid-nineteenth century. During the seventeenth century, other schools which served the needs of the church in training Sámi missionaries with basic literary skills and an understanding of the Bible were set up elsewhere in Sweden, in Jokkmokk, Åsele, Arjeplog, Jukkasjärvi, Gällivare and Utsjoki. This was followed in the mid-eighteenth century by the founding of a specifically itinerant school, with the aim of reaching all parts of Swedish Lapland, an establishment which only ceased its activities in the middle of the twentieth century. By then, other 'Lapp Schools' had been operating for up to a century, which included the first Sámi primary school in Finland (at that time a part of the Russian Empire) which opened its doors at Utsjoki in 1878. The school was later transferred to Outakoski, where the Sámi language was brought in as an occasional medium of instruction under the auspices of Josef Guttorm and Hans-Aslak Guttorm, both Sámi schoolmasters. For many years it remained the only school in Finland to use Sámi as a medium of instruction. Further plans to establish a similar school at Inari, however, were never realised.[95]

In Finnish Lapland, education in the eighteenth century traditionally remained in the hands of the catechist, a layman who lived in the church-village and was supervised by the local priest of the established Lutheran Church (Finland still belonged to Sweden at this time). His livelihood was provided by the religious authorities, but travel expenses to the nomadic Sámi encampments, which remained a common feature of Sámi life until 1792, were extracted from the Sámi themselves, local Sámi objections to the expense notwithstanding. However, during the nineteenth century, formal teaching for Sámi youth was increasingly made available in the towns and villages.[96] This was initially carried out through the private sector, but a state system of education for all, including the Sámi, was eventually established in Inari in 1894. The first such school opened there in 1902, followed by another at Kyrö (today's Ivalo) in 1909. The language of instruction was Finnish, both there and at the later Riutula School, founded in 1915 and run by the Young Women's Christian Association (YWCA) in Inari; home economics was the principal course offered and the girls were given practical training in the institute's vegetable garden. The YWCA also established an orphanage in Riutula, near Inari, in 1907. Among its first orphans were the children of a Sámi woman killed in an accident: frozen to death while trapping willow grouse.[97]

A revived interest in the Sámi language also began to take place during the following decades of the twentieth century, with proselytisation on behalf of the Sámi language spreading throughout Sápmi. For example, Tuomo Itkonen, rector of the parish church of Inari, was very active in encouraging the use of Sámi during the inter-war years. As a result of his initiative, an ABC primer in Northern Sámi was published in 1935. The Sámi Čuvgehussearvi (Society for the Promotion of Sámi Culture, founded in 1932) also took a prominent role, enabling the publication of Sámi literary books and educational material and, most significantly, of a Sámi-language magazine *Sápmelaš* from 1934 onwards. Yet despite these initiatives formal education among the Sámi still languished. True, compulsory education had been promulgated for the Sámi, as well as for all other Finnish citizens, in 1921. However, it only imposed the education of Sámi children who resided within 5 kilometres of a school, which meant that most Sámi children were not included in its remit. Only after the Second World War, in 1952, did the Sámi Committee ensure the establishment of a network of Sámi schools, using those in Sweden as an educational model for the rest of the Nordic region. The Sámi Christian Folk High School was established in Inari in 1953, and the Upper Lapland School in 1956. Other institutions for more specific educational purposes were also founded, including the Kemijärvi Teacher Training College, which had both Sámi and other students in attendance.[98]

Norway also undertook initiatives in the seventeenth century to train some of its Sámi youth for the priesthood and missionary activities. Isaac Olsen (c.1680–1730) arrived in Varanger as a schoolmaster in 1703 and in 1708 was made responsible for education in Tana, Laksefjord, Porsanger and Kvalsund. His religious tract *Vildfarelse og*

Overtro (Delusion and Superstition; 1716–17) exerted a considerable influence on Sámi religious life at the time. In 1716 he also collaborated with the Norwegian priest and missionary Thomas von Westen (1682–1727), whose numerous missionary initiatives in Trondheim earned him the popular title of 'Apostle to the Sámi'. He established the Seminarium Scholasticum as an adjunct to the Cathedral school there in 1717, later re-founded as the Seminarium Lapponicum, specifically for the purpose of training priests, missionaries and teachers for the Sámi, by the priest and missionary Knud Leem (1696–1774) in 1752. Von Westen himself went north from 1716 to 1723 establishing a church and school at Mo I Rana, in the centre of the country, for the southern Sámi. He also built a chapel in the mountains at Masi to serve them on their seasonal migrations.[99] Leem, who had been active in Vest-Finnmark in 1725–34, was also a major figure in these early days of Sámi education and published an ABC primer for the Sámi, as well as religious tracts. His noted *Finmarkens Lapper* (The Lapps of Finnmark, 1767), reached a large audience, especially when he worked as a professor at the Seminarium Lapponicum in Trondheim from 1752 to 1774, teaching the Sámi language, which he had learnt from Isaac Olsen. Leem also produced an anthropological work, *Epitomes Historiæ Missionis Lapponicæ* (1730), which is particularly valuable for the insights it gives into the Sámi drum and its religious significance. This reached a relatively wide readership, especially among the clergy, as did the writings of Johan Randulf, parish priest in Namdal in 1718–23, who also left interesting observations on the South Sámi in his manuscript on Nærøy from that period.[100]

Another priest, Nils Vibe Stockfleth (1787–1866), continued Leem's mission in the early nineteenth century, furthering the use of the Sámi language despite the increasing hegemony of Norwegian culture and language in the Sámi homeland. In consequence, the use of Sámi (and indeed Finnish) was not suppressed. Still, it was first in the 1940s that the Sámi language became a medium of instruction at schools and it took until 1999 for new laws to be promulgated by which not only the right to instruction in Sámi was offered to all children whose parents wished them to have teaching in the Sámi language wherever they lived in Norway, but also a specific Sámi curriculum as well.

One especially notable educational reformer with respect to the Sámi during the twentieth century was Per Fokstad (1890–1973), a member of the Sámi Committee during the late 1950s. With the exception of the teaching of the Norwegian language itself, he successfully encouraged the medium of Sámi as the language for teaching all subjects to Sámi children, although his advocacy of the use of Sámi for university courses proved less acceptable to the education authorities. Nonetheless, by the beginning of the twenty-first century, some 3,000 pupils were being educated through the medium of Sámi at comprehensive and senior secondary schools in Norway. South Sámi was now the primary language used by a minority of people in Nordland, North Trøndelag, South Trøndelag and Hedmark, while a further sixty individuals were taught it as a secondary language. Three South Sámi schools currently serve the Norwegian Sámi: the Hattfjeld South Sámi School, founded in 1951, the Snåsa Sámi School and the Målselv Sámi School, established in 1983 south-east of Tromsø, all further bolstered by a cultural centre which serves the needs of the Lule Sámi speakers.[101]

Of considerable importance in terms of linguistic studies specifically was the Norwegian schoolmaster and school administrator Just Knud Qvigstad (1853–1957). Devoted to Sámi studies, Qvigstad joined the Helsinki-based Finno-Ugric Society in 1910, publishing a large number of German-language studies including *Beiträge zur Vergleichung des verwandten Wortvorrates der lappischen und der finnischen Sprache* (Articles on the Comparison of Related Vocabulary in the Lappish and Finnish Languages) from 1881, as well as the Norwegian-language *Lappiske eventyr og sagn* (Lapp Adventures and Sagas), from 1927 to 1929.[102]

The Finn Paavo Ilmari Ravila (1902–74) was another significant figure with respect to the preservation of the Sámi language. A member of the Finnish Academy and professor of Finno-Ugric linguistics, his prime focus was on the Sámi language spoken in and around Petsamo.[103] The Russian Orthodox priest Konstantin Shekoldin (1845–1916), who was also an important figure with respect to the Sámi language, lived among the Skolt Sámi there and elsewhere on the Kola Peninsula. Having published an ABC primer in 1895, he went on to translate various education works into both Kildin and Akkala Sámi. He also provided considerable assistance to the renowned Russian ethnographer Nikolai Kharuzin, whose writings on the Russian Sámi appeared in 1890.[104]

The first Sámi school opened its doors at Pasvik, which formerly belonged to Finland, in February 1888, with further schools opening at Nuortijärvi in January 1889. More also opened some ten to twelve years later at Lovozero, at the Skolt Sámi village of Suonikylä (since

1944 in Finland) and at Jokanga. Yet the language of instruction was Russian and students were only in attendance for between four and six months per year.[105] In the school that opened in Lovozero in 1890 an Orthodox priest, M. Pochesersky, assumed responsibility for teaching the eight boys and five girls who subsequently enrolled.[106] Pupil numbers increased over the following years and by 1905 there were twenty-seven school pupils in attendance.[107]

Various Sámi literary endeavours for educational purposes were also undertaken in the late nineteenth century. In 1895 the Orthodox Missionary Society published a series of 'ABC Books for Lapps', which proved to be an important educational tool in the newly opened schools. The future of Sámi education looked promising, but with the outbreak of the Bolshevik Revolution these schools, so important to the Sámi community, were forced to close. However, in the 1920s, after the horrors of the Civil War, schools reopened and, unlike previously when Russian was the medium of education, the Sámi language took over this role for the first time, the lack of Sámi teachers notwithstanding. To rectify this situation, new initiatives were undertaken and in 1932 the first native Sámi teachers completed their educational training. The Russian educator Alymov shed light on the previous state of Sámi education and professional training on the Kola Peninsula in an official document from the time:

The Sámi people had not its own intelligentsia up to that time. No pedagogues, no one with medical training, no technicians had appeared from among these half settled fishermen and reindeer herders. Up to now the Sámi have been the least literate of all the peoples who inhabit the Kola Peninsula: according to a census carried out six years ago only 16.5 per cent of the population (over eight years of age) could read or write. Among the other people with whom they live, the Nenets and Komi, the literacy rate is higher; the former are twice as likely to be literate, the latter three times as likely. Moreover, education is not valued among the indigenous population, despite the fact that there have been schools for the last fifty years.[108]

Literacy among the adult Sámi population was also now encouraged. In 1921, for instance, a reading room was opened in a cabin in Lovozero.[109] It served a variety of purposes and in 1927 it was equipped with the appropriate technology to receive radio transmissions, highly advanced for its time. The school there began to thrive as never before, with sixty-four pupils in attendance, taught by three teachers, one of whom, the choirmaster and theatre director N.D.

Ushkevich, also undertook a variety of cultural initiatives both in the school and more widely in Lovozero.[110]

In the years that followed the number of Sámi schools grew considerably, first at Kildin; then at Notozero, Pulozero and Akkala, in Kola-Lapp Commune; and next at Lovozero, Ivanovka, Semostrovje and Voronje, in Lovozero Commune; and finally at Jokanga and Sosnovka, in Ponoi Commune. Further later initiatives established schools at Ozerko, Western Litsa, Grjaznaja Guba and Imandra, in the Poljarnyi and Kola-Lapska communes. Boarding schools, too, so important for a nomadic people, were also founded at Notozero, Akkala, Lovozero and Ivanovka. In consequence, by 1931–2, some 200 Sámi children were attending school in the region. Nor was higher education neglected, especially after 1925 when one Sámi man was sent to the Northern Peoples' Institute, recently founded in Leningrad, with others following suit shortly thereafter: by 1931–2, eighteen Sámi had commenced their studies there, six of whom were women. At about the same time, in 1931 a second school of higher education was established, the Murmansk Pedagogical Teknikum, which had its own Sámi faculty. In 1931–2 eleven Sámi students were in attendance there; ten boys and one girl. Instruction was provided in Sámi, using the Latin alphabet which began to be known as the 'Lapp Alphabet' since it was already in use in the Nordic countries. Twenty-nine Sámi studied there in the following year, of whom seven were girls, and there was now one Sámi teacher, Ivan Andreyevich Osipov, who had been born into a reindeer-herding family in Notozero. He had recently graduated from the Northern Peoples' Institute in Leningrad before his employment, and a female teacher, Anastasia Lukinitina Matrechina, from Jokanga, soon joined him. Three Sámi also attended the newly established Communist Party School in Murmansk. Altogether, therefore, fifteen Sámi were in higher education by this time.[111]

During the early 1930s the authorities in the Soviet Union began to favour Cyrillic over the 'foreign' Latin script, even though, in 1933, the Sámi Cyrillic alphabet was itself translated into a corresponding Latin one for use in Sámi-language instruction on the Kola Peninsula. A Sámi newspaper also appeared in 1935, *Lovozerskaya Pravda* (The Lovozero Truth) produced under the leadership of its editor-in-chief, N.D. Ryibkin. As for the school there, it had meanwhile grown to encompass some 172 pupils, many of whom became the newspaper's most avid readers.[112] However, after ethnic minorities began to be repressed with respect to their ethnic and linguistic identities in the Soviet Union during the mid- and later 1930s, the Sámi language was also subjected to repression and in the late 1930s the production of Sámi literature came to a complete standstill. Indeed, it was only in the 1980s that Sámi teaching books and dictionaries began to be published once again in the Soviet Union, leading to a re-emergence of Sámi as a literary language.[113]

In nineteenth-century Sweden, meanwhile, controversy reigned over which was the best type of education for the Sámi. One side feared that the Sámi way of life, focused as it was around reindeer herding, would be undermined by the establishment of permanent schools. The other side, conversely, was preoccupied by the low standards of Sámi education and the limited service provided to Sámi youth by the itinerant schools. The Sámi, who were by now a minority within the wider Swedish population, suffered severe discrimination in a variety of areas, but especially in education: when the Swedish parliament debated the matter of the nomadic Sámi's education in 1913, few deputies were keen to raise the educational level of teaching provided to them.[114] Indeed, Sámi children from nomadic families were often expressly forbidden to enter the *folkskolan* (folk high school), but rather were obliged to remain in the nomadic schools where educational levels were lower and the teaching hours more limited. This situation only changed in the late 1930s.[115] Nonetheless, the Nomad School Reform of 1913 provided some increased educational benefits, albeit segregated and of modest scope. Olof Bergqvist, Bishop of Luleå, summed up the 'enlightened' view of the time by stating succinctly: 'Let a Lapp be a Lapp' (Lapp skall vara lapp). This view, however, did not extend to the use of the Sámi language in schools, for the medium of instruction remained Swedish, even though the first three years of schooling were provided at itinerant schools and only the later years at fixed ones. It was partly for this reason that, when the Sámi National Assembly was held in 1918, the flaws of these 'Nomadic Schools' were considered, not only in terms of their poor educational quality but their poor record of hygiene, as a result of which new measures were introduced during the 1920s which led to significant improvements on a variety of levels.[116] Still, the schools which the Sámi attended began to improve and by 1939 these schools were put on a par with non-Sámi ones and the length and quality of education available to the Sámi had increased. The use of the Sámi language as a medium of education also improved, owing in part to the agency of the Sámi Israel Ruong (1903–86), inspector of the nomad schools from 1947 to 1967. From 1957 onwards any Sámi child whose parents desired it could attend the nomad schools, which now provided compulsory education for nine years. A Sámi folk high school had meanwhile been established at Sorsele in 1942, although it was transferred to Jokkmokk in 1945.[117] Ruong, who came from Harrok near Arjeplog, was a leading academic and professor of the Sámi language and culture at the University of Umeå, and his initiative was also instrumental in securing the establishment of a centre for Sámi studies at the University of Umeå.[118] A quarter of a century later, Vaartoe—the Centre for Sámi Research—would also be established there, today directed by Professor Peter Sköld.

In Finland, new initiatives with respect to the young were also undertaken in the inter-war years. For example, Johan Nuorgam founded the Iijärven Nuorisoseura (Iijärvi Youth Club) in 1936, but its doors were forced to close for financial reasons shortly thereafter. Boarding schools continued to play an important role as late as the 1970s, especially in Finnish Lapland. Indeed, 80 per cent of children in the Sevettijärvi area attended them throughout their school years, some returning home for the weekends, others only for longer holidays. The situation was similar in Nellim. Since Skolt Sámi children were taught only in Finnish until the 1970s, their ties with the Sámi language and culture were also thereby loosened. Recently, however, the situation has changed dramatically, with primary schools now established in Sevettijärvi (there is also a lower school there), as well as Nellim and Keväjärvi. Most important, teaching in the Skolt Sámi language is provided at both Sevettijärvi and Nellim, while adult education in Skolt Sámi is also offered in Inari.[119]

In Finnish Lapland, the comprehensive school system which prevailed elsewhere in the country was introduced for the Sámi in early 1972. Language played an important role and in 1973 the Sámi Language Curriculum Planning Committee, which focused upon linguistic issues in this regard, stipulated that the Sámi language should be taught in all areas where the Sámi resided. Instruction in the language was also now offered to the wider population as an optional subject, with special funding for Sámi literature and teaching materials. As a result, in 1980 North Sámi (the term 'Lappish language' ceased to be used from 1983) became the second language in the important matriculation examination for secondary schools. This was followed in 1986 with the creation of the Council for Sámi Educational Affairs, which was tasked with supervising these developments in Sámi education and fostering their implementation. By 1990, therefore, Sámi, in its various forms, was taught in all schools in the regions in Finland where the Sámi resided. For example, along with Northern Sámi, Inari and Skolt Sámi became languages of instruction and, with respect to the first two, the languages of the matriculation examination. Thus every year some 150 pupils are now taught through the medium of Sámi each year, while elsewhere in Finland—in Rovaniemi, Sodankylä, Oulu and even Helsinki—Sámi has become an educational option.[120] An upper comprehensive school was founded at Sevettijärvi in 1990.

A more recent major development in this context was the passing of the 1998 Act on Comprehensive Education in Finland, which brought in the obligatory use of the Sámi language as a means of instruction for Sámi children.

Similar developments were taking place elsewhere in Sápmi. In Swedish Lapland, the *Sámij Álmmukallaskåvllå* (Sámi Folk High School) was another important early Sámi educational establishment, and it spawned other offshoots including the Sámij åhpadusguovdás (The Sámi Centre for Education), which opened in the 1942–3 academic year. Although its services were restricted to Sámi pupils over the following twenty years, it also provided educational resources for others beyond the Sámi community from 1968 to 1969. Another important figure in education during this period was the Sámi schoolteacher Karin Stenberg (1884–1969) who saw her educational role as encompassing the preservation of local Forest Sámi sites, such as Lappstan, near her native Araksuolo, by Arvidsjaur.[121] Also of note in this regard was *Sáminuorra* (Sámi Youth), set up in Gällivare, in Sweden, in 1969, one of a number of bodies subsumed within the Svenska Samernas Riksförbund, itself a subsidiary of the Swedish Youth Organisation.[122]

During the post-war period a number of new schools were established in Sápmi, not only in the Nordic countries but also in the Soviet Union. For example, a new three-storied boarding school was built in Lovozero in 1959, which opened its doors in the following year.[123] Also of importance was the founding in 1973 of the Nordic Sámi Institute in Finnish Lapland, under the directorship of the Sámi Aslak Nils Sara (1934–96), a native of Kautokeino where it was situated; today it forms a part of Sámi University College, established in 1989. Until 1986, when Sara left that position, he enjoyed a wide, even international, reputation as a supporter not only of Sámi interests, but of those of indigenous peoples worldwide, a task in which he collaborated with Georg Manuel, a Canadian of Native Peoples ethnicity. Both prominently supported the rights and interests of indigenous peoples, in particular after the Conference of Arctic Peoples which was held in Copenhagen in 1973 and brought such issues into the public limelight.[124]

In 1976 Sámi-language instruction was introduced into the wider Swedish public school system in the wake of a growing awareness of Sámi ethnic identity in Sweden. In the following year the nomad schools were renamed the Sámi schools and a range of other Sámi schools began to serve local people, including a Sámi upper comprehensive school or joint middle school in Gällivare (1964–84). Another Sámi school opened in Kiruna in 1986 and six further ones in Karesuando, Lannavaara, Gälivare, Jokkmokk and Tärneby, administratively supported by the Sámi Schools Board, which corresponded to the Sámi Oahpahusráddi (in Norwegian: Sámisk Utdanningsråd or, in English, Sámi Education Council) based in Kautokeino in Norway, which was founded by the Ministry of Education in 1975, and which today is under the purview of the Sámi Parliament. The Board for School and Educational Materials in Finland also functioned similarly and continues to this day. A variety of Sámi day-care centres and kindergartens was also established. The Swedish national government now made a strong political commitment to the Sámi, providing one million Swedish krona to support these educational endeavours, which although large in local terms were small by comparison to the ten to twelve million krona provided by the Norwegian government to the Sámi Parliament and the quarter of a million euros eventually given by the Finnish government. Significant funds were also made available for the publication of educational material. This has so far led to the publication of no less than 800 volumes of textual material, much of it serving primary educational needs, and mostly written in the majority North Sámi dialect.[125]

The Education Act of 1985, later amended in 1997, further strengthened the position of Sámi schools, making them competitive alternatives to mainstream comprehensive education. Henceforth, Sámi children in Sweden acquired not only the right to be taught in Sámi in their homeland, but for at least two hours per week anywhere else in the country, that is, on a par with other children in Sweden who were granted similar rights to be taught in the mother tongue of one of their parents.[126]

Higher Education among the Nordic Sámi

In twentieth-century Norway, it was not just educational institutions and schools, but also administrative bodies like the Sámi *Oahpahusráddi* and local day-care centres that began to enjoy increasing financial and political support under the purview of the Ministry of Education. This was the result not only of political will and Sámi pressure, but of the upsurge in profits from the oil industry which flowed into the public coffers, and made Norway, in the late-twentieth century, the envy of the Sámi in the other Nordic countries, and, even more so, of those in the Russian Federation.[127]

As for the higher educational system in Finnish Lapland, even the far-flung Skolt Sámi had already been fully integrated into the state school system by the early twentieth century.[128] Even here, though, dramatic improvements were occurring, especially at the higher levels, by the third-quarter of the twentieth century. The University of Lapland was established in Rovaniemi in 1979, with an intake of 312 students, twenty-four researchers and a staff of forty-five. Yet in just over two decades, by 2002, the numbers of its students, researchers and staff had increased more than tenfold to 3745, 391 and 534, respectively.[129]

Other institutions of higher education were also being established, among them the Nordic Sámi Research Institute, which was founded in 1973 at Kautokeino for the purpose of carrying out social science research with respect to Sámi life and culture.[130] As such, it was one of the first of these bodies to be founded under auspices of the Nordic Council of Ministers. Its broader aim is to foster Sámi interests, economically, culturally, socially and ecologically, on a global, as well as a Fenno-Russo-Scandinavian, stage. Its research periodical *Diedut*, first issued in 1974, serves to further its international profile. More recently, in 1989, the *Sámi Allaskuvla* (Sámi University College) was established in Kautokeino (Guovdageaidnu) to provide the Sámi with a university education in linguistics, law and social science, in a specifically Sámi cultural context.[131] Áran, the Lule Sámi centre located in Drag, in Norway, is also of note, not least because of its role since 1999 in publishing *Bárjås*, a popular scientific periodical, various articles of which are written in Lule Sámi.[132]

In Russia, an agricultural and animal husbandry college opened its doors in Lovozero in 1991.[133] Lovozero was 'twinned' with Karasjok in Norway in 1992. This relationship especially benefited the former, not least through generous medical and educational assistance, so needed in the straitened economic circumstances of that time.[134]

Even on the Kola Peninsula, opportunities for higher Sámi education were improving and Sámi students at certain universities and high schools were even accorded precedence over others.[135] From 1960 the Sámi boarding school at Lovozero opened dependent institutions elsewhere in the area, at Kanevka, Sosnovka and Krasnoshelye. Lovozero also benefited, and in 1970 an art and crafts school was established there.[136]

The Role of Women

In traditional Sámi society there was a sharp distinction between the social and work roles of men and women. Thus if reindeer herding was the purview of Sámi men, the execution of many crafts was carried out by the women. One such craft was the making of containers, boxes and pouches for use by the men, made from the roots of pine and other trees.[137] Women were often also directly involved in farming, especially in the river valleys, which allowed the men to devote themselves to the traditional tasks of reindeer herding and fishing, both of which were far more important economically and culturally than farming.[138] The labour of women was also constantly needed to support their men in a plethora of other ancillary ways. For example, the Swedish government official Hans Hansen Lilienskiold wrote in his book *The Speculum Boreale* of 1698 that Sámi women frequently accompanied their husbands to sea on fishing trips, which were generally considered a male activity.[139] Religious ritual, however, was off-limits to them. Indeed, according to Acerbi:

No woman was allowed to have any concern in the preparation or solemnisation of these sacrifices; they were exclusively performed by a privileged class of men amongst the Laplanders called *Noaaids*.[140]

Another subsequent visitor, the late nineteenth-century Italian Paulo Mantegazza, went as far as to lament that Sámi men were condescending and exploitative towards their women.[141] On the other hand, the attitudes of these foreign visitors were full of admiration for Sámi women. The Frenchman Albert Joseph Comte d'Alviella (1790–1873), for example, lauded their familial devotion, noting:

We well remember our surprise when, at Komagfjord, we encountered the daughters of the (Sámi) merchant—two charming persons educated at Trondhjem amongst all the refinements of urban life—informed us without the least affectation that each year they passed the most trying winter months in Finnmark attending to their father amongst the reindeers and Lapps of Karasjock.[142]

Within the Sámi community itself, on the other hand, the status of women remained that of dependants and rose or fell according to that of their husbands. Indeed, from 1917 until 1971, a woman who married a man without the right to herd reindeer lost her own right to do so.[143] However, by this period some Sámi women were beginning to stand up for their rights. One of the most significant was Elsa Laula Renberg, a native of Tärnaby in Sweden, and the daughter and wife of reindeer herders, who became a Sámi politician and activist after training as a midwife in Stockholm. In Russian Lapland, by way of contrast, politics among the Sámi remained in the hands of men until the post-war years, when, in 1969, the first session of the Lovozero Women's Society took place, giving them a greater voice in the wider political arena.[144]

An indication of the new-found prominence of women in Finland, in terms of their careers, was the first temporary exhibition to be held at SIIDA in Inari. Entitled *Geaidit—Conjurers*, this art exhibition of Sámi women artists, which opened on 24 April 1998, achieved considerable acclaim throughout the Nordic region.[145]

Sámi women's organisations have blossomed in recent years, often arising out of other earlier bodies. For example, the Kárásjoga Sámiid Nissonlista (the Karasjok List of Sámi Women), which had asserted the role of women in the first Sámi Women's Forum, led to the foundation of an offshoot, the Sámi Nisson Forum (The Sámi Women's Forum), in 1993. As a member organisation of the Norwegian Forum for Women and Development, it was closely integrated with others throughout the country. Among its activities was the publication of the periodical *Gába*. Similar work was also carried out by the women's group Sáráhkka, just one of many which have arisen in today's Sápmi.[146] Sámi women are now active in almost all areas of Sámi life and society, taking an especially prominent role in the national and international Sámi parliaments. Thus if, in the past, Europeans most frequently noted such quaint customs as the fact that the Skolt Sámi rubbed cheeks as a usual ceremony of parting,[147] today they are more likely to notice the independence and prominent role Sámi women play in almost all aspects of Sámi political, cultural and economic life.

4

SÁMI DWELLINGS, ARTS AND CRAFTS

Early Sámi Settlements

Varieties of Sámi craftsmanship were expressed in the construction of their dwellings, both temporary and permanent. The earliest Sámi settlements seem to have been composed of arched turf dwellings, formed around wooden frameworks. The intriguing remains of some of these have been found at Grasbakken, near Varangerfjord, which appear to date back some three millennia (i.e. to the end of the Stone Age) and evince the skills of Sámi builders.[1] This tradition persisted in some areas for many centuries; a number of cabins at Enontekiö, for example, were still covered by turf in the twentieth century.[2]

Sites of Sámi settlements from the eleventh and twelfth centuries AD—the so-called *stállo* sites—in turn evince the ruins of houses with oval-shaped foundations, storage pits and associated pit systems for hunting wild reindeer. Many of these tend to be situated at mountainous sites, interposed among large lakes, such as that of Badjelánnda, close to lakes Virihávrre, Vastenjávrre, Sállohávrre and Guvtjávrre.[3]

Migratory Habits

The Sámi were long known as a nomadic people. Yet journeying throughout the coastal regions of northern Lapland, Acerbi found that the degree of this nomadism varied considerably:

The maritime Laplanders only change their habitations twice a year ... in spring and autumn: in doing this they leave their huts standing until their return; but this rule is not observed by the mountain Laplanders, who, like the ancient Scythians or the modern Tartars and Arabs, are continually wandering from place to place.[4]

In fact, the actual movement of the Sámi across the mountains and hills followed a strict regimen, which, according to Acerbi, involved the use of a type of sledge with boat-like characteristics:

The following is the order of the winter march: the husband proceeds in the leading sledge, and is followed by the wife in the second, which she drives herself; and if she give suck, she has her child in the cradle by her side, carefully wrapped up in furs ... The rest of the family follow the sledges on foot, having in charge to drive the rein-deer the way they go.[5]

(Alas, few Sámi today make these boat-like sledges, even if the art of the craft is still taught.)[6]

Not unlike Alpine herders, Acerbi found that 'They fix bells to the harness of the rein-deer ... in order that they may be kept together by hearing, when they cannot see one another, after the light of their short day fails them.'[7]

Sámi Dwellings and Tents

One of the earliest depictions of a Sámi tent, with an adjacent food storage hut fixed on to a tree, was provided by the academic Johannes Schefferus in the seventeenth century.[8] In a contextual sense, this *njalla* (i.e. the object in which food was stored for the winter) was kept on a pole elsewhere, even in the tundra, much as was done by many other northern indigenous peoples as far east as Siberia.[9] Storehouses were of great importance in the late eighteenth century, not least for the Sámi who needed to store their food in order to maintain their lengthy migrations. Acerbi noted:

On the road by which they pass to the sea-coast, the mountain Laplanders construct a sort of hovel for the purpose of depositing provisions and such necessaries as they may have occasion for in their journey. In their return to the mountains in autumn, the rein-deer being in that season particularly fat, they kill as much venison as they judge necessary, and lay it up in these storehouses, where it remains during the winter, being intended as a supply for themselves and household in the following spring, when they shall be on their progress to the coast.[10]

At the Nukkumajoki winter village of the Inari Sámi, archaeological excavations have revealed a wealth of information concerning the construction of Sámi dwellings from the middle of the sixteenth century. The excavations have demonstrated that the Sámi there lived in huts typical of the Forest Sámi (i.e. in huts made of sod imposed on a framework made of log tiers). These buildings were situated on the high ground of the sandy river terraces and provided the home base from which the men went off on fishing, hunting and trapping expeditions, leaving the womenfolk behind.[11]

Yet values changed and by the end of the 1500s dwellings with rectangular hearths were no longer constructed in the mountainous areas and the Sámi *goahti* or tent, often covered in sod, became commonplace because of the relative ease with which they could be transported on the seasonal migrations undertaken by the Sámi. In forested areas, and especially in Finnish Lapland, the old and flimsy winter *gámme* were now abandoned and the more long-lasting six- or eight-sided timber tents, whose base was partly framed by logs, came to be constructed, with the exterior covered by sod. This was a trend encouraged by central government which saw religious and secular advantages in the establishment of fixed Sámi winter villages. Most importantly, they also served to encourage trade and so the winter villages of Utsjoki, Inari, Sodankylä, Sompio, Kemikylä, Kola Lake, Kitka and Näätämö all took root, becoming important trading centres. Later, during the course of the eighteenth century, in the heavily forested areas where hunting abounded, as in the Russian and Finnish parts of the Sámi homeland, log cabins were introduced as winter dwellings—for example, at Sompio—where they followed a wider, more southerly Scandinavian tradition of construction.[12]

In the Russian areas of the Sámi homeland, the *chum* was a traditional tent of skin or bark. Each strip was usually about 6 metres in length and some twenty-four to forty made up the tent, with an open hearth at its centre. The *vezha*, of roughly conical form—sometimes four-cornered, sometimes pyramidal—and supported by poles, was a typical winter home for the Sámi for centuries, often three metres square within. Two doors were common, at least one of which faced south, which were usually made of iron, wood or fur. An open space at the top allowed the smoke to escape from the hearth below. In ancient times there was an additional door of smaller size facing north which is said to have had religious significance, auguring well for the fishing and hunting expeditions that began by exiting through it. Women, however, were barred from using them. Another type of hut was the *tupa*, smaller in size and generally made of logs, with a basically flat, if slightly pitched, turf roof, door and small window. Smoke was emitted through a pipe leading through the roof. The two sexes were separated both here and in the *vezha*, with the men and boys sleeping in the front, the women and girls behind. Household valuables, both religious and material, were stored at the front. These huts were reasonably spacious since the *tupa* generally enclosed a space of some 10 to 15 square metres, with benches lining the walls. The spirit protecting the house was thought to reside along the wall by the hearth, an area of the house which the women of the household were obliged to avoid.

A wooden granary elevated on one sturdy post to store comestibles and prevent their consumption by animals became usual by the turn of the nineteenth century. In more modern times, however, greater physical stability was sought after and they began to be built on four short feet, the geographical situation permitting.[13] The Sámi of the Kola Peninsula occasionally lived in earthen holes, known as *kovvas*, which they dug out for use when in fear of attack or in bad weather. These were some some seven to eight metres square and dug at considerable distance from one another. Each had an opening at the top for light to enter and from which smoke could escape. A hearth was situated in the centre formed of a plate of iron on which the fire was laid. They would also contain a few small chairs.[14] Yet these were rare since the extreme cold of the region during the winter tended to make their usage impracticable.[15] The Porsanger missionary Knud Leem recorded in his writings, aided by carefully prepared illustrations, that the inhabitants of a Sámi dwelling each had their allotted place around the hearth. The head of the household's place, with his wife, was in the centre just to the right on the far side of the hearth, with any of his small children slightly in front. Adult children, both male and female, were just to the left of the hearth. Domestic animals, including dogs, lambs and calves, resided by the front entrance. The rear entrance was forbidden to women.[16] These winter homesteads were known as dálvadis.[17]

As for the Sámi tent, Acerbi noted that 'The summer tent of the mountain Laplander resembles, in every respect, that which he uses in winter, except that the covering of it is canvas cloth, and that it has no snow wall ...'[18] Proximity to the necessary materials for making them was of considerable importance, since 'For the brushwood with which he carpets the inside of his tent, as well as firewood, he trusts to what he may be able to procure within a little distance.'[19]

During the periods when the herders were in their tents, the reindeer were fastened to nearby trees, rather than being permitted to roam freely.[20] Much later, at least in Norwegian Finnmark towards the end of the nineteenth century, it was the government itself that began to provide field cabins for travellers, whether transporting animals or for the purposes of trade.[21] Unlike these, however, traditional Sámi dwellings consisted fundamentally of a variety of types. Their best description has been provided in *The Saami: A Cultural Encyclopaedia*, published by the Finnish Literature Society in 2005:

Portable dwellings: the wikiup and the vaulted tent.

The former consisted of a framework made up of 2.5 metre forked poles and one unforked pole, brought together in the shape of a pyramid, enclosed an oval space of almost four metres square, with two extra poles at the intersections. This framework was traditionally covered by birch or spruce bark. However, towards the end of the eighteenth century, canvas and sackcloth came into vogue. At the top of the pyramid a smoke hole was formed, beneath which there was a rectangular fireplace, bordered by stones. Archaeological remains of such dwellings date back as far as to the middle of the eighth century. Such wikiups were set up both in isolation and in groups. There were also semi-circular wikiups, that is, lean-tos formed by slanting poles.

Vaulted tents tended to be conical, constructed of four poles three and half to four metres in length, curved at one end where they were fixed to create a double vaulted space. These, in turn, were marked out by horizontal ribs, against which two long forked poles, with curved ends, were lent. There was about five metres of floorspace within the oval interior. Goods were stored behind the fireplace, with living space on either side. Above this fireplace was an open smoke hole at least a metre in width. The rear entrance had enjoyed special significance with respect to hunting prey. The tent was covered by mats of wood, for winter use, and burlap or sackcloth for summer use. Their usage coincided with the development of large scale reindeer herding amongst the Mountain Sámi from the seventeenth century and they came to replace the *wikiup* for such purposes.

Permanent dwellings included not only wickiups and conical vaulted tents but log-framed conical tents and timbered tents. The permanent wickiups differed from the temporary in having a covering of turf sods over the bark. The conical vaulted tents differed from the portable in having a floor of hexagonal shape, whilst the covering also included a central layer of boarding. The log framed tent was abandoned in

favour of the timbered tent. Both of these, from the seventeenth century, tended to have floors subdivided into nine sections.

As for the turf hut, two types predominated. One was the *stallotomt*,
with walls of turf sods, resting on earthen banks. This ancient form,
used from about 750 to 1300, predominated in interior mountainous
areas. Turf huts, by contrast, tended be employed along the Arctic coast,
rectangular in shape and formed around a four poster frame, upon
which the roof beams rested. The walls leaned towards the central axis
and were formed of vertical boarding or birch bark sheets. Turf sod,
sometimes weighed down by stone, covered the exterior. The interior
space varied from six to ten metres by five metres, and was crowned by
a smoke hole. Other dwellings included the one room wooden cabin,
formed by interlocking timbers, which came into use in the 1740s,
under Finnish influence, only to disappear in the early twentieth century. They tended to be smaller in scope than the others, only about 4.5
x 4 metres in space, whilst a fireplace, surmounted by a chimney, to the
side, provided warmth and cooking facilities. As such they corresponded to northern Scandinavian and Finnish archetypes. Between the
ceiling and the roof sand or moss was provided for insulation.[22]

Fixed Housing

With the spread of large farms along the valleys of the River Torne and
other northern rivers, Sámi families increasingly lived in growing isolation from one another. The days on which they attended church and
market days therefore became increasingly important occasions of
social intercourse.[23] The French painter and traveller Reginald Outhier
provided an illustration of one such farm in his copper engraving *A
Large Farm Near Torne River* (1736), which depicts a courtyard of
rectangular log cabins with pitched roofs, the walls of which are broken here and there by several windows. As such they are austere in
appearance, inward-looking and isolated, but supporting a prosperous
and self-reliant way of life.[24]

Many others, though, lived in more humble accommodation devoid
of any openings. However, Sommier, who visited the region in the
1880s, some 150 years later, noted that already by the time of his visit
the Sámi had ceased to live in such one room chimney-less huts without windows.[25]

By the 1970s, modernity had arrived in even the remotest areas of
the Sámi homeland, and even in the reindeer-herding communities on

the Kola Peninsula hardly any traditional peat huts or conical tents remained. Instead, the wooden cottages typical of the wider Russian rural population and the Komi had been virtually universally adopted, interspersed in more urbanised areas with cheaply constructed buildings of low-quality bricks.[26] That said, some of the buildings constructed in the mining research centre first built by Fersman continued to impress visitors in the beginning of the twenty-first century, in particular the mainly single-storey wood and stucco cottages with steeply pitched roofs, grouped picturesquely in a birch wood which was now in the middle of town. Built by prisoners earlier in the twentieth century, these buildings provided the laboratory and research facilities which in time evolved into today's Kola Science Centre. As far back as 1935, *kotedzhy* (wooden cottages with pitched roofs), were built along the side of the smaller lakes to accommodate the administrative offices of the smelting company Severonikel (the company's name means Northern Nickel). This led to the creation of the new town of Monchegorsk, famed for its Stalinist classical architecture on the one hand, but notorious on the other for the dead and blackened countryside which came to surround it in the late twentieth and early twenty-first century, making it a byword for ecological mismanagement.[27]

Early Sámi Duodji

The production of *duodji* (handicrafts) has been integral to Sámi life and culture for millennia. The hearths of dwellings in settlements from around Lake Virihávrre and the hunting pits found in the vicinity of Lake Sállohávrre, both from around 3000 BC, have given up the archaeological remains of the tools and other *duodji* which were made there.[28] One of the most interesting of such ancient items is a boat-shaped hammer axe, pierced with a rimmed circular hole, which was uncovered in the vicinity of Rovaniemi and dates back to between 3000 and 2000 BC. Other items included a red slate knife, in the stylised shape of a bird from about 3000 BC, found at Sodankylä, and an intricately decorated silver ring of the same period. The latter has had a somewhat controversial history: when it was discovered by the British archaeologist Sir Arthur Evans—most famous for his work on the Minoan civilisation of ancient Greece—on a visit in 1873 to the island of Ukonsaari, in Lake Inari, he secreted it away and departed home, giving it to the Ashmolean Museum in Oxford shortly thereafter. In recent years, this circumstance led to a dispute about its legal ownership, resulting in its recent restoration to the Sámi people: it is now owned by SIIDA, the museum of Sámi culture in Inari, where it has been put on public display, just one of the many artefacts which make this museum a treasure-trove of Sámi culture.[29] The earliest Sámi jewellery so far uncovered are bronze necklaces and other metal objects which date from as far back as about 900 BC, examples of which are also included in the collection.[30]

Sámi Culture Museums

Along with SIIDA, the Swedish Mountain and Sámi Museum at Ájtte, which opened in 1989, is one of the most important museums of Sámi culture, and is actually run by the Sámi themselves. It focuses in particular on Sámi culture in northern Sweden, and especially that of the Lule Sámi. Along with exhibition, conference and performance space, it provides 'a national presentation of Sámi cultural history', albeit often with artefacts, such as drums, borrowed from various major museums.[31] One of these, the Nordiska Museet, founded in Stockholm in 1873, remains the world's most important collection of Sámi artefacts and culture. For this reason, in 1988 it was officially declared an *ansvarmuseum*, that is, a museum responsible for the preservation of historical Sámi culture and, in particular, of some thirty-four rare ancient Sámi drums. Most of these have been deposited by the National Historical Museum in Stockholm, after an exchange effected in the mid-twentieth century according to which all artefacts made after 1520 were to be transferred there. According to the curator Rolf Kjellström, it became important to form a new display of Sámi artefacts and culture in 1981, since 'the installations made in the early and mid twentieth century romanticised the Sámi and, while they were attractive to look at, were neither realistic nor educational'.[32]

Already in the early post-war years, the Sámi Ätnam Association sought to protect the interests of Sámi craftsmen against an onslaught of inauthentic 'native crafts' which actually had no connection to the Sámi and were produced abroad, often in East Asia. This control was made more stringent in 1982 when the Nordic Sámi Council adopted a specific handicraft trademark, which confirmed such craft artefacts as actually being Sámi in origin. This trademark, confirming that the object is a Sámi *duodji*, has proved increasingly important as mass tourism and the import of 'false Sámi souvenirs from the far corners of the globe' have threatened Sámi cultural identity.[33] That said, today one of the quandaries confronting the production and sale of Sámi *duodji* is economic: original Sámi artefacts are very expensive to produce, as a result of which original Sámi works are often sold mixed with 'Sámi-like' products from China, produced at a fraction of the cost.[34] Nonetheless, native handicrafts, such as those produced at Gaaltije near Östersund—a centre of South Sámi culture—began to enjoy the financial support not only of the Sámi themselves but also of the European Union, which sought to bring the peripheries and minority peoples of Europe into the limelight.[35]

Early Sámi Ceramics

One of the principal crafts in which the Sámi excelled was ceramics. As early as around 5000 BC the so-called Pitted Ceramics, which originated in central Russia, began to spread north-westward and northward into eastern Karelia and thence amongst the Sámi who were settled in the area. From about 3900 to 3500 BC, the so-called Comb Style came to dominate, not only in Sápmi but from as far afield as what is present-day Latvia in the south, the Arctic Circle in the north, the Gulf of Bothnia in the west and the shores of Lake Onega in the east. This style of ceramic ware was in turn transplanted by the so-called Late Comb Ceramic, from about 3600 to 2800 BC. Strikingly, this style correlates with those regions of what is today north-western Russia and Finland, in which early proto-Finnic was spoken. Thus the spread of the Comb Ceramic Culture in Finland and north-western Russia seems to have been introduced and carried on by those who spoke the ancestral language of both the Sámi and Finnish people. An elk carving, decorated in this style, possibly the figurehead of a boat, discovered near Rovaniemi and dating back to 6000 BC, is a prime example of an object spread by the nomadic people who produced it, although in the Scandinavian part of the Sámi homeland no pottery from this period has been found. In any case, from about 1900 BC a dramatic shift occurred in the nature and style of the region's ceramic ware because of the introduction of asbestos ceramics (as well as broad-edged arrowheads) which was soon in production not only in the Finnic-speaking areas but in much of northern Scandinavia as well.[36]

Already by the end of the late Stone Age and in the Bronze Age (from about 2000 BC to AD 400), asbestos, mined from mountainous quarries, provided a crushed raw material which, when mixed with clay, was used for pottery. Among the earliest ceramic remains to have been uncovered are those from Lovozero which date back to around 1700 BC. Others, from Vardö, have been dated to about 1300 BC.[37] Textile decoration was impressed upon the pottery which, by the final century of the first millennium, seems to have been of two specific types—*Risvikkeramik* from the north Norwegian coastal region and *Kjelmøykeramik* from the north-east of Fenno-Scandia, in particular the north of Sweden. This latter type evinces elaborate motifs apparently influenced by contemporary Russian decorative forms, possibly a result of close trading links between the Sámi, Karelians and Russians, among others.[38] Beadwork, too, was another ancient craft among the Sámi, particularly among the Skolts,[39] and in a similar fashion examples of this craft clearly evince the influence of south-eastern styles of ornamentation, especially those of the Russians, Karelians and Komi, with whom they lived in ever closer proximity.[40]

Antler Ornamentation

Another area of Sámi decorative craftsmanship was, and to some degree still is, antler ornamentation. This decorative ornamentation was based on two regional styles, with a transitional area in between. The former style derived from the south and centre of Scandinavian Lapland. Broad surfaces there were frequently decorated with banded motifs of zigzag patterns and carefully carved geometrical shapes. Magical drum figures were also prominent. Above the zone of transition in which elements from the two styles intermingle is that of the northern part of Scandinavian Lapland, as well as Finnish Lapland and Russian Lapland (i.e. the remainder of the traditional Sámi homeland). This northern style, by contrast, is composed of ornamented surfaces which alternate with surfaces devoid of decoration. The ornamented surfaces were largely composed of floral motifs similar to those found on medieval metal artefacts from what is now Russian Karelia. Sometimes, in later carvings, recognisable plants and flowers can be discerned. In other examples reindeers are incised, sometimes solitary, at other times pulling a sled or driven. In the most eastern areas, that is, in the east of Finnish Lapland and in Russian Lapland, the decoration is simple and geometrical, albeit interspersed with decorated surfaces.[41]

Objects of Birch Bark and Pine Root

Sámi crafts also encompassed the decoration of objects of birch bark, a craft similarly carried out by their Karelian neighbours. These were usually constructed using sheets of birch bark, each of which was made by a single piece. Other objects such as containers were made of root work—in the Skolt region it was of pine—and were to be found from the four corners of the Sámi homeland, inspired by decoration and design from what must originally have been mainstream European examples.[42]

Pre-Christian Era Artistic Remains

Pictorial art, usually with some spiritual context, has played a prominent role in Sámi cultural and religious life for thousands for years. Among the earliest pictorial artistic remains in the Sámi homeland are those at Nämforsen in Sweden. These are petroglyphs—rock engravings—which depict some 366 boats, 306 of which are rhomboid in shape with the remainder defined by single lines, and which date from as far back as 4000 BC. Prominent in these are figures of people, indicated by simple strokes, travelling in boats. The most notable among the later rock engravings, at the mountainous site of Badjelánnda (the term means 'upper level' in the Lule Sámi language) in Sweden, were discovered not by archaeologists but by Sámi reindeer herders themselves coming from the Sirges/Sirkas settlement (Sameby, Sweden), in the vicinity of Jokkmokk in 1990. These also include anthropomorphs (images of people without specific identities), as well as boats—including sailing vessels, rarely depicted among the North Sámi in such rock art—and animals, some dating back to around 2000 BC.[43] There is also one of the oldest images of a man, made of horn, which was discovered at Karlebotn in Nesseby Commune, which is today exhibited at the Varanger Sámi Museum in Norway.[44] Many of the earlier petroglyphs in this area were made on soapstone, probably by using a sharp stick or a piece of bone, while those made later were most likely executed with a sharp metal implement.[45] In Norway, among the Coastal Sámi, images of sailing boats have been found at Mount Álda, along Varangerfjord, and at Gylland in Melhus, Trøndelag. However, these latter examples are late medieval in date.[46]

There are also examples of petroglyphs at Flatruet in Härjedalen and at Áhusjgårsså in the Lule Valley of the north of Sweden. However, ancient examples of petroglyphs—both paintings and engravings—are more usually prevalent in the northern coastal or lowland forested areas of Sweden and Norway, close to bodies of water.[47] These include waterfalls and rapids, such as Nämforsen, situated on the Ångerman River, Norrfors on the Ume River, and Laxforsen on the Öre River, all in northern Sweden. Other such cliff or rock sites adjacent to lakes are the older ones of Värikallio in Suomussalmi in Finland; Brattberget, Hällberget, Fångsjön and Hästkottjärn in the north of Sweden; and Sasskam in the Lule Valley, and Ruksesbákti in Porsangerfjord, both of which were more recently uncovered. All of these were formerly located far nearer the coast than they are now, after a dramatic change of sea level caused the waters to recede.[48] The Nämorsen site, dating back to about 4000 BC, is among the richest in cultural artefacts; no less than 2,000 figures have been revealed in this site, including elks, boats, humans, footprints, fish and birds.[49]

The site at Flatruet in Härjedalen, probably from about 2000 BC and situated less usually on the summit of a mountain rather than near water, recently revealed some twenty figures of animals, mainly elks but also a reindeer, a bear and five human figures. Images of up to six animals, including elk, reindeer and what may be a bear, have also been uncovered at the Sasskam site, which is located by a rock face overhanging some water.[50] Yet the greatest renown as a Sámi archaeological site has been earned by Badjelánnda in Swedish Lapland. This ancient site appears to have had great sacred significance, predominantly used in the summer months,[51] unlike others in the north of Sweden and Norway which now appear to have been primarily winter residential sites. Of immense importance not only in Fenno-Scandinavia but internationally as well, it is today protected as an official UNESCO heritage site and is claimed as such by both the Sámi and Norwegian peoples alike.[52]

The archaeological horde from the site is enormous, for no less than 2,500–3,000 figures have been found there depicting elk, reindeer, boats and people. After initial uncertainty, it now seems that they were made in four different phases, from 4200 BC to 500 BC, with a particular flourishing in the late Neolithic period (c.2300–1800 BC).[53] That said, other sites deriving from a different cultural tradition on the nearby Norwegian coast of Troms, Nordland and Nord-Trøndelag seem to have been produced in three quite diverse phases, separated by considerable intervals: the ground rock art of the Mesolithic Age

(7900–6500 BC), illustrating bear, elk and reindeer; the carved rock art of the Neolithic Age (3600 and 2500 BC) with similar animals, but also people and their accoutrements (including boats), as well as sea mammals and fish; and finally the painted figure art of the Bronze and Early Iron Ages (1800 BC–AD 1), which is often found in caves. With respect to the latter, human 'stick figures' are prominent, while maritime mammals or fish hardly make an appearance.[54] Finally, the Swedish site near Ahutjkårså, in the Lule River valley, where a human figure engraved on a quartzite boulder has recently been uncovered, should also be mentioned.[55]

All the engravings and paintings described above are from the north of Scandinavia. However, far to the east, in what is now north-western Russia, there are also similar archaeological remains, although considerable uncertainty remains with regard to the dating of all of them, not least because stylistic affinities do not always coincide with the previous ascriptions. For example, in Karelia, to the north of St Petersburg, there are the so-called Karelian Petroglyphs—one near Belomorsk, on the southern White Sea Coast, at Zalavruga near the mouth of the Vyg River, and the other far to the south-east, along the eastern shore of Lake Onega. At the former, some of the 2,100 figures are images of homosexual activity, the symbolism or significance of which has not been ascertained, with other images being of animals and birds. With respect to the latter, it has been recorded that 1,176 of the rock carvings focus prominently on swans. Their dating has been traced to the Neolithic period (c. 4000–2000 BC). Yet while their relationship to shamanistic ritual seems incontrovertible, specific Sámi links as such are limited, although their origins can be traced back to the dawn of the Christian era.[56] Specifically Sámi rock art has, however, been found on the Kola Peninsula, dating back to the beginning of the Christian era and continuing up to the early modern period, possibly as late as the seventeenth century. These tend to be decorated by shallowly incised images of people, humanoid beings and animals.[57] There are also other smaller rock carving sites in this region at the Ivanovka *siida* on the Ponoi River, in the interior of the Kola Peninsula, where human and animal figures, in particular of wild reindeer and elk, cover the entire rock face.[58] Yet it must be accepted that very few examples of specifically Sámi rock art have been confirmed.[59]

Personal Possessions

It was the seventeenth-century Johannes Schefferus who provided some of the earliest illustrations of Sámi artefacts, including boots, boxes and jugs, picturesque and full of exotic local colour.[60] However, a century later, Acerbi noted the Spartan material world of the Sámi in terms of personal possessions:

Chairs, tables, and things of this kind, which other people require, are to them totally unnecessary, and therefore they have them not. … A few copper vessels, tin kettles, wooden bowls, and horn spoons, form the whole for their kitchen utensils. To this scanty and inexpensive catalogue, a few of the richest individuals add two or three pewter dishes, and some silver spoons. The mountain Laplander has no light in his hut during the night but what the fire affords him: the maritime Laplander uses a lamp.[61]

Some household pieces did however take pride of place:

The most ornamental piece of furniture the Laplander possesses is his child's cradle: this is a piece of wood properly shaped, and hollowed with his own hand. It has a recess for the infant's head. Cords are fixed to go round it, and fasten occasionally to the mother's back when she travels; and a ring with beads is suspended from the upper part, to amuse the child as it lies on its back with its hands at liberty.[62]

Perhaps surprisingly, tin remained the only metal with which the Sámi have worked in historic times.[63]

Sámi Artists

The attraction of Sápmi for non-Sámi artists was long-standing, yet the Sámi themselves had little tradition of painterly art in the continental European sense of the term. The ancient Sámi tradition of pictorial rock art aside, the artistic profession as such is quite recent among the Sámi—it only began at the turn of the twentieth century and rapidly developed its own unique stylistic aspects. This has been noted by the Norwegian academic Bodil Kaalund who has claimed that Sámi art has no closed space, and consequently planned compositions play little role in it.[64] Among its first practitioners were Johan Turi and Nils Nilsson Skum, both of whom are particularly well known for their book illustrations.

Johan Turi (1854–1936), a native of Kautokeino in Norway, an important winter centre of residence for the Sámi, came from a reindeer-herding family. However, he spent much of his childhood in

Talma Sameby, in the Torne region, and, although at first he had herded, fished and hunted himself, having suffered the loss of his reindeer he eventually abandoned herding in favour of a bohemian lifestyle. Taking up residence at Lattilahti, in 1904 he became acquainted with the Danish artist Emilie Demant (1873–1958), who was keenly interested in the Sámi, leading to a literary and artistic collaboration that resulted in the work *Muittalus Sámid birra* (*Tales of the Sámi*), published in both Danish and Sámi. This volume included an atlas, as well as Turi's own charming illustrations, executed in a naivist style, which won Turi not only considerable artistic acclaim, but also a gold medal and a state pension.[65]

His fellow Sámi artist Nils Nilsson Skum (1872–1951), who was born in Norrkaitum near Gällivare in Swedish Lapland to a family originally from northern Finnmark in Norway, was obliged to abandon reindeer herding during the Great Depression of the 1930s, and took up painting as an autodidact, establishing himself at Sjisjkavare in Swedish Lapland in order to pursue an artistic career which drew inspiration from everyday Sámi life and traditions. He soon achieved considerable popularity when two of his works were exhibited at the 1937 World Exhibition in Paris. Although most of his life was beset by financial difficulties, he eventually achieved great international acclaim in old age after the publication of his autographical book *Sáme sita* (The Sámi Village), published in 1938 in Sámi, accompanied by a Swedish-language version provided by the Sámi professor of Sámi language Israel Ruong (1903–86). This is a work which not only focuses on the cultural elements of Sámi life, but also emphasises the importance of the seasons of the year in informing Sámi reindeer herding. His foreign exhibitions in the 1930s, in particular, attracted international attention, not only for their exotic subject matter which featured reindeer herding, but for their expressiveness in capturing the geographical beauties of the Sámi homeland. Along with his book illustrations, Skum also produced paintings in oil and carved wood, many examples of which are now exhibited at the Nordiska Museum (Nordic Museum) in Stockholm.[66] His works bear his own strongly idiosyncratic style, which tends to stress the collective aspects of Sámi life as well of the reindeer herds that are so central to it. Thus, he infuses them with organic, even pantheistic quality. With artistic recognition achieved abroad, financial security followed at home through the provision of a state pension. The posthumous publication of *Valla renar*

(*Reindeer Herding*) in 1955 further secured his place in the pantheon of Sámi artists.[67]

Another Sámi artist was Nikolaus Bind (1926–72), a great nephew of Skum who was his grandmother's brother. He spent most of his life at Ratekjokk, near Norrkaitum, where his family herded reindeer. He took up drawing at an early age and later entered the Swedish artist Otto Sköld's painting school, before attending the Kungliga Konstakademien (Royal Academy of Art) in Stockholm. In 1947–9, he exhibited there at the young artists' exhibition, held at the Nationalmuseum (National Museum), and in 1948 at the Liljevalchs konsthall (Liljevalchs Art Gallery). Although he returned to Ratekjokk to herd reindeer for two years after his time in the academy, he intermittently continued to paint and even travelled to Paris on an artistic visit. Only in 1968, though, did he hold his first solo exhibition, achieving considerable acclaim, and many of his works are now exhibited in both the Nationalmuseum and Moderna Muséet (Museum of Modern Art) in Stockholm.[68]

Less naivist in style, indeed, more Western European in artistic vision, are the paintings of the Sámi John Andreas Savio (1902–38), a native of South Varanger in Norway, who, unlike the artists previously discussed, received a good formal education, albeit after surviving a troubled childhood aggravated by chronic illness. A student at the School for Arts and Crafts in Oslo during the 1920s, he was one of the first Sámi to study art in the capital. Although his life was cut short by tuberculosis at the age of thirty-six, he achieved a modicum of international success after he exhibited some of his works in Paris, to which he travelled in 1933–4. Savio primarily worked in oils, watercolour and graphics, yet he is more noted for his woodcuts and linoleum cuts, focusing on themes which illustrate various aspects of Sámi life and culture, still popular today and frequently used to illustrate the works of other Sámi writers.[69] Indeed, some consider him to have been the most important Sámi artist altogether, even if, in his own lifetime, he failed to earn a livelihood from his art. For all the Sámi themes of his art, however, he was a man of his time, highly influenced by other contemporary Nordic artists, including the Norwegian abstract expressionist Edvard Munch, most famous for *The Scream*, produced and reproduced in both paintings and woodcuts. This influence is evident in Savio's own woodcuts, for example, *Øen Lillemolla, Svolvær* (The Island of Lillemolla, Svolveara), in which a wintry fjord in northern Finnmark is depicted, full of expressionist energy. The fact that he generally preferred to draw inspiration from wider European themes rather than Sámi ones aroused some disapproval from his fellow Sámi who felt he would have done better by focusing on exclusively Sámi themes. Nonetheless, he remains an eminence of the Sámi world of pictorial art and today many of his works are exhibited at the Tromsø Museum in Norway.[70]

Yet another artist of this generation was Andreas Alariesto (1900–89), a native of Riesto near Sodankylä in Finland, who settled for many years at Sompio, in Finnish Lapland, and worked in a naivist style. Although he was hardly conscious of being Sámi in an ethnic sense, he nonetheless devoted much of his art to themes from traditional Sámi life and mythology. Many of the works of this autodidact painter are exhibited at the Alariesto Museum, which opened in Sydankylä in 1986. The American art critic Thomas Dubois has commented upon Alariesto's skill in 'depicting a Lapland that is being destroyed by modern development and social change, a way of life threatened by advancing modernity'.[71] Certainly, there is a mystical allegorical quality in his paintings which seem to hark back to a lost golden age, and such works have found considerable resonance among viewers longing for the sureties of a more traditional and rural way of life.[72]

Contemporary Artists

Two later artists from reindeer-herding families, Lars Pirak (1932–2008) and Iver Jåks (1932–2007), successfully combined both painterly and craft elements in their work and are among the most gifted and acclaimed of all Sámi artists. Pirak came from Jokkmokk in Sweden, and Jåks from Karasjok in Norway, but, after a serious reindeer-herding accident, the latter went on to study art in Oslo and Copenhagen, attracting considerable attention with his explicit erotic images, before returning home in the 1960s. Both went on not only to become honorary members of the *Sámi Dáiddačehpiid Searvi* (Association of Sámi Artists), but also to exhibit their work internationally, not only in Scandinavia but elsewhere in Europe, the United States and Australia. This association was founded in 1979 at Páttikkä, north of Karesuando, and its first annual meeting, attended by fourteen artists, was held at Jokkmokk in February 1980. In June of that year it staged its first exhibition in Tromsø in the far north of Norway, *Vår kunst i dag* (Our art today), with thirty-five artists exhibiting some seventy-five examples of their works.[73] Their works were also promoted in its art journal *Čehppodat Áiti*, which commenced publication in 1981.[74]

As for Pirak, he had meanwhile abandoned reindeer herding during a period of economic hardship, taking up the study of a wide range of the arts, including oil painting, water-colours, graphic design and sculpture. Drawing upon his earlier experience in assisting the artisan Johan Pavval, he also applied himself to a variety of crafts and went on to combine them to produce his characteristic bird-shaped dishes in which the spoon forms the 'tail' of the bird. Other works by him have a more symbolic character. These include such works as *Beive Niedia*, a figure made of wood and bone. Jåks had suffered an accident in childhood which resulted in a convalescence of five years in hospital. Despite only partially recovering from the accident, he learned to draw and eventually enrolled in several art schools in southern Norway and Copenhagen, enabling him to employ painterly, sculptural and graphic techniques. He began to teach design after the completion of his studies, before becoming an independent artist. Like Pirak, he has turned his hand to public works of art, but he has also been successful as a book illustrator. His personal artistic success enabled him to win a state art stipend in 1988.

Hans Ragnar Mathisen (born 1945), from the Tana Valley, was yet another artist of the period to spend a lengthy sojourn in hospital—in his case eleven years, as a result of tuberculosis—before going on to become a successful artist. The Finnish Merja Aletta Ranttila (born 1960) similarly endured a lengthy period of difficulty, in her case enduring what she perceived to be a childhood oppressed by religious fundamentalism, in particular by Læstadianism, an experience further aggravated by an unhappy time at boarding school. However, out of this cauldron of trauma, her so-called 'devil's pictures' were produced which glorify shamanism and old Sámi spirituality. Many of her works make use of lino-cuts, such as her so-called 'Pictures of Distress', pictorial explorations of her own anxieties and quest for release, using Finnish language titles. *Sininen kettu* (Blue Fox) is one such work which seems to have provided the painter with catharsis. *Haavoittunut enkeli* (The Wounded Angel) is also personal to her experiences while, at the same time, it looks back to the iconic work of the turn of the twentieth-century Finnish painter Hugo Simberg. Other works are purely modern or contemporary in theme, drawing upon numerous traumatic events such as the 1986 Chernobyl disaster and the First

Gulf War of the following decade.[75] Her oeuvre is characterised by a sharp dichotomy between her 'day works' and her 'night works'. Whereas the former are joyful, delicate acrylic paintings, book illustrations and postcards (unthreatening 'meat and potatoes' works which bring her an income), the latter are eccentric images from a world of dreams, in which devils play a prominent role, full of foreboding and gloom. For this reason, some people have commented on a shamanistic aspect of her works which expresses the needs of the human psyche. Others link it to a Freudian psychological framework. However, Ranttila herself rejects the connections to both, professing ignorance of Sámi shamanism and Freudian psychology.[76]

These artists began their artistic careers early, but for the Swedish Sámi Maj-Lis Skaltje artistic blossoming only commenced in middle age. A tailor of leather clothes, her artistic works have a modern twist, for she explores the conflict between conceptual and folk art.[77]

Synnøve Persen (born 1950), from Bevkop, on Porsangerfjord in Norway, studied for a year at the art school in Trondheim. Thereafter, for a further five years she attended the school of the Statens Kunstakademi (National Academy of Art) in Oslo. Of particular note, she was a member of the Masi Group of artists or Sámi Dáiddarjoavku during the 1970s, which preferred a global vision of art that played down the local and regional. It was also somewhat politicised in that the group was forged during the Alta dispute and Persen took an active part in the hunger strike in 1979 which sought to promote Sámi interests. After studying at the National Academy of Fine Art in Oslo, her activism led her to be elected the chairman of De Sámiske Kunstnares Forbund (The Sámi Union of Artists). Many of her paintings, such as the oil painting *Skábman* (Dark Time) (1978), are now exhibited in the *De Sámiske Samlinger* (The Sámi Collections) in Karasjok.[78] Other members of the Masi Group included Rose-Marie Huuva (b. 1943, previously mentioned), noted for her textile works along with Outi Pieski and Satu Natunen, and Hans Ragnar Mathisen, who, in addition to traditional imagery, looked to maps for inspiration. He studied at the Statens Kunst- og Hantverksskole (School of Arts and Crafts) for two years, and then at the Statens Kunstakademi in Oslo for a further five years, where he concentrated on graphics. One of the works he produced is *Sápmelas-girku Gilevuonas* (The Sámi Church at Kjøllefjord), which is now exhibited at Den Sámiske folkehøgskola (Sámi Folk High School) at Karasjok.[79]

Maj-Lis Skaltje studied at the Academy of Fine Arts in Helsinki, but she also trained in the industrial arts. Much of her work is rooted in traditional handicrafts. Sissel Sofie Zahl, from the vicinity of Varanger, however, is more interested in focusing on human relationships in her art. By contrast, the Swedish Sámi Eva Aira, who lives in Karasjok, takes a different approach from the latter two artists and is noted for her abstract graphic art, rejecting realism and tradition in art in favour of elements of nature which are infused with symbolic elements.

Textile art, in turn, is a principal focus in the works of Britta Marakatt-Labba (born in 1951), a native of Vittangi in Sweden, who today lives in Övre Soppero. Having studied at Södra Sunderby Folkhögskola (Södra Sunderby Folk High School) in 1971–3, she went on to study textiles at the Konstindustriskola (School of Art Industry) in Gothenburg in 1974–8. Nature plays a key role in her oeuvre, while still being highly political in tone. This political symbolism is obvious in *The Big Pike*, for example, a work in which a large fish is shown devouring a smaller one, dressed in traditional Sámi apparel. In *The Swimming Witches*, the biblical story of Jonah and the Whale forms the theme, but is given a Sámi context, with Sámi shamans swallowed up whole, rather than Jonah.[80] With such spiritual allusions, her work bears comparison with those of Ranttila, some of whose work, as we have seen, also has deep spiritual overtones. Some of her work has been exhibited, in 1979 and 1980, at the Scandinavian Exhibition, held at the *Nordisk Textiltriennal*. She is also a gifted pedagogue and has taught at both the Karasjok Barneskole (Karasjok Children's School) and the Samernas Folkhögskola (Sámi Folk High School) in Jokkmokk.[81]

With respect to plastic works of art, the sculptor Aage Gaup (born 1943) is active in a variety of media, including wood, cement, aluminium and iron. His early works are composed of large tree trunk driftwood, probably from Russia, which he himself fished out of the Arctic Ocean. One such work is *The Heavenly Arch*, almost of ceiling height, which seems to reach upwards and outward, as if towards the heavens. On the other hand, *Gravity* is downward-looking and earth-based. Gaup also works as a producer of some of the musical works of the famed contemporary Sámi folk singer Mari Boine (discussed in Chapter 6), a role that has involved creating stage scenery, including sets for the Beaivváš Sámi Theatre, and most importantly the internationally famed film *Pathfinder*.[82] The sculptor Elly Mathilde Johnsen from the vicinity of Varanger also creates installations using stone and other materials.

While some contemporary Sámi artists focused on family or personal relations and others on the workings of the natural world, a third group adopted strident political tones in their works. One such artist is the Swedish Sámi Rose-Marie Huuva, who came from a Sámi village near Kiruna and, after learning handicraft from her parents, went on to study it at both the Sámi High School and the Jämtslöjds Vävskola (Jämtslöjd School of Weaving). Her first exhibition was held in 1963 and today her works are to be found in numerous museums, including the Nationalmuseum, Stockholm, the Ethnographiska Museet, Oslo, the Jokkmokks museum and the Museum of International Folk Art, Sante Fe, in New Mexico.[83] Much of her work has a strong political agenda. Indeed, although the study of modern clothing and textile design particularly fascinates her, she has found it difficult to express herself through these media, and therefore prefers to concentrate more on her painting, especially after the growing political confrontation between the Sámi and the Norwegian government, in which the latter won the battle. In this sense, the Alta Conflict was pivotal for her, since, as she herself put it, 'I stood there, crying and painting.'[84]

In many of her paintings Huuva stridently defends the political, social and economic rights of the Sámi. This stance is evident in the series *This is Our Land*, in which a Sámi woman can be seen disappearing behind fence posts, leaving only reindeer antlers behind. Huuva has also been critical of some Sámi politicians whom she sees as too ready to abandon their Sámi dress and interests to pursue their own careers. In one of her paintings, *I Must Leave*, traditional Sámi clothing hangs feebly in the deserted landscape. Huuva also paints subjects in which Sámi themes, though not explicit, are none the less inherent in these works by virtue of their symbolism. For example, she often paints mummy-like figures which seem to be arrested in their development, and more recently she has turned to a growing abstraction of forms and symbols.[85]

Another artist, Ingunn Utsi (born 1948), a Norwegian Sea Sámi, sought her inspiration not from the outside world, but from the intimate world of her childhood on Porsangerfjord. She is particularly taken by the local sea, the landscape and its wildlife, in particular puffins, which have a special symbolic significance in her works. She eschews traditional Sámi symbols in favour of letting wood and stone 'speak for themselves', although she is not adverse to using plexiglass as well. As she has put it:

Plexiglass reminds me of something that is and is not. It is like a dream; it creates a view of the world which differs from the one we normally see. It is like the attic window of my childhood when one looks through it, the world is different from what it used to be. It is like the wind which one can see and yet not see.[86]

Murals

Along with individual paintings, monumental murals also became a popular form of art among contemporary Sámi artists. At the winter market held in Jokkmokk in February 2000, the Sámi artist Lars Pirak and the Swedish artist Bengt Lindström displayed their series of murals *Doors Westward*, produced for the inauguration of the Akkats Dam on the Lule River by Jokkmokk. The traditional Sámi drum plays a key thematic role, especially in Pirak's *Reindeer Caravan Westward*, while Lindström's designs evince a more general inspiration derived from ancient Sámi shamanism and religious belief. Two of his murals are actually displayed on the dam locks themselves, namely *Seite*, which represents a place of sacrificial offering, and *The Shaman's Eye*, with a more overt reference. A third mural, located on the south side of the building above the dam which receives the water, depicts *Sáráhkká*, one of the goddess *Máttaráhkká's* three daughters, who succoured women and children in the traditional Sámi religious pantheon. The north side, by contrast, is decorated by Lars Pirak, Bengt Lindström and Lars Johansson Nutti with a drum, specifically influenced by those of Lule Sámi design. The image includes the sun, with two other spheres. The whole project was made possible by financial support from the Luleå Arts Council in cooperation with Vattenfall (Waterfall), the corporation which runs the hydro-electric dams, and Jokkmokk municipality. Roland S. Lundström, in *Norbottens Kuriren*, referred to the drum depicted as a symbol of the dreams, hopes and visions which are paving the road toward the realisation of the role of the Jokkmokk area as a cultural centre for Sámi culture. The three would later collaborate again in 1995, while on retreat at Vaisaluokta, and in 1999 they painted further mural works for the local dam, which focus upon the Sámi drum, the whole of which was finally revealed to the public in 2000.[87] This proved controversial, as by no means all the local Sámi were happy with the project. Indeed, some members of the Sirkas Sameby, a traditional reindeer-herding community in the Lule River region, complained that the works of Pirak in particular, and especially his *Reindeer Caravan Westward*, were false in the sense that they gave a positive gloss to the relationship of Sámi reindeer herders to the Swedish government, rather than showing that many herders were deeply unhappy that their traditional herding routes had been ruined by the very dams on the Lule River that were being decorated. The fact that several of the *seite* themselves, located, as they had been, on the shores of the Lule River, were now obliterated by the waters of the dams further heightened the tension.[88]

Artists' Societies

Today there are a number of Sámi artists' societies, including the Artists' Society of Lappi, which by 1990 had some sixty-two members,[89] and the Association of Sámi Artists, already mentioned, which by 1994 had grown to include some forty-four members, coming from a wide range of artistic fields, include including painting, sculpture, graphic art, photography and crafts. Even Russia joined the Nordic countries in encouraging the establishment of a decorative and applied arts society for the Sámi, Chepes Sam (meaning 'skilful Sámi'), which has become prominent not only in north-western Russia, but in the whole of Scandinavia as well.[90]

Art Museums

Art galleries began to blossom in Sápmi during the mid- and late twentieth century. In 1945, despite the outbreak of the Lapland War in neighbouring Norway and Finland, the art gallery Same Ätnam (Sámi Land) was established in Arvidsjaur in Sweden for the promotion not only of Sámi handicrafts, but also other Sámi cultural media, including the literary, theatrical and artistic.[91] Almost fifty years later, in 1990, an important art museum was founded in Finnish Lapland, the Rovaniemi Art Museum, which attracts thousands of visitors.[92] There were even improvements in this context in the Soviet Union, albeit of a modest scope. For example, in 1956 the first stone building in Lovozero was constructed to accommodate the local House of Culture and a sauna, in which aspects of Sámi culture were represented.[93] A small district museum, administratively linked to that in Murmansk, was also set up at the school under the direction of P.P. Uryev in 1962, and in 1968 the autonomous Lovozero District Museum opened its doors. The National

Ethnic Culture Centre in Lovozero was also established, and this now has some thirty working places.[94] In the 1980s a period of thaw compared with the cold treatment previously given to the culture of indigenous minorities in the Soviet Union was now underway, and in 1984 Café Chum opened its doors as a centre of Sámi cultural activities in Lovozero, followed, in the subsequent year, by a new House of Culture. This enabled its former site to be turned over for use as a school for Sámi children and the establishment of another local museum, the Sámi Museum, which holds fascinating exhibitions of ancient Skolt Sámi art and artefacts, much of which is infused with religious and mythological images.[95]

Photography

As well as being the subjects of anthropological photography, some Sámi also began to take an interest in photographing themselves. One of the earliest of these Sámi photographers was Nils Anton Thomasson (1880–1975), who published his first image in 1905 and provided a plethora of photographic work for the Jämtland Provincial Museum in Östersund in Sweden.[96] Today there are numerous Sámi photographers and video producers in the region who reach an international audience not only through local exhibitions but also through the virtually ubiquitous medium of the Internet.

5

LITERATURE

Early Transcriptions of Sámi

Early transcriptions of Sámi have a long history. They were first referred to in the late nineteenth-century work of Nikolai Kharuzin and appear to be up to 4,000 years old. In the twentieth century, the ethnographer Yakov Alekseyevich Komshilov went on to compile what remains the largest collection of Sámi alphabetic markings, which many scholars initially viewed as being closely related to Viking runes.[1] Others, however, do not accept this runic link, and instead consider their meaning more practical, as labels relating to ownership and such like.[2] Be that as it may, in terms of transcription into the Latin or Russian alphabets, among the earliest of Sámi prose (albeit in translation) was the Swedish *ABC Book på Lappska Tungmål* (*ABC Book in the Lappish Language*), an educational primer, and the hymnbook *En liten sångebook* (*A Little Songbook*).[3] J. Qvigstad and K.B. Wiklund's *Bibliographie der Lappischen Literatur* in the *Mémoires de la Société Finno-Ougrienne XIII*, published in Helsinki in 1899, provides exact information about the oldest books in Sámi. However, the oldest Sámi text altogether, a vocabulary of ninety-five words in both Sámi and English, was composed by the English sailor Stephen Borough during a stay among the Sámi on the Kola Peninsula in 1557.

It was the publication of Sámi poetry by Johannes Schefferus (1621–79), professor at Uppsala University, which first disseminated such

179

works throughout Europe. Also of great antiquity are the Sámi poems *Moarsi fávrrot (Oarrejárvi)* and *Guldnasaš*, written by the Sámi seminarian Olaus Sirma (1650–1719), who studied for the Lutheran priesthood at Uppsala University. Sirma's poems achieved such a degree of international recognition that they merited a review in the English periodical *The Spectator* in 1711, and his fame was to spread even further over the course of the eighteenth century and beyond. The first Sámi books published were those by the Swedish parish priest Nicolao Andreæ, in Piteå, in 1619. One was an ABC, the other a Lutheran service book, but the Sámi grammar with which they were expressed was highly corrupted. A small catechism based on South Sámi was published in 1633 and another ABC based on Lule Sámi appeared in 1638. These were tentative projects, but in 1643 Johannes Jonæ Tornæus, in Piteå, was commissioned by the Swedish king himself to translate the Lutheran Service Book into Sámi. This *Manuale Lapponicum*, a tome of over 1,000 pages, was published in 1648 using the Northern Sámi dialect of the Torne Valley. Tornæus strove at consistency in its literary transcription and much assistance was provided to him in these undertakings by the Sámi Lars Pålsson. But the transcription was deeply flawed nonetheless. A shorter version of the *Manuale Lapponicum* was published in 1669 based on the Ume Sámi dialect, transcribed by the Finnish vicar, Olaus Sephani Grann, the first director of the newly established Sámi school in Lycksele. More widely read at this time, however, was Schefferus's *Lapponia*, a book which focused on the exoticism of Lapland and its peoples: first published in Latin in 1673, it subsequently appeared in English in 1674, German in 1675, French in 1678 and Dutch in 1682.[4]

One of the most important philologists working with the Sámi language in the eighteenth century was the Finn Henrik Ganander (c.1700–52), whose *Grammatica Lapponica* served to codify the Tornio dialect of Northern Sámi. Although Ganander mistakenly maintained that Sámi was a linguistic descendant of Hebrew, he was nonetheless correct in stressing its close relationship to Finnish.[5]

Anders Fjellner and Other Authors

Among the earliest to record the narratives of the Sámi—in this case those from the Tana River valley, situated on both sides of the Finnish–Norwegian border—was Stuorra-Jovna Jomppanen (1794–1874), a deer hunter from Utsjoki.[6] In his own lifetime he became an important social and cultural focus for his fellow Sámi by encouraging the establishment of permanent villages, one of the houses of which is decorated by his own collage, dating from the middle years of the nineteenth century,[7] and still enjoying a certain degree of popularity to this day in Sámi literary circles.[8] Those currently influenced by his work include Marjut Huuskonen, who has focused on the much more recent narratives of Pedar Jalvi, a teacher from Utsjoki, who had come under Jomppanen's influence. Jalvi was the first author in Finland to use the Sámi language as his literary language. These narratives were recorded in 1913–15 and now form a part of the wider Sámi Folklore Research Project, based at the University of Turku.[9] Many of these tales are set in landscapes which are sometimes historically ieal, like the 'sacred fells' Rastikaisa and Nuvvuksen Ailikas, and which at other times are mythical, the products of fertile imaginations nurtured in ancient Sámi spirituality.[10]

Also of considerable note are the writings of the famous missionary of Lapland, Lars Levi Læstadaeus. Having devised a Lule Sámi written language in the 1830s (known as Nord-lapska Bokspråket in Swedish and 'Tent Lappish' colloquially), Læstadaeus vividly captured the language spoken by the nomadic Lule Sámi, living in their tents. Indeed, he later went on to publish four Sámi literary works including *Tåluts suptsasah, Jubmela birra ja almatji birra* (1844), which drew particular inspiration from the Old Testament. Twelve other publications in written Lule Sámi eventually followed, covering a wide range of religious, legal and practical subjects, even if the language failed to take hold as a wider linguistic medium at that time and for the decades that followed.[11]

Arguably the most important figure with respect to Sámi literature in the nineteenth century, however, was Anders Fjellner (1795–1876), a Lutheran priest of the Swedish Church who studied theology at Uppsala University before moving first to Jukkasjärvi and then to Karesuando where he carried out his ministry. He later returned to his native parish of Sorsele, residing there from 1842 to 1876, where he began to publish his Sámi poetry in 1843 in the newspaper *Norrland Tidningar*, on the occasion of a royal commemoration. He also compiled a wide range of *yoiks* (Sámi chants) in the hope of putting together a Sámi epic, much as the Finn Elias Lönnrot had done with the *Kalevala* in Finland. As a result of his endeavours, one of the earliest of the epic Sámi poems is today preserved as *Biejvve bárdni*. Set in high mountains, the poem tells the tale of the son of the sun, as written by Fjellner in the mid-nineteenth century.[12] The quest for treasures in the mountains provides the theme, which is likely an allusion to the quarrying of asbestos and soapstone in ancient times at Badjelánnda, a sacred site of the Sámi.[13] Although they were first published in 1876 in the German compilation *Lappische Lieder* (*Lapp Songs*), edited by Otto Donner, the most famous of the *yoiks, Pieven Parneh* (*The Son of the Sun Goes a-Wooing in the Land of the Giants*) appeared in Swedish as early as 1849. Taken as a whole, this epic compilation traces the mythical history of the Sámi and their ancestors with a great panoramic sweep, encouraging classical Greek comparisons which led many in the Nordic countries to label him the Homer of the Sámi. It also greatly influenced such cultural (and political) figures as Isak Saba. The latter's *Sámi soga lávlla* (*Song of the Sámi People*), which was composed in 1906, achieved such popularity among the Sámi that it is today used as their national anthem. His influence among the Sámi remains strong; he continues to provide other Sámi poets with considerable inspiration, and not least Sápmi's most famous modern poet, the late Nils Aslak Valkeapää.[14] The Norwegian Sámi Matti Aikio (1872–1929), from Karasjok, also exerted a political as well as literary influence on his and the following generation. Originally a student of theology in Finland, he is most noted for his *I dyreskind* (*In Deerskin*) (1906), which considers the problems confronting a young man, one of whose parents are Sámi, in becoming a priest.[15] Finally, the Finn Jussi Lainio (1898–1957) should also be mentioned. Lainio is noted for his collection of Finnish short stories *Pohjolan elinkautisia* (*Life in the North*) (1935), which focus upon a wide range of issues relating to Finnish Lapland and its people.[16]

The Arrival and Development of Newspapers

Yet it was the newspaper, rather than more literary forms, that played the most important role in moulding Sámi political identity in the late nineteenth century. Among the earliest was the Norwegian Sámi-language newspaper *Muitalaegje*, which was first published in 1873 but was forced to close for financial reasons only two years later. However, the Free Church of Norway, which attracted many Sámi followers, provided financial support for what proved to be a far more lasting venture: the Sámi-language magazine *Nuorttanaste* (*The Eastern Star*), based in Nesseby, which is still published today. Another publication, *Sagai Muittalægje* (*The News Teller*), which was directed by Sámi editor Anders Larsen, was active from 1904–11. Although short-lived, it served as a powerful voice for the Coastal Sámi, and was of key importance in drumming up support for the Sámi politician Isak Saba.[17]

In more recent years a variety of newspapers specifically addressing Sámi issues have been published in Norway, most of which are published either in Norwegian or in the North Sámi language. These include the Norwegian-language newspaper *Ságat*, which has been of note in drawing attention to Sámi issues because of its wide Sámi readership, totalling some 2,500 readers in Finnmark alone, as well as the weekly periodical *Sámi Aigi*, which first emerged in response to the Alta dispute (see Chapter 1) and was published in North Sámi from 1979 onwards. Although the latter newspaper was forced to close owing to financial difficulties in 1989, it was subsequently re-established as *Min Áigi* in 1993. In August 2007 it merged with its rival, the twice-weekly newspaper *Áššu*—published in Karasjok and the largest of all such papers published in Sámi, with a subscribed readership of at least 2,000 Sámi—in order to form a new daily publication in the North Sámi language, *Ávvir*. The only newspaper to appear in Skolt Sámi, *Sää 'moddaz*, which was published from 1978 as a result of a joint venture between the Association of Border Regions (1979–83) and the European Cultural Foundation (1985–6), with Satu Moshnikoff serving as its principal editor, has since gone out of business.

Today the biggest newspaper in Finnish Lapland is *Lapin Kansa*, but it is hardly Sámi in terms of its focus and in fact uses Finnish as its linguistic medium. Inari Sámi is, however, the medium for *Anarâš*, which began publication in 1986 and is the only periodical to use the Inari language; it publishes three times a year, relying on financial support from the Anarâškielâ servi (the Inari Sámi Language Association).[18] As such, it relies heavily on the linguistic work originally carried out by the Finnish philologist Frans Äimä (1875–1936), who specialised in the Inari Sámi language. First studying under the linguist Eemil Nestor Setälä, he later became professor of phonetics at Helsinki University during the second and third decades of the twentieth century.[19]

In Sweden, a mouthpiece for the Sámi was provided for a few years through the party newspaper of the Lapparnas Centralförbund, which had been established in Sweden in 1904. However, of somewhat longer-term importance was another Swedish Sámi newspaper, *Waren Sardne*, founded by the Swedish Sámi Daniel Mortenson and published between 1910 and 1913 and again from 1922 to 1925. It focused less on politics and more on matters of agricultural and economic interest to Sámi life, such as reindeer herding and fishing. Despite publishing articles predominantly in the medium of Swedish rather than Sámi, *Samefolket*, which was founded and edited by Torkel Tomasson, is also worthy of note. Based in Östersund, the newspaper is still published today, although its internet version, which was first launched in 1997, has achieved a far wider audience than its hard-copy version. These and other publications have all enjoyed the support of the Sámi Press Association, SÁLAS, which was founded in 1993 in order to further the interests of South Sámi and Lule Sámi journalists.[20]

With respect to Finland, the Lapin Sivistysseura (Lapland Education Society) began to publish *Sabmelaš* in 1934 (spelt *Sápmelaš* after 1979),which became an important mouthpiece for the Sámi. From 1951, this journal was jointly edited by Paavo Ravila and Erkki Itkonen, both professors active with the Sámi Liitto. Although it closed its doors for financial reasons in 1979, they were reopened in 1993 and publishing resumed under the name *Odđa Sápmelaš*. After 1995, it was printed in Kautokeino, which was also the seat of *Aššu*. Both publications were made financially viable by the Sámi Cultural Board which provides funds for both publication and distribution, not only in Lapland but throughout all of Finland.[21] More recently, however, *Odđa Sápmelaš* has again ceased publication.

Skolt Sámi Literature

Printed literature in the Skolt Sámi language arrived quite late by comparison with that written or published in the other Sámi tongues. A prayer book was published in 1893, but only in 1988 was a part of the New Testament, St John's Gospel, translated and published in the language. As a result, Skolt Sámi now plays a more important role in church services in Finnish Lapland than ever before, a role encouraged by the diocesan administration of the Finnish Orthodox Church in Lapland, situated in Rovaniemi.[22] It was not always thus, for the Skolt Sámi language was only given its own orthography in the early 1970s, based on the Skolt Sámi dialect spoken in Suonikylä. One of the first instances of its use was the publication of a Skolt grammar in 1973, which also included two short Sámi stories, accompanied by a glossary, and was soon followed by the appearance of the Skolt-language newspaper *Sää'moḍḍâz* between 1978 and 1986. Economic difficulties forced it to shut, despite the fact that it was run on a voluntary basis. Several Skolt dictionaries were also published, among them a Finnish–Skolt dictionary that was published in 1989 and includes some 6,000 entries.[23] In literary terms, however, it is Aune Kuuva's *Uáináh-uv* (*Oainnátgo*) (1992), a collection of poetry focusing on the Sámi, which achieved the greatest significance at this time, containing as it does musical and artistic elements as well. Kuuva is also a musical performer and creator of artistic installations.

Anders Larsen

Various Sámi journalists and educators were especially important in fostering Sámi political, cultural and social identity through the written word. One was Anders Larsen (1870–1949), a Norwegian Coastal Sámi, who played an important role in this regard as editor of the Sámi-language newspaper *Sagai Muittalaegje* during the years in which it was published from 1904 to 1911. He also became one of the first Sámi writers in a modern sense. His book, *Beaivve-Alggo* (*The Dawn*) (1912), not only examines issues of Sámi identity but helped foster his role as a political activist. This had political implications when he provided considerable assistance for Isak Saba in his election campaign for the Norwegian Storting (parliament) in 1906.[24]

Pedar Jalvi

This pioneering role of Larsen was also supported by another colleague, Pedar Jalvi (1888–1916). Jalvi, a native of Outakoski in the Tana Valley near Utsjoki, first worked as an educator, eventually taking a teaching post at Savitaipale, in South Karelia, after graduating from a teachers' college at Jyväskylä, in southern Finland, in 1915. However, he later went on to become the first Finnish Sámi poet, in the modern sense, publishing his anthology of wide-ranging poems *Muohtačalmmit* (*Snow Flakes*) to considerable acclaim in 1915.[25]

Hans-Aslak Guttorm

Another Sámi educator who devoted himself to literature was Hans-Aslak Guttorm (1907–92), a native of Outakoski who also attended

the same teacher training college in Jyväskylä as Jalvi, albeit a generation later, during the 1930s. His works are in essence a reaction to the
rise of the militant nationalism encouraged by the Lapua Movement
which was coming to dominate Finnish political and social life during
this period. His Sámi-language anthology *Koccam spalli* (*A Rising
Gust of Wind*), which was published in 1941, confirms his pioneering
role in developing the linguistic expressionist potential of his native
Sámi tongue.[26]

Anta Pirak

Some Sámi found their voice through the literary skills of others. This
was the case with the Lule Sámi reindeer herder and nomadic catechist
Anta Pirak (1893–1951), whose memoirs were recorded by the
Swedish priest Harald Grundström in the vicinity of Jokkmokk, where
Pirak lived. This was published in book form as *Jåhtte same viessom*
(*A Reindeer Herdsman and his Life*), with a Swedish-language edition
appearing in 1933 and a Lule Sámi edition in 1937.[27]

Vladimir Charnolusky

Others, especially in the Soviet Union, took inspiration from their nineteenth-century predecessors in doing fieldwork in the deepest countryside in an attempt to compile what they could find of the vestiges of historical epics. In 1927, for example, the Soviet author and ethnographer
Vladimir Charnolusky (Swedish spelling: Tjarnoluskij, 1894–1969) carried out research in the Kola Peninsula, hearing tales which he was convinced were the remains of an old Sámi *epos*. Many of these, with the
holy white reindeer and his golden horns at their heart, were subsequently published and are of literary as well as spiritual and ethnographic interest, with sources in various parts of the Kola Peninsula.[28]

Development of a Reading Public

The growth and development of a Sámi literary culture of course
depended on the creation and growth of a reading public. In the
Nordic countries, where the established churches had for centuries
encouraged the inculcation of reading skills in the interest of propagat-
ing the Lutheran catechism, this was no difficulty. However, the availability of books other than the Bible was limited in Lapland. To ame-

liorate this situation, Ida Hannula founded Rovaniemi's first bookshop in 1895, which carried on for a further quarter of a century until others supplanted it.[29] In Russian Lapland, however, the reading public was small. Only in the Soviet period did literacy finally spread throughout the region.

The publication of a Sámi dictionary fostered the use of Sámi by codifying a Sámi language, orthography and spelling which could be used by most, if not all, of the Sámi. Konrad Nielsen (1875–1953), a Norwegian professor of Finno-Ugric languages at the University of Oslo, furthered the cause of Sámi usage by his production of a three-volume *Lapp Dictionary* between 1932 and 1938, based on three North Sámi dialects. The fourth volume, with glossary, was published posthumously.[30] This dictionary was of considerable importance, for today the North Sámi language is the *lingua franca* of Sámi-speaking Sámi peoples.

Johan Turi

Sámi literary prose began to blossom from the beginning of the twentieth century onwards. Among the first of such Sámi authors was Johan Turi, whose most famous Sámi-language novel *Muittalus Sámid birra* (1910) (*Tale of the Sámi*) is still read today, not only by the Sámi themselves but many other people in various translations.[31] As a reindeer herder as well as an artist (he is discussed in this capacity in the previous chapter), he moved with his family from his native Kautokeino to Jukkasjärvi in 1870. This proved to be fortunate, for it was there that he later met the Danish artist Emilie Demant-Hatt, who encouraged him to write that book, which was accompanied by her own illustrations. The book proved highly popular, not only in the Nordic countries but also abroad, and was translated into a variety of European languages. He also wrote in Swedish, including *Från fjället* (*From the Fell*) (1913), and was ultimately awarded the Swedish Royal Gold Medal and a State Writer's Pension for his services.[32]

Samuli Paulaharju

Although not a Sámi, Samuli Paulaharju (1875–1944) was a significant author in early twentieth-century Finnish Lapland who focused on Sámi life and culture.[33] A teacher and writer who spent a considerable amount of time in the environs of Pechenga (then known as Petsamo in Finland), he brought the Sámi of the Russian Kola Peninsula to the attention of a wider academic audience through his Finnish-language publication *Kolttain mailla* (*In the Land of the Skolts*), which first appeared in 1914. Other books included *Lapin muisteluksia* (*Recollections of Lapland*) (1922) and *Taka-Lappia* (*Hinter Lappland*) (1927). The copious research material which he collected is still available to researchers in the Folklore Archive of the Finnish Literature Society in Helsinki.[34]

Evacuee Literature

Among the most traumatic upheavals to afflict the Sámi in recent centuries was their evacuation from their ancient homelands when the Petsamo region, a part of Finland during the inter-war years, was ceded back to the Soviet Union at the end of the Arctic War in 1945 (see Chapter 1). The Skolt Sámis Vassi Semenoja and Helena Semenoff wrote a Sámi song which looks back to their now long-lost *siida*.

Memories of Suonikylä

That's where we left the boats
made by our fathers and uncles,
that's where we left the seines and nets
made by our mothers,
that's where we left our reindeer does, those with beautiful antler,
and our draft reindeer, each one so gentle.

They cut our roots,
Through a swirl of snow,
they brought us across Lake Inari.
There were no cars, no gravel roads.
We were taken to the seaside,
Replanted like saplings
In the midst of the coldest winter,
leaving our roots in our childhood lands.[35]

Poetry in Russian Lapland

Russian literary interest in the Kola Peninsula and its peoples might be said to go back to 1873, when the author Vladimir Ivanovich Nemirovich-Danchenko (1858–1943) visited Lovozero as a boy.[36] Yet in reality it was in the work of the poetess Oktyabrina Vladimirovna

Voronova (1934–90), who wrote a collection of Sámi poems entitled *Yalla* which was published in Ter Sámi in 1989, that this literary form began to assume a new role among the Sámi in the later twentieth century. Her father, a Russian, was the son of the Orthodox priest of Lovozero, Mikhail Rasputin, who was shot during the repressions of the 1930s. A pupil at the Sámi boarding school in Lovozero, she was befriended by and came under the influence of the Murmansk poet Vladimir Alexandrovich Smirnov in 1975. Her poems were first published in the newspaper *Lovozero Pravda* in 1979; her language is the Iokang dialect of Skolt Sámi. Her first collection *Sneshnitza* soon appeared in 1986, followed by *Volaya Ptiza* in 1987. She was accepted into the Union of Soviet Writers in 1989.

Askold Alekseyevich Bazhanov (1934–), who was born into a family of reindeer hunters in Notozero, is another important Sámi poet. His poems in the collection *The Sun Over the Tundra* (*Solntse nad Tundroi*, in Russian) focus on the life of the Sámi in the tundra and were first published in 1982.

Three Sámi women poets also came to the fore during the 1980s. The scientist and educator Alexandra Andreyevna Antonova (born 1932) is a native of the Teribersk district who later studied at the Institute of Northern Peoples and is best known for such collections of poems as *My Sorrows* (*Moi bol*, in Russian). Elvira Galkin, from Lovozero, on the other hand, studied at the State Pedagogical Institute at Murmansk. Her grandfather played a particularly important role in her life. She wrote, 'My childhood—it was my grandpa. I was always to be found around him, listening as he spoke of Sámi wisdom, how he learned of life.' The wildness of nature also plays a major part in her imagery, in particular that of the forest and its wildlife, full of its own mysterious soul. There is, moreover, an aural quality in much of her work which gives them a musical dimension—the musical dimension of nature itself, she suggests. Today she is widely known far beyond Russian Lapland itself. Sophia Yakimovich, born 1940, in turn, is a noted Sámi singer and storyteller (born 1940), particularly renowned for her Sámi fairy tales, such as *Beautiful Nastya* (*Krasivaya Nastya*, in Russian), published at the turn of the millennium. She also writes poems, and among these perhaps the most admired is *The Banquet of the Bears* (*Prazdnik medvedya*, in Russian), which evinces musical qualities. Such aural focus clearly ran in the family, for her sister Anna Effimova Navokhatko went on to achieve considerable fame as a singer in Russia.[37]

Not surprisingly, then, since the Second World War, poetry, infused with aural qualities, has been the most prominent of Sámi literary forms, appealing to a broad international audience.[38] Paulus Utsi (1918–75) is an example of one such successful figure from Finnish Lapland. His first Sámi-language poems were published in the 1950s in the magazine *Samefolket* (*The Sámi People*). This was followed in 1974 by *Giela giela*, a compilation of poems written together with his wife, Inger Huuva-Utsi (1914–84), but only published posthumously in 1980. Focusing upon such topical issues as ecology and the vulnerability of the natural world, these collections have proven very popular, dovetailing, as they do, with the values of a global 'green' movement.[39]

Late Twentieth-Century Authors

In the late twentieth century, Sámi authors tended to become increasingly politicised in their writings. This was especially true of Kirsti Paltto (born 1947), from Finnish Lapland, whose polemical Finnish-language political pamphlets acquired a certain notoriety among the wider population of the country. Yet of greater literary significance is her series of novels, *Beaivváža bajásdánsun* (1985), *Guhtoset dearvan min bohccot* (*Dig Well, Our Reindeer*) (1986) and *Guržo luottat* (*Tracks of an Evil Spirit*) (1991). Their predominant interest lies in the panoramic imagery they provide of Sámi life and culture from the 1930s to the outbreak of the Winter War in 1940, and the hardships caused by the obligatory evacuation of many Sámi which followed in its wake. Whereas the first volume focuses upon the confrontational relationship of the Sámi and Finns, the second considers the relationships—sometimes also confrontational—among the Sámi themselves.[40]

In her novel *Goalsenjárga* (1994), Rauna Paadar-Leivo (born 1942) focuses upon the life of Sámi children in the boarding schools of the preceding period and the dislocation this caused with respect to family and community life. Similar themes are also found in the writings of Inghilda Tapio (born 1946), whose *Ii fan dan diht* was published in 1995. Other poets, however, have turned away from such localised and highly individualised experiences, seeking subject matter in the broader human emotional responses of humanity as a whole, which, because of their more general subject matter, resonate more widely with non-Sámi audiences on a global level. The poetry of Inger-Mari Aikio, a native of Utsjoki, and particularly the poems *Gollebiekkat almmi dieva*

(1989), *Jiehki vuolde ruonas gidda* (1993), *Silkeguobbara lákca* (1995) and *Máilmmis dása* (2001), all revolve around the subject of love; interestingly, her husband is from Mauritius, in the Indian Ocean. A similar theme informs the poetry of Stina Inga, including the work entitled *Ferten eallima joksat* (1995). Others, like Risten Sokki, have turned to historical subjects in a context of violence. As a descendant of one of the leaders of the Kautokeino Revolt, Aslak Jacobsen Hætta, who was executed for murder in 1852, she has used her 1996 bilingual publication *Bonán, bonán soga suonaid* (*Jeg tvinner tvinner slektas sener, in Norwegian*) to examine the historical context in which her ancestor played such a notorious role. Rose-Marie Huuva, on the other hand, uses such poetry as *Galbna rádna* (1999) to examine a private, existential theme: a woman confronting cancer and the expectation of death.

While these poets wrote in the Northern Sámi language, others, such as Stig Gaelok Urheim from Swedish Lapland, used the medium of the other Sámi languages. A number of his works have appeared in Lule Sámi including *O, Oarjjevuodna* (1983), *Vuonak* (*From the Fjord*) (1986) and *Soaje* (*Venger*) (1993). In 1994, he and fellow poet Kari Waag Gaelok turned to a wider national audience by publishing a work in Swedish, entitled *Det doppelte hjerte* (*The Double Heart*), which focuses on a wider variety of Sámi themes. Other poets, though, continued to prefer to use the media of their respective Sámi languages, including Gaebpien Gåsta (Gustav Kappfjell), who published the first poem ever to appear in print in the South Sámi language, *Gaaltije* (1987). Kati-Claudia Fofonoff, in turn, used the Skolt Sámi language for her poetry and stories, which include *Pââsjogg Laulli* (*Songs of Paatsjo*) (1988) and *Jännam muttum nuu'bbioo'ri* (1998). Both deal with Sámi life in and around Suonikylä. She published two children's books, *Ä'nn-Mää'rj mue'rjjreiss* (1999) and *Öhtt ee'kk O'lssee da Såålla mie'ldd* (2000), before her anthology of poetry, *Jännam muttum nuu'bbioo'ri*, appeared in 1998. Works in other, more obscure Sámi languages also saw the literary light of day, including those in Russian Sámi.[41] Finally, the Finnish Sámi Veli-Pekka Lehtola (born 1957), professor of Sámi culture at the University of Oulu, should also be mentioned.[42] His English-language book, *The Sami People: Traditions in Transitions*, which was published in Alaska in 2005, has reached a wide international public and further served to bring the Sámi people and their culture to a wider reading audience.

Feminist issues have also featured in Sámi literature. The Finnish Sámi feminist writer Vuokko Hirvonen concentrates on feminist issues in her works, while the Finnish author Annikki Kariniemi acquired a considerable following on related issues through her novel *Laulu Lapin papista* (The Song of the Sámi Priest) (1972), even though she herself was not Sámi. Both were from the first generation of feminist authors in Finnish Lapland, taking inspiration from the American literature of the time.

Čeppári čáráhus, a Bildungsroman by Kerttu Vuolab (born 1951) is also of particular note, as are the works of Jovnna-Ánde Vest (born 1948), a Sámi man now living in Paris whose wife is a French professor. He takes a humorous approach to his early novels. She explores similar themes by using irony to set the tone in works which are filled with sardonically critical imagery; the unrealisable yearnings of an idealistic father in the grips of a hard reality create a humorous but insightful picture of the changes that took place in the Tana Valley from the 1950s onwards. Later works, by contrast, move away from local Sámi issues. Indeed, Vest's later novels no longer even mention Sámi ethnicity. Rather they consider the development of people, in general, in unfamiliar settings, and their only connection to 'Sáminess' is the fact that they are written in Sámi. Only in the late 1990s did Vest's latest novels once again begin to focus on Sámi life in the Tana Valley and the recent political, cultural and economic events impacting upon it. Among these is the novel *Čáhcegáddái nohká boazobálggis* (The Reindeer Path Ends by the Water) (1998). Highly autobiographical in subject matter, it is played out against a backdrop of the 1950s, 1960s and 1970s, taking as its subject his father and the way in which he adapted to the radical changes of Sámi society.[43]

The Sámi Theatrical Blossoming of the 1970s

Although theatre was not a Sámi tradition, in the 1970s performance companies were established and rapidly began to blossom. One of the first such Sámi theatre companies—albeit amateur rather than professional—was Dálvadis, which was founded in 1971 and was initially based in Jokkmokk. The Sámi actress Harriet Nordlund (born 1954) and the textile designer Maj-Doris Rimpi (born 1943) played key roles in its foundation and development. Its repertoire includes *Rajden går* (The Reindeer Caravan Travels), first performed in 1979, which gives a key role to the *yoik* in its productions. *Min duoddarat* (*Our Extents*), *Čuovga Čiehka* (*Eight Minutes from the Sun*), in 1987, and *Dálveniehku*

(*Winter Dreams*) are other plays examining Sámi themes, some of them mythological. This was the case with the latter play, which was first performed on the ice of Lake Talvadis, rather than in a theatre, in 1982–3. The Sámi actress and singer Åsa Simma, born 1963, took the leading role as the *urmutter* (i.e. ancient mother). The American Norman Charles became an important influence in their plays in the following years, as did the cultural influences of the North American indigenous peoples, including both the Arctic Inuit and various Third Nation tribes. The theatre company has not, however, abandoned its earlier Sámi themes and roots, as is clear from the decision to rename Dálvadis as the Sámiska Teatern (Sámi Theatre) when it moved to Kiruna in 1992, a rebranding that has made it more easily recognisable internationally as one of the leading Sámi theatrical companies. Nordlund, Rimpi and Christer Helander went on to stage another noted theatrical production at the Lama-Hado Theatre in the following year.[44] Yet it was the Beaivváš Company, based in Kautokeino and founded in 1981, that achieved the status of a national theatre in 1995. Its successful productions were provided by a plethora of playwrights including John Gustavsen (born 1943), Marry A. Somby (born 1953), Rauni Magga Lukkari (born 1943), Inger Margarethe Olsen (born 1956) and Nils Utsi (born 1943). Beaivváš has also become a touring company, and has never hesitated to explore disturbing themes. For example, *Dearvvuođat* (*Regards*) (1999), with a monologue script by Magga Lukkari, examines the troubling issue of suicide among young people. By that time she had also published a number of other works to international acclaim, including *Jienjat vulget* (*The Ice Leaves*) (1980), *Losses beaivigirji* (1986), *Mu gonagasa gollebiktasat* (1991) and *Árbeeadni* (1997). Other works, however, are more conventional in form, such as *Gumpegoddi* (*The Wolf Slayer*), written by John Gustavsen, which presents the life of the author Johan Turi.[45]

With respect to South Sámi theatrical productions, it was the Åarjelhsaemien (Sydsamisk Teater, in Swedish; South Sámi Theatre in English) which achieved the greatest importance during the 1980s. The theatre staged at least ten productions, with the most acclaimed arguably being that which focused on the life of the South Sámi political activist Elsa Laula-Renberg (1877–1931). The production was subsequently broadcast on Norwegian television in 1997, before being performed shortly thereafter at the eightieth anniversary celebration of the foundation of the Sámi Movement in Trondheim. Another significant amateur theatre company, the Rávgoš Group, was formed in 1981. The members of Rávgoš (the Sámi word for the bird, the English Ruff) came together in Outakoski, in Finnish Lapland, where works by Eino Guttorm, dealing with religious fanaticism, were performed.[46] *Árbeeatnan luohti* (*The Yoik of the Inherited Land*), also by Guttorm, was published that same year and became something of a cult book owing to its focus on a new, politicised sense of Sámi cultural and social identity.[47]

Although the first Sámi language plays were written and performed at schools, professional ones soon became popular, and many even drew large audiences when they were performed in one of the Nordic languages rather than the Sámi language. For example, Kirsti Paltto, one of the first Sámi playwrights, wrote *Liemmajoen Anni* in Finnish in 1976, after which it was performed at the Rovaniemi City Theatre for a mainly Finnish-speaking audience. Paltto's works have been aired in Finnish by the Finnish Broadcasting Company on radio throughout the country, and they have also been performed by the Rávgoš Group in the Sámi language, in conjunction with the stage director Eino Guttorm.

Although Margarethe Olsen's rock musical *Earálágan* took up a controversial theme among the Sámi, namely the issue of homosexuality, her other works are much more conventional in scope, including *Giegat guhkket* (1993) which considers the difficulties endured by the Skolt Sámi whose homeland was devastated during the Second World War.

The actor turned playwright Nils Utsi preferred themes with a historical and political focus. His play *Eatni váibmu vardá* focuses upon Sámi politics in Norway in and around the time of Norwegian independence in the early twentieth century. His *Skoavdnji*, in turn, is feminist in focus and deals with the subject of 'battered wives' and domestic violence among the Sámi. Yet other authors have turned to children's literature, in particular, Marry Ailonieida Somby (born 1953). Her play *Ráhkisvuoða soahki* (1996) eschews the modernist literary forms adopted by other modern Sámi playwrights in favour of a more traditional format. However, Sámi literature in no way exists in any form of splendid isolation and so, with the advent of numerous translations of world literature, whether mainstream or by indigenous peoples, influences are exerted from around the world.[48]

The Norwegian poet Stig Riemmbe Gælok (born 1961) published his noted collection of poems *O, Oarjjevuodna* in Lule Sámi in 1983, one of the first collections ever to appear in that language. However, the first Lule Sámi novel was *Tjaktjalasta* (*Autumn Leaves*), written by Lars Matto Tuolja (1925–96). His sister Sigga Tuolja-Sandström is also a noted Lule Sámi writer. Her writings include *Ja jage gållin* (*And the Years Went By*), *Måno niejdda* (*The Moon's Daughter*) and *Soldottern Biejveniejdda* (*The Sun's Daughter*). Other works written in Lule Sámi include the novella *Stuorlådde* (*The Large Bird*), by Gøran Andersen, and the children's book *Gålmmå giehto*.[49] Although more famous as an artist, Iver Jåks (born in 1932), from Karasjok, has also written short stories, plays and poems.[50]

Nils-Aslak Valkeapää

The most famous of all modern Sámi literary figures is undoubtedly Nils-Aslak Valkepää (known as Aillohaš in Sámi, 1943–2001), a native of Pättikkä, in Finnish Lapland, and a man whose cultural talents and range were vast. Although primarily a poet and a writer of polemical pamphlets (published in Finnish), he also worked as an actor, painter, photographer, composer and musician.[51] Indeed, he chanted *yoiks* at the opening ceremony of the Winter Olympic Games held at Lillehammar in Norway, which he opened in 1994, when a caravan of reindeer came on stage, by which time he had become one of Sápmi's most famous cultural figures internationally.

Among his early literary works was *Lávllo vizar biellocizáš* (1967), followed by *Giđa ijat čuovgadat* (1974) and *Ádjaga silbasuonat* (1981), which together were republished as an epic trilogy in *Ruoktu váimmus* (*My Home is my Heart*) in 1985, richly accompanied by illustrations. The trilogy presents a sweeping panorama of Sámi history, its society and culture, while at the same time focusing on one individual's progress through life, from the bosom of a secure and stable family, through the rough and tumble of boarding school, to a wider awareness of the issues confronting indigenous peoples worldwide. The work also has a musical dimension, *yoiks* seeming to exert a strong influence on linguistic tonality. His later work, *Beaivi Áhčážan* (*The Sun, My Father*) (1988), draws on the post-war traumas of one Sámi man, and seeks to create an epic for all the Sámi people, against a spiritual backdrop of the old Sámi religion, its mythology and relevance for today. It has proven so popular amongst the Sámi themselves, as well as an international reading public, that he was awarded the Nordic Literature Award in 1991.[52] By this time he had settled at Skibotten, on the Lyngenfjord in Norway, where he built a house and became naturalised as a Norwegian citizen. Other works followed, including *Nu guhkkin dat mii lahka* (1994), *Jus gazzebiehtár bohkosivččii* (1996) and *Girddán seivvodan* (1999). Yet the most successful, because it encompassed not only the Sámi but other indigenous peoples, was *Eanni, Eannážan*, published in Kautokeino (Guovdageaidnu), in 2001. A deeply lyrical as well as richly illustrated work, it found a warm global reception rarely vouchsafed to works by Sámi poets and authors.[53] But his appeal was not only to a wide general audience, but to Sámi literary figures as well. Indeed, his poems served as models for other Sámi poets, including Synnöve Persen (born 1950), as is clearly apparent in the poems *Alit lottit girdilit* (1981), *Biekkakeahtes bálggis* (1992), and *Ábid eadni* (1994), in terms not only of their poetry, but of the illustrations which accompany them and the graphic format in which they were produced. Thomas Marainen's *Duddjojun Sánit* (1997) is yet another example of a Sámi poem deeply influenced by Valkepää.[54] His legacy might have become even greater had he not suffered a motor car accident in 1996, from the complications of which he finally died on his way back from a visit to Japan.

Many Sámi writers enjoyed the assistance of the international Sámi association for representing the needs and aspirations of Sámi authors, the Sámi Girječálliid Searvi (Association of Sámi Writers), which was founded in 1979.[55] In the following year the Sámi Teáhtersearvi was also established to promote the interests of Sámi actors and theatre people.[56]

With respect to Lule Sámi literary culture, it was Árran, the Sámi Centre in Drag, which was of considerable importance. Since commencing publication of the popular scientific periodical *Bårjås* in 1999, it is unique in using the medium of Lule Sámi as its main language. It also publishes some articles in Norwegian and Swedish, a role also played by Ájtte, the Swedish mountain and mining museum, and the Silver Museum in Arjeplog. These latter institutions also published some articles in Lule Sámi.[57]

Kola Sámi of the Twenty-First Century

The Russian part of the Sámi homeland has also enjoyed an increasingly rich literary life in which natural imagery plays a major role. Oktyabrina Voronova (1934–90), the Ter Sámi poet from the village of Chalmni Varre (the name signifies 'eyes of the forest') by the Ponoi River on the Kola Peninsula, studied at the Pedagogical Institute, in Leningrad, after the Second World War. She chose to focus her lyrical poetry on snow which relates to everyday elements of Sámi life:

> it lies in magnificent snowdrifts
> Light, wet, like a young reindeer ...[58]

The bard Ivan Matrekhin, on the other hand, considers the more inclement side of the Kola climate:

> In the mournful tundra, the wind torments the clouds,
> The grey mists creep from the swamp,
> And sink, the sounds of foul weather,
> The Polar Circle, The Polar Circle.
> The tundra—full of the mournful autumn.
> The tundra—the silence looses its way in it.
> The tundra—its extent knows no limits.
> The tundra—herds of deer, flocks of birds.[59]

Feminist Literature

Among Sámi Feminist writers—and these have mainly been from the Nordic parts of Sápmi, for the Russian areas remain deeply traditional with respect to the role of women—Rauni Magga Lukkari has taken a prominent place, especially with regard to her later works. On the one hand, they look back on the cultural heritage of the Sámi through the ages, while on the other, they consider how the role of women has changed from generation to generation. The problems she uncovers remain topical, not least because, as she perceives it, Sámi women have been hindered by their own community and traditions from fully developing their identities and thereby achieving their rightful place, with respect not only to Sámi society, but to the wider world as well. Less confrontational in this context is the poetry of Inger-Mari Aikio, mentioned above. Rather than promoting women's rights through an aggressive feminist ideology, she prefers a more nuanced approach, in which the role of young women in twentieth-century Sámi society is expressed through a powerful, but delicate linguistic imagery.[60] Her first collection of poetry was *Gollebiekkat almmi dievva* (1989), with her most recent being *Máilmmis dása* (2001). Some of these poets found their forum in Sámi women's magazines, including *Gába* (*Sámi Nissonfierpmádat*), which began publication in Sámi, Norwegian and English in 1996.[61]

Sámi Literature Today

Sámi literature today is a hybrid formed out of two complementary traditions, the oral one of the Sámi, the written one of modern European and American literature.[62] Two Sámi publishing houses have played a key role in the preservation and promotion of Sámi language and literature, namely, Davvi Girji and DAT. The former is located in Karasjok, in Norway, and is the largest of the Sámi publishers, focusing on literature and textbooks. The latter is based at Kautokeino, and along with book publishing it also sells recordings. Books for children are given a strong focus, not least because of the central role which childhood education plays in the preservation of Sámi culture—children's books have come to compose the overwhelming majority of the Sámi literature published over the last few years.[63] Today teaching in Lule Sámi is provided periodically at the Bodø Teacher Training College, in Norway, while university level teaching in the language is available at the University of Tromsø, also in Norway, as well as at Uppsala University in Sweden. In consequence of this development, well over 150 books were published in Lule Sámi between 1976 and 2002, the majority for teaching the language.[64] In Finland, the universities of Rovaniemi, Oulu and Helsinki remain highly important centres of Sámi education and learning. In Russian Lapland, in turn, it is the Sámi Museum of Literature and the Written Language, which opened its doors in Revda on the Kola Peninsula in 1994, that has primary importance in preserving Sámi literary culture, rather than academic institutions in Moscow or St Petersburg.[65]

6

MUSIC, SPORT AND FILMS

Perceptions of Sámi Music

The Swedish prelate Olaus Magnus was among the first of scholars writing about the Sámi and their homeland to comment upon their bardic tradition and the epic way in which they recounted heroic stories from their past.[1] Yet some foreign visitors, such as the Italian diplomat Giuseppe Acerbi, falsely perceived the inhabitants of Lapland, both Sámi and Finnish, as devoid of musical culture. 'It is very remarkable,' he wrote, 'that the Finlanders settled here, like the pastoral Laplanders, know nothing either of poetry and music, or musical instrument'.[2]

Indeed, he made so bold as to claim that:

Music and dancing are entirely unknown amongst the Laplanders, on these or any other festivities; nor are they even acquainted with the use of any one musical instrument; and seem to be totally incapable of learning to sing in tune.[3]

His perceptions, however, did not correspond to the reality, for the *Fádnu*, a whistle flute made of the shoot of an angelica plant without its stalk (after which it was named), was traditionally used in Sámi music, the player using between three and five finger holes to modify the sound.[4] Furthermore, it was singing—the traditional Sámi *yoik*—and the Sámi drum which really informed the heart of Sámi life, spiritual as much as musical. And this Sámi musical tradition continued long after the decline of Shamanistic ritual and shamanistic ritual singers. The church sexton Pehr Gullsten (1770–1825), for example, was

199

one of the most noted runic singers of his time and place. Born in Niska, in the vicinity of Oulu, he moved to Rovaniemi where he spent the rest of his life and from where he deeply influenced the father of the famed Finnish man of letters Zachris Topelius, who took a keen interest in this musical genre—albeit not in any Sámi context (although he did write a children's book, *Sampo the Lapp*)—which was especially fashionable in this national romantic period.[5] Indeed, as the nineteenth century progressed, this runic tradition spilt over into popular vernacular music, leading to such popular folk songs as 'Beaivvi bártnit' ('Sons of the Sun') and 'Ráfi ruohtas'('The Root of Peace'), the appeal of which extends to an audience far beyond the boundaries of Sápmi.[6]

Armas Launis

This growing interest in Sámi musical culture increased after the turn of the twentieth century among musicians and ethnographers, as well as a wider learned public. One of the most important and influential figures to focus upon Sámi music in the twentieth century was the composer and ethno-musicologist Armas Launis (1884–1959), a Finn from Hämeenlinna in the south of Finland. When Launis travelled to Lapland in 1904 and 1905 he became acquainted with ancient Sámi melodies which in turn served to influence his own musical output in 1908. During the former visit he went to Ivalo, Inari and Utsjoki in Finnish Lapland, even venturing to Polmak, on the Norwegian side of the border, after which he published his noted reminiscence *Lapin matka 1904* (Journey to Lapland 1904).[7] Other works focusing specifically on Sámi music include: *Sibelius-Akatemian Yoikukokelma* 1904 (The Sibelius Society's Collection of Yoiks)[8] and *Suomalaisen kirjallisuuden seuran yoikukokoelma 1904* (The Finnish Literature Society Collection of Yoiks),[9] both of which attracted considerable international interest.

During the second trip, his travels took him around Finnmark, in Norway, from Alta and Bossekop, in the west, up to the North Cape and eastwards to Vadsø. These journeys were highly productive and have left us with a fascinating legacy not only of photographs of a vanished age and society,[10] but, most importantly, of a series of publications including the general reminiscence *Lapin matka 1905* (Journey to Lapland 1905),[11] as well as musical collections such as the *Sibelius-Akatemian Joikukokoelma 1905* (The Sibelius Academy Yoik Collection of 1905),[12] *Kertomus Sävelkeruumatkasta Norjan ja Suomen Lapissa Kesällä vuonna 1905* (Story of a Composing Journey in Norwegian and Finnish Lapland in the Spring of 1905)[13] and *Suomalaisen kirjallisuuden seuran Yoikukokoelma 1905* (The Finnish Literature Academy's Collection of Yoiks of 1905).[14] Launis's most influential work was perhaps the German-language *Lappische Juoigos-Melodien* (Lappish Yoik Melodies) (1908) which meticulously recorded and otherwise documented who the *yoik* singers were, the music they sang and where they were recorded at that time.[15] At some point around 1921 Launis even composed an opera, *Aslak Hetta*, about one of the leaders of the nineteenth-century Kautokeino Revolt, which was performed for the first time a few years ago.

Although Launis returned to the Sámi homeland again in 1922, it was his studies in Germany, under Wilhelm Klatte and then Waldemar von Baussenern, that thereafter shaped his musical oeuvre. He eventually found his attention drawn to the music of the Mediterranean, as a result of which he settled in Nice in 1930 and from there made forays into the Arab world, especially North Africa and the Middle East, where its traditional music began to preoccupy him and during his remaining years he devoted himself to its study. Nonetheless, the legacy from his earlier period remains of incomparable importance for Sámi music.[16]

The Sámi Drum

Sámi music has its own special elements and characteristics, with the Sámi drum, more than any other instrument, playing a particularly important role in the Sámi musical tradition. The Sámi drum was much more than a mere musical instrument: it was a primary tool of spirituality and the expression of man's place in the universe. It is not surprising, therefore, that its many usages were constrained by strict traditions. The drum was traditionally played with a Y-shaped hammer or stick made of the root of a reindeer antler, a tool known as the *Veažir*. The *Veažir* was used to beat both ends of the drum, but it could also be used as a means of divination, when it would be placed on the drum-head, formed by a tanned reindeer hide decorated with a variety of symbolic figures, the most common of which was the sun. The manner in which this stick 'jumped' along the drum's surface provided the spiritual and practical information sought, but few were vouchsafed the right to play it. For its use was usually reserved for the *noaidi* (shamans), who were always male, even if sometimes, as among the more southern Sámi, the male heads of households might also play them. Their design and composition varied regionally. In southern Sámi areas, the wet tanned reindeer hides which formed the coverings of the drums were usually placed around frames, but in the northern areas bowl drums predominated as the interior framework, with a wider range of symbolic features, some abstract, but many naturalistic, with depictions of reindeer, bears and serpents. The Åsele type—or segmental ones—are most frequently to be found in the Finnmark, Torneå and Kemi regions of the north. Only about seventy historical drums are still known to exist, and none have been found from the Kola Peninsula, in Russian Lapland. Yet although few historical drums have survived, the modern reincarnation remains vibrant; indeed, newly constructed Sámi drums and their usage today have taken on new life. No longer the butt of Christian hostility, they are often used at Sámi religious services in the most Christian of contexts, or as key instruments within Sámi popular music. Indeed, musical instrument makers as far abroad as Eastern Asia have turned their industrial potential to reproduce them, leading to a further revitalisation of the art with which many Sámi are unhappy: their expropriation for decorative, commercial and touristic purposes by people with no direct links to Sámi culture other than its profitability has left them dismayed.[17]

Yoiks

Whether traditional or modern in form and context, Sámi *yoiks* have proven to be less controversial. As such they remain one of the most characteristic features of the Sámi musical tradition, which is so unlike the musical song traditions of the other peoples of Scandinavia, Norwegian or north-western Russia; indeed, there is considerable diversity in the way *yoiks* are sung even among the Sámi, reflecting the different Sámi languages and cultures themselves. For example, around Kautokeino, in Norway, the singers traditionally 'shouted' the *yoik* with 'sharp' voices after entering their shamanistic trances, which was supposed to enable them to travel between the spiritual and material worlds that made up the Sámi cosmos.[18] Carl Axel Gottlund (1796–1875), a Finnish ethnographer at the University of Helsinki, became the first academic to publish an analysis of these *yoiks*, accompanied by an illustration which was drawn by the notable nineteenth-century Finnish artist of Scottish descent Magnus von Wright.[19] More recently, in the first half of the twentieth century, the most noted traditional *yoik* singer was Jouni Aikio (1875–1956),[20] while the multi-talented artist and writer Iver Jåks (1932–2007), who devoted himself to the singing of *yoiks*, was also able to earn a small but keen following.[21] But their singing represented only one genre of this spiritual chant—as the famous Sámi poet, photographer and musician Nils-Aslak Valkeapää has written, 'The yoiks of the forest areas are quite unlike those of the Teno Valley—not to mention the wild yoiks sung in the freedom of the fell country.'[22]

Nonetheless, throughout the middle decades of the twentieth century, the *yoik* remained suspect to many on religious grounds as its implicit paganism conflicted with the Protestant Christian system of belief which permeated Sápmi at that time. Indeed, municipal centres in the Sámi homeland continued to ban its singing and many local educational boards prohibited its musical expression in schools, in administrative decisions confirmed in 1953, 1961, 1976 and 1977.[23]

However, in the final quarter of the twentieth century the singing of *yoiks* underwent a major revitalisation, aided by the highly personal interpretation with which they increasingly came to be sung. This enabled them to reach and appeal to an ever-growing international audience, not only in Europe but in the wider world. Thus, towards the end of the twentieth century, Wimme Saari, born 1959, from Enontekiö achieved considerable international acclaim for his *yoiks*, especially after his tour of the United States in 1996 where he found a particularly receptive audience in Texas.[24] To a large degree, this new global fascination with *yoiks* is the result of their adaptation to contemporary musical rhythms and modalities, a development which had begun in the early 1970s. This trend was aided by the fact that many Sámi children had been educated at boarding schools in the previous decade, when international popular music had been all the rage. Furthermore, since its establishment in 1982, the Sámi Musihkariid Searvi (Association of Sámi Musicians) has fostered a wide variety of Sámi music, including not only the traditional *yoik* but a variety of contemporary musical forms as well.[25]

Nils-Aslak Valkeapää

When the poet, musician, artist and photographer Nils-Aslak Valkeapää (Big Áilu, 1943–2001) turned his attention to the Sámi *yoiks,* he also used modern musical elements to give them a new edge, making them more palatable to the younger generation while ensuring that they remained highly diversified, even going so far as to include jazz elements. In consequence, his album *Vuoi, Biret-Máret, vuoi!* (1974), proved a great success. Others followed, including Sápmi *lottážan 1–2* (*Sápmi, My Dear Little Bird*) from 1982, in which Valkeapää mixed elements of *yoiks* with other sounds. Such music could acquire overt, even radical, political overtones; one song included what was purported to be the sound of police helicopters, intended to allude to the confrontation with the national government that the Sámi had faced at Alta when such surveillance vehicles were used. If, during the 1980s, he helped to make Sámi 'ethno' music popular, he also served to fuse more classical forms of Western music with those of the Sámi and of wider 'Mother Nature' as well. For example, he incorporated elements of symphonic orchestral music into his radiophonic production *Goase dušše,* together with the sounds of the forest and tundra, winning him an award in the category of radio music at the Prix Italia in 1993.[26]

The 1980s Generation of Sámi Musicians

The new phenomenon of pop bands also played an increasingly important role. One of the most prominent was Deadnugátte nuorat (the Teno Valley Youths), who were greatly influenced by Valkeapää and his approach to Sámi culture. Not only did they blend traditional *yoiks* with modern Western European musical elements, they also introduced European guitars, drums and flutes to give their music new dimensions, previously rejected by traditional musical purists. Experimentation became the norm in this the period as groups such as Máze nieiddat (The Girls from Masi) began to play tangos (since the early twentieth century an extremely popular genre in Finland), polkas and the Máze waltz, music which many had thought to belong to an older generation. Others, such as Ámmun Johnskareng and Halvdan Nedrejord, took a more radical line, turning to the latest trends in pop and rock. The latter certainly influenced Áilu Gaup, whose band Ivnniiguin (Colours) became a byword for such music. By the 1980s, electric guitars had become common in much Sámi music, reinforced by the ubiquitous synthesisers to create a new and energised genre of Sámi songs, and they were one of the basic elements of 'Sámi sound' in the early 1980s. Ann-Jorid Henriksen became very popular, sometimes as part of a duet with Johnskareng, and she went on to become a regular performer at the Beaivváš Theatre.[27]

New Yoiks

Today *yoiks* remain a highly important symbol of Sámi identity, but with an important difference with respect to the past—they have lost their anti-Christian associations. As Kjell Olsen has put it, they are now even suitable for Christian assemblies.[28] Indeed, over the last few decades, *yoiks*—as folk music rather than religious expression—have again taken centre stage in Sámi cultural life, and are increasingly appreciated by tourists and musical audiences. Establishment bodies like the ministries of tourism and education, as well as the national Lutheran churches, often encourage their singing, while music companies foster them because compact discs and music files of them sell.[29]

These new *yoiks* evince a tendency to absorb elements from modern popular music and tend to favour melody and a more a 'Western European' use of the voice. Among the modern Sámi singers of *yoik* living in the western parts of the Nordic countries are Mattis Haetta (born 1959), Áilu Gaup (Little Áilu) (born 1960), Inga Juuso (born 1945) and Lars-Anders Baer (1952), who have reduced the number of words sung compared with the more traditional *yoik*. Others, from the more eastern regions of Finland's Teno River, Norway's Varangerfjord and Russia's Kola Peninsula have also been successful, including the highly traditional Skolt Sámi, singers of *leu'dd*, an eastern Sámi form of *yoik* (said to have Siberian, rather than Sámi roots), and the Kola Sámi song and dance group Oijar.[30]

The Influence of Traditional Sámi Music in the Late Twentieth Century

If Valkepää was one of the first to marry elements of the Sámi *yoik* with modern music in his musical compilation *Joikuja* (1968), an approach which continued with his release of *Vuoi, Biret-Máret* (*Oh, Biret-Maret, Oh!*), later music groups such as the highly politicised Dœdnugádde Nuorat, Máze Nieddat and Ivnniiguin, in which Ailu Gaup was prominent, also turned to his music for their own inspiration, but by no means exclusively. Indeed, Gaup collaborated with the Finn Seppo Paroni Paakkunainen (born 1943) on his recording *Sámi eadnam duoddariid* (*The Fells of Sápmi*) in 1978. Further joint ventures followed, including *Davás ja geassi* (*To the North and Summer*) and *Sápmi, vuoi Sápmi* (*Sápmi, Oh, Sápmi*) in 1982. Following this, the double album *Sápmi lottǎzan* (*Sápmi, My Bird*) was recorded, drawing inspiration not just from the *yoik*, but from the sounds of northern nature itself.[31]

Mari Boine

Today, the queen of Sámi Songs is undoubtedly Mari Boine (born Mari Boine Persen, in 1956), from Gamehisnjarga, on the river Anarjohka, in Norwegian Finnmark. By integrating elements of traditional Sámi music, jazz and disco rock she has created a form of modern Sámi music which has won her international acclaim to a degree never before achieved by a Sámi musician. Her family were devoted members of the Læstadian movement, which rejected not only 'heathen' *yoiks* but radio music as well. This might sound an unlikely milieu in which to blossom musically. However, the early musical influences of Christian hymn-singing which she surreptitiously experienced as a child served her well, even after she began to listen to modern rock and disco on the radio, the influences of which can be found in many of her songs. Boine's first album *Jaskatvuoða maŋŋá* (After the Silence), which was issued in 1985, clearly reveals a youthful defiance which found resonance among the younger generation of Sámi who became her ardent fans. Her second album was *Gula gula* (Listen, listen) (1989), which brought her to the attention of the wider world beyond the Sámi homeland and, indeed, the Nordic countries. Since then other elements of world music have been integrated into her performances, including not only the blues, but the music of the American Indians. Later albums show an increasing preference for softer music and deeper tones than were heard in her more rock influenced performances. Traditional Sámi themes have also now come to the fore in such albums as *Goaskinviellja* (The Eagle Brother) from 1993 and *Leahkastin* (The Opening) from 1994. The ancestors of the Sámi, their culture, philosophy of life and even religion have since become central themes. Boine herself thus calls her album *Bálvvoslatnja* (*Shrine*) (1998), 'her holy spiritual room', because of the mystical dimension in which her lyrics consider the cultural and spiritual history of the Sámi people.[32]

Other Sámi Groups of the 1990s

Musicians of note from Finland include Tuuni and Ursula Länsman, who performed as the duet Angelit, a name adopted from that of their native village of Angeli, some 62 kilometres from Inari. *Dolla* (*The Fire*), which appeared in 1992, was their most successful early release, but their later collaboration with the heavy rock band Waltari won them an even greater following among Sámi youth. The internationally acclaimed work of Wimme Saari (born 1959), which draws upon traditional Sámi *yoiks*, is also highly popular in Finland—although principally a soloist, he has also contributed to a number of performing groups, including Tallari, Pohjantahti and Hedningarna. In 1995 he was awarded the title of 'Folk Musician of the Year' in Finland, before going on to produce *Gierran* (*Spell*), which appeared in 1997, and *Cugu* (*Whelp*) two years later, both of which were highly popular.[33] His skill resides in part in his ability to draw on the formalised musical framework of traditional *yoik*, even in its most archaic forms, in combination with modern instruments like the saxophone or high-tech electronics.

As Finland was the northern European country in which the tango—at least as far back as the 1920s—became one of the most popular musical genres, it is not surprising that some Sámi Finns also took inspiration from it. This is apparent in *Beaivvášeana* (*The Land of the Sun*), by Eero Magga (born 1953), which came out in 1995. *Sámi váimmus* (*Lapland in my Heart*) by Tiina Aikio also evinces a similar inspiration, as do the chants sung with tango cadences by Liisa and Olavi Jomppanen, from Lemmenjoki.

In Sweden and Norway, the Frode Fjellheim Trans *Yoik* Ensemble have also utilised the South Sámi musical tradition in their music, while in Finnish Lapland Jaakko Gauriloff has made his own significant eastern Sámi musical contribution, in particular with his *leu'dd* genre of singing.[34]

Twentieth-Century Russian Sámi Music

Western European music was also not unknown in the Sámi heartland of the Kola Peninsula. Indeed, the first piano arrived in Lovozero[35] as far back as 1936, and a European style school of music was established there in 1966.[36] Yet long before Sámi music had been fostered in the region the folk ensemble Lujavvr had been established in Lovozero already in 1929 by Nikolai Dmitriyevich Ushkov, and after his death in the Second World War, the directorship was assumed by a variety of individuals including P.N. Bekrenev, S.S. Sokolov, L.A. Bessonova and, from 1966, Valentin Danilovich Gurinov. Pavl Ivanovich Konykov was one of the most popular of these singers, performing songs like 'I sing to you my North' and 'Lapp Rhythms' at festivities held at the Sámi *kolkhoz* (collective farm), organised by the Communist Party. The group not only toured in Leningrad and Moscow, but also gave performances at international venues in Norway and Finland in 2004 that proudly celebrated the seventy-five years since Lujavvr's foundation. Another folk ensemble, Oiyar (meaning 'circles in the water') was established in 1985. Maria Gavrilovna Medvyedeva became its director in 1990, whereupon it continued to focus on traditional Sámi songs, folk tales and games. The Skolt Sámi have also enjoyed a tradition of dance, originating at least as far back as the eighteenth century, accompanied by the accordion,[37] and so it is not surprising that Sámi dance was also given a sharp focus, in particular by Tantsuyushchie Saamy (The Dancing Sámi) which took centre stage under the leadership of Galina Yakovleva. It was chosen to perform at an event in 1998 in celebration of the foundation of Murmansk province some sixty years earlier, in which the Sámi homeland in Russia lies. One *obshina* (a community group) known as 'Sámi Families', which was established in 2000, focuses upon fostering cultural creativity within families on the Kola Peninsula. It has helped to organise performances that have been enjoyed not only in Russian Lapland but at various venues in northern Finland and Scandinavia, not least through the international 'family' cultural event known as Polyarnye Svedzy (The Polar Stars), in which musical groups from all of Sápmi compete.[38]

Sport

Sport has also long enjoyed an important cultural and social role among the Sámi. As far back as the late eighteenth century, Acerbi found the Sámi to be a people very much taken by games, although not the ones generally popular in Europe or even the Nordic countries and Russia:

They know nothing, or very little, of playing cards. They exercise themselves in throwing at a mark with a javelin: the prizes in these games, for those who come nearest the mark, are sometimes pieces of money, at other times tobacco, or such like articles. Besides this diversion, they have another with a leathern ball stuffed hard, which is struck in the air, and caught before it falls to the ground.

A certain amusement called *gaase spil*, or the game of fox and geese, is in great request with them. This is played by the two parties, on a board marked with square divisions for the purpose; one of the parties managing thirteen pegs, called geese, about this labyrinth; and, as may be imagined, in the dexterity of pursuit and escape consists the skill of the players.

Leaping over a stick held in an horizontal position by two Laplanders, is another diversion with which they pass their time. Sometimes two Laplanders, having each of them a stick in his hands, from the end of one rope being extended to the other, will drive to disengage the stick from each other's grasp; and in this, perhaps, they are assisted on each side by an equal number of the bystanders: this occasions a smart struggle, till at length the rope breaks, or the weakest party gives way, which at once decides the contest ... Another exercise consists in two of them fastening their hands in each other's belt, striving to raise one another from the ground, and thus to give each other a fall. They are besides excellent wrestlers; and these kind of exercises are found necessary to keep their bodies warm, as well as to fill up their intervals of leisure, when they are upon a journey, during the stoppages requisite to be made to give their rein-deer an opportunity of baiting; for which purpose ... those animals must dig up the snow in quest of moss, as it is not possible to carry forage with them in their sledges.[39]

The Sámi also have their own special forms of competition, for example with respect to skiing and shooting. Indeed, the sport of skiing while throwing a lasso seems to be unique to the Sámi. Of course, there are also many forms of reindeer races throughout the Sámi homeland, while the Russian Sámi have their own special sports, which include jumping over sledges and throwing hammers.[40]

Swimming seems also to have been popular among some of the Sámi. The Russian geologist Wilhelm Böhtlingk wrote that, during his visit in 1839, he observed that it was the custom of the Sámi youth to spend the day cooling off by swimming in the Arctic Ocean when the midday temperature hovered at between 20 and 23 degrees Celsius, as measured in our own time.[41]

Among the Skolt and Kola Sámi the traditional rope game was a popular sport. The game began with people forming a ring in the village field, some of whom would take hold of a lasso. One of the villagers was sent blindfolded into the middle of the circle, where he or she then had to try and catch those holding the rope as they escaped. Whoever was caught in this way then had to go into the centre as the one before him or her had done.[42]

In the twentieth century, however, many Sámi began to take up European sports, often to the neglect of their own. It was partly in order to counteract this trend that the Sámiid Valástallan Lihttu (Sámi Sports Association) was established in 1969, an organisation which focused upon encouraging Sámi activity in sports as a means to encourage Sámi cultural and social identity. In the 1940s a similar organisation was also set up in Sweden, the Svenska Samernas Skidförbund (Swedish Sámi Ski Association), but in contrast to the Sámiid Valástallan Lihttu its purpose was solely to develop Sámi achievements in the ancient Sámi activity of skiing, so central to their practical life.[43]

Although football is a relatively new sport in Sápmi, the Sámi now have their own team of football players who have gone on to compete not only locally but as far afield as the Åland Islands, off the southern coast of Finland, as well as in Estonia and even Greenland. Indeed, special Sámi games are held every winter drawing large crowds.

Films

While the film industry arrived late in Sápmi, it nonetheless achieved a modest development in the second half of the twentieth century. During the post-war years, *Valkoinen peura* (The White Reindeer), by the Finnish cinematographer Erik Blomberg (1913–96), proved to be a successful film on the life of the Sámi when it appeared in Finland in 1952. Shot in Sarriselkä with a lyrical slant, it won considerable acclaim internationally in Cannes and Hollywood for its romantic vision of Lapland and the Sámi people. A Sámi girl competing with her admirer, the reindeer herder Aslak, in a reindeer race, forms its subject. In particular, though, it is the way in which she turns to Sámi shamanism, a Sámi drum from Kemi and the *yoik* to resolve her marital unhappiness that heightens its exotic, mystical appeal.[44] Other displays of affection were muted. Indeed, the Sámi who played Aslak, Jouni Tapiola (1924–2012), a native of Utsjoki, confessed in an interview that when asked to kiss the actress as a part of the performance he had refused out of shyness, declaring that kissing was not a Sámi custom.[45]

When the Midnight Sun Film Festival was first held at Sodankylä in Finland in the summer of 1986 some called it 'anti-Cannes'.[46] First staged by the world famous Finnish film directors Aki Kaurismäki, Mika Kaurismäki and Peter von Bagh, it has more recently numbered the American film director Francis Ford Coppola and the Czech-born Miloš Forman among those who have taken part.

The first film actually made by a Sámi, one which won acclaim not only in the Nordic countries but globally, was *Ofelaš* (The Pathfinder)

(1987). Produced by the Norwegian Sámi film director and script-writer Nils Gaup (born 1955), and starring his son Mikkel Gaup (born 1968), this is undoubtedly the most internationally famous of Sámi films—it was even nominated for an Oscar. Nils Gaup, a native of Kautokeino where he had attended drama school, later went on to direct the Norwegian film *Hodet over vannet* (Head above Water) (1993), which won the Amanda Award, Norway's most famous prize for films. More recently, in 2008, he produced a film about the Kautokeino Rebellion (See Chapter 1), in which his son Mikko once again took a prominent role.

A new initiative was also undertaken to promote films dealing with Sámi issues in Finnish Lapland. One of the outcomes of this was the festival *Skábmagovat—Reflections of the Endless Night*, which was held at SIIDA in Inari in January 1999. The festival, which was organised by the Friends of Sámi Art, the Sámi Museum and the Northern Lapland Nature Centre, broadcast a number of important films relating to indigenous peoples.[47]

Films on related themes also began to be produced in the Russian part of Sápmi. The most notable of these was the Sámi–Finnish–Russian production *Kokushka* (in Russian, *Kukushka*; in English, *The Cuckoo*, 2002). Directed by the Russian Aleksandr Rogozhkin (born 1949), this tragicomedy focuses upon the confrontation between a Russian (Ivan, played by Viktor Bychkov) and a Finnish soldier (Veikko, played by Ville Haapasalo), who find themselves stranded at the farmhouse of a lone Sámi woman (Anni, played by the Finnish Sámi Anni-Kristiina Juuso, born 1979) after the Continuation War, the second military confrontation between Finland and Russia during the course of the Second World War. The name of the film itself refers to the Russian slang term used to denote a Finnish sniper, perched on the branch of a tree. The plot is more complicated than at first might appear, since the Russian was already accused by his own side of anti-Soviet activity. Romance, or at least sexual relations, are first shown with Anni and Veikko, then with Anni and Ivan, while the two former adversaries find themselves increasingly bound into a friendship formed by the need to collaborate in order to survive the harsh Lapland winter. Sámi religious healing rituals also play a role when Anni uses them to bring back the ailing Veikko from the threshold of death. The film subsequently won the Golden Griffin Grand Prize of the Festival of Festivals in St Petersburg in July 2002, and the Main Prize for Best

Film of the Europa Cinema Festival in Viareggio, Italy, in October of that same year, among many other awards. Juuso herself won the Best Actress Award at the Window to Europe Festival, held in Viborg in August 2002, where the film also won the Grand Prize for Best Film. These achievements were eventually recognised in Russia when the entire crew was awarded the Russian Federation's National Award for Art and Literature in June 2004.

Agitprop Films

Among the most interesting recent agitprop films of the last few years is *Last Yoik in Sámi Forests?* a video report for the UN. The film was published by the Sámi Council and Osuuskunta Marjarinteen Metsäpuutarha, and was produced by the Signs of Life Video Workshop. The film puts forward the Sámi case for the preservation of semi-natural forests for reindeer herding because of their rich ground and tree-hanging lichen, ruined, from a Sámi perspective, by intensive logging. The culprits, according to this report, are the decision-makers of the state-owned Metsähallitus (Forest Board of Finland) and the Stora Enso Company, specialising in wood and paper products, which they feel give priority to economic returns and jobs over the preservation of the forests and the traditional lifestyle of the Sámi people. The accompanying *yoik* music by Wimme Saari, Ulla Pirtijärvi, Niilas Somby and the late Nils-Aslak Valkeapää heightens the emotional impact of the film, which does not shy away from focusing upon the most violent elements of the ensuing confrontation.[48]

Radio and Television

The first ever broadcast in the Sámi language took place on Christmas Day 1936 at Polmak Church in the north of Norway. However, it took a further ten years for another Sámi radio programme to be broadcast, which on this occasion was devoted to the latest events that had occurred in the wake of the Second World War and the Nazi occupation and destruction which followed. This broadcast was to be the first of many transmitted over a period of thirty years there, made memorable by 'the Voice of Sámi Radio', Katherine Johnsen, from Vadsø. Additional, regular scheduled radio broadcasts in and for the Sámi began in the early 1960s. Other Sámi speakers, in Sweden, first in

Jokkmokk (1953), then in Luleå (1966) and later in Kiruna (1971), also became active in running radio transmissions. Transmission from Gällivare followed in the 1980s. All of these broadcasts were eventually amalgamated into the Swedish Sámi Radio.

In Finland, radio presentations first began in 1948 with broadcasts from Oulu. The Finnish Sámi Radio became autonomous in 1985 and by the beginning of the 1990s it had opened branches in Utsjoki and Kaaresuvanto. Since the creation of the joint Nordic Sámi Radio initiative, there has also been almost daily transmission of programmes in the Inari and Skolt Sámi languages. This resulted in the broadcast of a modest news programme from Tromsø in 1964, which eventually became a more thorough and regularly scheduled current affairs programme, broadcast from Kiruna, in 1974. In 1984 another radio station was established, this time in Karasjok, in Norway, which today employs over 100 people. Broadcasts in North Sámi, South Sámi and Lule Sámi are transmitted for some ten hours each day in the Nordic countries.[49]

The first Russian Sámi radio programme was broadcast in Lovozero in 1983.[50] This was followed by the introduction of regular broadcasts produced by Sámi Radio in 1990, with the assistance of A.A. Antonova, which focused on a wide range of aspects of Sámi culture. However, the station closed down in 2000 when 'Radio Murman' assumed some of its functions. The Sámi Council increasingly came to provide financial and administrative assistance from Norway, Finland and Sweden, which led to the production of short Sámi programmes.

Although radio broadcasts began in the twentieth century, Sámi-language television programmes were not introduced until relatively recently. Sweden and Norway introduced Sámi broadcasts in August 2001, while the Finnish Broadcasting Company (YLE) began to use Sámi for some of its news coverage in January 2002. Building upon these modest initiatives, Nils Johan Heatta, the director of Sámi Radio (a subsidiary of the Norwegian Broadcasting Corporation [NRK]), let it be known at the World Indigenous Television Broadcasting Conference that he hoped to launch the world's first Sámi-language television channel, which would broadcast to the whole of Sápmi from 2012/13 onwards. Today there are daily evening television news broadcasts in the Sámi language, some 95 per cent of which are in a Northern Sámi version and are broadcast to viewers in Norway, Sweden and Finland (albeit at different times), of fifteen minutes duration. There was also a project which established a television broadcast centre in Lovozero

for the benefit of Russian Sámi viewers and speakers, but it only functioned for a couple of years owing to a collapse in the Nordic financial
support which had sustained it, due in part, it has been said, to the
pressures of Russian governmental bureaucracy. The internet is also
playing an increasingly important part in Sámi media by bringing Sámi
broadcasts and other forms of transmission into homes, workplaces
and schools in Sápmi and all places in the world where there are those
interested in Sámi language and culture.

7

REINDEER HERDING AND OTHER LIVELIHOODS

Reindeer Herding

In the wake of the retreat of the glaciers which covered what became the Sámi homeland in Fenno-Scandia and the Kola Peninsula, groups of hunters arrived in the river valleys in pursuit of the rich game and fishing stocks. Their presence has been confirmed at Arjeplog, in Sweden, in the period between 7100 and 7700 BC, the latter date just 100 years after the ice had retreated.[1] The earliest evidence of reindeer hunting has been uncovered at Enontekiö, in Finnish Lapland, from about 6000 BC.[2] At Áhusjgårsså, in northern Sweden, hunting pits have been found which date back, according to radiocarbon dating, to about 3500 BC. As a later pit has been uncovered from 1450, it would appear that the area was used for similar purposes for thousands of years.[3]

In what is today north-western Russia, the Sámi or their forebears were for millennia engaged in hunting wild reindeer and fishing in the tundra of the Kola Peninsula in the Neolithic period, in particular around Lovozero. The Sámi also appear to have inhabited sites along the southern shores of Lake Ladoga in the vicinity of Oreshek as late as the fifteenth century.[4] Certainly, by 2000 BC, reindeer hunting was of primary importance for the inhabitants of these regions, albeit only in those areas covered in boreal forests and mountain foothills.[5]

The Sámi hunted wild reindeer virtually exclusively up until the ninth century. However, not long thereafter, probably from as early as the

890s (i.e. around the time of Ottar's death: see the introduction to this book), the domestication of reindeer had begun.[6] Indeed, some maintain that reindeer husbandry, at least on a limited scale, can be traced back to around AD 500.[7] Traditionally only reindeers and dogs were tamed, but some Sámi settlements also kept cattle, sheep and goats as domesticated animals. Indeed, the Sámi in the vicinity of Enontekiö became noted for the goats which grazed on their summer pastures.[8]

The Coastal Sámi of what had already become Norway became increasingly sedentary from about 1100, devoting themselves to fishing, animal husbandry and sometimes agriculture.[9] The Mountain Sámi, on the other hand, continued to pursue a nomadic life in which wild reindeer hunting and fishing were the primary activities. Yet the increasing domestication of reindeer was well underway in the new millennium, even if actual large-scale reindeer herding is said to have first been adopted by some of the Sámi during the thirteenth century.[10]

Among the first to record the hunting habits of the Sámi with respect to reindeer was Olaus Magnus, in the early sixteenth century.[11] By then a specific type of hunter-gathering society was established, prevalent in Lule Lappmark in the mid-1500s, and which survived up to the late nineteenth century in the east Sámi area.[12]

In the 1500s, east Lule Lappmark was composed of four *siida*. Those closest to Tysfjord were the mountain communities of Sierkaluokta and Tuorpun. Further east were Dálvadis, Jokkmokk and Vuollesiida. Although wild reindeer disappeared first in the coastal areas, it was in the mountain areas that domestic reindeer holding first began. Sámi from the two former *siida* began to take the reindeer with them to the coast during the summer. There were practical reasons for this since cheese was made from reindeer milk. *Juopmu* (sorrel) helped to clot it, which preserved it for longer periods than would otherwise have been the case.[13] But the production of cheese and reindeer milking were by no means ancient Sámi customs: like so often in Sámi homeland, the Sámi and those among whom they resided lived in symbiosis, and both practices were in fact introduced under Scandinavian influence in the modern period.[14]

It was King Karl IX of Sweden who first took a reindeer census in Swedish Lapland in 1605. From this it became clear that domestic reindeer had come to dominate the whole of the southern region where the Sámi lived in Sweden.[15] This had major social and economic repercussions because domestic reindeer herding encouraged the private, individual ownership of the reindeer, rather than that of the entire community.[16]

Reindeer were of course not the sole focus of Sámi hunting and herding. Fishing, in particular for cod, grew in importance during the eighteenth century, while whales and otters were also sometimes hunted. Furs of great trading value, and marten and deer, were just some of the valuable commodities obtained by the Sámi from the interior. Giuseppe Acerbi noted that the Sámi were excellent marksmen.[17] Trapping could also be a lucrative activity. In Russian Lapland, hundreds of peregrine, gyr, merlin and goshawk were trapped annually to satisfy the market, with the trade proving highly profitable for the Sámi who were intimately familiar with the breeding grounds of these birds.[18]

Furthermore, domestic animals other than reindeer were also introduced, as we have seen, towards the end of the sixteenth century, supplemented by limited agriculture in the region. Indeed, Swedish tax archives from 1559 confirm that agriculture had become widespread, especially at the mouth of the fjords on which the Sámi had increasingly settled. Despite the fact that domestic reindeer hunting had been introduced in the Tysfjord region as early as the end of the sixteenth century, wild reindeer hunting persisted as a major form of livelihood in the mountains.[19]

Traditionally, wild reindeer hunting had been the mainstay of the Sámi and was practised in three forms. In one method, in use from the seventeenth to the nineteenth century, fences made from tree trunks steered the animals down specific paths to be caught in traps, constructed by pointed stakes, nooses or pits. The second—which continued in some areas until the twentieth century—was a form of seasonal winter hunting that took place in February and March, the Sámi pursuing their game on skis when snow lay on the ground. This method enabled the Sámi to pursue their prey rapidly, often more quickly than in the warmer snow-free months. The third, also persisting until the twentieth century, was the most labour intensive form of wild reindeer hunting, involving many kilometres of fenced runs, culminating in pits, into which the animals were ultimately driven and killed.[20]

Wild reindeer hunting was carried out in the early autumn on the Varanger Peninsula, especially at Gollevárri, in the vicinity of the Teno (Tana, in Finnish) River. Driving the wild reindeer into ditches was the primary means used for hunting them. Some 2,700 such ditches have been uncovered between Varangerfjord and the Teno. The *Vuopman* or corridor through which they were propelled was encompassed by stone barriers, the largest by Noaidečearru, on the Varangerfjord, some 500 to 600 metres in length. Hidden posts from which to shoot were set up from the sixteenth century when guns were introduced, while provisions were also made for protected storage places for meat. These hunting grounds, which were still in use in the seventeenth century, date back through the Viking period, deep into the Stone Age. However, although the arrival of the gun increased the catch, it also served to deplete the wild stocks from the beginning of the seventeenth century onwards.[21]

Nonetheless, reindeer-herding nomadism, as records indicate, was firmly established by the beginning of the 1600s.[22] Indeed, as Jukka Pennanen has pointed out, the Sámi were the first people in the world to herd reindeer on a large scale, most probably in the area stretching from the Nordland Fjord, in central Norway, to the fjords of Troms, in the north, by the Kølen Mountains.[23] The Skolts were among the last of the Sámi to take up reindeer herding.[24] In the eastern regions in which they lived stocks of wild reindeer remained more plentiful than in the west. Some of the earliest illustrations of such herding are to be found in the work of Johannes Schefferus, with lengthy descriptions of their domestication.[25]

Domestic reindeer herding actually began among the Sámi of the Varangerfjord in Norway, along with the holding of domestic animals. Doubtless, the arrival of Norwegian settlers in the thirteenth century had long provided models of more settled modes of animal husbandry. Those Mountain Sámi who had not as yet adopted domestic herding now came to be called Varanger mountain Finns, and the province in which they resided Finnmark. Here wild reindeer had become a depleted commodity and the adoption of domestic reindeer herding reflected this unhappy ecological situation, in which the animals were over-taxed and over-hunted. By the end of the seventeenth century, the use of the *Vuopman*, fenced hunting enclosures to trap the reindeer, was a thing of the past, although wild reindeer hunting on the Varangerfjord carried on in ever more limited scope to at least some degree until the middle of the nineteenth century, when finally the practice was legally prohibited.[26]

By the sixteenth century the Sámi had long established their winter residence at Varanger, a valley of the fjord in the vicinity of which fuel was readily available. Assemblies took place here and bailiffs visited to organise the collection of taxes. Karlebotn, situated nearby, was the region's most important centre of trade, as a Swedish royal letter from 1571, confirming its wealth, mentions.[27] Of considerable importance for the taxes it generated, Karlebotn was placed under direct royal supervision from 1688. According to the government official Niels Kang in 1694, traders came from as far afield at Torneå in Sweden and Kola in north-western Russia, making it one of the Sámi's most important entrepôts.[28]

In the inland mountainous northern areas of Sweden, unlike the Varangerfjord region of Norway, wild reindeer hunting and fishing continued to predominate, with the largest reindeer herds, of up to seventy animals, being held at Tuorpun. Elsewhere the herds were considerably smaller: thirty reindeer were held at Sierkaluokta and twenty at Dálvadis. The Sámi who arrived at the Norwegian coast—usually Tysfjord—with their reindeer were obliged to pay tax on them, a burden ever more stringently imposed at least from the beginning of the seventeenth century. More than forty Sámi arrived at Tysfjord in 1605, as is recorded in the tax register, while others went to Saltenfjord. Tysfjord and Jokkmokk also became important trading centres for the Sámi, and all of them increasingly had much in common, as trade became ever more important for both the Mountain and Coastal Sámi. This situation changed, however, when the herds grew larger in the course of the seventeenth century, demanding more time from the Sámi herders who migrated less and less to the coast during the summer months. Only in the 1670s did domestic reindeer herding come to dominate the economic lives of both the Mountain and Forest Sámi in the south. First restricted mainly to trading contacts, relations between the Mountain and Forest Sámi grew more intertwined with contact, until a network of intermeshing relationships had developed, a social and economic *verddevuohta* (friendly arrangement) which continues up to this day.[29]

By the late seventeenth century wild reindeer herding was drawing to a close and with it the domestication of reindeer which had begun in the first half of the century and even before was nearing completion. In consequence, by 1660 there were virtually no wild reindeer hunts in the Varanger *siida*. Moreover, already from the end of the 1660s, Norwegian settlers and their descendants also began to acquire and keep reindeer, leading to a growing conflict with the Sámi.[30] This competition for limited resources was of course already old with respect to fishing. For while the Sámi still had their own fishing grounds at Kiberg and Vardø,[31] they had for centuries found their mastery eroded by Norwegian, English and Dutch fishermen.

In the later eighteenth century many Sámi increasingly began to take up settled agriculture in preference to reindeer herding. As a result, the old hunting *siida*, in Diggevárri and Siggevárri, for example, began to disintegrate. This obliged some migratory Sámi to settle in nearby forest valleys or on the isthmuses of Evenes and Skånland, in northern Norway. New settlements also came into being for those Sámi who still went on migrations. Thus Gállogieddi became a base by the coast for those Sámi arriving from Jukkasjärvi for the summer.[32] Reindeer herding continued, even in coastal areas where competition for land with Norwegian settlers continued to grow. Indeed, it was carried out on Langøya, off the coast of Ofoten, until the 1970s.[33] As for Russian Lapland, by 1858 the Sámi in Lovozero, whose numbers had grown to 120, had some 210 reindeer in their herds.[34] Reindeer animal husbandry has continued in this region despite the vagaries of politics, famine and war up to our own day.

Lands Subjected to 'Lapp Taxes'

For many centuries the Sámi were subject to onerous taxation from all of the states which laid claim to the Sámi homeland. This circumstance led to the careful recording of the demography of the Sámi, including details of their livelihoods, information which was of considerable importance in facilitating their taxation and exploitation. In consequence, we know that Varanger was one of the largest *siida* in Lapland towards the end of the Middle Ages. One-third of the Coastal Sámi registered in Finnmark lived there. In 1601 it had some sixty-seven recorded taxable households, a figure that subsequently rose to 101 in 1690 and 108 in 1769. By contrast, in Vestertana there were five taxable households in 1601, thirteen in Laksefjord and thirty-five in Lakselv. Thirty taxable Norwegians also lived at Varanger, but their number increased dramatically after the arrival of waves of missionaries and the increased trade which accrued to the region.[35]

Higher taxes were imposed in Swedish Lapland after the Kalmar War (1611–13), forcing many Sámi to flee to the Norwegian coast. The Swedish tax register of 1614 confirms that seven Sámi from Ávjovárri and four from Deatnu did so. This trend burgeoned after 1730, for the number of Sámi households increased significantly, leading to ever heavier tax burdens.[36]

Lappskatteland (land subject to Lapp taxes) was an important element of Sámi land ownership. Such land was inherited and passed from generation to generation within individual families. Hence, this land was private, although it was generally owned not by an individual, but by a family or extended clan. Highly variable in size, it was also subject to the state's laws of inheritance.

During the second half of the seventeenth and the first half of the eighteenth century, rates of taxation were high, and unusually severe weather, as well as growing competition for land resources, made life difficult for many Sámi. Indeed, this was a period of extreme mortality for the Sámi and the other inhabitants of the Nordic countries and north-western Russia, as well as other northern Europeans. Many of the Lule Sámi in Sweden, and especially those from the district of Kaitum, were obliged to leave their homeland. The situation was at its worst in the 1660s, when all of the Sámi in Kaitum were obliged to depart during a two year period. Many of those forced to migrate moved northwards into Torne Lappmark in 1702. Many areas formerly occupied by the Sámi thus became almost emptied of them. In 1726, in the vicinity of Sjokksjokk, relatively few Sámi were recorded in the tax records, probably because of the difficult conditions which had forced them to abandon their ancestral lands. Similarly, in Kaitum, between 1695 and 1750 no new *lappskatteland* was recorded, although reindeer herding across the border with Norway is known to have been significant. New *lappskatteland* was added in Sjokksjokk after 1695, although hunting and fishing continued to predominate. The arduous circumstances led to conflict, and so the Sjokksjokk Sámi seem to have been involved in considerable local legal litigation with respect to their rights over land and lakes. Matters came to a head after 1750 with the arrival of more 'colonists' from the south, many of whom were involved in a wide range of economic activities, including mining, which infringed upon the Sámi and their ancestral lands. Moreover, as borders were redrawn and a more intrusive ecclesiastical infrastructure was established, bringing in growing governmental as well as religious intrusions, the old order of *lappskatteland* soon found itself undergoing revolutionary changes, which largely worked against the well-being of the Sámi vis-à-vis the newcomers.[37]

In Finland, the payment of the 'Lapp Tax' had largely ceased by the early nineteenth century, around the time of its transfer to the Russian

Crown, although it continued to be collected in the vicinities of Utsjoki, Inari and Enontekiö for some years to come.[38] In Russia itself, however, taxation and state pressures upon the Sámi were even more burdensome, although colonisation was far less of a problem. Indeed, it was only in 1778 that the Sámi regained their full property rights over their hunting and fishing grounds, which had long been usurped from them.[39]

For all the hardships of their life and livelihood, the Sámi were a hard-working people who eschewed exploitation of the weak. As Giuseppi Acerbi noted, they were permeated by a sense of fairness with respect to sharing their labours:

We left it to them to divide our baggage into seven parcels, one for each, including the girl, who was to be made to carry her proportion. We remarked a degree of equality in the distribution of the burthens, which impressed us with no unfavourable idea of the character of these people. We observed that they gave the lightest packets to such as appeared unequal to a heavier load.[40]

He also noted approvingly that 'Norway swarms with beggars, but begging is unknown amongst the Laplanders.'[41]

Mining

Intensive silver mining first began in 1635 at Nasafjäll, about a kilometre east of the Norwegian border in Sweden, after the discovery of this precious metal by the Sámi Jöns Persson and Peder Olafsson in 1634 during the reign of Queen Christina of Sweden. Rather than importing labourers for the endeavour, the Sámi themselves were conscripted and set to work hauling the ore by reindeer from the mines to Silbojokk, where the smelting was carried out. Severe measures were used against the Sámi who refused this conscription, including such punishments as dunking through one hole in the ice before being lifted out through another. However, proximity to the Norwegian border meant that flight to Norway was an option and many Sámi sought refuge from this *corvée*. Not surprisingly, some of these assisted the Norwegians when a military incursion was made into Sweden in 1659. The smelting works were attacked on 15 August of that year, when those who guarded and worked it were at the spring market at Arjeplog. Only the local clergyman was taken as captive, from which perspective he left his own record of the event: movable goods from the smelting works were removed to Norway and that physical infrastructure which could not be transferred was burnt or otherwise destroyed. The mine itself suffered a similar fate several days later. For this and other economic reasons, this mining of silver proved a major disappointment to the Swedish Crown and government.[42] It also heightened hostilities between Sweden and Norway.

In 1673 emigration to Norway was prohibited altogether, a measure severely damaging Sámi interests, for it hindered the seasonal movement of the Sámi with their reindeer. The introduction of other laws also harmed them. The *Skogsloven* (Forest Law) of 1695 declared that untaxed and 'under-utilised' forest lands belonged to the Swedish state, while it also encouraged the development of mining.[43] The *Lappmarksplakat* of 1695, on the other hand, benefited the Sámi because it sought to restrict the rights of the mainly newly arrived colonists to burn woodlands, so important for reindeer sustenance, which even in Stockholm was considered to have been deleterious to the region's economy and ecology. Nonetheless, the *Lappmarksreglementet* of 1749 further encouraged colonial settlements. As in previous cases, although stipulations were made to minimise conflict between the new arrivals and the Sámi, their practical benefits were limited. In consequence, many Sámi took up a sedentary way of life, taking advantage of the privileges granted to the new settlers from which they too could now benefit. The new settlers were, however, dissuaded from hunting and fishing—activities of central importance to the Sámi—and encouraged instead to develop their permanent farmsteads, in conjunction with animal husbandry. Local clergymen, many of whom took a keen interest in fostering the well-being of their Sámi flock, frequently encouraged this development, in particular Pehr Högström at Gällivare,[44] where, according to lists recording the occupations of the inhabitants of Torne Lapland in 1750, 303 Sámi continued their traditional way of life, herding more than 25,500 reindeer.[45] Individual families were allotted hunting and fishing areas by the Sámi village's local administration. During the eighteenth century, these were actually listed by the Swedish government under the names of the families to whom they were allotted. The village administration also decided on when the fishing and hunting were to be carried out.[46]

Colonisation proceeded apace, but even by the end of the eighteenth century settlers from the south, though numerous, had not succeeded in dominating Lapland in terms of population. For example, the village of Enontekis, which comprised some 930 residents in total, had 258 'colonists' and 672 nomadic Sámi, living in the mountains where they herded reindeer.[47] The area had by then become an important trading centre, at least from the early seventeenth century, when a bonded warehouse had been constructed at Markkina, incorporated in the residence of the local official appointed to administer law and order, along with twenty-two houses and storerooms for tax collectors and merchants to reside, during the Candlemas Fair held in early February which lasted ten days. Later, in 1809, the market was transferred to the village of Palojoensuu, slightly to the south, by which time Finnish settlers were starting to arrive. Nonetheless, well into the nineteenth century Markkina and Palojoensuu only had seasonal residents, with the exception of its Lutheran priest who farmed the land, maintained meadows for hay, fished and kept cows to maintain himself. Indeed, even the local police chief only came there in times of market activity, residing predominantly in Karesuando. Only in the early nineteenth century did Finnish settlers finally appear in Markkina, making their presence ever more felt.[48]

The importance of these fairs and the goods sold or bartered were noted by Acerbi with respect to the winter fair in Kautokeino:

In the small village of Kautokeino, there is in the month of February an annual fair, which is frequently by the neighbouring Laplanders and the merchants from Torneå, who come thither for the purpose of purchasing rein-deer skins, furs, and other articles. In those fairs the medium of trade is barter. The Laplanders give the skins of rein-deer, foxes, wolves, and bears, with gloves and shoes, or rather short boots, in exchange for coarse flannels, but above all for brandy, tobacco, meal, and salt.

They have a few cows and sheep, which in some degree supply them with milk and wool. For fodder to their cows, when they have not hay enough, they gather the moss that the rein-deer feeds upon, and which the cows, for want of better nourishment are glad to live upon. ... As sheep do not form any article of barter or commerce, they are to be purchased at a very low price.[49]

Kautokeino was by now clearly an extremely important centre of Sámi mercantile and cultural life, something also confirmed by Yrjö Kortelainen in his recent research.[50]

Yet a seasonal nomadic lifestyle remained characteristic of the Sámi. This was also noted by Acerbi, who was taken by their predilection for a nomadic lifestyle in preference to the sedentary habits of the Nordic settlers. He wrote:

It would not be difficult for the few families of Kautokeino to raise grain sufficient for their wants: but they choose rather to fish, and hunt wild rein-deer, than to undergo the wearisome toils of husbandry. They exchange for grain what fish they can spare, or barter for it the skins of bears or other animals which they may happen to kill.[51]

Other Forms of Hunting

While reindeer hunting had historically been the principal focus of traditional Sámi life, bear hunting had also been an important activity and remained so as late as the mid-eighteenth century, in particular in the more southerly parts of Lapland. Pehr Fjellström, a priest in Swedish Lapland, published a book in 1755 which examined bear hunting and the celebrations which followed. These included the threading of brass rings upon string which was then hung around the necks of the hunters. Special food and drink were provided to the men and the women—separately—and for three nights carnal congress was forbidden. As elsewhere in Finno-Ugric cultures, the naming of the bear directly was taboo.[52]

Beaver hunting, an ancient tradition in Kemmi Lappmark, was traditionally carried out from early December to early January. From early June to early July, the Sámi there fished at Kemijärvi, among other sites. From early August to early October, they devoted themselves to hunting wild reindeer, after which the herds of reindeer were rounded up for the winter. Early January to the end of February was a period in which trade was carried out, as well as the payment of taxes and other practical matters often involving assemblies. From early March until the end of May, wild reindeer hunting was again carried out, along with the hunting of other animals.[53] Yet beaver hunting remained important too and not only for an individual, since it was frequently carried out inter-communally, as at Skoarojohka in Teno, where both Utsjoki and Varanger *siida* went on hunts in a coordinated form. The fish and prey obtained were divided among the Sámi, as the village administration of each *siida* saw fit, whether or not the individual families had actually participated. Wild reindeer herding was also a communal activity, not least because it required an infrastructure of fencing. With respect to beaver hunting, those young men new to taking part might be required to swear oaths to confirm that they would provide the beaver brought in to the benefit of the whole *siida*, rather than to them individually. This was of considerable importance, since beaver pelts provided an important element in the *siida's* payment of taxes. This was the case at

Beaverbukt (in Norwegian; 'Beaver Bay' in English), near Karasjok, which was an important site of beaver hunting.[54]

Unfortunately, by the end of the seventeenth century, beavers had been largely exterminated in the northern Sámi areas and the supply of otters was markedly reduced. The end of wild reindeer hunting also meant a sharp diminution in communal activities by the *siida*, as well as its political and social power. The growth of domestic reindeer herding in the interior also created pressure on land and the intrusions of one *siida* into the area of another. This led to a growing movement of people from the interior to the coast. This had happened in Pite and Lule Lappmark already towards the end of the sixteenth century and began to take place a century later at Kautokeino, Ávjovárri, Teno and Utsjoki. Although, in Norway, the Coastal Sámi requested protection from Copenhagen, the seat of the Danish Crown and state government, the latter encouraged the movement of domestic reindeer herders from the interior, which, the authorities felt, strengthened Denmark's political and economic profile in the region. Yet as both Coastal and interior Sámi went over to domestic reindeer herding, seasonal migration patterns strengthened whereby many Sámi spent the winters in the interior and the summers on the coast. The heads of the *siida* also achieved greater significance since they increasingly represented their people in dealings with government authorities.[55]

Seal, whale and walrus hunting on the Norwegian coast had long been of importance for the Coastal Sámi. In Varanger, where whaling was at its best along the coast, whales were generally hunted not on the open sea but when they became embedded in local groundwater.[56] But the Sámi had to contend with international competition: not only Norwegian whalers, but Dutch and even sometimes English ones, based on their ships, also hunted whale by Varanger.[57]

Border Closures and the Disruption of Sámi Life

A major blow struck the way of life and economic livelihood of Sámi reindeer herders when the borders between Norway and Finland were closed in 1852. The Court of Appeal, at Vaasa, in Finland, decided that reindeer herders living in Norway who brought their herds to Finland would suffer the confiscation of 10 per cent of their reindeer, the monies raised to be utilised by the provincial governor 'for the enhancement of Lapland's economy'. This 'enhancement' might include the construction of reindeer pasture fences, encouragement of agriculture or the building of schools and libraries. A similar approach was also taken in Norway. As a result, in the 1880s many Varanger Sámi moved to Finland where they settled in Näätämö, to the north-east of Inari. Other reindeer herders from Utsjoki then settled to the west of Inari, on land which was as yet 'unoccupied'. Immigration to the area was further encouraged, if only seasonally during the summer months, by a gold-rush along the shores of the Ivalo River in the 1870s. At such times, the population could double. However, by the early 1900s the quest for gold had shifted to Lemmenjoki, attracting people, in reverse, from Inari. Not surprisingly, given the remarkable growth of Inari at this time, the village was made a municipality in 1876, a status which reflected its wealth. A Sámi, Paavali Valle, was elected chairman of both the local council and the municipal assembly.[58] The Sámi of Inari had 7,311 reindeer in 1870, but this number more than quadrupled to 32,000 by 1900. The Finns there, by contrast, had 1,214 reindeer in 1870 and 2,612 by 1900, thus only doubling their share, and so, in this instance, the Sámi role in reindeer herding became more dominant.[59] In that same year one Sámi reindeer herder, Niilo Magga, had no less than 2,800 animals himself and three others had 2,000 or more reindeer.[60]

According to the Census of Reindeer conducted by the visiting ethnographer Paulo Mantegazza in 1881, there were 220,800 reindeer in Sweden in 1870 (165 per family group), 101,768 in Norway in 1865 (130 per family group), 40,200 in Finland in 1865 (325 per family) and 232 in Russia in 1859.[61]

During the late nineteenth century the Sámi were granted a monopoly on reindeer herding in Sweden. (Although they also came to enjoy this privilege in Norway, they have never done so in Finland or Russia.) This monopoly was undoubtedly welcomed by many Sámi who thereby perceived their traditional livelihood to be better protected, but it also served to further isolate them and cut them off from other forms of activity, traditional as well as new.[62] Moreover, the unwanted corollary of this was the exclusion of the non-reindeer-holding Sámi in the later nineteenth century in Sweden from being considered a 'proper Lapp', since reindeer herding no longer played a role in their lives, and it hindered freedom of movement. Alarik Dahlqvist, in charge of Sámi affairs in Jämtland, considered it beneficial and claimed:

I support the measures which were introduced to prevent the Lapps from moving about on one another's land as a useful beginning in encouraging good reindeer herding. With the passing of the reindeer herding law of 1886, the right to move onto reindeer herding land—considered to be a right by the Lapps—was removed, and therewith was eliminated one of the major factors which encouraged poor management and disorder.[63]

Others, however, saw it as a devastating intrusion into Sámi identity and livelihood. 'With one blow,' as Lennart Lundmark has put it, 'the Swedish crown had split Sámi society in two. Those who were not reindeer herders could no longer be considered Sámi.'[64]

Be that as it may, many Sámi had already adopted a largely sedentary form of life. Erik Grape, a rector of Karesuando, has left us an account of life there among the farming population:

The Farms contain both cattle and sheep, each averaging from four to ten cows and between fifteen and forty sheep ... To stretch out their food, lichen is at times included in their winter feed. From June to mid September the cows are sent into the woods to graze. On summer evenings smudge fires have to be lit in order to protect them from the plagues of mosquitoes ... Barley is the only grain sown ... Of the last thirty years only six have seen fully mature harvests, but four others have been reasonably rewarding. From the church village northwards only turnips are cultivated, since the prospects for corn are so poor. The priest normally has eight cows and a horse, as well as smaller livestock.

In the peasant homes bread is often replaced by dried whitefish, milk, meat or porridge.[65]

Similar acts were also promulgated in Russia with respect to the Sámi and reindeer herding. Centralised control from St Petersburg was increasing throughout the Russian Empire and, in particular, with respect to the Grand Duchy of Finland. Indeed, the Russian imperial government decreed in 1898 that reindeer were henceforth to be herded exclusively by members of cooperatives from within the Finnish reindeer-herding area.[66]

Reindeer Cooperatives

Cooperation between *siida* had long been a feature of the Sámi in social and especially economic terms. Sámi *siida* sometimes shared hunting areas, such as in Jávrrešduottar for both Kautokeino and Ávjovárri. Occasionally even fishing resources were shared, as at Suonikylä and Notozero to the east.[67] Yet state governments increasingly considered it their prerogative to interfere and reorder the arrangements as they felt appropriate with respect to nationwide interests. For example, in 1898, the Finnish Senate ordered the establishment of a system of reindeer-herding cooperatives, granting reindeer herders 'free grazing and tree felling rights on the Crown's lands'. In consequence, five cooperatives were formed at Muddusjärvi, Paatsjoki, Paadar, Ivalo and Inarin Kyrö, and the land devoted to pasture was increased significantly. By 1900, there were some 32,000 reindeer in the area, the greatest in any single municipality.[68] Thus, by the end of the nineteenth century, the various states in which the Sámi lived all enacted laws encouraging the creation of reindeer-herding cooperatives. By 1928 they, in turn, established a mutual interest administrative body that eventually became the Association of Reindeer Herding Co-operatives, and which helped to create an initiative that led to the passing of the first Reindeer Herding Act in 1932.[69] Instead of flourishing, however, reindeer herding diminished. Although there were some 10,631 reindeer in and around Rovaniemi by 1910, the numbers began to decline dramatically thereafter, to only some 6,279 by 1930.[70] Interestingly, though, other forms of animal husbandry increased significantly during that period, with the number of pigs there rising from forty to 214, and fowl from 169 to 575.[71]

The 1928 law defining the right to reindeer herding in Sweden expounded:

The right to reindeer herding, as here laid out, is granted to those of Lapp ancestry, in so far as his father or mother or grandparents have been consistently engaged in the carrying out of reindeer herding ... The term Lapp, in the context of this law, refers to those who have the right to carry out reindeer herding ...

Those Sámi whose parents or grandparents were not engaged in reindeer herding were now barred from being considered as Sámi.[72]

Thus, during the 1930s, in Sweden, discrimination increasingly affected non-herding Sámi, because government officials preferred that the 'nomadic' Sámi continue to live in their tents rather than in permanent settled housing, in the interest of more efficient reindeer herding. However, this created problems, not least for the poor Sámi, who no longer had any reindeer herds or who had adopted a settled way of life, as we have seen. It also discouraged the Sámi from taking up agriculture, which in some areas would have provided a more secure and lucrative return. There was, moreover, a racial aspect to the discrimination which persisted well into the post-Second World War years.[73]

The re-fixing of national borders in the wake of the Second World War, not to mention the Iron Curtain which now divided Finland and Norway from the Soviet Union, also traumatised the Sámi, and life continued to be difficult even in the subsequent period when the Nordic countries worked together in ever closer cooperation and the borders between them were no longer contested. The construction of a fence along parts of the Finnish northern and western borders with Sweden and Norway in the 1950s, for example, severely restricted the movements of the Sámi with their herds. Henceforth, the Sámi no longer migrated with the reindeer in the summer, but increasingly became settled all year round. Reindeer milk became an exotic commodity as the milking of the animals virtually ceased. Technology also brought about its own changes. Today reindeer herding, especially in Finland, has become a much less time-consuming activity, for the herds are now permitted to roam around the *siida* throughout most of the year, albeit in different grazing areas at different seasons for ecological reasons, so as not to overexploit the pastures. During the spring months, the reindeer are released in anticipation of their calving. As a result of this, the herders have direct contact with their animals on just a few occasions (i.e. calving in spring, the earmarking of calves in summer or autumn, which provides information on ownership, and the slaughtering and tallying season in autumn and early winter).[74]

Earmarks play a major role in reindeer herding, both culturally and in practical terms, throughout the Sámi homeland. Its usage was first recorded in documents from the seventeenth century, which show that even then the Sámi carried out their herding on the basis of the individual ownership of each animal, as opposed to any form of collective ownership. This remains the case in modern times, with neither the *siida* nor families owning reindeer as a collective unit, although family members continue to use an earmarking system in which the symbols making up the marks often allude to the common relationship of the animal's owners.[75] Reindeer herders know that the reindeer are attracted by the odour of urine and they make use of this fact to bring them together for earmarking and control. This is highly important in reindeer herding since earmarks play a key role in the ascertaining to whom an animal belongs. The art of herding is quite complex and the rounding up of the reindeer requires the skilful use of a lasso. Skis were formerly also a necessity for tending herds in the winter,[76] although now snowmobiles have taken over this role virtually exclusively.

Ancillary shacks for temporary accommodation at the time of the round-up and slaughtering, often not very picturesque but 'practical', have also made their appearance. In Finnmark, for example, most of these shacks are clustered together on the summer pastures of the owners, where it is convenient to park cars or buses, and near to where the animals are slaughtered.[77]

Decision making and implementation have also become more bureaucratic. The long established Association of Reindeer Herding Cooperatives, now located in Rovaniemi, is today partly funded by the Finnish government, and continues to manage and promote reindeer husbandry in Finland on the basis of the fourteen districts and fifty-six cooperatives that compose it. It also publishes the Finnish journal *Poromies* (Reindeer Herder), with information on a wide variety of relevant subjects useful to its readership.[78]

Important changes also occurred with respect to reindeer herding in Finland in 1969, when a new law regarding the homesteads of herders was introduced to facilitate modernisation. This provision was subsequently built upon in 1994 with the 'Law on Nature-Based Occupations', which was passed to further encourage the Sámi's livelihood and their traditional way of life. As a result, the construction of houses—usually modernist bungalows—in isolated and remote areas was encouraged. At the same time, paradoxically, the implementation of Finnish models of municipal planning led to the breakdown of homogeneous Sámi communities, fostering instead a concept of the village based on bringing together Sámi people from what had previously been a variety of diverse *siida* backgrounds. For example, what had been two different winter villages were brought together at the large hill of Sakkaravaara, near Karesuando.[79]

By the beginning of the third millennium, there were four reindeer-herding cooperatives in the vicinity of Vätsäri, Näätämö, Paatsjoki and Ivalo. The economic importance they had for the local Sámi was considerable since some thirty households received a major part of their income from their activities. Fishing of course continued to play a small role in Sámi livelihoods, albeit not on a commercial level, along with berry picking, which although also had a primarily domestic purpose, did provide an income for about eighty local people.[80]

Collectivisation on the Kola Peninsula

During the 1920s the Soviet government introduced the so-called 'New Economic Policy' which, although it allowed certain capitalist features to re-enter the economy, nonetheless obliged the collectivisation of the Sámi on the Kola Peninsula, as of other indigenous peoples, and the setting up of cooperatives. The first of these was agricultural and was established in 1927. Later, after the adoption of Stalin's First Five Year Plan, Ribkoop, a fishing cooperative, was set up at Lovozero in 1931. It proved without doubt the most successful of such ventures, and in contrast to others in the region, it continues in this function to this day. Four other cooperatives were also set up at Ponoi and Jokanga. These cooperatives collectivised reindeer herding, although the reindeer themselves, as well as the equipment needed for their herding, remained privately owned. Yet the growing reliance of herders on the provision of reindeer by the government, which was reluctant to enrich privately owned herds, led to a weak response, thereby damaging the productivity and quality of the herding. Thus the establishment of *kolkhoz* (collective farms) in Lovozero in 1928, for both Sámi and Komi reindeer herders, signalled the end of a traditional herding system that was already in terminal decline. Adrian Ionovich Gerasimov, a former student at the Northern Peoples' Institute, in Leningrad, was now appointed to supervise the collectivisation of reindeer herding among the Sámi. He was also appointed vice chairman of the Kolkhoz League of Kola-Lapp Commune.[81]

The first official reindeer *kolkhoz* in the Kola Peninsula was established in 1929 at Kamensk, in the vicinity of the former Resurrection Monastery.[82] The Lapp *kolkhoz* was founded at Lovozero[83] and several opened elsewhere, one notably at Semiostrovy, in the eastern part of the Kola Peninsula. At first named Olenovod (The Reindeer Herder), it later acquired a name more suitable to its new political orientation and natural geography: Krasnaya Tundra (Red Tundra). One of the largest, it had at least 2,000 head of reindeer, divided into two herds, which straddled the Zapadnaya (Western) Litsa River that separated them.[84]

Barter, rather than cash, had by now become one of the principal forms of exchange. Moreover, from 1929 a newly established voluntary reindeer herding association, Lopari, began to represent all the reindeer-herding peoples of the north-west of Russia, based in Lovozero, including not only the Sámi but also the Komi, Nenets and Russian herders.

Yet shortly thereafter, it too was collectivised and more succinctly renamed Tundra.[85] By contrast with the large reindeer herds of the Komi, which gave them a full-time occupation in the region encouraged by the Soviet authorities, Sámi herds were small and seasonal.[86]

Some Sámi, like the Kamenka, particularly suffered from the imposition of the new cooperative system, since rich families like the Matryokhin, some of whom managed to survive the Soviet period, were dispossessed of their large herds, augmented over several hundred years, in the east of the Kola Peninsula by the coastal settlement of Lumbovka.[87]

By the time of its heyday in 1940, therefore, there were some eleven reindeer-herding *kolkhoz* functioning on the Kola Peninsula. Their herds were larger than had traditionally been the case, often containing 2,000 to 3,000 reindeer each. So-called brigades, composed of eight to twelve men, herded them all year round, but it was the Komi rather than Sámi tradition, that now dominated, because the authorities were convinced that the Komi were less sullied by foreign contacts and more committed to the Soviet system.[88]

Closure of Collective Farms of the Kola Peninsula

As with so much in the Soviet Union, the nightmare reality of what was created did not correspond to the ideological propaganda about the benefits the communist system propagated. Thus, by the 1950s, it had already become clear to many that the collectivisation of reindeer herding had brought about its ruination. Its ecology was poor and the grazing grounds required by the reindeer for sustenance had become severely depleted. Only seasonal herding could now be maintained with any productivity and that was only achieved by reintroducing a modest level of private reindeer ownership. Even Sámi fishing languished, although it eventually made a slow recovery, as did reindeer herding from the 1960s onwards, when a renewed capitalisation occurred, albeit at the expense of a growing centralisation and concentration of the *kolkhoz*. This, however, had dire social consequences since many Sámi villages were now emptied and the small *kolkhoz* were gobbled up by the large ones. For example, Krasnaya Tundra was united with Krasnoshelye, creating the new and powerful Pamyat Lenina (Lenin's Memorial) *kolkhoz*. This led to the marginalisation of large numbers of Sámi reindeer herders, who increasingly abandoned their traditional occupations to take up industrial work in the cities and towns of the Kola Peninsula or were forced into other lines of employment in the bleak, poorly constructed dormitory towns that places like Lovozero had become.[89] This process had commenced in the 1970s, when large blocks of tenement flats were built, accommodating some 70 per cent of the population of the town by 1980. Moreover, this social engineering was further strengthened by new living regulations promulgated by the Soviet authorities that forced the Sámi to reside in the four main towns and villages of the region, Lovozero, Krasnoshelye, Jona and Tuloma, all of which had become centres of cattle husbandry and agriculture, now fostered on the Kola Peninsula.[90]

With the complete integration of these *kolkhoz* into the state farm system of the 1970s, the future of the Sámi with respect to reindeer herding seemed dismal. However, the growth of an unofficial modest market-based economy led to the creation of a more successful 'community economy' in which barter and reciprocity were of greater importance than was previously the case even during the early Soviet period.[91] Nonetheless, by 1989 there were only seventy-four Sámi on the Kola Peninsula who continued to work as reindeer herders and Lovozero had truly become a 'dormitory town' for sedentary urban workers, rather than a winter home of Sámi herders.[92]

With the collapse of the Soviet Union and Russia's transformation into a full market economy during the early 1990s, however, a brighter future seemed to be on the horizon for the Sámi. Old traditions were revived and old names were retaken: the old *sovkhoz* at Krasnoshelye once again became known as 'The Reindeer Herder'. More importantly, the herders now became shareholders in the newly established market cooperatives. Some level of bartering remained, but money now became the primary means of exchange.[93] On the other hand, during the lawless period of the mid- and late 1990s, crime, as elsewhere in the former Soviet Union, increased dramatically, and even reindeer herds suffered from criminality, especially the theft of their animals and equipment.[94]

Reindeer Herding and the Growing Conflict with Ecologists

In the Nordic countries, despite the better developed ecological and technological infrastructure, other forms of conflict were coming to the fore. For example, in an interview in the newspaper *Altaposten* (4 June 1997), Kurt Oddekalv, the leader of Norges Miljøvernforbund

(Norway's Environment Association), claimed that he was prepared to prosecute reindeer herders, accusing them of allowing a substantial number of reindeer to starve to death during the extremely cold and snowy winter of 1996-7. He not only said it was a myth that the Sámi reindeer herders were living in harmony with nature, but also argued that their approach to the modernisation of the reindeer-herding industry was destroying the tundra of Finnmark itself. In consequence of such accusations, and the rise of an ever more vociferous Green movement, the Sámi—who saw themselves as the indigenous caretakers of their homeland—found themselves accused of destroying it. Despite their protests, these circumstances have often led to the implementation of political initiatives from central government which have used these 'justifications for the preservation of Mother Earth' to limit the number of reindeer herders altogether.[95]

Other sources of conflict exist within the Sámi community itself. For example, after the Sámi Rights Commission suggested the re-establishment of a reindeer-herding *siida* among the Skolt Sámi, based on old Skolt reindeer-herding traditions (described by the Finnish ethnographer Väinö Tanner in 1929, see Chapter One, p.53) that were no longer followed in Norway, other Sámi groups protested because this entailed the establishment of small herds under collective ownership, rather than large herds owned by individuals, which would be worked more intensively than previously. Others objected to the reintroduction of processes like the milking of reindeer and their use for transport, which had long since fallen into abeyance. While these revived activities might foster a growth in tourism, with visitors keen to experience and see the 'traditional Sámi reindeer herding way of life', the critics complained that the Sámi of today who were already utilising the pastures for their herding, assisted by modern technology, would be put out of business. 'Sámi heritage' would thus become an artificially created monoculture, in conflict with the 'real life' needs and values of the modern world.[96]

In Sweden, where the Ruota Sámiid Riikkasearvi (National Union of the Swedish Sámi), based in Jokkmokk, has played an important role in administering and regulating reindeer herding since 1950, conflicts were more muted. It has also supported a wide range of legal actions in support of Sámi interests. Of particular note in this context was the fifteen-year court case it undertook in the pursuance of Sámi land rights in northern Jämtland, a judicial landmark in the sense that the

Sámi now had a political voice, despite the fact that the Supreme Court of Sweden eventually issued a judgement which supported the land claims of others over those of the Sámi.[97]

Agriculture and Animal Husbandry

Agriculture and settled farming arrived in the north of Fenno-Scandinavia in the first half of the first millennium, but as late as the early Iron Age, towards the end of the fourth century AD, they were carried on only in the outer coastal areas. Analyses of pollen confirm that farming, in particular the cultivation of barley, was particularly extensive by the sixth century. However, in the following century many farms in the region came to be abandoned. Yet in centres of political power like Borg on Vestvågøy they carried on and, in the inner fjord vicinities of Ibestad and Arstad, were even extended.[98]

By the late Middle Ages, the Sámi of northern Norway had probably become familiar with the raising of sheep, goats and cattle from their Norwegian neighbours, settled on nearby islands and fjords, since as far back as the early Viking Age, as loan words in Sámi concerning animal husbandry evince.[99] Agriculture had meanwhile become firmly established in Varangerfjord by the end of the seventeenth century.[100]

In Finnish Lapland animal husbandry had also become firmly established by the sixteenth century, in part through the arrival of Finnish colonists. In 1571, one Antti Niilonpoika had at least fourteen cows, more than anyone else in the vicinity of Rovaniemi. Eighteen others had between five and ten each.[101] Certainly, by the seventeenth century, the increasing stream of Finnish settlers arriving in the Sámi homeland fostered the extension of such animal husbandry.[102] Indeed, thereafter, the practice of both agriculture and animal husbandry began to spread, in growing waves from the south, first reaching the southernmost Sámi *siidas* by the early 1700s.[103] Some Sámi now began to take up farming and animal husbandry themselves, in particular along the Alta and Kautokeino rivers in Norway and the Teno, Utsjoki, Inari and Karasjok rivers in Finland. Documents confirm that Juhani Aikio, a Sámi originally from Enontekiö, was the first to start farming in Inari, at Muddusniemi, to which he introduced cattle in 1745. Henrik Kyrö came from Kittilä but established his farm at Kyrö, on the Ivalo River, in 1758, while Iisak Paadar, from Inari, took up farming on the Vaskojoki River that same year. This transition was facilitated by the granting of tax-free years by central government. A new law of 1762 enabled the taxes paid by the Sámi to be deducted from the collective *siida* tax to which they belonged.

Yet as Acerbi noted, the practice of agriculture, at least in the Norwegian part of Sápmi, was poor.

No horses are employed in West Finmark, the labour everywhere else performed by those useful animals, being there done by men. In this respect the mountain Laplanders are better accommodated, as they use their rein-deer for that purpose. Since agriculture is not attended to, except on some few spots near the river Alten, the Laplanders consume by fire all the dung collected from their cows, sheep and goats.[104]

Taxation with respect to agriculture also persisted, but only after this had become worthless for the government towards the end of the nineteenth century did the debate over its abolition begin (the taxation was finally abolished in 1925).[105] The Skolt Sámi were raising sheep at the latest by the 1920s, but by then animal husbandry was undergoing a series of expansions and contractions, with some Skolt Sámi raising sheep at Nellim in the 1950s.[106]

Crop Innovations

Agriculture continued to prosper in the early eighteenth century but with only modest degrees of success. The introduction of potatoes in the Sámi homeland was quite late compared to the rest of the Nordic countries, if not Russia, and proved to be a mixed blessing. In 1830 the Oulu Household Association of Ostrobothnia introduced the potato, distributing it among the inhabitants of Inari as part of a government initiative. Shovels and hoes were also provided, and guidance given on how best to cultivate the crop. The plough was introduced fifteen years later and farmers were encouraged to sow turnips and barley, too. Unfortunately, the climatic conditions were hardly suitable and frost frequently wiped out the crops. Nonetheless, attempts to develop agriculture continued and in 1877 a model farm, Toivoniemi (Hope Peninsula), was established at Uulankotaniemi by the mouth of the Kaamasjoki River, under the initiative of the local chief of police Xenofon Nordling. Clergymen, often Sámi themselves, also played a role in its fostering, and among the first to cultivate land in Utsjoki were the Helanders and Högmans, families of Lutheran priests, who, along with the catechism, taught their flock about the latest agricultural innovations of which they were aware as they travelled around the countryside.[107]

In the 1920s, the first associations of small farm-holders were founded which took an interest in all aspects of agriculture and animal husbandry. The overwhelming majority of farms remained small. By the 1950s and 1960s, the average field size was no more than 2.4 hectares, out of a total of some 400 hectares of fields in cultivation divided up among 150 farmers who often engaged in other forms of livelihood as well. Thus many Sámi people continue to derive income from making boats, sleighs and skis, increasingly popular throughout the region in the tourist industry.[108] Spring was the time to build boats, whether of skin or wood, before they were used in the summer.[109]

Horses

Horses were a rarity in the Sámi homeland until well into the modern period, but by the eighteenth century they had become fairly common in the largest town of Finnish Lapland, Rovaniemi. Enbuske has recorded that there were twenty-one horses in the town and over five times that number—124—in the whole of the parish in 1786–90.[110] This compares with a total human population in Rovaniemi of 1,421 in 1800, a number which almost doubled to 2,208 by 1840 and had again risen to 18,324 by 1900.[111] But Rovaniemi was now a Finnish, rather than a Sámi, town.[112]

Further north in Sápmi, however, horses continued to be a rarity. For example, the visiting Frenchman Count Goblet d'Alviella observed that there were no horses at all at Kautokeino in 1868.[113] Yet by the twentieth century, they had become almost ubiquitous throughout the Sámi homeland.[114] By 1905, there were some forty-two horses (and 503 cows) among the Inari Sámi and their numbers continued to burgeon.[115] Thus by 1930 there were 123 horses and 513 cows belonging to the Inari Sámi.[116] By the turn of the twentieth century, horses had become thoroughly commonplace in Rovaniemi, reaching their highest number by around 1910—some 1,223 horses. However, with the advent of motorised transport over the following decades, their numbers declined slightly to 1,175 by 1930.[117]

Cattle, Sheep and Goats

Cows had also become a more common animal, although reindeer herds of course predominated.[118] Although the Inari Sámi had only twenty horses and eighty cows in 1855, these numbers increased dramatically over the following ten years and by 1865 had grown to twenty-one horses and 205 cows.[119]

In the mid-1700s seven houses in Utsjoki maintained cattle and sheep. That said, it was first in the 1820s, in the Teno Valley, that animal husbandry became more lucrative, when butter and other dairy produce were exported significantly to the copper miners in Alta. Here, too, reindeer herding continued to be central to the life of the Sámi, but flocks of sheep were also maintained and played an important economic role for them until at least the 1850s. Thereafter, however, cattle became more important. Whereas, in 1870, there were 392 in Inari, by 1900 there were no less than 594 cattle there and, at Utsjoki, in 1897 some forty cattle. Indeed, within the first decade of the following century, agriculture and cattle husbandry were even introduced in the Teno Valley, which was previously largely devoid of such activities.[120]

Over the following decades cattle husbandry increased still further, with the first cattle show in the region being held in Utsjoki in 1935. However, by the 1950s and 1960s, the number of cattle had fallen to 350, though 500 to 600 sheep were also kept.[121]

Additionally, many Sámi households kept three or four goats for their milk, at least from the 1800s up to the 1950s. During the summer, the reindeer-herding Sámi tended their goats themselves. However, during the other months, when they were in migration looking for pastures for their reindeer, the goats were given out to small farm-holders to look after.[122]

During the immediate post-war period agriculture in Finnish Lapland languished. Animal husbandry particularly suffered, as the traditional Sámi cow was increasingly displaced by larger imported types. However, in the following decades, at least until the 1970s, agriculture again became viable, albeit in a different way from before, since dairy farming involving cows and goats assumed a new-found importance, along with the production of meat from beef cattle and lambs. State subsidies allowed for major infrastructural improvements, not least of which was a new macadam road to Utsjoki in the 1960s. Henceforth, the leading dairy producing firm Valio began to export milk through Finland. Other types of farming also became more capital intensive, unfortunately undermining the traditional small landholders in the process. Thus, in the longer term, the age-old agriculture of the region was undermined, rather than encouraged,[123] although new farms were set up in Finnish Lapland during the second half of the 1970s, including eighty-five in the Sevettijärvi, Keväjärvi and Nellim districts.[124] By 2002 there were only 200 purebred Lapland cows used for breeding purposes. However, subsidies are now provided to encourage the raising of these cattle.[125]

Today, agriculture and animal husbandry in the Sámi homeland are based on potatoes, growing hay for cattle fodder, dairy produce, in particular cow's milk, and meat processing. However, its profitability is still low, not only for climatic reasons but for economic ones as well—animal husbandry requires a substantial capital outlay and is highly vulnerable to a range of threats, biological and market-based. It is a full-time occupation and no longer part of 'an economy of multiple livelihoods'.[126] In consequence, like much of the European agricultural industry, it requires massive state subsidies. On the Swedish–Finnish border, animal husbandry is largely confined to about fifty cattle farms on the Teno River (five are on the Finnish side), along the lower course of the Inari River, and in the valley of the Utsjoki River.[127]

Fishing

In 1555 Olaus Magnus wrote that fishing was a mainstay of the Sámi, and this remained equally true long thereafter.[128] In the Lule Sámi area of Sweden, in the vicinity of Sjokksjokk, fishing was the most important livelihood for the Sámi from about 1550 to 1750, by contrast with the district around Kaitum, where semi-nomadism was more widespread. However, even there reindeer herding was still only a complement to fishing and hunting.[129]

The fish caught varied from locality to locality. Salmon fishing was, until the second quarter of the eighteenth century, important at Teno. More than one *siida* exploited these resources, which in Teno were utilised by the Sámi of Utsjoki and Vestertana.[130]

As the visitor Wilhelm Böhtlingk put it in 1839, using the term 'Finn' for the Sámi:

The right to sell the fish one caught to whoever one wished belonged to the Finns only a few weeks a year, for all the rest of the time, they must resign their catch to the Norwegian merchants, who possess a monopoly of trade and therefore also in part to determine the price of fish. The Finns also practice animal husbandry and, along with their reindeer, which they utilise for travel and clothing, even maintain cows and sheep. Their winter feed distinguishes itself from that of the reindeer by a broth of boiled fish heads which is poured over the reindeer moss.[131]

Fishing was a mainstay of the Coastal Sámi, but it was also highly important in the heartland of the Sámi homeland around Lake Inari, Finland's third largest lake, some 1,153 square kilometres in extent. Far to the south, along the North Bothnian coast, fishing records from 1639 in Kemi Lapland give insight into the Sámi tradition there of fishing with a seine, a method used throughout the year and which was especially productive in exploiting the rich fish resources under the ice in winter. It also records the Sámi as fishing with hooks, at that time made of juniper, which proved especially useful for catching burbot. Documents also show that by the 1860s hooks and lines were employed to catch trout as well. Partly in consequence of this, as well as the introduction of more efficient gill nets, the older form of seine fishing had considerably declined by the 1910s. Indeed, by the end of the 1920s, seine fishing in enclosed waters ceased altogether. However, from the 1930s large open-water seines and whitefish trap nets and fyke nets were introduced there by deep sea fishermen, but in 1951 the unsustainable exploitation of fishing stocks led to the introduction of a law restricting the use of these nets. Instead, by the 1950s, surface gill nets had come to be popularly employed. By then a far more dramatic intrusion had occurred with respect to Lake Inari than the use of seines and traps, for during the 1940s, a major hydro-electric power plant had been built on the Paatsjoki River, which severely lowered local water levels. This in turn led to a sharp reduction in fish stocks, particularly those of whitefish which spawn in the autumn, since the spawning areas were no longer under water. As a result, members of commercial fishermen on the lake decreased from 139 in the early 1950s to half that number in only two decades. By the early 1980s, there were less than fifty.[132]

Yet not everything on the horizon was bleak with respect to fishing, because the accidental introduction of vendace into Lake Inari in the 1980s proved to be a major boon, as stocks increased naturally. This benefit was offset at the same time, however, by intensive trawling and the reintroduction of winter fishing with seines. Unsurprisingly, therefore, vendace stock suffered severe depletion in just a few years.[133] Since the Sámi were, of course, not the only ethnic group who enjoyed fishing rights, and as they often hired these rights out or sold them,

241

competition for the limited resources remained high, which also had a negative impact on the fishing stocks.[134]

In Russia, the Kola Sámi who resided near the mouth of the Kharlovka River were chiefly occupied with salmon fishing.[135] Off the coasts of the Kola Peninsula, where the stocks were richer than further west off Norway, confrontation between Russia and its Nordic neighbour for the fish could be quite sharp. During the 1860s, Norwegian fishermen made many incursions into Russian waters in pursuit of cod, which forced the governor of Arkhangelsk, under whose authority the Kola Peninsula was then subsumed, to complain to the tsar. In reaction, Alexander II issued a decree providing new settlers in the region, whether Russian or foreign, with a six-year tax exemption, among other privileges and benefits, so as to reinforce Russian imperial territorial claims.[136] Development followed, and immediately prior to the revolution such places as Teriberka had become significant settlements, with a church, a post office and telegraph. The Russian hydrologist Knipovich, who surveyed the coasts of the Barents Sea at the turn of the twentieth century, commented on its burgeoning mercantile development, mentioning that it even traded directly with businesses not only in St Petersburg and Moscow, but in Hamburg as well. After the Russian Civil War Teriberka went on to become the site of Russian Lapland's first collective fishing station in the 1920s. It later became a major base for Norwegian as well as Russian trawler fleets. However, since the fall of the Soviet Union it has been completely abandoned.[137]

The main fishing activities of the Skolt Sámi were, of course, not only carried on inland but on the Atlantic and Arctic coasts as well. Those residing in Norway migrated to the vicinity of Kiberg on the northern coast of the Varangerfjord, where they traditionally took up seasonal residence in huts of sod and used their gill nets and seines to catch not only salmon, their mainstay, but herring and coalfish as well. Then, in the early summer, when the ice broke up on the larger inland lakes and rivers, they returned inland with their drift nets.[138] Driftnet and dragnet fishing were generally carried out by more than one Sámi *siida*.[139] However, these types of fishing were prohibited in Norway in 1872–3, along with spear fishing, which was carried out in the autumn, just before the ice formed. This method used nets which would extend across the whole width of the river and drifted with the current to catch the salmon upstream shortly after the break-up of the ice, though in the past it could also take place at other times of the year. Today its use has been restricted to limited periods in the spring and only one boat is permitted to take part.[140] By the autumn, whitefish became an important catch and, to a lesser degree, pike and perch. The fishing methods employed by the Sámi at the Skoltefossen Falls in Neiden were unusual in that they entailed throwing light seines into the falls in the places where salmon rested while migrating upstream. There, at the Padun Falls on the Tuulomajoki River, located on the territory of the Notozero *siida*, the Sámi had constructed a great salmon weir which was used not only by this *siida* but others as well. The best of the salmon catch was then sold on to merchants, with the less valuable stock used for local consumption by the Skolt Sámi themselves or their flocks of sheep. That which had not been consumed by the autumn was then salted or dried and kept for the winter. Fishing on Lake Ala-Akkajärvi, a popular summer site for the Sámi, has in recent years been protected by the introduction of a quota of three fish per day per person in order to help preserve the fish stock.[141]

A Historical View of Fishing among the Tana Sámi

A closer focus on the Tana Valley provides a microcosm of changes in the fishing habits of the Sámi over the last two centuries. Fishing weirs played an important role in inland Sámi fishing and took a variety of forms. The most usual were cross weirs, like that at Outakoski at Nuorpiniemi Point in Finland, which transects the river. These facilitated the collection of fish in fish bags (i.e. natural pools) located downstream, where the fish could be killed by stoning or bludgeoning with poles. Such weirs were constructed and utilised by cooperatives, some of which had as many as forty members. The weir was used for almost 100 years, from the 1770s to the 1860s. However, their use was subsequently forbidden in Norway in 1872 and then in Finland in 1873. There were also other types of weirs, including the kick weir—which is still in use, and in which the vertical poles or trestles form the barrier (today they tend to be made of iron) and run contrary to the current, the fish being caught downstream in sack-like nets several metres in length—and the trap weir, the last example of which was utilised on the lowest of the Yläköngäs Rapids until 1949.[142]

King Charles IX of Sweden commissioned the building of weirs on both the Teno and Alta Rivers as early as 1596. Documents from the years following confirm that they were in use on the Teno River by

1607 and that the Mountain Sámi had been obliged to pay the Crown a tithe of their income from the sale of salmon in 1629. Another document, from 1638, makes clear that the reindeer-herding Sámi of Utsjoki, Outakoski and Ávjovárri, as well as some Inari Sámi, fished for salmon on the Teno River in summer. With so many different Sámi groups, taxable by the various states which had dominion over Sápmi, a treaty was clearly needed to keep conflicts to a minimum. The Strömstad Border Treaty was thus enacted in 1773 which gave the rights to fish salmon to the Sámi on different sides of the border. In the following century, other local residents were also given fishing rights which entailed the use of private weirs, but their joint fishing rights were not enforced. In consequence, the quantity of fish caught increased. Whereas in the 1700s at least 100 barrels of salmon were caught yearly in the Teno River, by the 1920s this quantity had increased dramatically from 500 to 1,000 barrels in the same period. Half of this was freshly consumed during the summer and half was dried or salted for winter use. Among the Tana Sámi, during the 1800s, cross weirs, torch-fishing, and goldin or seine fishing were the methods employed to maximise the catch of fish on the Teno River. However, by the second half of the century the need for more stringent fishing regulations was realised: in 1873 various restrictions were imposed and the use of cross weirs, goldin fishing and torch-fishing now came to be forbidden.[143]

During the middle decades of the nineteenth century, a form of touristic fishing flourished along the Teno River, beginning about 1840. The English aristocrats who introduced this new method of salmon fishing proved so successful in catching fish that their method was adopted by the Sámi themselves, as Aage Solbakk, in 'The Salmon Lords', makes clear.[144]

Fishing in the Teno Valley went hand in hand with the development and spread of agriculture. Both brought in considerable prosperity and provided considerable taxable resources. In the course of the twentieth century, methods changed again and, whereas in the past gill net fishing was the most common method, by the later twentieth century rod and reel fishing predominated. Indeed, less than half of the salmon currently caught are obtained by the older methods, and the materials used as tackle have changed: formerly the gill nets were made of hemp, but in the post-Second World War period they are generally made of synthetic fibres. Fishing rods have also changed; whereas formerly they were made of wood or bamboo, they are now constructed of fibreglass or carbon fibre. As for the reels, previously of simple, wooden club-shaped form, wound with hemp, they are now 'high-tech' devices with ball-bearings.[145]

Fishing in the Teno Valley in the Late Twentieth Century

As a result of these and other innovations, some 50 tonnes of salmon have been caught on average each year during the last few decades. In Finland, 70 tonnes were caught in just one year (during the 1970s) and 180 tonnes in Norway, largely because of the use of drift nets at sea. Unfortunately, this overstretch severely depleted fish stocks; by 1979 the Finnish catch had fallen to only 25 tonnes and the Norwegian to 50 tonnes. At sea, because of the use of drift nets, the overexploitation of fish stocks was colossal: whereas 2,000 kilos of salmon had been caught in 1975, this figure had multiplied two hundred fold to an extraordinary 218,000 tonnes by 1981, 40 per cent of which was caught by tourists. Not surprisingly, the size of the salmon that are caught has also diminished significantly.[146]

Other problems have also arisen. With the establishment there of wild salmon and salmon farms cheek by jowl, there is the possibility that the highly sought after wild Teno salmon might interbreed with the farmed ones or become infected by farm-associated pathologies, such as anaemia, pancreatic necrosis, kidney disease and furunculosis. These have already struck fish farms on the coast of Norway. The salmon parasite *Gyrodactylus salaries* has already wiped out more than thirty salmon rivers there and has appeared elsewhere in the Sámi homeland in both Finland and Russia. To deal with contemporary issues relating to the salmon-fishing industry Norway and Finland agreed to regulate it and, in 1993, the Finnish Game and Fisheries Research Institute established a milt bank to insure the preservation of the salmon stock of the Teno River in the event of an ecological disaster.[147]

Other methods of fishing included long-line fishing, prohibited since the 1800s, and torch fishing, banned since the 1950s. This latter method, utilised in the late autumn, focused on the salmon that were spawning in shallow waters. The fishermen built a fire out of resinous pinewood on a grid at the prow of the boat or placed a petroleum lamp there that attracted the fish, which were then killed by fish spears. Finally, there was the grayling board which, with a fishing line and flies or shrimps attached, floated freely from the one end held on shore. This method was prohibited in 1960 because of the damage it did to the fish's mouths. However, traditional burbot fishing through a hole in the ice is still carried out on the Teno River in winter. Trolling for salmon is also still permitted, albeit with strict regulations regarding the days in the week and the hours in the day when it can be carried out.[148]

This was not the case with the goldin method of fishing. With a tradition of over 200 years, its use among the Sámi was first recorded in 1751 in the form of a complaint: the Sámi of Karasjok, Ávjovárri and Inari lamented that certain people from Utsjoki had employed the technique, closing the mouth of the Inari River and using a seine across the river above the Teno cross weir. This resulted in bottling up of the salmon which could no longer migrate upriver. Nonetheless, the practice continued legally at least until it was prohibited in 1873, and it continued well beyond that illegally at night at least until the 1950s. (Even a local police chief was known to have engaged in the activity.) This form of fishing involved the construction of two cross weirs divided by a space of from a few hundred metres to 40 kilometres. A downstream weir was then left open for several days to admit the fish before it was closed, enabling the salmon to be caught. The Sámi term for the seine was *goldda*. Weights prevented it from drifting, so, along with the tackle, it had to be pulled downstream.[149]

Barter, rather than money, also sometimes characterised Sámi fishing. Indeed, in the nineteenth century the Sámi were often paid for their fish with alcoholic beverages. During his visit to Lapland in the summer of 1820 the English traveller Sir Arthur de Cappell Brooke noted that Norwegian fishermen from Helgeland were:

actively employed in exchanging the produce of their fishery with the Russians for flour, which they carried with them to the south; and the Laplander was no less eager in parting with his fish in exchange for brandy.[150]

Indeed, even as late as the 1930s in Sweden, along with their subsidiary rights to fish and hunt, went the perquisites of taking wood for fires and building materials.[151]

Boats and Shipping

The Coastal Sámi people had learned how to build sea worthy sail boats from their Nordic neighbours by the first millennium AD, and by the turn of the second millennium they were even selling them to others. As the researchers Borgos and Torgvaer have suggested, the

Sámi may have been the first to employ the typical 'Nordland' boat which ploughed these northern seas for almost 1,000 years, as late as the early twentieth century.[152] Mulk and Bayliss-Smith have noted that these boats were characterised by a single mid-ship mast, a square sail, and six or seven oars per side, and were open from end to end, with high stem and stern posts. Moreover, they have pointed out that only the novel feature of the stern-rudder distinguishes the twentieth-century Nordland boats from the ancient stone depictions found at the archaeological site of Badjelánnda. The excavation of nine boats from the seventh to the nineteenth century seems to confirm this view.[153]

Wood from the local pine forests was used by the Coastal Sámi for their boats. The boats were made through the use of so-called 'clinker construction', accomplished without the use of nails, in which willow roots were used to sew the planks together.[154] According to the Norse epic *Heimskringla* of Snorre Sturlason (AD 1138–9), the Norse chief on Hinnøya, at his base 100 kilometres to the north of Tysfjord, purchased two boats which were made during the winter months by Sámi living by Gljuvrafjord. They accommodated twenty-four oarsmen, twelve on each side.[155] One such boat has been excavated at Bårset from Nord-Kvaløy, Troms, and appears to have been made around the year 700.[156]

Mercantile Activity

In the far north-west of Russia Arkhangelsk and Kholmogory—birthplace of the early eighteenth-century Russian scientist and academician Mikhail Lomonosov—were the hubs of economic and mercantile activity. As the writer Maureen Perrie has put it:

In fact Archangel's seventy shops in the 1620s (not counting the trading spaces in the merchants' bazaar) and limited number of trades contrast poorly with nearby Kholmogory which had 316 shops and a much wider variety of craft activities. The latter was the true centre of the region for local commerce.[157]

Much of the trade carried out on the Arctic and the White Sea coasts involved the Russian Pomors (i.e. coastal fisherman—the word signifies people living 'on the sea'), who sailed to the coast of Finnmark in northern Norway and beyond to buy fish and to sell a wide variety of goods. However, a significant amount of trade was also carried out by the Sámi. The Inari Sámi were especially active in Karlebotn, by the mouth of Varangerfjord, after the latter trading post was re-established following a seventy-year interval in 1831. New trading agreements between Russia and Norway in 1838 served to facilitate trade, since they enabled the Inari Sámi to import goods from Norway without paying duty. As trade expanded during the later nineteenth century, the Norwegian trading post of Bugöyfjord, in Finnmark, became one of the most important in the region.[158]

Industry

Sámi industry is as ancient as its material culture. Early stone tools have been found from 2000 BC, while slate, quartz, quartzite and asbestos, which were used for a variety of different purposes, were mined in such mountains areas as Badjelánnda.[159]

Factory-based industrial production in Sápmi began in the early modern period. One of the first industrial enterprises, sawmills, arrived in the late eighteenth century.[160] Potash production in Lapland followed in the early 1830s,[161] and was only one of the reasons why Læstadius claimed that Lapland was a land of considerable economic opportunity rather than being the wasteland of popular perception.[162] Indeed, Læstadius encouraged the government to provide financial assistance for its development, which led to even further immigration from the south, a process some have described as a form of *de facto* colonisation.[163] In Russian Lapland, factory industry arrived much later in the nineteenth century when workers were employed in Lovozero at I.N. Terentyev's small factory.[164] The conditions under which they worked in all of the Sámi homeland were poor, and in 1931 five workers from a timber mill in Ångermanland in Sweden—the so-called 'Ådalen martyrs'—were shot by soldiers suppressing a strike over wages.[165]

Transport Development

From the transitional period of reindeer pastoralism—indeed, in some instances, from prehistoric times—the Sámi transported themselves in their migrations by the use of sledges and domesticated reindeer which served as pack animals. Reindeer facilitated the transport of food and skins from the hunting grounds down river valleys and back to the winter settlements, made easier once the ground was covered by snow during the autumn migration.[166]

From time immemorial ships and boats had been of the greatest importance in linking the Sámi homeland to Western and Central

Europe, but a closer and more modern connection was established in the 1860s, when a weekly postal service by ship was established in the north of Norway, between Vadsö and Hammerfest.[167] Henceforth, access to the region was made not only rapid but regular. Yet by far the most exotic form of transport to arrive in Sápmi was the hot air balloon used during the visit of the English mineralogist and Cambridge academic Edward Daniel Clarke in 1789 to Enontekiö, in Finnish Lapland.[168]

Of great importance, in practical terms, was the arrival of the first freight train to Rovaniemi, which began service in August 1909.[169] This service allowed passengers and goods from the south to be transported at ease to the rest of Finland and to the harbours of the gulfs of Bothnia and Finland, a role which it retains to this day. Other novel developments followed. In Ivalo, for example, a ferry made of logs was introduced to provide transit across the Ivalojoki River during the 1910s.[170] Thus with access facilitated to the far north of Sápmi, various forms of urban development began to gather pace. One place to benefit was Inari, by the mouth of the Juutua River, where municipal offices, a gaol, a shop, a pharmacy, a hospital, a doctor's medical station and a school dormitory were rapidly built.[171] The construction of an astronomical observatory in Rovaniemi was also undertaken in 1910 and began to function in 1914.[172]

Although the first motor cars arrived in Varanger in the 1890s, they only really began to make a permanent appearance in the region in the 1910s, despite the paucity of suitable roads. That same decade also saw the introduction of motor boats along the Arctic coast. Inland, however, their introduction was delayed: they were first used in the Teno Valley during the 1930s.[173]

The number of cars subsequently multiplied as the network of roads improved, and by the second half of the 1940s they had become quite common in the Nordic part of Sápmi. Tractors were also introduced around the same time, and they soon became generally utilised throughout the region, in particular in the Teno Valley. Of particular importance were snow tractors, manufactured by the Canadian company Bombardier which had been developing them since the 1920s, and which now enabled snow bound villages to be easily reached.[174] Motorboats also began to ply the waterways of Inari, providing an efficient postal service during the warmer months.[175]

Industrial Development in Soviet Lapland

In the 1880s the geologist Wilhelm Ramsay (1865–1928), whose family had originally come to Finland from Scotland, had discovered that the Khibiny and Lovozero massifs, on the Kola Peninsula in Russian Lapland, were rich in minerals. The Northern Science Research Expedition of the All-Russia Council for the National Economy organised by the Russian-German geologist and chemist Aleksandr Yevgenevich Fersman, accompanied by eleven female researchers, visited the area in August and September 1920. It was then that two of Fersman's colleagues discovered major deposits of apatite, an important source of phosphate for fertiliser, for which Morocco had previously been the principal source. This led to the development of the Khibiny mines in 1926, the first of many such industrial developments in the region which, for all their practical usefulness to the Soviets, had dire consequences for the Sámi. Some of the Soviet Union's most eminent scientists and engineers joined the project and a college-like lodge was erected there, called 'Tietta', provided with a study centre, library, cafeteria and ancillary accommodation. As Sergey Mironovich Kirov, first secretary of the Leningrad Communist Party, expressed it in 1930, ignoring the existence of the Sámi altogether, 'This severe, barren, useless, northern wilderness has emerged in reality as one of the richest.'[176]

Meanwhile, the construction of the Murmansk Railway had been completed in 1916 and this aided the development of mining which sought to exploit the recent discovery of copper and nickel deposits at Monchegorsk, now notorious for the ecological disaster which turned its environs into a blackened moonscape. Modern technology and motorisation also encouraged the expansion of the Murmansk fishing industry.[177]

Other technological developments included the introduction of telephone and telegraph services in the late nineteenth and early twentieth centuries in the Nordic regions of the Sámi homeland and finally at Lovozero, which was connected to the telephone service of Murmansk in 1932. The first motor car and tractor arrived in Lovozero that same year and an independent telephone exchange was opened in the following year.[178] In 1962 its streets were asphalted, a boon in the spring and autumn when melting snow and mud made the use of any form of transport extremely difficult.[179]

Much of the technology thus benefited the Sámi in a plethora of ways. However, others proved extremely detrimental to their life and livelihoods, especially during the 1960s when a variety of hydro-electric projects were carried out in the region. In fact, at least twenty Sámi settlements were destroyed on the Kola Peninsula alone. Adding insult to injury, their inhabitants were then resettled in four villages, in the midst of the Lovozero district reindeer-breeding grounds.[180]

The technological innovation of the snowmobile has had an enormous impact throughout the Sámi region, and particularly in those parts of the Sámi homeland within the Nordic countries.[181] Snowmobiles first appeared in Norway and Sweden in 1961 and in Finland the following year, revolutionising the life of the reindeer herders.[182] Even in the more backward Soviet Union, during the 1970s snowmobiles and Caterpillars were introduced, becoming relatively common during the state farm era. However, shortages of fuel, so typical of the Soviet period, meant that Komi and Nenets reindeer teams and sleighs, rather than those of the Sámi, were often used, as they had been before in the 1930s, when they had become suspect to the government authorities.[183]

The introduction of electricity in parts of the far north of Finnish Lapland in 1979 was another improvement, which in 1989 was followed by the extension of the road from Kaamanen to Näätämö, allowing direct access to the new Skolt Sámi areas from Norway. A café-cum-post office, as well as a grocery, was also opened and internet service soon came to be provided.[184]

The technological development of the nuclear submarine industry, which made Soviet Lapland a nuclear powerhouse and the area one of the most militarised in the world, should also be noted. Indeed, by the late 1980s 245 nuclear submarines and four nuclear-powered battle cruisers were commissioned by the Soviet Navy, eighty-two of them specifically for its Northern Fleet. At one time, in 1989, no less than 120 were in operation with these providing over one-fifth of the world's entire nuclear reactor capability.[185]

Growth of an Urban Infrastructure

It was the Nordic areas of Sápmi that were the first to undergo a major development of urban infrastructure, as we have seen, albeit in modest ways. The first chemist's shop opened, for example, in Rovaniemi in 1885.[186] Other places, however, especially in Russian Lapland, like

Lovozero, remained highly isolated; in the late nineteenth century it still took three days to make the journey there from Kola during the winter.[187] Yet when Aleksandr Engelhardt, governor of the province of Archangel, visited Russian Lapland in 1896 he was convinced that the region was on the verge of development, supported by the fact that the telegraph had been laid between Karelia and Kola. Moreover, a railway link was also being planned, having first been envisioned in the 1860s. In 1914, with the impetus of the First World War, the Murmansk railway project got underway. Some 15,000 Chinese navvies arrived from Harbin and during the war 20,000 German and Austro-Hungarian prisoners of war were also set to work on the project, using timber from Karelia. Little ballast was used in laying down the line and much of the foundations proved to be unsatisfactory since the rods that were rammed through the snow during the winter months to test for rock caused the engineers to confuse it with the solidity of ice. Yet the project continued and the new railway line crossed no fewer than 1,100 rivers and streams in the process, although the cost was high in human suffering, as so often was the case in Russia: the mortality rate was incredibly high, with deaths numbering in the tens of thousands—ranking with that of the later Belomorsk–White Sea Canal, in which cold, disease and scurvy took a horrendous toll.[188] The initiative of Vasilii V. Alymov in laying a telegraph line between Murmansk and Lovozero, on the other hand, was an expenditure that rapidly proved its worth.[189]

In Finland, Inari's importance as a Sámi administrative centre grew, particularly after 1909 when the office of the chief of police chief and the post office were moved there from Toivoniemi, by Lake Muddusjärvi, as was the official residence of the Kaamanen officer for forestry. Tourism was also on the rise. Ranta-Antti, the son of Yrjänä Morottaja, built a small hotel, with local mercantile activity expanded by local businessman Frans Kangasniemi.[190]

All this was made possible by the development of a growing network of roads which increasingly criss-crossed the Sámi homeland. During the 1930s a road finally reached Ivalo, which then became the centre of a new municipality, part of a string of such urban developments intended to lead on to Petsamo, on the Arctic coast, which had been ceded by Russia to Finland after the First World War. The road, which was built during the Finnish period, provided access to a nickel mine, with both the road and the mine itself having made use of Sámi workers in their construction.[191]

Although Petsamo and its environs were lost to the Soviet Union in the wake of the Second World War, Ivalo assumed greater importance, becoming one of the principal towns in the north of Finnish Lapland especially for the Sámi who gathered there for festive occasions and shopping.[192]

Nuclear and Mining Threats

The increasing militarisation of the Kola Peninsula after the Soviet Union became a nuclear power had a major effect on the Sámi who found themselves living and working in what had become one of the state's most fortified regions. Indeed, during the late Soviet period, the nuclear tests which were carried out at Kuelpor in 1974 were perceived by many not only as an ecological threat to the region, but as a factor which, in the case of a nuclear confrontation, would lead to its complete annihilation. Though less apocalyptic, the burgeoning mining industry was also posing an increasing threat to reindeer herding, since it was based in the Sámi grazing heartlands. The discovery of bauxite deposits in a variety of locations throughout the reindeer-herding grazing areas provided new sources of confrontation between the Sámi and the other nomadic peoples, on the one hand, and the Soviet industrial complex, on the other.[193] Moreover, the effects were long-lasting. A bore hole, one of the world's deepest at some 12.261 kilometres deep, still remains in the north-west of the region, although the mine ceased operations in 1993.[194]

Unexploited minerals also continue to be found, as there are some 900 minerals present in the peninsula (i.e. around a quarter of all known minerals). A fifth of these were discovered first in the Murmansk region. In the Khibiny massif alone there are some 350 different types of mineral, in the Lovozero massif 340, with seventy-three recorded as first-time discoveries. Niobium, zirconium (eudialyte), tantalum, uranium and thorium are just some of the minerals needed for the high-tech requirements of the defence industry.[195]

Tourism

Another industry growing in Sápmi, with a different type of ecological impact, is tourism. The village of Inari had become an important centre for tourism in the Sámi homeland as early as the 1930s. In 1936, for example, a hotel was built by the banks of the Juutua River; it has since undergone a number of enlargements and renovations and is currently one of northern Finland's most popular hotels.[196] The Suomu Hotel, located beneath the ski slopes of Suomutunturi Fell in a part of Finnish Lapland where the Sámi do not reside, is visited by many tourists from throughout the world, attracted by the surrounding nature and sporting amenities, along with its exotic roof, surmounted by tepee-like formations. Although it is not located in a Sámi area, many visitors stay in the hotel in order to make excursions to visit Sámi areas.[197]

In Sweden, the national park created on state land at Badjelánnda in 1962 also attracts a wide international clientele. In 1966 the Laponia World Heritage Site was also established, thereby protecting for posterity a region of a high plateau, as well as parts of the Sarek Mountain range. Of especial note as an attraction, though, is its inclusion of the noted sacred and archaeological site of Badjelánnda, which forms the heart of the Badjelánnda National Park, covering some 2,000 square kilometres. However, the presence of tourists remains rare and the area continues to be an important traditional summer grazing area for the reindeer-herding Sámi of Sirges Sameby.[198] In 1996 the Badjelánnda National Park became part of Laponia and was placed by UNESCO on its World Heritage list. Registered as a mixed cultural and natural landscape, it is a highly protected area in which hunting and fishing are forbidden.[199] Yet the local government's desire for increased tourist development, which it was hoped would increase jobs and revenue, has led to conflict in this region of declining industry; as a result, many Sámi have become disenchanted with its status, which they want to see revoked.[200] Yet tourism has continued apace and in 1996 there were no less than 140,000 visitors to so-called Sámi attractions in Norway alone.[201]

Tourism has also experienced major development in Finnish Lapland over the last few decades. This was in part a result of the fact that the infrastructure of the region was improving and, at Nellim and Keväjärvi, near Ivalo, postal and banking services were provided, even if Sevettijärvi remained devoid of such amenities—its closest post office is at Inari, some 130 kilometres away. Nonetheless, it remains the centre of the Skolt Sámi community. Indeed, it is this very isolation that has served to attract tourists, who usually stay at camping sites in order to explore local handicrafts and visit the local museum and heritage house, as well as new Finnish settlers, many of which are seasonal. Both groups are now served by a grocer's shop, a school, a health centre and café. Similar development has occurred at Neillim where there is a grocer's shop, a café and lodging facilities, along with a small museum and handicrafts shop.[202] In 2011 a Dutch eco-tourism company opened Pan Village Oulanka, in an eastern part of Finnish Lapland near the Arctic Circle, which has since attracted many people from the heart of Europe. Its location in the vicinity of Salla Reindeer Park, Ski Village Salla and the Aatsinki-Onkamon Natura Site has helped to make it a popular venue.

Reindeer Herding versus Forestry

Although in many respects the rights of the Sámi have been most protected in Norway, Finland has also come out well in looking after Sámi interests, at least with respect to land. In fact, as of 2006, Finland had the highest proportion of protected land and wilderness reserves in Europe, totalling some 2.8 million hectares (i.e. about 11 per cent of the total land area of the country). Strictly protected forests comprise over 1.5 million hectares (6.6 per cent of the total land area), while protected old-growth forests comprise approximately 10,000 acres.[203] Considerable though this protected expanse may be, it has, nonetheless, proven unsatisfactory for the majority of its Sámi residents who continue to regret the loss of reindeer-grazing forests, not least to the forestry industry. It is not yet clear how this will resolve itself over time and the impact it will have on reindeer herding. Already, well over half a century ago, in June 1948, Norgga Boazosámiid Riikkasearvi (the Reindeer Herders' Association of Norway) had been established to promote the interests of its members with the government.[204] A principal focus of this initiative was to foster the needs of the Sámi interests with respect to reindeer herding. While only the Sámi people are allowed to carry out reindeer herding in Norway and Sweden, in Finland any citizen of the European Union is permitted to do so.[205] Today there are about 300,000 reindeer in Finland at any one time, subdivided into cooperatives of 500 to 13,000 in size, with about 500 individuals owning at least 100 reindeer. Together they come from roughly 800 families, 600 of which practise full-time. In addition to the herds already mentioned, in Finland there are two and a half million semi-domestic reindeer. Sweden has the second largest number of reindeer: about 275,000, owned by 2,500 people, while in Norway there are just over 200,000 reindeer currently being herded.[206] In Russia the number is more difficult to ascertain.

By 2002 the number of reindeer herders in Finnish Lapland evinced a sharp decline: only 5,700 reindeer herders, both Sámi and Finnish, remained. Moreover, almost half the country's Sámi now lived outside the Sámi homeland, many in big urban conurbations, some abroad; whereas 38 per cent lived outside Sápmi in 1992, this figure had risen to 45 per cent ten years later.[207] There are other issues as well, since new regulations issued by the European Union no longer permit grants to reindeer herders once they have reached the age of sixty-five.[208] The old slogan from numerous demonstrations in the Nordic countries, 'A Sámi is a Sámi even without reindeer', is now more pertinent than ever.[209] Many Sámi have also intermarried, not only with their Nordic neighbours, but with people from other continents; yet they, too, remain Sámi.

In the past, the Sámi of the Kola Peninsula have without doubt suffered the greatest economic and social hardship of all the Sámi people. Yet despite this fact, the Sámi of the Kola Peninsula today form a community of about 1,600 people, a population broadly equivalent to that at the beginning of the twentieth century.[210] So the situation there is by no means as bleak as it may previously have seemed.

In many respects, the Sámi have indeed become a global people with a global perspective. In recent times, Sámi reindeer herders, possessed of a deep knowledge of the natural world in which they reside and with a keen desire to protect their patrimony, have been commissioned and sent to Alaska to teach the indigenous Inuit (Eskimo) hunters how to herd reindeer.[211]

Yet it is equally true today to maintain that Sámi statehood and ethnic identity, on both the domestic and the international stage—like those of other indigenous peoples—depend on the resolution of one principal dilemma: namely, whether the equality of individuals or the membership of an ethnic community should be considered more paramount. Should the indigenous origins and claims of the ethnic community take priority over the perceived rights of those whose ancestors arrived much later, but who are far more numerous? Should the wrongs and persecutions of the past permit a compensation which today favours positive discrimination for the historically injured and disadvantaged party? Almost two generations ago, Tim Ingold cogently wrote with respect to the Skolt Sámi that:

It seems rather fruitless to be overly concerned that the community should persist as an exclusive reserve of Skolt Culture. The implementation of such a view would mean laying down in advance the constituent attributes of culture, investing the available resources to ensure a repetitive, traditional performance. The effect of blocking local but non-traditional alternatives would be to hasten cultural collapse through the emigration of personnel and stagnation among those left at home. More important is that the groundwork be laid through overall policies of regional development for a sound economy in the community, which would allow opportunities for constructive self-expression and personal fulfilment according to values held by the people themselves.[212]

In practical terms the answers to the questions outlined above will no doubt lie in the degree to which powerful nation states, whose overwhelming population lies outside the indigenous community, will feel themselves to be in a position to make sacrifices and to what degree the minority group will feel that their uniqueness and wider value to the world has been appreciated. However, the opposite is also true: if Sámi culture is perceived as offering benefits not only to the wider communities of the Nordic countries and Russia but also beyond, enhancing the status of the nation states in which they live, they will be cherished at least to some degree. If not, good will may dry up quickly, especially in times of growing economic hardship and ever more limited economic opportunities for growth. The Sámi would then be in danger of finding themselves relegated to an increasingly restricted periphery, one in which not only their cultural identity but their economic existence is in danger of being extinguished.[213]

CONCLUSION

Sápmi and the indigenous Sámi who have resided there for thousands of years still continue to fascinate the wider world, their exoticism being retained in the popular imagination despite the arrival of mass travel and modern technological infrastructure in the Sámi homeland many years ago. But today this fascination has gone global. Japanese and Chinese tourists are just as likely to visit the Sámi homeland as the Germans and the British. True, these visits are more likely to be linked to childhood fantasies connected to an American version of Santa Claus—a figure with virtually no resonance in Sámi culture—than with any indigenous cultural element. Yet the connection is there and more and more people from around the world now have at least some contact with the reality of Sámi life. The Sámi, in turn, have themselves become far more travelled than their forefathers, albeit by way of holidays and student years abroad rather than the nomadic migrations of the past. Some have even married into families with roots or homelands as far afield as Southern and Eastern Asia. Those Sámi who work abroad are even greater in number. The Sámi, in short, have become an integral component of the global economy with all of its blessings and ills.

On a political level life for the Sámi has improved dramatically since the beginning of the twentieth century. Indeed, with the notable exception of the Russian Federation, the Sámi now have their own parliaments, even if their legislative powers are inevitably limited by the national governments and parliaments of the Nordic countries in which they reside. However imperfect this situation may be, and their small numbers notwithstanding, it is political developments such as these which have finally enabled the Sámi to take their rightful place in the roll-call of nations, a proud people whose unique social, cultural and economic identity is important not only for themselves and other indigenous peoples, but for all the peoples of the world, and especially those concerned with maintaining a sustainable ecology in a time of dramatic climate change. The Arctic homeland of the Sámi, after all, can no longer be viewed as part of the periphery of the 'civilised world': the fate of its delicate ecology has worldwide implications.

On the economic plane an increasing number of Sámi are working in areas unrelated to their traditional pursuits of reindeer hunting and fishing. Many have not only moved away from Sápmi but eschewed rural areas altogether, often settling and raising their families in national capitals where work opportunities are greater and the maintenance of their traditional ethnic identity more difficult. In these environments the Sámi are often indistinguishable from their neighbours, with whom they frequently share a language and religion or, as is more common today, their secularism.

The picture that emerges with respect to religion in Sápmi itself is slightly more complex. Whereas a symbiosis has occurred in the Scandinavian and Finnish parts of the Sámi homeland, in which an appreciation of the elements of the old Sámi religion no longer meets with the disdain and abhorrence of the Protestant churches, the Russian Orthodox Church has sought to maintain a more 'pure' form of traditional Christian practice among the Sámi, partly as a response to the Protestant evangelising of the Nordic countries during the 1990s. In more recent years, however, the Nordic churches and the Russian Orthodox Church have found common ground in defending Christian belief against the secularist and atheistic values primarily emanating from Western Europe and North America, their differences regarding the interpretation of Christian doctrine notwithstanding. But in the final analysis it is the Russian Orthodox Church that has had the most success in this regard: while churchgoing among the Sámi youth in the Scandinavian and Finnish parts of Sápmi has continued to decline, as it has elsewhere in Europe, Christianity in the Russian part of Sápmi has experienced something of a revival, with more and more young people attending church services.

Feminism has also made inroads, particularly in the Nordic region of the Sámi homeland. The independence and equality of many Sámi women at home and in the workplace have become central features of contemporary Sámi life. In recent years women's organisations have blossomed in a wide range of areas, including the political, cultural and economic spheres, and play a particularly prominent role in the Sámi parliaments both nationally and internationally.

Sámi art, film and photography have increasingly been presented to a wider public, not only in Sápmi, the Nordic countries and Russia, but throughout the world in exhibitions and in an ever wider variety of media. The growth of the internet and its presence in billions of homes throughout the world now make Sámi culture available to most people at the click of a mouse. The internet has also proved beneficial for the use of the mainstream Sámi languages, providing both teaching materials and dictionaries online. Sámi television programmes, videos and radio broadcasts are now readily available almost everywhere.

The Sámi have clearly become a global people with a global perspective in other respects as well. Health, hygiene and nutrition have improved dramatically; life expectancy among the Sámi has reached its highest ever level. Hospitals and medical care are now of the highest standard, while the speed with which these services can be accessed in Sápmi has also increased significantly.

Sámi reindeer herders are now able to share their knowledge of the natural world with like-minded indigenous peoples as far away as Alaska and Australia. This has had numerous practical benefits for the indigenous peoples in question; the Sámi have been able, for example, to teach the indigenous Inuit (Eskimo) hunters of Alaska how to herd reindeer, which are not native to this region.

Yet global communications, demographic pressure and competition for resources inevitably bring in their wake the sharpening of old conflicts and new dilemmas. Indigenous peoples continue to do battle in the courts and on the cultural plane with those who arrived later (although sometimes these *arrivistes* settled as far back as a millennium ago): should the equality of individuals be paramount or do the claims of indigenous ethnic communities have priority? What compromises are acceptable to both and, in case of continued conflict, how should they be resolved? Does 'might make right' and do the wishes of a demographic majority of newcomers trump a numerically small minority with greater historical claims? Furthermore, do the wrongs and persecutions of the past demand contemporary compensation? How successfully these questions will be resolved with respect to Sápmi and the Sámi people remains to be seen by future generations.

NOTES

INTRODUCTION

1. Tim Moore, 'Family Adventures in the Arctic Wilderness', *Daily Telegraph*, 4 Feb. 2009.
2. Aage Solbakk, *Sápmi Sameland. Samenes historie fram til 1751*, Karasjok: 2007, pp. 13, 18.
3. Leif Rantala, unpublished message to the author, Jan. 2012.
4. Ulla-Maija Kulonen, Irja Seurujärvi, Kari and Risto Pulkkinen (eds), *The Saami: A Cultural Encyclopaedia*, Helsinki: Suomalaisen Kirjallisuuden Seura, 2005, p. 5.
5. Klemetti Näkkäläjärvi and Jukka Pennanen, 'The Assimilation of Sámi Reindeer-Herding Administration into the Finnish Government', in Jukka Pennanen and Klemetti Näkkäläjärvi (eds), *Siidastallan: From Lapp Communities to Modern Sámi Life*, Inari: 2002, p. 118.
6. P.A. Yur'eva, *skazka o solntse*, Murmansk: 1978, p. 1.
7. Nadezhda Zhizn' Bolshakova, *Obychai i Mify Kol'skikh Saamov v Proshlom i Nastoyashchem*, Murmansk: 2005, p. 29. (It should be noted that many academics specialising in Sámi life and culture are highly critical of this author's scholarship.)
8. Jari Ojala, Jari Eloranta and Jukka Jalava (eds), *The Road to Prosperity: An Economic History of Finland*, Suomalaisen Kirjallisuuden Seuran Toimituksia 1076, Helsinki: Suomalaisen Kirjallisuuden Seura, 2006, pp. 69–70.
9. Ibid., p. 90.
10. Matti Mela, 'Adaptation to Northern Conditions', in Pennanen and Näkkäläjärvi, *Siidastallan: From Lapp Communities*, p. 11.
11. Kulonen et al., *The Saami*, p. 403.
12. Larisa Pelle, 'Off to See Father Christmas', *Taleon Club Magazine, St Petersburg*: Jan. 2007, p. 13.
13. Leif Rantala, unpublished message to the author, Jan. 2012.
14. Solbakk, *Sápmi Sameland*, p. 51.

15. Ibid., p. 210.
16. Johannes Schefferus, *Lapponia*, Frankfurt: 1674; Irja Seurujärvi-Kari (ed.), *Beaivvi Mánná*, Saamelaisten Juuret ja Nykyaika Suomalaisen Kirjallisuuden Seuran Tietolipas 164, Helsinki: 2000.
17. Solbakk, *Sápmi Sameland*, p. 107.
18. Ibid., p. 119.
19. Knud Leem, *Beskrivelse over Finmarkens Lapper, deres Tungemall, Levemaade og ferrige Afgudsdyrkelse,... med J.E. Gunneri... Anmærkninger: og E.J. Jassen-S... Afhandling om de Norske Finnen og Lappers hedenske Religion. C.L....de Lapponibus Finmarchiæ...commentatio, etc. Dan. & Lat.* 2 pt., Copenhagen: 1767
20. Joseph Acerbi, *Travels through Sweden, Finland, and Lapland, to the North Cape in the Years 1798 and 1799*, vol. II, London: 1802, p. 15.
21. Paulo Mantegazza, *Un Viaggio in Lapponia*, Milan: 1881, p. 82.
22. Ibid., p. 85.
23. Ibid., p. 86.
24. Acerbi, *Travels through Sweden*, p. 106.
25. Mantegazza, *Un Viaggio in Lapponia*, p. 88.
26. Anders Hesjedal, C. Damm, B. Olsen and I. Storli, *Arkeologi på Slettnes: Dokumentasjon av 11.000 års bosetning*, Tromsø Museums Skrifter 26, Tromsø: Tromsø Museum, 1996, p. 154.
27. Inga-Maria Mulk, *Sirkas—ett Sámiskt fångstsamhälle i förändring Kr.f. -1600 e. Kr.*, Studia Archaelogica Universitatis Umensis 6, Umeå: 1994, p. 87.
28. Inga-Maria Mulk and Tim Bayliss-Smith, *Rock Art and Sámi Sacred Geography in Badjelánnda, Laponia, Sweden: Sailing Boats, Anthropomorphs and Reindeer*, Archaeology and Environment 22. Kungl. Skytteanska Samfundets Handlingar 58, Umeå: 2006, p. 17.
29. Christian Carpelan, 'The Cultural Background of Being Sámi: A Look at the Sámi and their Cultural Eras in the Light of Archaeological Research', in Pennanen and Näkkäläjärvi, *Siidastallan: From Lapp Communities*, pp. 22–3.
30. Solbakk, *Sápmi Sameland*, p. 20.
31. Ibid., p. 21.
32. Ibid., p. 17.
33. Bolshakova, *Obychai i Mify Kol'skikh Saamov v Proshlom i Nastoyashchem*, p. 13.
34. Solbakk, *Sápmi Sameland*, p. 19; Knut Helskog, *Helleristningene i Alta: Spor etter ritualer og dagligliv i Finnmarks forhistorie*, Alta: Alta Museum, 1988.
35. Mulk and Bayliss-Smith, *Rock Art and Sámi Sacred Geography*, p. v.
36. Ibid., p. 31.
37. Mulk, *Sirkas—ett Sámiskt*, p. 287.
38. Mulk and Bayliss-Smith, *Rock Art and Sámi Sacred Geography*, p. 17.
39. Ibid., p. 18.
40. Solbakk, *Sápmi Sameland*, p. 36.
41. Ibid., p. 27.
42. Veli-Pekka Lehtola (ed.), *Inari, Aanaar* Oulu: 2003, p. 63.

43. Solbakk, *Sápmi Sameland*, p. 29.
44. Ibid., p. 30.
45. Mulk and Bayliss-Smith, *Rock Art and Sámi Sacred Geography*, p. 78.
46. Näkkäläjärvi and Jukka Pennanen, 'The Assimilation of Sámi Reindeer-Herding Administration', p. 117.
47. Solbakk, *Sápmi Sameland*, p. 32.
48. Ibid., p. 35.
49. Ibid., p. 37.
50. Ibid., p. 36.
51. Bolshakova, *Obychai i Mify Kol'skikh Saamov v Proshlom i Nastoyashchem*, pp. 11–12.
52. Leif Rantala, unpublished message to the author, Jan. 2012.
53. Bolshakova, *Obychai i Mify Kol'skikh Saamov v Proshlom i Nastoyashchem*, p. 14
54. Solbakk, *Sápmi Sameland*, p. 38.
55. Ibid., pp. 41–2.
56. Klemetti Näkkäläjärvi and Jukka Pennanen, 'The Dimensions of Movement', in Pennanen and Näkkäläjärvi, *Siidastallan: From Lapp Communities*, p. 96.
57. Solbakk, *Sápmi Sameland*, p. 199.
58. Ibid., p. 47.
59. Olao Magno, *Storia de Costvmi de'Popoli Settentrionali*, translated by M. Remigio Fiorentino, Vinegia: 1561, p. 118.
60. Ibid., pp. 426 and 504.
61. Solbakk, *Sápmi Sameland*, p. 106.
62. Ibid., p. 138.
63. Ibid., p. 220.
64. Ibid., pp. 42–3.
65. Ibid., pp. 44–5.
66. A. Outakoski (ed.), *Rovaniemen Historia i Rovaniemen Seudun Vaiheita Vuotten 1631*, Rovaniemi: 1965, p. 52.
67. Ibid., p. 98.
68. Mulk and Bayliss-Smith, *Rock Art and Sámi Sacred Geography*, p. 109.
69. Outakoski, *Rovaniemen Historia*, p. 5.
70. Neil Kent, *The Soul of the North: A Social, Architectural and Cultural History of the Nordic Countries, 1700–1940*, London: Reaktion, 2000, pp. 153–5.
71. Sverker Sörlin, 'Fransmans resor idet exotiska Lappland', in Pontius Grate (ed.), *Solen och nordstjärnan: Frankrike och Sverige på 1700-talet*, Stockholm: National Museum, 1993, p. 214.
72. Kent, *The Soul of the North*, p. 155.
73. Joseph Acerbi, *Vues de la Suede, de la Finlande, et de la Lapponie, depuis le Detroit du Sund jusqu'au Cap Nord*, Paris: 1803, p. 15.
74. N.N. Kharuzin, *Russkie Lopari—Ocherki*, Moscow: 1890.
75. Pelle, 'Off to See Father Christmas', p. 10.

1. ETHNICITIES, THE LAW, REPRESSIONS AND WAR

1. Samuli Aikio, 'Samernas historia—med vems ögon?' in Tuula Puisto (ed.), *Sámi Dáidda*, Helsinki: Davviriikkaid Dáiddaguovddaš, 1981, p. 12.

2. Johannes Schefferus, *Lapponia*, Frankfurt: 1674, p. 248.

3. Christian Carpelan, 'The Cultural Background of Being Sámi: A Look at the Sámi and their Cultural Eras in the Light of Archaeological Research', in Pennanen and Näkkäläjärvi, *Siidastallan: From Lapp Communities to Modern Sámi Life*, Inari: 2002, p. 24.

4. Aage Solbakk, *Sápmi Sameland. Samenes historie fram til 1751*, Karasjok: 2007, p. 10.

5. Inga-Maria Mulk and Tim Bayliss-Smith, *Rock Art and Sámi Sacred Geography in Badjelánnda, Laponia, Sweden: Sailing Boats, Anthropomorphs and Reindeer*, Archaeology and Environment 22. Kungl. Skytteanska Samfundets Handlingar 58, Umeå: 2006, p. 18.

6. Carpelan, 'The Cultural Background of Being Sámi', p. 25.

7. Ibid., p. 25.

8. Solbakk, *Sápmi Sameland*, p. 131.

9. Ibid., p. 128.

10. Ibid., pp. 132–3.

11. Johan Ingvald Borgos and T. Torgvaer, 'Samer og båtbygging', in *Människor och båtar i Norden. Sjöhistorisk Årsbok 1998–1999*, Stockholm: Föreningen Sveriges Sjöfartsmuseum, 1998, p. 110.

12. Thorleif Sjøvold, *The Iron Age Settlement of Arctic Norway: A Study of the Expansion of Iron Age Culture within the Arctic Circle. II. Late Iron Age* (Tromsø Museums Skrifter, X, 2), Tromsø, Oslo and Bergen: Norwegian Universities Press, 1974, p. 335.

13. Mulk and Bayliss-Smith, *Rock Art and Sámi Sacred Geography*, p. 77.

14. Niels Lund (ed.), *Two Voyagers at the Court of King Alfred: The Ventures of Ohthere and Wufstan Together with the Description of Northern Europe from the Old English Orosius*, York: William Sessions, 1984, p. 19.

15. Mulk and Bayliss-Smith, *Rock Art and Sámi Sacred Geography*, p. 85.

16. Lars Ivar Hansen, 'Trade and Markets in Northern Fenno-Scandinavia A.D. 1550–1750', *Acta Borealia*, 1, 2 (1984), pp. 47–79.

17. Martti Linkola, 'Art for Decoration and Everyday Use', in Pennanen and Näkkäläjärvi, *Siidastallan: From Lapp Communities*, p. 170.

18. Solbakk, *Sápmi Sameland*, p. 58.

19. Ulla-Maija Kulonen, Irja Seurujärvi, Kari and Risto Pulkkinen (eds), *The Saami: A Cultural Encyclopaedia*, Helsinki: Suomalaisen kirjallisuuden seura, 2005, pp. 38–9.

20. Nadezhda Zhizn' Bolshakova, *Obychai i Mify Kol'skikh Saamov v Proshlom i Nastoyashchem*, Murmansk: 2005, p. 229.

21. Ibid., p. 25.

22. Solbakk, *Sápmi Sameland*, pp. 52–3.

23. Ibid., p. 55.

24. T.V. Luk'yanchenko, *Rasselenie kol'skikh saamov v XVI vv. K istorii malykh narodnostei Evropeiskogo Severa SSSR*, Petrozavodsk: 1979, p. 19.

25. *Khrestomatiya po istorii Karelii s derevneishikh vremen do kontsa XVII veka*, Petrozavodsk: 1939, pp. 172–3.

26. V. Slavyanski, *Ocherki Severa*, V. pustynakh Laplandii Delo. god vozmoi, 1874: aprel', p. 16.

27. Peter Sköld, *Samerna och deras Historia, Metodövninger i Sámisk 1600- och 1700-talshistoria*, Umeå: 1993, p. 9.

28. Klemetii Näkkäläjärvi, 'The *Siida*, or Sámi Village, as the Basis of Community Life', in Pennanen and Näkkäläjärvi, *Siidastallan: From Lapp Communities*, p. 117.

29. Kulonen et al., *The Saami*, p. 384.

30. Carpelan, 'The Cultural Background of Being Sámi', p. 26.

31. Samuli Aikio, Teuvo Lehtola and Klemetti Näkkäläjärvi, 'Agriculture—a Sámi livelihood as of the 1700s', in Pennanen and Näkkäläjärvi, *Siidastallan: From Lapp Communities*, p. 55.

32. Bolshakova, *Obychai i Mify Kol'skikh Saamov v Proshlom i Nastoyashchem*, p. 116. Leif Rantala, however, considers this figure too high.

33. Joseph Acerbi, *Travels through Sweden, Finland, and Lapland, to the North Cape in the Years 1798 and 1799*, vol. II, London: 1802, p. 284.

34. Teuvo Lehtola, 'The History of the Inari Sámi', in Pennanen and Näkkäläjärvi, *Siidastallan: From Lapp Communities*, p. 124.

35. Solbakk, *Sápmi Sameland*, p. 75; Sköld, *Samerna och deras Historia*, p. 124.

36. Israel Ruong, *Lapps in Sweden*, Stockholm: 1867, p. 17.

37. Asjbørn Nesheim, *Samene. Historie og kultur*, Oslo: 1966, p. 34.

38. Kulonen et al., *The Saami*, p. 185.

39. Solbakk, *Sápmi Sameland*, pp. 264–5.

40. Stephen Sommier, 'Sui Lapponi e sui Finlandesi', *Settentrionali Archivo per l'Antropologia e l'Etnologia*, XVI, I (1886), p. 115.

41. Ibid., p. 115.

42. Paulo Mantegazza, *Un Viaggio in Lapponia*, Milan: 1881, pp. 115–16.

43. Sommier, 'Sui Lapponi', pp. 14–15.

44. Ibid., p. 37.

45. Solbakk, *Sápmi Sameland*, pp. 265–7.

46. Aleksei Venediktovich Kozhevnikov, *Solntse ezdit na olenyakh* [The Sun Travels by Reindeer], Moscow: 1972, p. 242.

47. Solbakk, *Sápmi Sameland*, p. 203.

48. Kulonen et al., *The Saami*, p. 384.

49. Solbakk, *Sápmi Sameland*, p. 75.

50. Bolshakova, *Obychai i Mify Kol'skikh Saamov v Proshlom i Nastoyashchem*, pp. 62–3.

51. Sköld, *Samerna och deras Historia*, p. 15.

52. Kulonen et al., *The Saami*, p. 327.

53. Schefferus, *Lapponia*, pp. 103, pp. 125–39.

54. Ibid., pp. 157 and 160–7.

55. Ibid., pp. 180–2 and 186–7.
56. Kulonen et al., *The Saami*, p. 338.
57. Nicolavs Hackzell, *Lula*, Uppsala: 1731.
58. Samuli Aikio, 'Epilogue', in Pennanen and Näkkäläjärvi, *Siidastallan: From Lapp Communities*, p. 217.
59. Acerbi, *Travels through Sweden*, vol. 2, p. 43.
60. Ibid., p. 103.
61. Ibid., p. 105.
62. Mantegazza, *Un Viaggio in Lapponia*, p. 90.
63. Ibid., p. 116.
64. Johannis J. Tornæi, *Beskrifning, ofver Tornå och Kemi Lappmarker*, written in 1672 but first published in Stockholm: 1772, p. 63.
65. Tomasz Kamusella, *The Politics of Language and Nationalism in Modern Central Europe*, Basingstoke/New York: Palgrave, 2009, p. 475.
66. Sköld, *Samerna och deras Historia*, p. 14.
67. Lehtola, 'The History of the Inari Sámi', p. 125.
68. Schefferus, *Lapponia*, p. 214.
69. Le Comte Goblet d'Alviella, *Sahara et Laponie*, Paris: 1873, p. 286.
70. Olov Isaksson and Folke Isaksson, *Gammelstad Kyrkby vid Luleå Älv*, Stockholm: 1991, p. 162.
71. Edward Rae, FRGS, *The White Sea Peninsula: A Journey in Russian Lapland and Karelia*, London: 1881, p. 37.
72. Kulonen et al., *The Saami*, p. 162.
73. Leif Rantala, *Kuolaan. Venäjän vallan aikana Kuolan niemimaalla käyneet suomalaiset tiedemiehet ja heidän kirjoituksensa*, Lapin yliopiston kasvatustieteellisiä raportteja 5, Rovaniemi: 2008, p. 9.
74. 'Berättelse om W. Böhtlingks Resa Genom Finland och Lappmarkerne [=Kolahalvön År 1839]', in Leif Rantala (ed.), *Dokument om de ryska samerna och Kolahalvön Lapplands*, Universitets Pedagogiska Publikationer, 15, Rovaniemi: 2006, p. 10.
75. Roger Took, *Running with Reindeer: Encounters in Russian Lapland*, London: John Murray, 2003, p. 67.
76. N.N. Kharuzin, *Russkie Lopari—Ocherki*, Moscow: 1890, pp. 92–4.
77. D'Alviella, *Sahara et Laponie*, p. 172.
78. Ibid., p. 176.
79. Ibid., p. 228.
80. Solbakk, *Sápmi Sameland*, p. 100.
81. Acerbi, *Travels through Sweden*, vol. 2, pp. 315–17.
82. Lennart Lundmark, *Samernas skatteland i Norr- och Västerbotten under 300 År*, Stockholm: 2006, p. 175.
83. Solbakk, *Sápmi Sameland*, p. 126.
84. Lundmark, *Samernas skatteland*, p. 175.
85. Näkkäläjärvi, 'The *Siida*, or Sámi Village, as the Basis of Community Life', p. 117.
86. Ibid., p. 114.

87. Ibid., p. 115.
88. Ibid., p. 119.
89. Ibid., pp. 121–2.
90. Lehtola, 'The History of the Inari Sámi', p. 123.
91. Näkkäläjärvi, 'The *Siida*, or Sámi Village, as the Basis of Community Life', p. 116.
92. Ibid., p. 118.
93. Lehtola, 'The History of the *Inari* Sámi', pp. 123–4.
94. Veli-Pekka Lehtola (ed.), *Inari*, Aanaar Oulu: 2003, p. 167.
95. Näkkäläjärvi, 'The *Siida*, or Sámi Village, as the Basis of Community Life', p. 116.
96. Lehtola, 'The History of the Inari Sámi', p. 124.
97. Sommier, 'Sui Lapponi', p. 114.
98. Lundmark, *Samernas skatteland*, p. 34.
99. Solbakk, *Sápmi Sameland*, p. 98.
100. Neil Kent, *A Concise History of Sweden,* Cambridge: Cambridge University Press, 2008, p. 201.
101. Leif Rantala in an unpublished letter to the author in Jan. 2012.
102. Anni Linkola and Martti Linkola, 'The Skolt Sámi—A Minority within a Minority', in Pennanen and Näkkäläjärvi, *Siidastallan: From Lapp Communities*, pp. 129–30.
103. Ibid., p. 133.
104. Leif Rantala, in an unpublished letter to the author, Jan. 2012.
105. Linkola and Linkola, 'The Skolt Sámi—A Minority', pp. 129–31.
106. Leif Rantala in an unpublished letter to the author in Jan. 2012.
107. Linkola and Linkola, 'The Skolt Sámi—A Minority', pp. 133–4.
108. Anni Linkola, 'The Skolt Sámi Today', in Pennanen and Näkkäläjärvi, *Siidastallan: From Lapp Communities*, p. 204.
109. Leif Rantala, unpublished letter to the author, Jan. 2012.
110. Ibid.
111. Ibid.
112. Linkola and Linkola, 'The Skolt Sámi—A Minority', p. 122.
113. Ibid., p. 133.
114. Kulonen et al., *The Saami*, 2005, p. 147. Leif Rantala, however, estimates their number at only 400 at this time; unpublished letter to the author, Jan. 2012.
115. Lehtola, 'The History of the Inari Sámi', pp. 129–30.
116. Linkola and Linkola, 'The Skolt Sámi—A Minority', p. 135.
117. Kulonen et al., *The Saami*, p. 398.
118. Leif Rantala, unpublished letter to the author, Jan. 2012.
119. Linkola and Linkola, 'The Skolt Sámi—A Minority', p 136.
120. Ibid., p. 137.
121. Leif Rantala, unpublished letter to the author, Jan. 2012.
122. Kulonen et al., *The Saami*, p. 89.
123. Ibid., pp. 90–1.

124. Linkola, 'The Skolt Sámi Today', p. 204.
125. Kulonen et al., *The Saami*, p. 148.
126. Acerbi, *Travels through Sweden*, vol. 2, p. 281.
127. Matti Enbuska, 'Samerna som Nybyggare I Kemi Socken och I Kemi Lappmark', Presentation at Nordic Sami History Symposium in Lövånger, 13–14 February 1995, Umeå: 1995, p. 45.
128. Lundmark, *Samernas skatteland*, p. 107.
129. Eino Jutikkala, *Bonden i Finland genom Tiderna*, Helsinki: 1963, pp. 149–51.
130. Neil Kent, *The Soul of the North: A Social, Architectural and Cultural History of the Nordic Countries, 1700–1940*, London: Reaktion, 2000, p. 153.
131. J. Engström, *Resa genom Södra Lappland, Jemtland, Trondhem och Dalarne, år 1834 Första Delen Om S. Lappland och Jemtland*, Stockholm: 1835, p. 3.
132. Lennart Lundmark, *Protest och Profetia: Korpela-rörelsen och drömmen om tidens ände*, Lund: 1985, p. 90.
133. Lundmark, *Samernas skatteland*, p. 46.
134. Ibid., p. 72.
135. Ibid., p. 117.
136. Ibid., p. 118.
137. Ibid., p. 133.
138. Ibid., p. 145.
139. Lennart Lundmark, 'Lappen är ombytlig, ostadig och obekväm', Svenska Statens Samepolitik i Rasismens Tidevarv, Umeå: 2002, p. 165.
140. Lennart Lundmark, *Så länge vi har marker. Samerna och staten under sexhundra år*, Stockholm: 1998, p. 108.
141. Lundmark, *Samernas skatteland*, pp. 160–1.
142. Lundmark, *Så länge vi har marker*, p. 110.
143. Lundmark, *Samernas skatteland*, p. 177.
144. Lundmark, 'Lappen är ombytlig, ostadig och obekväm', p. 168.
145. Mikko Korhonen, *Johdatus lapin kielen historiaan*, Suomalaisen Kirjallisuuden Seuran Toimituksia 370, Helsinki: Suomalaisen Kirjallisuuden Seura, 1981, p. 50.
146. Marjut Aikio, *Saamelaiset Kielenvaihdon Kierteessä. Kielisosiologinen tutkimus viiden saamelaiskylän kielenvaihdosta 1910–1980*, Suomalaisen Kirjallisuuden Seuran Toimituksia 479, Helsinki: Suomalaisen Kirjallisuuden Seura, 1988, p. ix.
147. Kulonen et al., *The Saami*, pp. 151–2.
148. Jukka Pennanen, *Jos ei ole poropaimenia, kansa häviää, Kuolan poronhoitajen sosiokulttuurinen adaptaatio 20. vuosisadalla*, Suomalaisen Kirjallisuuden Seuran Toimituksia 779, Helsinki: Suomalaisen Kirjallisuuden Seura, 2000, p. 100.
149. Bolshakova, *Obychai i Mify Kol'skikh Saamov v Proshlom i Nastoyashchem*, p. 234.
150. Kulonen et al., *The Saami*, p. 12.

151. Linkola, 'The Skolt Sámi Today', p. 212.
152. Kulonen et al., *The Saami*, p. 180.
153. Bolshakova, *Obychai i Mify Kol'skikh Saamov v Proshlom i Nastoyashchem*, p. 231.
154. Rae, *The White Sea Peninsula*, p. 25.
155. Ibid., p. 104.
156. Lehtola, 'The History of the Inari Sámi', p. 24.
157. Took, *Running with Reindeer*, p. 126.
158. Ibid., p. 141.
159. S.N. Dasjtjinskij, 'Den Samiska Republikens President', in Rantala, *Dokument om de ryska samerna och Kolahalvön*, p. 69.
160. V.I. Nemirovich-Danchenko, *Strana Kholoda*, Moscow: 1877, p. 279.
161. Bolshakova, *Obychai i Mify Kol'skikh Saamov v Proshlom i Nastoyashchem*, p. 231.
162. Kulonen et al., *The Saami*, p. 326.
163. Bolshakova, *Obychai i Mify Kol'skikh Saamov v Proshlom i Nastoyashchem*, p. 231.
164. Kulonen et al., *The Saami*, p. 66.
165. Ibid., p. 165.
166. Bolshakova, *Obychai i Mify Kol'skikh Saamov v Proshlom i Nastoyashchem*, p. 231.
167. Samuli Paulaharju, *Kolttain mailta*, Helsinki: 2nd Edition, 2009, p. 6.
168. Ibid., pp. 8, 11–12.
169. Kulonen et al., *The Saami*, p. 327.
170. V. Tanner, *Antropogeografiska studier inom Petsamo-område[...]. 1. Skolt-Lapparna*, Fennia 49, no. 4, Helsinki: 1929.
171. Took, *Running with Reindeer*, p. 96.
172. Ibid., p. 193.
173. Ibid., pp. 195–207.
174. Jelena Porsanger, 'The Eastern Sámi and the Missionary Policy of the Russian Orthodox Church', in Anna-Leena Siikala, Barbro Klein and Stein R. Mathisen (eds), *Creating Diversities: Folklore, Religion and the Politics of Heritage*, Studia Fennica. Foklorista 14, Helsinki: Finnish Literature Society, 2004, p. 118.
175. V. Alymov, 'Om Samernas Assimilering', in Rantala, *Dokument om de ryska samerna och Kolahalvön Lapplands*, p. 41.
176. Kulonen et al., *The Saami*, p. 165.
177. V.V. Sorokazjerdjev, 'Vasilij Alymov—Samernas Vän—Folkets Fiende', in Rantala, *Dokument om de ryska samerna och Kolahalvön Lapplands*, p. 61.
178. Alymov, 'Om Samernas Assimilering', p. 43.
179. V.V. Sorokazjerdjev, 'Alymov och den Nordliga Kommittén', in Rantala, *Dokument om de ryska samerna och Kolahalvön Lapplands*, pp. 29 and 36.
180. 'Alymovs Brev Till Prof. Wiklund', in Rantala, *Dokument om de ryska samerna och Kolahalvön Lapplands*, p. 21.
181. Leif Rantala, unpublished letter to the author, Jan. 2012.

182. Sorokazjerdjev, 'Alymov och den Nordliga Kommittén', p. 39.
183. Ibid., pp. 33–4.
184. Ibid., p. 61.
185. Tomasz Kizny, *GULAG*, New York: Firefly Books, 2004, p. 78.
186. Ibid.
187. Ibid., p. 79.
188. Ibid., p. 78.
189. Ibid., pp. 78–9.
190. Ibid., p. 79.
191. Ibid., p. 80.
192. Bolshakova, *Obychai i Mify Kol'skikh Saamov v Proshlom i Nastoyashchem*, p. 232.
193. Ibid., p. 176.
194. S.N. Dasjtjinskij, 'Den Sámiska Republikens President', in Rantala, *Dokument om de ryska samerna och Kolahalvön Lapplands*, p. 68.
195. Took, *Running with Reindeer*, p. 239.
196. Bolshakova, *Obychai i Mify Kol'skikh Saamov v Proshlom i Nastoyashchem*, p. 63.
197. Sorokazjerdjev, 'Vasilij Alymov—Samernas Vän', pp. 64–5.
198. V. Alymov, 'Samernas Skolundervisning på 1930-talet', in Rantala, *Dokument om de ryska samerna och Kolahalvön Lapplands*, p. 27.
199. Dasjtjinskij, 'Den Sámiska Republikens President', in Rantala, *Dokument om de ryska samerna och Kolahalvön Lapplands*, pp. 70–1, 74–5.
200. Ibid., pp. 68–9.
201. Ibid., p. 69.
202. Leif Rantala, unpublished letters to the author, Jan. 2012.
203. Linkola and Linkola, 'The Skolt Sámi—A Minority', p. 135.
204. Bolshakova, *Obychai i Mify Kol'skikh Saamov v Proshlom i Nastoyashchem*, p. 232.
205. Linkola and Linkola, 'The Skolt Sámi—A Minority', pp. 134–5.
206. Ibid., p. 135.
207. Ibid.
208. Jukka Pennanen, 'From the Ice Age to the Present', in Jukka Pennanen and Klemetti Näkkäläjärvi (eds), *Siidastallan: From Lapp Communities to Modern Sámi Life*, Inari: 2002, p. 20.
209. Niilo Aikio, *Liekkejä pakoon: Saamelaiset evakossa 1944–1945*, Helsinki: Suomalaisen Kirjallisuuden Seura, 2000, p. 20.
210. Dasjtjinskij, 'Den Sámiska Republikens President', in Rantala, *Dokument om de ryska samerna och Kolahalvön*, p. 68.
211. Marja Tuominen, 'Lapin sodan tuhot ja jälleenrakennus', in Ilmo Massa and Hanna Snellman (eds), *Lappi: Maa,kansat, kulttuurit*, Helsinki: Suomalaisen Kirjallisuuden Seura, 2006, p. 115.
212. Pennanen, 'From the Ice Age to the Present', p. 20.
213. Lehtola, 'The History of the Inari Sámi', p. 122.
214. Kjell Olsen, 'The Touristic Construction of the "Emblematic" Sámi', in Siikala et al., *Creating Diversities*, p. 293.

215. Leif Rantala, 'Den Ryska Samen Maksim Antonovs Öde', in Rantala, *Dokument om de ryska samerna och Kolahalvön Lapplands*, pp. 129–33 and 137–8.

216. Bolshakova, *Obychai i Mify Kol'skikh Saamov v Proshlom i Nastoyashchem*, p. 84.

217. Andreas Sarri and Margareta Sarri, *Welcome to Shittown. En fotodokumentär*, Kiruna: 2006, p. 61.

218. Pennanen, *Jos ei ole poropaimenia, kansa häviää*, p. 99.

219. Ibid., pp. 99–100.

220. Bolshakova, *Obychai i Mify Kol'skikh Saamov v Proshlom i Nastoyashchem*, p. 177.

221. Pennanen, *Jos ei ole poropaimenia, kansa häviää*, p. 98.

222. Ibid., p. 99.

223. Ibid., p. 100.

224. Sarri and Sarri, *Welcome to Shittown*, p. 55.

225. Bolshakova, *Obychai i Mify Kol'skikh Saamov v Proshlom i Nastoyashchem*, p. 83.

226. Sarri and Sarri, *Welcome to Shittown*, p. 56.

227. Kulonen et al., *The Saami*, p. 10.

228. Anna-Riitta Lindgren, *Helsingin saamelaiset ja oma Kieli*, Suomalaisen kirjallisuuden seuran Toimituksia 801, Helsinki: Suomalaisen Kirjallisuuden Seuran, 2000, p. 273.

229. Ibid., p. 274.

230. Kulonen et al., *The Saami*, p. 267.

231. Ibid., p. 234.

232. Ibid., p. 162.

233. Stein R. Mathisen, 'Hegemonic Representations of Sámi Culture: From Narratives of Noble Savages to Discourses on Ecological Sámi', in Siikala et al., *Creating Diversities*, p. 20; Kulonen et al., *The Saami*, p. 11.

234. Klemetti Näkkäläjärvi, 'The Sámi Flag', in Pennanen and Näkkäläjärvi, *Siidastallan: From Lapp Communities*, p. 21.

235. Zoë Hateehc Durrah Scheffy, 'Sámi Religion in Museums and Artistry', in Siikala et al., *Creating Diversities*, p. 253.

236. Näkkäläjärvi, 'The Sámi Flag', p. 21.

237. Kulonen et al., *The Saami*, p. 269.

238. Tarmo Jomppanen, 'The Sámi Museum—Past and Present', in Pennanen and Näkkäläjärvi, *Siidastallan: From Lapp Communities*, p. 213.

239. Kulonen et al., *The Saami*, p. 207.

240. Ibid., p. 273.

241. Sarri and Sarri, *Welcome to Shittown*, p. 57.

242. Siikala et al., *Creating Diversities*, p. 10.

243. Mathisen, 'Hegemonic Representations of Sámi Culture', p. 26.

244. Durrah Scheffy, 'Sámi Religion in Museums and Artistry', n. 4, p. 256.

245. Olsen, 'The Touristic Construction of the "Emblematic" Sámi', p. 301.

246. Mikael Svonni, 'The Future of Sámi: Minority Language Survival in

Circumpolar Scandinavia', in Robert P. Wheelersburg (ed.), *Northern People, Southern States: Maintaining Ethnicities in the Circumpolar World*, Umeå: 1996, p. 23.

247. Ibid., p. 28.

248. Bolshakova, *Obychai i Mify Kol'skikh Saamov v Proshlom i Nastoyashchem*, p. 220.

249. Kulonen et al., *The Saami*, p. 165.

250. Bolshakova, *Obychai i Mify Kol'skikh Saamov v Proshlom i Nastoyashchem*, p. 60.

251. Leif Rantala, unpublished letter to the author, Jan. 2012.

252. Kulonen et al., *The Saami*, p. 89.

253. Bolshakova, *Obychai i Mify Kol'skikh Saamov v Proshlom i Nastoyashchem*, p. 219.

254. Kulonen et al., *The Saami*, p. 165.

255. Bolshakova, *Obychai i Mify Kol'skikh Saamov v Proshlom i Nastoyashchem*, p. 222.

256. Ibid., p. 236.

257. Kulonen et al., *The Saami*, p. 279.

258. Bolshakova, *Obychai i Mify Kol'skikh Saamov v Proshlom i Nastoyashchem*, p. 226.

259. Kulonen et al., *The Saami*, pp. 192–3.

260. Solbakk, *Sápmi Sameland*, p. 67.

261. Veli-Pekka Lehtola, 'Towards a United Sápmi', in Pennanen and Näkkäläjärvi, *Siidastallan: From Lapp Communities*, p. 201.

262. Ibid., pp. 201–2; Kulonen et al., *The Saami*, p. 344.

263. Linkola and Linkola, 'The Skolt Sámi—A Minority', p. 130.

264. Kulonen et al., *The Saami*, p. 377.

265. Ibid., pp. 153–4.

266. Ibid., p. 184.

267. Ibid., p. 150.

268. Ibid., pp. 18–19.

269. Ibid., p. 128.

270. Lehtola, 'Towards a United Sápmi', p. 202.

2. RELIGION

1. Inga-Maria Mulk and Tim Bayliss-Smith, *Rock Art and Sámi Sacred Geography in Badjelánnda, Laponia, Sweden: Sailing Boats, Anthropomorphs and Reindeer*, Archaeology and Environment 22. Kungl. Skytteanska Samfundets Handlingar 58, Umeå: 2006, p. 25.

2. Ibid., p. 26.

3. Acerbi, *Travels through Sweden*, vol. 2, p. 312.

4. Mulk and Bayliss-Smith, *Rock Art and Sámi Sacred Geography*, p. 57.

5. Vladimir Charnolusky, *Den Vilda Renen i myt och rit*, Jokkmokk: 1993, pp. 7 and 9.

6. V. Charnolusky, *O kul'te Myandasha. Skandinaviski sbornik*, Tallinn: 1966, p. 308.

7. Aage Solbakk, *Sápmi Sameland. Samenes historie fram til 1751*, Karasjok: 2007, p. 127.

8. Veli-Pekka Lehtola, 'The Heritage of the Ancient World-View', in Pennanen and Näkkäläjärvi, *Siidastallan: From Lapp Communities*, p. 163.

9. Neil Kent, *The Soul of the North: A Social, Architectural and Cultural History of the Nordic Countries, 1700–1940*, London: Reaktion, 2000, p. 42.

10. Jelena Porsanger, 'A Close Relationship to Nature—The Basis of Religion', in Pennanen and Näkkäläjärvi, *Siidastallan: From Lapp Communities*, p. 151.

11. Jukka Pennanen, 'The Sacred Sieidi—A Link between Human Beings and the Divinities of Nature', in Pennanen and Näkkäläjärvi, *Siidastallan: From Lapp Communities*, p. 156.

12. Ulla-Maija Kulonen, Irja Seurujärvi, Kari and Risto Pulkkinen (eds), *The Saami: A Cultural Encyclopaedia*, Helsinki: Suomalaisen kirjallisuuden seura, 2005, p. 7.

13. Ibid., p. 152.

14. Peter Sköld, 'Sámi and Smallpox in Eighteenth Century Sweden: Cultural Prevention of Epidemic Disease', in Robert P. Wheelersburg (ed.), *Northern People, Southern States: Maintaining Ethnicities in the Circumpolar World*, Umeå: 1996, pp. 97–8.

15. Kulonen et al., *The Saami*, p. 32.

16. Ibid., pp. 8–9.

17. Ibid., p. 10.

18. Bolshakova, *Obychai i Mify Kol'skikh Saamov v Proshlom i Nastoyashchem*, p. 241.

19. Kulonen et al., *The Saami*, pp. 155–7.

20. Ibid., p. 215.

21. N.N. Kharuzin, *Russkie Lopari—Ocherki*, Moscow: 1890, p. 139.

22. Kulonen et al., *The Saami*, p. 327.

23. Ibid., p. 413.

24. Mulk and Bayliss-Smith, *Rock Art and Sámi Sacred Geography*, p. 36.

25. Ibid., p. 63.

26. Inga-Maria Mulk, 'Sacrificial Places and their Meaning in Sámi Society', in David Carmichael, Jane Hubert, Brian Reeves and Audhild Schanche (eds), *Sacred Sites, Sacred Places*, London: Routledge, 1994, pp. 123–31.

27. Pennanen, 'The Sacred Sieidi', p. 156.

28. Joseph Acerbi, *Travels through Sweden, Finland, and Lapland, to the North Cape in the Years 1798 and 1799*, vol. II, London: 1802, pp. 303–4.

29. Stein R. Mathisen, 'Hegemonic Representations of Sámi Culture: From Narratives of Noble Savages to Discourses on Ecological Sámi', in Siikala et al., *Creating Diversities*, p. 21.

30. Kulonen et al., *The Saami*, p. 12.

31. Mulk and Bayliss-Smith, *Rock Art and Sámi Sacred Geography*, p. 45.

32. Solbakk, *Sápmi Sameland*, p. 219.

33. Ibid., p. 229.
34. Ibid., p. 123.
35. Ibid., pp. 221–2.
36. Kulonen et al., *The Saami*, pp. 431–2.
37. Solbakk, *Sápmi Sameland*, pp. 231–2.
38. Ibid., p. 204.
39. Ibid., pp. 232–4.
40. Ibid., p. 237.
41. Ibid., pp. 243–4.
42. Ibid., p. 245.
43. Jukka Pennanen, 'From Natural Religion to Christianity: The Clash of Different Religious Views', in Pennanen and Näkkäläjärvi, *Siidastallan: From Lapp Communities*, p. 149.
44. Solbakk, *Sápmi Sameland*, p. 212.
45. Ibid., p. 214.
46. Kulonen et al., *The Saami*, p. 209.
47. Solbakk, *Sápmi Sameland*, p. 19.
48. Leif Rantala, unpublished letter to the author, Jan. 2012.
49. Solbakk, *Sápmi Sameland*, pp. 241–9.
50. Kent, *The Soul of the North*, p. 35.
51. Anders Åman, *Om den Offentliga Vården. Byggnader och verksamheter vid svenska vårdsinstitutioner under 1800-och 1900 talen, En arkitekturhistorish underskning*, Uppsala: 1976, p. 75.
52. Kulonen et al., *The Saami*, p. 416.
53. Solbakk, *Sápmi Sameland*, p. 157.
54. Ibid., p. 214.
55. Ibid., pp. 212–17.
56. Kent, *The Soul of the North*, p. 43.
57. Pennanen, 'From Natural Religion to Christianity', p. 150.
58. Bolshakova, *Obychai i Mify Kol'skikh Saamov v Proshlom i Nastoyashchem*, p. 31.
59. Ibid., p. 440.
60. Solbakk, *Sápmi Sameland*, p. 205.
61. Aage Solbakk, *Solovetskii Pyaterik*, Moscow: 1991, p. 42.
62. Bolshakova, *Obychai i Mify Kol'skikh Saamov v Proshlom i Nastoyashchem*, p. 33.
63. Porsanger, 'The Eastern Sámi and the Missionary Policy of the Russian Orthodox Church', in Siikala et al., *Creating Diversities*, p. 114.
64. Kharuzin, *Russkie Lopari*, p. 210.
65. Acerbi, *Travels through Sweden*, vol. 2, p. 305.
66. Kharuzin, *Russkie Lopari*, p. 258.
67. A.A. Zhilinskii, *Krainii Sever Evropeiskoi Rossii*, Petrograd: 1919, p. 163.
68. Solbakk, *Sápmi Sameland*, pp. 206, 209.
69. Ibid., p. 209; Kulonen et al., *The Saami*, p. 26.
70. Porsanger, 'The Eastern Sámi and the Missionary Policy of the Russian Orthodox Church', pp. 110, 112.

71. Bolshakova, *Obychai i Mify Kol'skikh Saamov v Proshlom i Nastoyashchem*, pp. 32–3.
72. Porsanger, 'The Eastern Sámi and the Missionary Policy of the Russian Orthodox Church', pp. 115–16.
73. Bolshakova, *Obychai i Mify Kol'skikh Saamov v Proshlom i Nastoyashchem*, pp. 32–3, p. 65.
74. Took, *Running with Reindeer*, p. 110.
75. Ibid., p. 110.
76. Jukka Pennanen, 'The First Church in Finnish Lapland in Enontekiö', in Pennanen and Näkkäläjärvi, *Siidastallan: From Lapp Communities*, p. 158.
77. Seija Pulkamo (ed.), *Rovaniemen Seurakunta 350 Vuotta*, Rovaniemi: 1982, p. 15.
78. Ibid., p. 33.
79. Ibid., pp. 36–40.
80. Klemetti Näkkäläjärvi and Jukka Pennanen, 'The Assimilation of Sámi Reindeer-Herding Administration into the Finnish Government', in Pennanen and Näkkäläjärvi (eds), *Siidastallan: From Lapp Communities*, Inari: 2002, p. 118.
81. Acerbi, *Travels through Sweden*, vol. 2, p. 306.
82. Ibid., p. 54.
83. Ibid., p. 55.
84. Ibid., p. 56.
85. Karin Granqvist-Nutti, 'Samerna och den Kristna Missionen i 1600-talets Sverige', Presentation at the Nordic Sami History Symposium in Lövånger 13–14 February, Umeå: 1995, p. 63.
86. Ibid., pp. 60–1.
87. Teuvo Lehtola, 'The History of the Inari Sámi', in Pennanen and Näkkäläjärvi, *Siidastallan: From Lapp Communities*, p. 127.
88. Veli-Pekka Lehtola (ed.), *Inari*, Aanaar Oulu: 2003, p. 161.
89. Granqvist-Nutti, 'Samerna och den Kristna Missionen i 1600-talets Sverige', p. 60.
90. Acerbi, *Travels through Sweden*, vol. 2, p. 70.
91. Ibid., p. 77.
92. Ibid., p. 124.
93. Mulk and Bayliss-Smith, *Rock Art and Sámi Sacred Geography*, p. 106.
94. Kharuzin, *Russkie Lopari*, p. 181.
95. Solbakk, *Sápmi Sameland*, p. 143.
96. Veli-Pekka Lehtola, 'Folklore and its Present Manifestations', in Pennanen and Näkkäläjärvi, *Siidastallan: From Lapp Communities*, p. 181.
97. Acerbi, *Travels through Sweden*, vol. 2, p. 305.
98. Ibid., p. 312.
99. Mulk and Bayliss-Smith, *Rock Art and Sámi Sacred Geography*, p. 26.
100. Bolshakova, *Obychai i Mify Kol'skikh Saamov v Proshlom i Nastoyashchem*, p. 8.
101. Mulk and Bayliss-Smith, *Rock Art and Sámi Sacred Geography*, p. 62.

102. Kulonen et al., *The Saami*, p. 418.
103. Håkan Rydving, 'The Sámi Drums at Religious Encounter in the 17th and 18th Centuries', in Tore Ahlbäck and Jan Bergman (eds), *The Sámi Shaman Drum*, Scripta Instituti Donneriani Aboensis XIV, Stockholm: Donner Insitute, Turku and Almqvist & Wiksell, 1991, pp. 28–51, see p. 35.
104. Klemetti Näkkäläjärvi, 'The Sámi Flag', in Pennanen and Näkkäläjärvi, *Siidastallan: From Lapp Communities*, p. 21.
105. Veli-Pekka Lehtola, 'The Heritage of the Ancient World-View', in Pennanen and Näkkäläjärvi, *Siidastallan: From Lapp Communities*, p. 164.
106. Acerbi, *Travels through Sweden*, vol. 2, p. 309.
107. Zoë Hateehc Durrah Scheffy, 'Sámi Religion in Museums and Artistry', in Siikala et al., *Creating Diversities*, p. 226.
108. Ibid., p. 228.
109. Kulonen et al., *The Saami*, p. 213.
110. Solbakk, *Sápmi Sameland*, p. 223.
111. Ibid., p. 248.
112. Israel Ruong, *Lapps in Sweden*, Stockholm: 1867, p. 18.
113. Solbakk, *Sápmi Sameland*, p. 151.
114. Jens C.V. Johansen, 'Faith Superstition and Witchcraft in Reformation Scandinavia', in Olle Grell (ed.), *The Scandinavian Reformation: From Evangelical Movement to Institutionalisation of Reform*, Cambridge: Cambridge University Press, 1995, p. 202.
115. Solbakk, *Sápmi Sameland*, pp. 224–9.
116. Ruong, *Lapps in Sweden*, p. 75.
117. Leif Rantala, unpublished letters to the author, Jan. 2012.
118. Acerbi, *Travels through Sweden*, vol. 2, p. 311.
119. Mathisen, 'Hegemonic Representations of Sámi Culture', p. 21.
120. Acerbi, *Travels through Sweden*, vol. 2, p. 281.
121. Ibid., p. 288.
122. Ibid., p. 304.
123. Mantegazza, *Un Viaggio in Lapponia*, p. 91.
124. Acerbi, *Travels through Sweden*, vol. 2, p. 182.
125. Åman, *Om den Offentliga Vården*, p. 75.
126. Lehtola, 'The History of the Inari Sámi', p. 126.
127. Kulonen et al., *The Saami*, p. 60.
128. Kent, *The Soul of the North*, p. 43.
129. Ibid., p. 51.
130. Kulonen et al., *The Saami*, pp. 171–2.
131. Ibid., p. 215.
132. Ibid., p. 143.
133. Ibid., p. 14.
134. Ibid., p. 279.
135. Jukka Pennanen, 'From the Ice Age to the Present', in Pennanen and Näkkäläjärvi, *Siidastallan: From Lapp Communities*, p. 19.
136. Leif Rantala, unpublished letter to the author, Jan. 2012.

137. Le Comte Goblet d'Alviella, *Sahara et Laponie*, Paris: 1873, pp. 240–4.
138. Kulonen et al., *The Saami*, p. 158.
139. Lennart Lundmark, *Protest och Profetia: Korpela-rörelsen och drömmen om tidens ände*, Lund: 1985, p. 172.
140. Stephen Sommier, 'Viaggio in Norwegia ed in Lapponia', Bolletino del Club Alpino Italiano, 45, Turin: 1881, p. 16.
141. Lehtola, 'The History of the Inari Sámi', p. 128.
142. Kent, *The Soul of the North*, p. 63.
143. Anders Åman, 'Kyrkornas norrländska landskap', Provins. Norrländsk Magasin, 4, Piteå: 1990, pp. 27–8.
144. Martti Linkiola, 'The Skolt Sámi become Orthodox', in Pennanen and Näkkäläjärvi, *Siidastallan: From Lapp Communities*, p. 160.
145. Bolshakova, *Obychai i Mify Kol'skikh Saamov v Proshlom i Nastoyashchem*, pp. 37–8 and 231.
146. Linkola and Linkola, 'The Skolt Sámi—A Minority', p. 134.
147. Kulonen et al., *The Saami*, p. 269.
148. Kizny, *GULAG*, p. 78.
149. Ibid., p. 25.
150. Ibid., p. 78.
151. Ibid., p. 79.
152. Ibid.
153. Bolshakova, *Obychai i Mify Kol'skikh Saamov v Proshlom i Nastoyashchem*, pp. 40–1.
154. Kizny, *GULAG*, p. 80.
155. Bolshakova, *Obychai i Mify Kol'skikh Saamov v Proshlom i Nastoyashchem*, p. 42.
156. Minna Riikka Järvinen, *Armas Launis. Tunturisävelmiä Etsimässä. Lapissa 1904 ja 1905*, Helsinki: 2004, p. 42.
157. Lehtola, *Inari*, p. 461; Porsanger, 'The Eastern Sámi and the Missionary Policy of the Russian Orthodox Church', p. 119.
158. Lehtola, *Inari*, p. 456.
159. Lehtola, 'Folklore and its Present Manifestations', pp. 193, 195.
160. Kjell Olsen, 'Heritage, Religion and the Deficit of Meaning in Institutionalized Discourse', in Anna-Leena Siikala, Barbro Klein and Stein R. Mathisen (eds), *Creating Diversities: Folklore, Religion and the Politics of Heritage*, Studia Fennica. Foklorista 14, Helsinki: Finnish Literature Society, 2004, pp. 35–6.
161. Linkola, 'The Skolt Sámi become Orthodox', pp. 160–1.
162. Kulonen et al., *The Saami*, p. 400.
163. Porsanger, 'The Eastern Sámi and the Missionary Policy of the Russian Orthodox Church', p. 120.
164. Bolshakova, *Obychai i Mify Kol'skikh Saamov v Proshlom i Nastoyashchem*, p. 236.
165. Ibid., p. 239.
166. Kulonen et al., *The Saami*, p. 207.
167. Audhild Schanche, *Graver i ur och berg. Sámisk gravskikk og reliigion fra forhistorisk tid til nyere tid*, Karasjok: 2000, p. 173.

168. Nils Storå, *Burial Customs of the Skolt Lapps*, Folk-lore Fellows Communications 210. Suomalainen Tiedeakatemia, Academia Scientiarum Fennica, Helsinki: 1971, pp. 161–231.

169. Kulonen et al., *The Saami*, p. 64.

170. Solbakk, *Sápmi Sameland*, p. 183.

171. E.J. Kleppe, 'Archaeological material and ethnic identification: A study of Lappish material from Varanger, Norway', *Norwegian Archaeological Review*, 10, 1–2 (1977), pp. 32–46.

172. Storå, *Burial Customs of the Skolt Lapps*, p. 129.

173. Ernst Manker, *Lappmarksgravar, Dödsföreställningar och gravskick i lappmarkerna*, Acta Lapponica 17, Nordiska Museet, Stockholm: 1961, pp. 176–8.

174. Acerbi, *Travels through Sweden*, vol. 2, pp. 292–3.

175. Solbakk, *Sápmi Sameland*, p. 183.

176. Ibid., p. 185.

177. Bolshakova, *Obychai i Mify Kol'skikh Saamov v Proshlom i Nastoyashchem*, p. 221.

3. HEALTH, FAMILY, SEXUALITY AND EDUCATION

1. Leif Rantala, unpublished letter to the author, Jan. 2012.

2. Ulla-Maija Kulonen, Irja Seurujärvi, Kari and Risto Pulkkinen (eds), *The Saami: A Cultural Encyclopaedia*, Helsinki: Suomalaisen kirjallisuuden seura, 2005, p. 339.

3. Joseph Acerbi, *Travels through Sweden, Finland, and Lapland, to the North Cape in the Years 1798 and 1799*, vol. II, London: 1802, pp. 43–4.

4. Ibid., p. 21.

5. Leif Rantala, unpublished letter to the author, Jan. 2012.

6. J. Engström, *Resa genom Södra Lappland, Jemtland, Trondhem och Dalarne, år 1834 Första Delen Om S. Lappland och Jemtland*, Stockholm: 1835, pp. 4, 49.

7. Teuvo Lehtola, 'The History of the Inari Sámi', in Pennanen and Näkkäläjärvi, *Siidastallan: From Lapp Communities*, p. 24.

8. Le Comte Goblet d'Alviella, *Sahara et Laponie*, Paris: 1873, p. 197.

9. Jouko Vahtola, 'Spanska Sjukan i Enare Socken 1920', Presentation at Nordic Sámi History Symposium in Lövånger 13–14 Feb. 1995, Umeå: 1995, p. 185.

10. Acerbi, *Travels through Sweden*, vol. 2, p. 34.

11. Leif Rantala, unpublished letter to the author, Jan. 2012.

12. Acerbi, *Travels through Sweden*, vol. 2, p. 179.

13. Ibid., p. 180.

14. Jukka Pennanen, 'Reindeer Herding—The Defining Cultural Element in the Circumpolar Region', in Pennanen and Näkkäläjärvi, *Siidastallan: From Lapp Communities*, p. 60.

15. Leif Rantala, unpublished letter to the author, Jan. 2012.

16. M.M. Priivin, *Vesna sveta, Izbrannoeyu*, Moscow: 1955, p. 242.

17. Peter Sköld, 'Sámi and Smallpox in Eighteenth Century Sweden: Cultural Prevention of Epidemic Disease', in Wheelersburg, Northern People, *Southern States: Maintaining Ethnicities*, p. 104.

18. Ibid., pp. 96–8.

19. Ibid., pp. 99–101.

20. Acerbi, *Travels through Sweden*, vol. 2, p. 290.

21. Ibid., p. 305.

22. Sköld, 'Sámi and Smallpox in Eighteenth Century Sweden', pp. 107–8.

23. Ibid., pp. 3–7, 102 and 106.

24. Ibid., pp. 102–3.

25. William R. Mead, *An Experience of Finland*, London: Hurst, 1993, pp. 100 and 104.

26. Lehtola, 'The History of the Inari Sámi', p. 24.

27. Lehtola, 'Folklore and its Present Manifestations', pp. 192–3.

28. Sköld, 'Sámi and Smallpox in Eighteenth Century Sweden', p. 105.

29. V. Slavyanski, *Ocherki Severa*, V. pustynakh Laplandii Delo. god vozmoi, 1874 aprel'., p. 14.

30. F.G. Ivanov-Dyatlov, *Nablyudeniya vracha na Kol'skom Poluostrove (11 Yanvarya–11 Maya 1927 god)*, Leningrad: 1927, p. 105.

31. Kulonen et al., *The Saami*, p. 121.

32. Leif Rantala, unpublished letter, Jan. 2012.

33. Ivanov-Dyatlov, *Nablyudeniya vracha na Kol'skom Poluostrove (11 Yanvarya–11 Maya 1927 god)*, pp. 112–13.

34. Vahtola, 'Spanska Sjukan i Enare Socken 1920', pp. 185–9.

35. Acerbi, *Travels through Sweden*, vol. 2, p. 84.

36. Ibid., pp. 291–2.

37. Kulonen et al., *The Saami*, p. 76.

38. Leif Rantala, unpublished letter to the author, Jan. 2012.

39. Acerbi, *Travels through Sweden*, vol. 2, p. 290.

40. Klemetii Näkkäläjärvi, 'The *Siida*, or Sámi Village, as the Basis of Community Life', in Pennanen and Näkkäläjärvi, *Siidastallan: From Lapp Communities*, p. 119.

41. Lehtola, 'The History of the Inari Sámi', p. 128.

42. Kulonen et al., *The Saami*, p. 31.

43. Edward Rae, FRGS, *The White Sea Peninsula: A Journey in Russian Lapland and Karelia*, London: 1881, p. 39.

44. Acerbi, *Travels through Sweden*, vol. 2, p. 84.

45. Rae, *The White Sea Peninsula*, p. 19.

46. Linkola and Linkola, 'The Skolt Sámi—A Minority', in Pennanen and Näkkäläjärvi, *Siidastallan: From Lapp Communities*, p. 132.

47. V.I. Nemirovich-Danchenko, *Strana kholoda*, Moscow: 1877, p. 269.

48. Lehtola, 'The History of the Inari Sámi', p. 122.

49. Ibid., p. 152.

50. Nadezhda Zhizn' Bolshakova, *Obychai i Mify Kol'skikh Saamov v Proshlom i Nastoyashchem*, Murmansk: 2005, p. 231.

51. Ibid., p. 153.
52. D.A. Zolotarev, *Loparskaya ekspeditsiya*, Leningrad: 1927, p. 22.
53. T.V. Luk'yanchenko, *Profilaktika i lechenie boleznei u narodov Krainevo Severa Evropeiskoi Rossii (saamy i nentsy) Sibirskii etnograficheskii sbornik. Vypusk 9, Narody Rossiiskogo Severa i Sibiri*, Moscow: 1999, p. 147.
54. Bolshakova, *Obychai i Mify Kol'skikh Saamov v Proshlom i Nastoyashchem*, p. 153.
55. Jukka Pennanen, *Jos ei ole poropaimenia, kansa häviää, Kuolan poronhoitajen sosiokulttuurinen adaptaatio 20. vuosisadalla*, Suomalaisen kirjallisuuden seuran toimituksia 779, Helsinki: Suomalaisen kirjallisuuden seura, 2000, p. 99.
56. Z.E. Chernyakov, 'Kol'skie Lopari', *Spravochnik po narodam SSSR*, Leningrad: 1931, p. 3.
57. Lehtola, 'The History of the Inari Sámi', p. 128.
58. Bolshakova, *Obychai i Mify Kol'skikh Saamov v Proshlom i Nastoyashchem*, p. 232.
59. Acerbi, *Travels through Sweden*, vol. 2, pp. 49 and 290–2.
60. Solbakk, *Sápmi Sameland*, p. 250.
61. Acerbi, *Travels through Sweden*, vol. 2, p. 21.
62. Lehtola, 'The History of the Inari Sámi', p. 24.
63. Kjell Olsen, 'Heritage, Religion and the Deficit of Meaning in Institutionalized Discourse', Sikkala et al., *Creating Diversities*, p. 33.
64. Ibid., p. 37.
65. Ibid., footnote 1, p. 41.
66. Pennanen, *Jos ei ole poropaimenia, kansa häviää*, p. 99.
67. Bolshakova, *Obychai i Mify Kol'skikh Saamov v Proshlom i Nastoyashchem*, p. 69.
68. F. G. Ivanov-Dyatlov, *Nablyudeniya vracha na Kol'skom Poluostrove (11 Yanvarya–11 Maya 1927 god)*, Leningrad: 1927, p. 334.
69. Mulk and Bayliss-Smith, *Rock Art and Sámi Sacred Geography*, p. 19.
70. Olao Magno, *Storia de Costvmi de'Popoli Settentrionali*, translated by M. Remigio Fiorentino, Vinegia: 1561, p. 118.
71. Ibid., p. 120.
72. Acerbi, *Travels through Sweden*, vol. 2, pp. 284–9.
73. Asjbørn Nesheim, *Samene. Historie og kultur*, Oslo: 1966, p. 33.
74. Solbakk, *Sápmi Sameland*, p. 174.
75. Johannes Schefferus, *Lapponia*, Frankfurt: 1674, pp. 278–94.
76. Solbakk, *Sápmi Sameland*, p. 171.
77. Ibid., p. 171.
78. Ibid., p. 171.
79. Bolshakova, *Obychai i Mify Kol'skikh Saamov v Proshlom i Nastoyashchem*, p. 86.
80. G.I. Anokhin, *Sovremennaya sem'ya u saamov Kol'skogo poluostrova Skandinavskii sbornik VII*, Tallinn: 1963.
81. Bolshakova, *Obychai i Mify Kol'skikh Saamov v Proshlom i Nastoyashchem*, p. 87.

82. Pennanen, *Jos ei ole poropaimenia, kansa häviää*, p. 99.
83. Bolshakova, *Obychai i Mify Kol'skikh Saamov v Proshlom i Nastoyashchem*, p. 96.
84. N.B. Bogdanov, 'Protsess urbanizatsii korennogo naseleniya Kolskogo Poluostrova—saami v XX veke', *Lovozerskaya Pravda*, 18, 24 noyabrya, 2000.
85. Acerbi, *Travels through Sweden*, vol. 2, p. 182.
86. Ibid., p. 293.
87. Solbakk, *Sápmi Sameland*, p. 175.
88. Acerbi, *Travels through Sweden*, vol. 2, p. 52.
89. Solbakk, *Sápmi Sameland*, p. 176.
90. Stephen Sommier, 'Sui Lapponi e sui Finlandesi', *Settentrionali Archivo per l'Antropologia e l'Etnologia*, XVI, I (1886), p. 114.
91. V. Alymov, 'Om Samernas Assimilering', in *Rantala, Dokument om de ryska samerna och Kolahalvön Lapplands*, p. 41.
92. Bolshakova, *Obychai i Mify Kol'skikh Saamov v Proshlom i Nastoyashchem*, p. 231.
93. V.V. Sorokazjerdjev, 'Vasilij Alymov—Samernas Vän—Folkets Fiende', in *Rantala, Dokument om de ryska samerna och Kolahalvön Lapplands*, p. 62.
94. Andreas Sarri and Margareta Sarri, *Welcome to Shittown, En fotodokumentär*, Kiruna: 2006, p. 55.
95. Kulonen et al., *The Saami*, p. 93.
96. Ian Whitaker, 'Settler and Nomad in Northern Torne-Lappmark', *Polar Record*, XXI (1983), p. 337.
97. Lehtola, 'The History of the Inari Sámi', pp. 126, 128.
98. Kulonen et al., *The Saami*, pp. 93–5.
99. Solbakk, *Sápmi Sameland*, p. 142.
100. Ibid., p. 142.
101. Kulonen et al., *The Saami*, pp. 95–6 and 109.
102. Ibid., p. 289.
103. Ibid., p. 293.
104. Ibid., p. 388.
105. Bolshakova, *Obychai i Mify Kol'skikh Saamov v Proshlom i Nastoyashchem*, p. 172.
106. Ibid., p. 231.
107. Ibid.
108. V. Alymov, 'Samernas Skolundervisning på 1930-talet', in Rantala, *Dokument om de ryska samerna och Kolahalvön Lapplands*, p. 23.
109. Bolshakova, *Obychai i Mify Kol'skikh Saamov v Proshlom i Nastoyashchem*, p. 231.
110. Ibid., p. 232.
111. Alymov, 'Samernas Skolundervisning på 1930-talet', pp. 23–6.
112. Bolshakova, *Obychai i Mify Kol'skikh Saamov v Proshlom i Nastoyashchem*, p. 232.
113. Sorokazjerdjev, 'Alymov och den Nordliga Kommittén', p. 32.

114. Lennart Lundmark, 'Lappen är ombytlig, ostadig och obekväm', Svenska Statens Samepolitik i Rasismens Tidevarv, Umeå: 2002, p. 165.
115. Ibid., p. 166.
116. Kulonen et al., *The Saami*, p. 377.
117. Ibid., p. 9.
118. Ibid., pp. 338–9.
119. Veli-Pekka Lehtola, 'Towards a United Sápmi', in Pennanen and Näkkäläjärvi, *Siidastallan: From Lapp Communities*, pp. 204–5.
120. Kulonen et al., *The Saami*, p. 92.
121. Ibid., p. 408.
122. Ibid., pp. 377–8.
123. Bolshakova, *Obychai i Mify Kol'skikh Saamov v Proshlom i Nastoyashchem*, p. 234.
124. Kulonen et al., *The Saami*, p. 379.
125. Ibid., pp. 97 and 376.
126. Ibid., p. 95.
127. Joann Conrad, 'Mapping Space, Claiming Place: The (Ethno-) Politics of Everyday Geography in Northern Norway', in Siikala et al., *Creating Diversities*, p. 179.
128. Jari Ojala, Jari Eloranta and Jukka Jalava (eds), *The Road to Prosperity: An Economic History of Finland*, Suomalaisen kirjallisuuden seuran Toimituksia 1076, Helsinki: Suomalaisen kirjallisuuden seura, 2006, p. 229.
129. Riitta Kontio, 'Teemoja ja tendensejä pohjoisessa kirjallisuudessa', in Massa and Snellman, *Lappi. Maa,kansat, kulttuurit*, p. 231.
130. Lehtola, 'Towards a United Sápmi', p. 202.
131. Kulonen et al., *The Saami*, p. 246.
132. Ibid., p. 22.
133. Bolshakova, *Obychai i Mify Kol'skikh Saamov v Proshlom i Nastoyashchem*, p. 220.
134. Ibid., p. 224.
135. Sarri and Sarri, *Welcome to Shittown*, p. 55.
136. Bolshakova, *Obychai i Mify Kol'skikh Saamov v Proshlom i Nastoyashchem*, p. 234.
137. Veli-Pekka Lehtola, 'The Heritage of the Ancient World-View', in Pennanen and Näkkäläjärvi, *Siidastallan: From Lapp Communities*, p. 173.
138. Samuli Aikio, Teuvo Lehtola and Klemetti Näkkäläjärvi, 'Agriculture—a Sámi livelihood as of the 1700s', in Pennanen and Näkkäläjärvi, *Siidastallan: From Lapp Communities*, p. 58.
139. Solbakk, *Sápmi Sameland*, p. 88.
140. Acerbi, *Travels through Sweden*, vol. 2, pp. 304–5.
141. Mantegazza, *Un Viaggio in Lapponia*.
142. D'Alviella, *Sahara et Laponie*, p. 280.
143. Lennart Lundmark, *Så länge vi har marker. Samerna och staten under sex-hundra år*, Stockholm: 1998, p. 113.
144. Bolshakova, *Obychai i Mify Kol'skikh Saamov v Proshlom i Nastoyashchem*, p. 234.

145. Jukka Pennanen, 'The Sámi Museum—A Means of Strengthening Ethnicity', in Pennanen and Näkkäläjärvi, *Siidastallan: From Lapp Communities*, p. 215.
146. Kulonen et al., *The Saami*, pp. 433–4.
147. Rae, *The White Sea Peninsula*, p. 20.

4. SÁMI DWELLINGS, ARTS AND CRAFTS

1. Solbakk, *Sápmi Sameland*, p. 22.
2. Yrjö Kortelainen, *Entistä Enontekiötä*, Porvoo: 1995, p. 78.
3. Inga-Maria Mulk, 'Sacrificial Places and their Meaning in Sámi Society', in David Carmichael et al., *Sacred Sites, Sacred Places*, pp. 123–31.
4. Joseph Acerbi, *Travels through Sweden, Finland, and Lapland, to the North Cape in the Years 1798 and 1799*, vol. II, London: 1802, p. 208.
5. Ibid., pp. 209–10.
6. Kulonen et al., *The Saami*, p. 402.
7. Acerbi, *Travels through Sweden*, vol. 2, p. 210.
8. Johannes Schefferus, *Lapponia*, Frankfurt: 1674, p. 203.
9. Kulonen et al., *The Saami*, p. 243.
10. Acerbi, *Travels through Sweden*, vol. 2, pp. 208–9.
11. Teuvo Lehtola, 'The History of the Inari Sámi', in Pennanen and Näkkäläjärvi, *Siidastallan: From Lapp Communities*, p. 123.
12. Carpelan, 'The Cultural Background of Being Sámi', p. 26.
13. Bolshakova, *Obychai i Mify Kol'skikh Saamov v Proshlom i Nastoyashchem*, pp. 142–9.
14. Ibid., p. 141.
15. Leif Rantala, unpublished letter, Jan. 2012.
16. Solbakk, *Sápmi Sameland*, p. 74.
17. Ibid., p. 68.
18. Acerbi, *Travels through Sweden*, vol. 2, p. 176.
19. Ibid., p. 209.
20. Ibid., p. 211.
21. Le Comte Goblet d'Alviella, *Sahara et Laponie*, Paris: 1873, p. 249.
22. Kulonen et al., *The Saami*, pp. 78–81.
23. Olov Isaksson and Folke Isaksson, *Gammelstad Kyrkby vid Luleå Älv*, Stockholm: 1991, p. 107.
24. Neil Kent, *The Soul of the North: A Social, Architectural and Cultural History of the Nordic Countries, 1700–1940*, London: Reaktion, 2000 p. 157.
25. Stephen Sommier, 'Sui Lapponi e sui Finlandesi', *Settentrionali Archivo per l'Antropologia e l'Etnologia*, XVI, I (1886), p. 124.
26. Jukka Pennanen, *Jos ei ole poropaimenia, kansa häviää, Kuolan poronhoitajen sosiokulttuurinen adaptaatio 20. vuosisadalla*, Suomalaisen kirjallisuuden seuran toimituksia 779, Helsinki: Suomalaisen kirjallisuuden seura, 2000, p. 99.
27. Roger Took, *Running with Reindeer: Encounters in Russian Lapland*, London: John Murray, 2003, pp. 22, 224.

28. Inga-Maria Mulk, *Sirkas—ett Sámiskt fångstsamhälle i förändring Kr.f. -1600 e. Kr.*, Studia Archaelogica Universitatis Umensis 6, Umeå: 1994, p. 287.
29. Carpelan, 'The Cultural Background of Being Sámi', p. 24.
30. Lehtola, *Inari*, p. 53.
31. Zoë Hateehc Durrah Scheffy, 'Sámi Religion in Museums and Artistry', in Siikala et al., *Creating Diversities*, p. 228.
32. Ibid., p. 229.
33. Kulonen et al., *The Saami*, pp. 76 and 377.
34. Olsen, 'The Touristic Construction of the "Emblematic" Sámi', in Siikala et al., *Creating Diversities*, p. 299.
35. Kulonen et al., *The Saami*, p. 129.
36. Carpelan, 'The Cultural Background of Being Sámi', pp. 22–4.
37. Lehtola, *Inari*, p. 45.
38. Inga-Maria Mulk and Tim Bayliss-Smith, *Rock Art and Sámi Sacred Geography in Badjelánnda, Laponia, Sweden: Sailing Boats, Anthropomorphs and Reindeer*, Archaeology and Environment 22. Kungl. Skytteanska Samfundets Handlingar 58, Umeå: 2006, pp. 17–18.
39. Martti Linkola, 'Art for Decoration and Everyday Use', in Pennanen and Näkkäläjärvi, *Siidastallan: From Lapp Communities*, p. 168.
40. Ibid., pp. 176 and 178.
41. Ibid., p. 171.
42. Ibid., p. 173.
43. Mulk and Bayliss-Smith, *Rock Art and Sámi Sacred Geography*, pp. 1, 17, 36.
44. Solbakk, *Sápmi Sameland*, p. 22.
45. Mulk and Bayliss-Smith, *Rock Art and Sámi Sacred Geography*, p. 43.
46. Ibid., p. 36.
47. Per H. Ramqvist, 'Rock-Art and Settlement: Issues of Spatial Order in the Prehistoric Rock-Art of Fenno-Scandinavia', in George Nash and Christopher Chippindale (eds), *European Landscapes of Rock-Art*, London and New York: Routledge, 2002, p. 148.
48. Mulk and Bayliss-Smith, *Rock Art and Sámi Sacred Geography*, p. 33.
49. Lars Forsberg, 'The Social Context of the Rock Art in Middle Scandinavia during the Neolithic', in Antero Kare (ed.), *Myanndash—Rock Art in the Ancient Arctic*, Rovaniemi: Arctic Centre Foundation, 2000, pp. 60 and 65.
50. *Norrbottens-Kuriren*, 29 July 2005, p. 6.
51. Povl Simonsen, 'North Norwegian Rock Art', in Kare, *Myanndash*, p. 37.
52. Conrad, 'Mapping Space, Claiming Place', in Siikala et al., *Creating Diversities*, p. 171.
53. Mulk and Bayliss-Smith, *Rock Art and Sámi Sacred Geography*, pp. 34–5.
54. Anders Hesjedal, 'Hunter's Rock Art in North Norway: Problems of Chronology and Interpretation', *Norwegian Archaeological Review*, 27, 1 (1994), pp. 1–28, see p. 11.
55. Mulk and Bayliss-Smith, *Rock Art and Sámi Sacred Geography*, p. 35.
56. Ibid.
57. Ibid., p. 36.

58. Porsanger, 'A Close Relationship to Nature', in Pennanen and Näkkäläjärvi, *Siidastallan: From Lapp Communities*, p. 153.
59. Mulk and Bayliss-Smith, *Rock Art and Sámi Sacred Geography*, p. 36.
60. Schefferus, *Lapponia*, p. 259.
61. Acerbi, *Travels through Sweden*, vol. 2, p. 190.
62. Ibid., p. 191.
63. Lehtola, 'The Heritage of the Ancient World-View', p. 176.
64. Veli-Pekka Lehtola, 'Folklore and its Present Manifestations', in Pennanen and Näkkäläjärvi, *Siidastallan: From Lapp Communities*, p. 193.
65. Rolf Kjellström 'Johan Turi', in Puisto, *Sámi Dáidda*, p. 105.
66. Ibid., p. 107.
67. Lehtola, 'Folklore and its Present Manifestations', p. 183.
68. Nils Jernsletten and Iver Jåks, 'John Savio, kunstner eller "samekunstner"?' in Puisto, *Sámi Dáidda*, pp. 118–21.
69. Lehtola, 'Folklore and its Present Manifestations', p. 183.
70. Jernsletten and Jåks, 'John Savio, kunstner eller "samekunstner"?' p. 112.
71. Thomas A. Dubois, 'With an End in Sight: Sympathetic Portrayals of "Vanishing" Sámi Life in the Works of Karl Nickul and Andreas Alariesto', *Scandinavian Studies* (22 June 2003).
72. Jernsletten and Jåks, 'John Savio, kunstner eller "samekunstner"?' pp. 128, 130.
73. Ibid., p. 50.
74. Kulonen et al., *The Saami*, p. 23.
75. Ibid., p. 426.
76. Lehtola, 'Folklore and its Present Manifestations', pp. 193–5.
77. Ibid., pp. 191–3.
78. Jernsletten and Jåks, 'John Savio, kunstner eller "samekunstner"?' p. 128.
79. Ibid., p. 126.
80. Ibid., p. 124.
81. Lehtola, 'Folklore and its Present Manifestations', p. 193.
82. Ibid., p. 193.
83. Jernsletten and Jåks, 'John Savio, kunstner eller "samekunstner"?' p. 122.
84. Lehtola, 'Folklore and its Present Manifestations', p. 193.
85. Ibid.
86. Ibid.
87. Durrah Scheffy, 'Sámi Religion in Museums and Artistry', p. 225.
88. Ibid., pp. 226–7.
89. Kontio, 'Teemoja ja tendenssejä pohjoisessa kirjallisuudessa', in Massa and Snellman, *Lappi. Maa,kansat, kulttuurit*, p. 210.
90. Bolshakova, *Obychai i Mify Kol'skikh Saamov v Proshlom i Nastoyashchem*, p. 220.
91. Kulonen et al., *The Saami*, p. 376.
92. Kontio, 'Teemoja ja tendenssejä pohjoisessa kirjallisuudessa', p. 210.
93. Bolshakova, *Obychai i Mify Kol'skikh Saamov v Proshlom i Nastoyashchem*, p. 232.

94. Leif Rantala, unpublished letter to the author, Jan. 2012.
95. Bolshakova, *Obychai i Mify Kol'skikh Saamov v Proshlom i Nastoyashchem*, p. 234.
96. Kulonen et al., *The Saami*, p. 413.

5. LITERATURE

1. Nadezhda Zhizn' Bolshakova, *Obychai i Mify Kol'skikh Saamov v Proshlom i Nastoyashchem*, Murmansk: 2005, p. 135.
2. Leif Rantala, unpublished letter to the author, Jan. 2012.
3. Ulla-Maija Kulonen, Irja Seurujärvi, Kari and Risto Pulkkinen (eds), *The Saami: A Cultural Encyclopaedia*, Helsinki: Suomalaisen kirjallisuuden seura, 2005, p. 200.
4. Aage Solbakk, *Sápmi Sameland. Samenes historie fram til 1751*, Karasjok: 2007, pp. 239–41.
5. Kulonen et al., *The Saami*, p. 130.
6. Jomppanen's narratives are now in the archives of the Finnish Literature Society in Helsinki.
7. Marjut Huuskonen, *Stuorra-Jovnnan Ladut.Tenonsaamelaisten ympäristökertomusten maailmat*, Helsinki: 2004, p. 310.
8. Ibid., p. 308.
9. Ibid., pp. 308–9.
10. Ibid., p. 310.
11. Kulonen et al., *The Saami*, p. 411.
12. Gustaf von Düben, *Om Lappland och lapparne, företrädesvis de svenske, Ethnografiska studier*, Stockholm: Nordiska museet, 1977 [1873].
13. Mulk and Bayliss-Smith, *Rock Art and Sámi Sacred Geography*, p. 1.
14. Kulonen et al., *The Saami*, p. 115.
15. Kontio, 'Teemoja ja tendenssejä pohjoisessa kirjallisuudessa', in Massa and Snellman, *Lappi. Maa,kansat, kulttuurit*, pp. 220–1.
16. Ibid., p. 220.
17. Kulonen et al., *The Saami*, p. 283.
18. Ibid., p. 284.
19. Ibid., p. 9.
20. Ibid., p. 285.
21. Ibid., p. 283.
22. Linkola, 'The Skolt Sámi become Orthodox', in Pennanen and Näkkäläjärvi, *Siidastallan: From Lapp Communities*, p. 161.
23. Kulonen et al., *The Saami*, pp. 399–400.
24. Veli-Pekka Lehtola, 'Folklore and its Present Manifestations', in Pennanen and Näkkäläjärvi, *Siidastallan: From Lapp Communities*, p. 183.
25. Jukka Pennanen, 'From the Ice Age to the Present', in Pennanen and Näkkäläjärvi, *Siidastallan: From Lapp Communities*, p. 19.
26. Lehtola, 'Folklore and its Present Manifestations', pp. 183–4.
27. Kulonen et al., *The Saami*, pp. 271–2.

28. Vladimir Tjarnoluskij, *Den vilda renen i myt och rit*, Jokkmokk: 1993, pp. 7–8.
29. Matti Enbuske, Susanna Runtti and Turo Manninen (eds), *Rovaniemen historia. Jokivarsien kasvatit ja junantuomat vuoteen 1990*, Rovaniemi: 1997, p. 126.
30. Kulonen et al., *The Saami*, pp. 242–3.
31. Kontio, 'Teemoja ja tendensseja pohjoisessa kirjallisuudessa', p. 207.
32. Kulonen et al., *The Saami*, p. 419.
33. Kontio, 'Teemoja ja tendensseja pohjoisessa kirjallisuudessa', p. 210.
34. Kulonen et al., *The Saami*, p. 267.
35. Anni Linkola and Martti Linkola, 'The Skolt Sámi—A Minority within a Minority', in Pennanen and Näkkäläjärvi, *Siidastallan: From Lapp Communities*, p. 137.
36. Bolshakova, *Obychai i Mify Kol'skikh Saamov v Proshlom i Nastoyashchem*, p. 231.
37. Ibid., pp. 182–7.
38. Kulonen et al., *The Saami*, p. 276.
39. Ibid., p. 277.
40. Lehtola, 'Folklore and its Present Manifestations', p. 189.
41. Kulonen et al., *The Saami*, pp. 277–8.
42. Kontio, 'Teemoja ja tendensseja pohjoisessa kirjallisuudessa', p. 212.
43. Lehtola, 'Folklore and its Present Manifestations', p. 189.
44. Kulonen et al., *The Saami*, p. 412.
45. Ibid., p. 412.
46. Ibid., pp. 412–13.
47. Lehtola, 'Folklore and its Present Manifestations', p. 188.
48. Kulonen et al., *The Saami*, p. 69.
49. Ibid., p. 208.
50. Lehtola, 'Folklore and its Present Manifestations', pp. 191–2.
51. Kontio, 'Teemoja ja tendensseja pohjoisessa kirjallisuudessa', p. 207.
52. Lehtola, 'Folklore and its Present Manifestations', pp. 189–90.
53. Nils-Aslak Valkeapää, *Eanni, Eannážan*, Guovdageaidnu: 2001.
54. Kulonen et al., *The Saami*, p. 277.
55. Ibid., p. 23.
56. Ibid.
57. Ibid., p. 209.
58. Bolshakova, *Obychai i Mify Kol'skikh Saamov v Proshlom i Nastoyashchem*, p. 26.
59. Ibid., p. 27.
60. Lehtola, 'Folklore and its Present Manifestations', p. 189.
61. Kulonen et al., *The Saami*, p. 285.
62. Lehtola, 'Folklore and its Present Manifestations', p. 188.
63. Ibid., p. 190.
64. Kulonen et al., *The Saami*, pp. 205–6.
65. Bolshakova, *Obychai i Mify Kol'skikh Saamov v Proshlom i Nastoyashchem*, p. 224.

6. MUSIC, SPORT AND FILMS

1. Olao Magno, *Storia de Costvmi de'Popoli Settentrionali*, translated by M. Remigio Fiorentino, Vinegia: 1561, p. 120.

2. Joseph Acerbi, *Travels through Sweden, Finland, and Lapland, to the North Cape in the Years 1798 and 1799*, vol. II, p. 18.

3. Ibid., p. 286.

4. Ulla-Maija Kulonen, Irja Seurujärvi, Kari and Risto Pulkkinen (eds), *The Saami: A Cultural Encyclopaedia*, Helsinki: Suomalaisen kirjallisuuden seura, 2005, p. 107.

5. Matti Enbuske, Susanna Runtti and Turo Manninen (eds) *Rovaniemen historia. Jokivarsien kasvatit ja junantuomat vuoteen 1990*, Rovaniemi: 1997, p. 71.

6. Samuli Aikio, 'Epilogue', in Pennanen and Näkkäläjärvi, *Siidastallan: From Lapp Communities*, p. 217.

7. Minna Riikka Järvinen (ed.), *Armas Launis. Tunturisävelmiä etsimässä. Lapissa 1904 ja 1905*, Suomalaisen Kirjallisuuden Seuran Toimituksia 991, Helsinki: Suomalaisen Kirjallisuuden Seura, 2004, p. 11.

8. Ibid., pp. 57–129.

9. Ibid., pp. 137–76.

10. Ibid., p. 6.

11. Ibid., p. 177.

12. Ibid., pp. 237–84.

13. Ibid., p. 285.

14. Ibid., pp. 293–338.

15. Ibid., pp. 358–83.

16. Järvinen, *Armas Launis*.

17. Kulonen et al., *The Saami*, pp. 69–73.

18. Kjell Olsen, 'Heritage, Religion and the Deficit of Meaning in Institutionalized Discourse', Sikkala et al., *Creating Diversities*, p. 32.

19. Kulonen et al., *The Saami*, pp. 135–6.

20. Kontio, 'Teemoja ja tendenssejä pohjoisessa kirjallisuudessa', in Massa and Snellman, *Lappi. Maa,kansat, kulttuurit*, p. 222.

21. Veli-Pekka Lehtola, 'Folklore and its Present Manifestations', in Pennanen and Näkkäläjärvi, *Siidastallan: From Lapp Communities*, p. 192.

22. Nils-Aslak Valkeapää, 'Nature and its Meaning to the Artist', in Pennanen and Näkkäläjärvi, *Siidastallan: From Lapp Communities*, p. 180.

23. Olsen, 'Heritage, Religion and the Deficit of Meaning', p. 33.

24. Kontio, 'Teemoja ja tendenssejä pohjoisessa kirjallisuudessa', p. 223.

25. Kulonen et al., *The Saami*, p. 23.

26. Lehtola, 'Folklore and its Present Manifestations', p. 186.

27. Ibid., p. 186.

28. Anna-Leena Siikala, Barbro Klein and Stein R. Mathisen (eds), *Creating Diversities: Folklore, Religion and the Politics of Heritage*, Studia Fennica. Foklorista 14, Helsinki: Finnish Literature Society, 2004, p. 10.

29. Olsen, 'Heritage, Religion and the Deficit of Meaning', p. 31.
30. Lehtola, 'Folklore and its Present Manifestations', p. 187.
31. Kulonen et al., *The Saami*, p. 230.
32. Lehtola, 'Folklore and its Present Manifestations', p. 187.
33. Ibid.
34. Kulonen et al., *The Saami*, pp. 231–3.
35. Nadezhda Zhizn' Bolshakova, *Obychai i Mify Kol'skikh Saamov v Proshlom i Nastoyashchem*, Murmansk: 2005, p. 232.
36. Ibid., p. 234.
37. Anni Linkola and Martti Linkola, 'The Skolt Sámi—A Minority within a Minority', in Pennanen and Näkkäläjärvi, *Siidastallan: From Lapp Communities*, p. 130.
38. Bolshakova, *Obychai i Mify Kol'skikh Saamov v Proshlom i Nastoyashchem*, p. 223.
39. Acerbi, *Travels through Sweden*, vol. 2, pp. 288–9.
40. Leif Rantala, unpublished letter to the author, Jan. 2012.
41. 'Berättelse om W. Böhtlingks Resa Genom Finland och Lappmarkerne [=Kolahalvön År 1839]', in Leif Rantala, *Dokument om de ryska samerna och Kolahalvön Lapplands*, p. 9.
42. Linkola and Linkola, 'The Skolt Sámi—A Minority', p. 134.
43. Kulonen et al., *The Saami*, p. 377.
44. Ibid., p. 423.
45. Leif Rantala, unpublished letter to the author, Jan. 2012.
46. Kontio, 'Teemoja ja tendenssejä pohjoisessa kirjallisuudessa', p. 218.
47. Jukka Pennanen, 'The Sámi Museum—A Means of Strengthening Ethnicity', in Pennanen and Näkkäläjärvi, *Siidastallan: From Lapp Communities*, p. 215.
48. 'Last Yoik in Sámi Forests?' A video report for the UN published by the Sámi Council and Osuuskunta Marjarinteen Metsäpuutarha, produced by Signs of Life video workshop, 2007.
49. Kulonen et al., *The Saami*, pp. 291–2.
50. Bolshakova, *Obychai i Mify Kol'skikh Saamov v Proshlom i Nastoyashchem*, p. 234.

7. REINDEER HERDING AND OTHER LIVELIHOODS

1. Inga-Maria Mulk and Tim Bayliss-Smith, *Rock Art and Sámi Sacred Geography in Badjelánnda, Laponia, Sweden: Sailing Boats, Anthropomorphs and Reindeer*, Archaeology and Environment 22. Kungl. Skytteanska Samfundets Handlingar 58, Umeå: 2006, p. 17.
2. Ari Siiriäinen, 'The Stone and Bronze Ages', in Knut Helle (ed.), *The Cambridge History of Scandinavia*, vol. 1, *Prehistory to 1520*, Cambridge: Cambridge University Press, 2003, p. 45.
3. Ibid., p. 36.
4. V.K. Alymov, *Lopari kol'skogo poluostrova. Doklady I soobshcheniya*, Murmansk: 1927, p. 11.

5. Mulk and Bayliss-Smith, *Rock Art and Sámi Sacred Geography*, p. 17.

6. Aage Solbakk, *Sápmi Sameland. Samenes historie fram til 1751*, Karasjok: 2007, p. 87.

7. Ulla-Maija Kulonen, Irja Seurujärvi, Kari and Risto Pulkkinen (eds), *The Saami: A Cultural Encyclopaedia*, Helsinki: Suomalaisen kirjallisuuden seura, 2005, p. 125.

8. Ibid., p. 129.

9. Lars Børge H. Myklevold, 'Samisk båtbyggningshistorie i Nord-Salten', *Bårjås* (2005), pp. 17–26, Arran lulesamisk centre, Drag, pp. 17–26.

10. Pennanen, 'Reindeer Herding—The Defining Cultural Element in the Circumpolar Region', in Pennanen and Näkkäläjärvi, *Siidastallan: From Lapp Communities*, p. 60.

11. Olao Magno, *Storia de Costvmi de'Popoli Settentrionali*, translated by M. Remigio Fiorentino, Vinegia: 1561, p. 120.

12. Lennart Lundmark, *Uppbörd, utarmning, utveckling. Det Sámiska fångstsamhällets övergång till rennomadism i Lule Lappmark*, Malmö: 1982, p. 174.

13. Kulonen et al., *The Saami*, p. 153.

14. Ibid., p. 233.

15. Solbakk, *Sápmi Sameland*, p. 134.

16. Ibid., p. 188.

17. Joseph Acerbi, *Travels through Sweden, Finland, and Lapland, to the North Cape in the Years 1798 and 1799*, vol. II, p. 289.

18. Roger Took, *Running with Reindeer: Encounters in Russian Lapland*, London: John Murray, 2003, p. 61.

19. Solbakk, *Sápmi Sameland*, p. 130.

20. Kulonen et al., *The Saami*, pp. 432–3.

21. Solbakk, *Sápmi Sameland*, p. 135.

22. Lundmark, *Uppbörd, utarmning, utveckling. Det Sámiska fångstsamhällets övergång till rennomadism i Lule Lappmark*, p. 175.

23. Jukka Pennanen, 'Large-Scale Reindeer Herding brings Changes to the *Siidas*', in Pennanen and Näkkäläjärvi, *Siidastallan: From Lapp Communities*, p. 138.

24. Klemetti Näkkäläjärvi, 'Reindeer Earmarks as a Sámi Cultural System', in Pennanen and Näkkäläjärvi, *Siidastallan: From Lapp Communities*, p. 142.

25. Schefferus, *Lapponia*, pp. 321–35.

26. Solbakk, *Sápmi Sameland*, p. 119.

27. Ibid., p. 115.

28. Ibid., p. 118.

28. Ibid., p. 135.

30. Ibid., p. 10.

31. Ibid., p. 115.

32. Ibid., p. 254.

33. Ibid., p. 256.

34. Nadezhda Zhizn' Bolshakova, *Obychai i Mify Kol'skikh Saamov v Proshlom i Nastoyashchem*, Murmansk: 2005, p. 231.

35. Solbakk, *Sápmi Sameland*, p. 112.

36. Ibid., p. 100.
37. Peter Sköld, *Sámisk Bosäting i Gällivare 1550–1750*, Umeå: 1992, p. v.
38. Kulonen et al., *The Saami*, p. 187.
39. Porsanger, 'The Eastern Sámi and the Missionary Policy of the Russian Orthodox Church', in Siikala et al., *Creating Diversities*, p. 117.
40. Acerbi, *Travels through Sweden*, vol. 2, p. 46.
41. Ibid., p. 58.
42. Israel Ruong, *Lapps in Sweden*, Stockholm: 1867, p. 17.
43. Solbakk, *Sápmi Sameland*, p. 194.
44. Ibid., p. 196.
45. Klemetii Näkkäläjärvi, 'The *Siida*, or Sámi Village, as the Basis of Community Life', in Pennanen and Näkkäläjärvi, *Siidastallan: From Lapp Communities*, p. 118.
46. Solbakk, *Sápmi Sameland*, p. 95.
47. Acerbi, *Travels through Sweden*, vol. 2, p. 24.
48. Jukka Pennanen, 'The First Church in Finnish Lapland in Enontekio', in Pennanen and Näkkäläjärvi, *Siidastallan: From Lapp Communities*, p. 158.
49. Acerbi, *Travels through Sweden*, vol. 2, p. 79.
50. Yrjö Kortelainen, *Entistä Enontekiötä*, Porvoo: 1995, p. 78.
51. Acerbi, *Travels through Sweden*, vol. 2, p. 78.
52. Solbakk, *Sápmi Sameland*, p. 78.
53. Ibid., p. 82.
54. Ibid., p. 96.
55. Ibid., p. 252.
56. Ibid., p. 97.
57. Ibid., p. 126.
58. Teuvo Lehtola, 'The History of the Inari Sámi', in Pennanen and Näkkäläjärvi, *Siidastallan: From Lapp Communities*, p. 126.
59. Veli-Pekka Lehtola (ed.), *Inari*, Aanaar Oulu: 2003, p. 231.
60. Ibid.
61. Mantegazza, *Un Viaggio in Lapponia*, pp. 115–16.
62. Lennart Lundmark, '*Lappen är ombytlig, ostadig och obekväm': svenska statens samepolitik i rasismens tidevarv*, Umeå: 2002, p. 165.
63. Lundmark, *Så länge vi har marker. Samerna och staten under sexhundra år*, Stockholm: 1998, p. 105.
64. Ibid., p. 113.
65. Ian Whitaker, 'Settler and Nomad in Northern Torne-Lappmark', *Polar Record*, 21, 133 (Jan. 1983), p. 335.
66. Jukka Pennanen, 'From the Ice Age to the Present', in Pennanen and Näkkäläjärvi, *Siidastallan: From Lapp Communities*, p. 19.
67. Solbakk, *Sápmi Sameland*, p. 66.
68. Lehtola, 'The History of the Inari Sámi', p. 128.
69. Klemetti Näkkäläjärvi and Jukka Pennanen, 'The Assimilation of Sámi Reindeer-Herding Administration into the Finnish Government', in Pennanen and Näkkäläjärvi (eds), *Siidastallan: From Lapp Communities*, Inari: 2002, p. 66.

70. Enbuske, Runtti and Manninen, *Rovaniemen Historia*, p. 189.

71. Ibid.

72. Lundmark, *'Lappen är ombytlig, ostadig och obekväm'*, pp. 167–78.

73. Ibid., p. 166.

74. Klemetti Näkkäläjärvi and Jukka Pennanen, 'Reindeer Herding and the Cycle of the Seasons', in Pennanen and Näkkäläjärvi, *Siidastallan: From Lapp Communities*, pp. 62–3.

75. Näkkäläjärvi, 'Reindeer Earmarks as a Sámi Cultural System', pp. 140, 144.

76. Pennanen, 'Reindeer Herding—The Defining Cultural Element in the Circumpolar Region', p. 60.

77. Olsen, 'The Touristic Construction of the "Emblematic" Sámi', in Siikala et al., *Creating Diversities*, p. 298.

78. Kulonen et al., *The Saami*, pp. 25, 29.

79. Pennanen, 'Large-Scale Reindeer Herding brings Changes to the *Siidas*', pp. 138–9.

80. Linkola, 'The Skolt Sámi Today', in Pennanen and Näkkäläjärvi, *Siidastallan: From Lapp Communities*, p. 204.

81. V. Alymov, 'Samernas Skolundervisning på 1930-talet', in Rantala, *Dokument om de ryska samerna och Kolahalvön Lapplands*, p. 27.

82. Nadezhda Zhizn' Bolshakova, *Obychai i Mify Kol'skikh Saamov v Proshlom i Nastoyashchem*, Murmansk: 2005, p. 65.

83. Ibid., p. 232.

84. Z. Tjernjakov, 'Rapport om en Tjänsteresa till Räjongen Poljarnyj i Murmansk Krets 23.09.–17.10.1933', in Rantala, *Dokument om de ryska samerna och Kolahalvön Lapplands*, pp. 48–9.

85. Kulonen et al., *The Saami*, pp. 158–9.

86. Ibid., p. 327.

87. Took, *Running with Reindeer*, p. 72.

88. Kulonen et al., *The Saami*, p. 159.

89. Ibid., p. 160.

90. Ibid., p. 163.

91. Jukka Pennanen, *Jos ei ole poropaimenia, kansa häviää, Kuolan poronhoitajen sosiokulttuurinen adaptaatio 20. vuosisadalla*, Suomalaisen kirjallisuuden seuran toimituksia 779, Helsinki: Suomalaisen kirjallisuuden seura, 2000, p. 99.

92. Kulonen et al., *The Saami*, p. 160.

93. Ibid., p. 161.

94. Pennanen, *Jos ei ole poropaimenia, kansa häviää*, p. 100.

95. Stein R. Mathisen, 'Hegemonic Representations of Sámi Culture: From Narratives of Noble Savages to Discourses on Ecological Sámi', in Siikala et al., *Creating Diversities*, p. 25.

96. Ibid., pp. 27–8.

97. Kulonen et al., *The Saami*, p. 339.

98. K.D. Vorren, E. Nilsen and B. Mørkved, 'Age and Agricultural History of the "-stadir" Farms of North and Central Norway', *Norsk Geografisk Tidsskrift*, 44 (1990), pp. 98–9.

99. Samuli Aikio, Teuvo Lehtola and Klemetti Näkkäläjärvi, 'Agriculture—a Sámi livelihood as of the 1700s', in Pennanen and Näkkäläjärvi, *Siidastallan: From Lapp Communities*, p. 54.
100. Solbakk, *Sápmi Sameland*, p. 119.
101. A. Outakoski (ed.), *Rovaniemi Historia I Rovaniemen Seudun Vaiheita Vuotten 1631*, Rovaniemi: 1965, p. 144.
102. Aikio et al., 'Agriculture—A Sámi Livelihood as of the 1700s', p. 54.
103. Ibid.
104. Acerbi, *Travels through Sweden*, vol. 2, pp. 282–3.
105. Aikio et al., 'Agriculture—A Sámi Livelihood as of the 1700s', pp. 55–6.
106. Linkola and Linkola, 'The Skolt Sámi—A Minority within a Minority', p. 137.
107. Aikio et al., 'Agriculture—A Sámi Livelihood as of the 1700s', pp. 56–7.
108. Ibid., p. 58.
109. Solbakk, *Sápmi Sameland*, p. 85.
110. Enbuske et al., *Rovaniemen Historia*, p. 37.
111. Seija Pulkamo (ed.), *Rovaniemen Seurakunta 350 Vuotta*, Rovaniemi: 1982, p. 35.
112. Lehtola, *Inari*, p. 182.
113. Le Comte Goblet d'Alviella, *Sahara et Laponie*, Paris: 1873, p. 245.
114. Pennanen, 'From the Ice Age to the Present', p. 19.
115. Lehtola, *Inari*, p. 229.
116. Ibid., p. 301.
117. Enbuske et al., *Rovaniemen Historia*, p. 189.
118. Ibid., p. 182.
119. Ibid., p. 180.
120. Pennanen, 'From the Ice Age to the Present', p. 19.
121. Aikio et al., 'Agriculture—A Sámi Livelihood as of the 1700s', pp. 56–8.
122. Ibid., p. 58.
123. Kulonen et al., *The Saami*, p. 8.
124. Ibid., p. 398.
125. Ibid., p. 184.
126. Aikio et al., 'Agriculture—A Sámi Livelihood as of the 1700s', p. 58.
127. Ibid.
128. Ibid., p. 88.
129. Peter Sköld, *Sámisk Bosäting i Gällivare 1550–1750*, Umeå: 1992, p. v.
130. Solbakk, *Sápmi Sameland*, p. 116.
131. 'Berättelse om W. Böhtlingks Resa Genom Finland och Lappmarkerne [=Kolahalvön År 1839]', p. 12.
132. Jukka Pennanen, 'Lake Inari—The Centre of the Fishing Sámi', in Pennanen and Näkkäläjärvi, *Siidastallan: From Lapp Communities*, p. 46.
133. Ibid., p. 46.
134. Martti Linkola, 'Fishing Dictated the Rhythm of Life among the Skolt Sámi', in Pennanen and Näkkäläjärvi, *Siidastallan: From Lapp Communities*, pp. 47–8.

135. Rae, *The White Sea Peninsula*, p. 75.
136. Took, *Running with Reindeer*, p. 180.
137. Ibid., p. 183.
138. Linkola, 'Fishing Dictated the Rhythm of Life among the Skolt Sámi', pp. 47–8.
139. Solbakk, *Sápmi Sameland*, p. 94.
140. Pentti Pieski, 'The Teno Sámi and Fishing', in Pennanen and Näkkäläjärvi, *Siidastallan: From Lapp Communities*, p. 51.
141. Linkola, 'Fishing Dictated the Rhythm of Life among the Skolt Sámi', pp. 47–8.
142. Pieski, 'The Teno Sámi and Fishing', p. 51.
143. Ibid., p. 49.
144. Aage Solbakk, *'The Salmon Lords' Take Over Deatnu/the Tana River: English Angling 1850–1900*, Karasjok: 2011.
145. Pieski, 'The Teno Sámi and Fishing', pp. 49–50.
146. Ibid., p. 50.
147. Ibid., pp. 50–1.
148. Ibid., pp. 52–3.
149. Pentti Pieski, 'Goldin—An Old Fishing Method', in Pennanen and Näkkäläjärvi, *Siidastallan: From Lapp Communities*, p. 53.
150. A. De Capell Brooke, *Travels through Sweden, Norway and Finmark to the North Cape in the Summer of 1820*, London: 1823, p. 339.
151. Lundmark, *'Lappen är ombytlig, ostadig och obekväm'*, p. 167.
152. Borgos and Torgvaer, 'Samer og båtbygging', pp. 104–15.
153. Mulk and Bayliss-Smith, *Rock Art and Sámi Sacred Geography*, pp. 74 and 76.
154. Christer Westerdahl, *'Et sätt som liknar them uti theras öfriga lefnadsart'. Om äldre samiskt båtbygge och samisk båthantering*, Skrifter utgivna av Johan Nordlander-sällskapet 11, Umeå: 1987.
155. Borgos and Torgvaer, 'Samer og båtbygging', p. 11.
156. Mulk and Bayliss-Smith, *Rock Art and Sámi Sacred Geography*, p. 78.
157. Dennis J.B. Shaw, 'Urban Developments', in Maureen Perrie (ed.), *Russia: From Early Rus to 1689*, vol. 1, The Cambridge History of Russia, Cambridge: Cambridge University Press, 2006, p. 592.
158. Lehtola, 'The History of the Inari Sámi', p. 125.
159. Mulk and Bayliss-Smith, *Rock Art and Sámi Sacred Geography*, p. 17.
160. Acerbi, *Travels through Sweden*, vol. 2, p. 279.
161. J. Engström, *Resa genom Södra Lappland, Jemtland, Trondhem och Dalarne, år 1834 Första Delen Om S. Lappland och Jemtland*, Stockholm: 1835, p. 21.
162. L.L. Laestadius, *Om Möjligheten och Fördelen af Allmänna Uppodlingar i Lappmarken*, Stockholm: 1824, p. 1.
163. Ibid., p. 143.
164. Bolshakova, *Obychai i Mify Kol'skikh Saamov v Proshlom i Nastoyashchem*, p. 231.
165. Andrew Brown, *Fishing in Utopia*, London: Granta, 2008, p. 41.

166. Mulk and Bayliss-Smith, *Rock Art and Sámi Sacred Geography*, pp. 19–20.

167. D'Alviella, *Sahara et Laponie*, p. 282

168. Kontio, 'Teemoja ja tendenssejä pohjoisessa kirjallisuudessa', in Massa and Snellman, *Lappi. Maa,kansat, kulttuurit*, p. 229.

169. Enbuske et al., *Rovaniemen Historia*, p. 136.

170. Lehtola, 'The History of the Inari Sámi', p. 126.

171. Ibid., p. 127.

172. Kontio, 'Teemoja ja tendenssejä pohjoisessa kirjallisuudessa', p. 240.

173. Näkkäläjärvi and Pennanen, 'The Dimensions of Movement', in Pennanen and Näkkäläjärvi, *Siidastallan: From Lapp Communities*, p. 98.

174. Ibid., p. 99.

175. Lehtola, 'The History of the Inari Sámi', p. 127.

176. Took, *Running with Reindeer*, pp. 211–15, 222.

177. Kulonen et al., *The Saami*, p. 164.

178. Bolshakova, *Obychai i Mify Kol'skikh Saamov v Proshlom i Nastoyashchem*, p. 232.

179. Ibid., p. 234.

180. Pennanen, *Jos ei ole poropaimenia, kansa häviää*, p. 99.

181. Jari Ojala, Jari Eloranta and Jukka Jalava (eds), *The Road to Prosperity: An Economic History of Finland*, Suomalaisen kirjallisuuden seuran Toimituksia 1076, Helsinki: Suomalaisen kirjallisuuden seura, 2006, p. 79.

182. Pennanen, 'From the Ice Age to the Present', p. 20.

183. Pennanen, *Jos ei ole poropaimenia, kansa häviää*, p. 99.

184. Kulonen et al., *The Saami*, p. 398.

185. Took, *Running with Reindeer*, p. 270.

186. Enbuske et al., *Rovaniemen Historia*, p. 151.

187. Rae, *The White Sea Peninsula*, p. 61.

188. Took, *Running with Reindeer*, pp. 189–90.

189. V.V. Sorokazjerdjev, 'Vasilij Alymov—Samernas Vän—Folkets Fiende', in Rantala, *Dokument om de ryska samerna och Kolahalvön Lapplands*, p. 62.

190. Lehtola, 'The History of the Inari Sámi', p. 128.

191. Linkola and Linkola, 'The Skolt Sámi—A Minority within a Minority', p. 132.

192. Lehtola, 'The History of the Inari Sámi', p. 128.

193. Pennanen, *Jos ei ole poropaimenia, kansa häviää*, p. 100.

194. Took, *Running with Reindeer*, p. 227.

195. Ibid., p. 226.

196. Lehtola, 'The History of the Inari Sámi', p. 127.

197. Ojala et al., *The Road to Prosperity*, p. 123.

198. Mulk and Bayliss-Smith, *Rock Art and Sámi Sacred Geography*, pp. 1–2, 17.

199. Ibid., p. 110.

200. Ibid., p. 114.

201. Olsen, 'The Touristic Construction of the "Emblematic" Sámi', p. 296.

202. Linkola, 'The Skolt Sámi Today', p. 204.

203. Ojala et al., *The Road to Prosperity*, p. 41.

204. Kulonen et al., *The Saami*, p. 247.

205. Ibid., p. 251.

206. Ibid., pp. 304–7 and 322–3.

207. Tarmo Jompannen and Klemetti Näkkäläjärvi, 'Reindeer Herding under Pressure', in Pennanen and Näkkäläjärvi, *Siidastallan: From Lapp Communities*, p. 70.

208. Kaisa Korpijaakko-Labba, 'Threats to Reindeer Herding', in Pennanen and Näkkäläjärvi, *Siidastallan: From Lapp Communities*, p. 71.

209. Samuli Aikio, 'Epilogue', in Pennanen and Näkkäläjärvi, *Siidastallan: From Lapp Communities*, p. 216.

210. Dasjtjinskij, 'Den Sámiska Republikens President', in Rantala, *Dokument om de ryska samerna och Kolahalvön*, p. 67.

211. Pennanen, 'Reindeer Herding—The Defining Cultural Element in the Circumpolar Region', p. 60.

212. Tim Ingold, *The Skolt Lapps Today*, 1976, Cambridge: Cambridge University Press, p. 253.

213. Seija Tuulentie, *Meidän väemistömme. Valtaväestön retoriikat saamelaisten oikeuksista käydyissä eskusteluissa*, Suomalaisen Kirjallisuuden Seuran Toimituksia 807, Helsinki: Suomalaisen Kirjallisuuden Seura, 2001, pp. 310–11.

BIBLIOGRAPHY

Acerbi, Joseph, *Travels through Sweden, Finland, and Lapland, to the North Cape in the Years 1798 and 1799*, London: 1802.
———— *Vues De La Suede, De La Finlande, Et De La Lapponie, Depuis Le Detroit Du Sund Jusqu'au Cap Nord*, Paris: 1803.
Aikio, Marjut, *Saamelaiset kielenvaihdon kierteessä. Kielisosiologinen tutkimus viiden saamelaiskylan kielenvaihdosta 1910–1980*, Suomalaisen Kirjallisuuden Seuran Toimituksia 479, Helsinki: Suomalaisen Kirjallisuuden Seura, 1988.
Aikio, Niilo, *Liekkejä pakoon—Saamelaiset evakossa 1944–1945*, Helsinki: Suomalaisen Kirjallisuuden Seura, 2000.
Aikio, Samuli, *Olbmot ovdal min—sámiid historjá 1700–logu rádjái*, Ohcejohka: 1992.
d'Alviella, le Comte Goblet, *Sahara et Laponie*, Paris: 1873.
Alymov, V.K., *Lopari kol'skogo poluostrova. Doklady I soobshcheniya*, Murmansk: 1927.
Åman, Anders, 'Kyrkornas norrländska landskap', *Provins. Norrländsk Magasin*, 4, Piteå: 1990.
———— *Om den offentliga vården. Byggnader och verksamheter vid svenska vårdsinstitutioner under 1800-och 1900 talen. En arkitekturhistorisk undersökning*, Uppsala: 1976.
Anokhin, G.I. *Sovremennaya sem'ya u saamov Kol'skogo poluostrova Skandinavskii sbornik VII*, Tallinn: 1963.
Bergman, I., 'Vessels and Kettles: Socio-Economic Implications of the Cessation of Asbestos Pottery in Northern Sweden', *Arkeologi i Norr*, 10 (2007), pp. 1–14.
Bergman, I., L. Liedgren, L. Östlund and O. Zachrisson, 'Kinship and Settlements: Sami Residence Patterns in the Fenno-Scandian Alpine Areas around A.D. 1000', *Arctic Anthropology*, 45, 1 (2008), pp. 97–110.
Bjørklund, I., T. Brantenberg, H. Eidheim, J.A. Kalstad and D. Storm, *Sápmi—Becoming a Nation*, Tromsø: Tromsø University Museum, 2000.
Bogdanov, N.B., 'Protsess urbanizatsii korennogo naseleniya Kolskogo Poluostrova—saami v XX veke', *Lovozerskaya Pravda*, 18, (2000).

Bolshakova, Nadezhda, *Zhizn', obychai i mify kol'skikh saamov v proshlom i nastoyashchem*, Murmansk: 2005.

Borgos, Johan Ingvald and T. Torgvaer, 'Samer og båtbyggning', in *Människor och båtar i Norden*. *Sjöhistorisk Årsbok 1998–1999*, Stockholm: Föreningen Sveriges Sjöfartsmuseum, 1998, pp. 104–15.

Brooke, A. de Capell, *Travels through Sweden, Norway and Finmark to the North Cape in the Summer of 1820*, London: 1823.

Brown, Andrew, *Fishing in Utopia*, London: Granta, 2008.

Charnolusky, V. 'O kul'te Myandasha', *Skandinaviski sbornik*, Tallinn: 1966, pp. 301–15.

Chernyakov, Z.E., 'Kol'skie Lopari', *Spravochnik po narodam SSSR*, Leningrad: 1931.

Düben, Gustaf von, *Om Lappland och lapparne, företrädesvis de svenske. Ethnografiska studier*, Stockholm: Nordiska museet, 1977 [1873].

Dubois, Thomas A. 'With an End in Sight: Sympathetic Portrayals of "Vanishing" Sami Life in the Works of Karl Nickul and Andreas Alariesto', *Scandinavian Studies* (22 June 2003).

Enbuska, Matti, 'Samerna som nybyggare i Kemi socken och i Kemi Lappmark', Presentation at the Nordic Sami History Symposium in Lövånger, 13–14 Feb. 1995, Roger Kvist (ed.), Umeå: 1995.

Enbuske, Matti, Susanna Runtti and Turo Manninen (eds), *Rovaniemen historia. Jokivarsien kasvatit ja junantuomat vuoteen 1990*, Rovaniemi: 1997.

The English Atlas, vol. I–IV, Oxford: 1680–2.

Engström, J., *Resa genom Södra Lappland, Jemtland, Trondhem och Dalarne, år 1834, Första Delen Om S. Lappland och Jemtland*, Stockholm: 1835.

Forsberg, Lars, 'The Social Context of the Rock Art in Middle Scandinavia during the Neolithic', in Antero Kare (ed.), *Myanndash—Rock Art in the Ancient Arctic*, Rovaniemi: Arctic Centre Foundation, 2000.

Granqvist-Nutti, Karin, 'Samerna och den Kristna Missionen i 1600-talets Sverige', Presentation at the Nordic Sami History Symposium in Lövånger, 13–14 Feb. 1995, Roger Kvist (ed.), Umeå: 1995.

Hackzell, Nicolavs, *Lula*, Uppsala: 1731.

Hallström, Gustav, 'Lapska offersplatser', in Svenska Fornminnesföreningen, *Arkeologiska studier tillägnad H.K.H. Kronprins Gustaf Adolf*, Stockholm: 1932, pp. 111–31.

Hansen, Lars Ivar, 'The Saami Hunting Society in Transition: Approaches, Concepts and Context', in K. Julku (ed.), *Historia Fenno-Ugrica 1:1, Congressus Primus Historiae Fenno-Ugricae*, Oulu: Societas Historiae Fenno-Ugricae, 1996, pp. 315–34.

—— 'Trade and Markets in Northern Fenno-Scandinavia A.D. 1550–1750', *Acta Borealia*, 1, 2 (1984), pp. 47–79.

Hansen, Lars Ivar and Bjørnar Olsen, *Samenes Historie farm til 1750*, Oslo: 2007.

Helskog, Knut, Helleristningene i Alta: Spor etter ritualer og dagligliv i Finnmarks forhistorie, Alta: Alta Museum, 1988.

BIBLIOGRAPHY

Hesjedal, Anders, 'Hunter's Rock Art in North Norway: Problems of Chronology and Interpretation', *Norwegian Archaeological Review*, 27, 1 (1994), pp. 1–28.

Hesjedal, Anders, C. Damm, B. Olsen and I. Storli, *Arkeologi på Slettnes. Dokumentasjon av 11.000 års bosetning*, Tromsø Museums Skrifter 26, Tromsø: Tromsø Museum, 1996.

Holger, Lena, *Helmer Osslund*, Stockholm: 2008.

Huuskonen, Marjut, *Stuorra-Jovnnan ladut. Tenonsaamelaisten ympäristökertomusten maalimat*, Suomalaisen Kirjallisuuden Seuran Toimituksia 986, Helsinki: Suomalaisen Kirjallisuuden Seura, 2004.

Ingold, Tim, *The Skolt Lapps Today*, Cambridge: Cambridge University Press, 1976.

Isaksson, Olov and Folke Isaksson, *Gammelstad kyrkby vid Luleå älv*, Stockholm: 1991.

Ivanov-Dyatlov, F.G., *Nablyudeniya vracha na Kol'skom Poluostrove (11 Yanvarya–11 Maya 1927 god)*, Leningrad: 1927.

Järvinen, Min na Riikka (ed.), *Armas Launis. Tunturisävelmiä etsimässä. Lapissa 1904 ja 1905*, Suomalaisen Kirjallisuuden Seuran Toimituksia 991, Helsinki: Suomalaisen Kirjallisuuden Seura, 2004.

Johansen, Jens C.V., 'Faith, Superstition and Witchcraft in Reformation Scandinavia', in Olle Grell (ed.), *The Scandinavian Reformation: From Evangelical Movement to Institutionalisation of Reform*, Cambridge: Cambridge University Press, 1995.

Jutikkala, Eino, *Bonden i Finland genom tiderna*, Helsinki: 1963.

Kamusella, Tomasz, *The Politics of Language and Nationalism in Modern Central Europe*, Basingstoke/New York: Palgrave, 2009.

Kent, Neil, *A Concise History of Sweden*, Cambridge: Cambridge University Press, 2008.

——— *The Soul of the North: A Social, Architectural and Cultural History of the Nordic Countries, 1700–1940*, London: Reaktion, 2000.

Kharuzin, N.N., *Russkie Lopari—Ocherki*, Moscow: 1890.

Khrestomatiya po istorii Karelii s derevneishikh vremen do kontsa XVII veka, Petrozavodsk: 1939.

Kleppe, E.J., 'Archaeological material and ethnic identification: A study of Lappish material from Varanger, Norway', *Norwegian Archaeological Review*, 10, 1–2 (1977), pp. 32–46.

Korhonen, Mikko, *Johdatus lapin kielen historiaan*, Suomalaisen Kirjallisuuden Seuran Toimituksia 370, Helsinki: Suomalaisen Kirjallisuuden Seura, 1981.

Korhonen, Teppo, *Poroerotus. Historia, toiminta ja tekniset ratkaisut*, Suomalaisen Kirjallisuuden Seuran Toimituksia 1165, Helsinki: Suomalaisen Kirjallisuuden Seura, 2008.

Kortelainen, Yrjö, *Entistä Enontekiötä*, Porvoo: 1995.

Kozhevnikov, A.V., *Solntse ezdit na olenyakh*, Moscow: 1972.

Kulonen, Ulla-Maija, Juha Pentikäinen and Irja Seurujärvi (eds) *Johdatus*

BIBLIOGRAPHY

Saamentutkimukseen, Suomalaisen Kirjallisuuden Seuran Toimituksia 131, Helsinki: Suomalaisen Kirjallisuuden Seura, 1994.

Kulonen, Ulla-Maija, Irja Seurujärvi-Kari Pulkkinen and Risto Pulkkinen (eds), *The Saami: A Cultural Encyclopaedia*, Helsinki: Suomalaisen Kirjallisuuden Seura, 2005.

Lähteenmäki, Maria, *Kalotin kansaa. Rajankäynnit ja vuorovaikutus Pohjoiskalotilla 1808–1889*, Helsinki: Suomalaisen Kirjallisuuden Seura, 2004.

Læstadius, L.I., *Om Möjligheten och Fördelen af Allmänna Uppodlingar i Lappmarken*, Stockholm: 1824.

Læstadius, Lars Levi, *Fragmenter i Lappska Mythologien*. NIF Publications 37, Reimund Kvideland (ed.), Åbo: Nordic Institute of Folklore, 1997.

Launis, Armas, *Tunturisävelmiä etsimässä. Lapissa 1904–1905*, Suomalaisen Kirjallisuuden Seuran Toimituksia 991, Minna Riikka Järvinen (ed.), Helsinki: Suomalaisen Kirjallisuuden Seura, 2004.

Leem, Knud *Beskrivelse over Finmarkens Lapper, deres Tungemaal, Levemaade og ferrige Afgudsdyrkelse, ... med J.E. Gunneri ... Anmærkninger: og E.J. Jassen-S ... Afhandling om de Norske Finnen og Lappers hedenske Relgion. C.L. ... de Lapponibus Finmarchiæ ... commentatio, etc. Dan. & Lat.,2 pt.*, Copenhagen: 1767.

——— *Beskrivelse over Finmarkens Lapper, deres Tungemaal, Levemaade og forrige Afgudsdyrkelse, oplyst ved mange Kaabberstykker = Canuti Leemii De Lapponibus Finmarchiae, eorumqve lingva, vita et religione pristina commentatio, multis tabulis aeneis illustrata/med J.E. Gunneri Anmærkninger. Og E.J. Jessen-S Afhandling om de norske Finners og Lappers hedenske Religion*, Copenhagen: 1767.

——— *En Lappisk Grammatica, efter den Dialect, som bruges af Field-Lapperne udi Porsanger-Fiorden, samt et Register; ... hvorhos er føyet et Blad af ... L. Holdbergs Kirke-Historie oversat in det Lappiske Tungemall, med en Analysi over et hvert Ord, etc.*, Copenhagen: 1748.

Lehtola, Veli-Pekka (ed.), *Inari. Aanaar. Inarin historia jääkaudesta nykypäivään*, Oulu: 2003.

Lindgren, Anna-Riitta, *Helsingin saamelaiset ja oma Kieli, Suomalaisen kirjallisuuden seuran toimituksia 801*, Helsinki: Suomalaisen Kirjallisuuden Seura, 2000.

Luk'yanchenko, T.V., *Rasselenie kol'skikh saamov v XVI vv. K istorii malykh narodnostei Evropeiskogo Severa SSSR*, Petrozavodsk: 1979.

Lund, Niels (ed.), *Two Voyagers at the Court of King Alfred: The Ventures of Ohthere and Wulfstan together with the Description of Northern Europe from the 'old English Orosius'*, York: Sessions, 1984.

Lundmark, Lennart, *'Lappen är ombytlig, ostadig och obekväm': svenska statens samepolitik i rasismens tidevarv*, Umeå: 2002.

——— *Protest och Profetia. Korpela-rörelsen och drömmen om tidens ände*, Lund: Arkiv, 1985.

——— *Samernas skatteland*, Stockholm: 2006.

—— Så länge vi har marker. Samerna och staten under sex hundra år, Stockholm: 1998.

—— Uppbörd, utarmning, utveckling. Det samiska fångstsamhällets övergång till rennomadism i Lule Lappmark, Malmö: 1982.

Magnus, Olaus, Storia de Costvmi de'Popoli Settentrionali, Vinegia: 1561.

Manker, Ernst, Lappmarksgravar, Dödsföreställningar och gravskick i Lappmarkerna, Acta Lapponica 17, Stockholm: Nordiska museet, 1961.

Mantegazza, Paulo, Lapponie, Milan: 1881.

Massa, Ilmo and Hanna Snellman (eds), Lappi—maa, kansat, kulttuurit, Helsinki: Suomalaisen Kirjallisuuden Seura, 2003.

Mead, William R., An Experience of Finland, London: Hurst, 1993.

Mulk, Inga-Maria, 'Conflicts Over the Repatriation of Sami Cultural Heritage in Sweden', Acta Borealia, 26, 2 (2009), pp. 194–214.

—— From Metal to Meat: Continuity in Ritual Practices at a Saami Sacrificial Site, Viddjavárri, Lapland, Northern Sweden, Oulu: 2009.

—— 'Sacrificial Places and their Meaning in Saami society', in David Carmichael, Jane Hubert, Brian Reeves and Audhild Chanche (eds), Sacred Sites, Sacred Places, London: Routledge, 1994, pp. 123–31.

—— Sirkas—ett samiskt fångstsamhälle i förändring Kr.f. -1600 e. Kr., Studia Archaelogica Universitatis Umensis 6, Umeå: 1994

Mulk, Inga-Maria and Tim Bayliss-Smith, Rock Art and Sami Sacred Geography in Badjelánnda, Laponia, Sweden. Sailing Boats, Anthropomorphs and Reindeer, Archaeology and Environment 22. Kungl. Skytteanska Samfundets Handlingar 58, Umeå: 2006.

Myklevold, Lars Børge H., 'Samisk båtbyggningshistorie i Nord-Salten', Bårjås, pp. 17–26, Arran lulesamisk centre: Drag, 2005.

Näkkäläjärvi, Klemetti and Jukka Pennanen (eds), Siidastallan: From Lapp Communities to Modern Sámi Life, Inari: 2002.

Nemirovich-Danchenko, V.I., Strana kholoda, Moscow: 1877.

Nergaard, Jens Ivar, 'Ghosts and Psychiatrists in Sápmi [Lapland] North Norway', sections from a book manuscript delivered at a Magic Circle Seminar, organised by Piers Vitebsy in Cambridge, 4 June 2010.

Nesheim, Asjbørn, Samene. Historie og kultur, Oslo: 1966.

Nils Storå, Burial Customs of the Skolt Lapps, Folk-lore Fellows Communications 210. Suomalainen Tiedeakatemia, Academic Scientiarum Fennica, Helsinki: 1971.

Norrbottens-Kuriren, 29 July 2005.

Ojala, Jari, Jari Eloranta and Jukka Jalava (eds), The Road to Prosperity: An Economic History of Finland, Suomalaisen Kirjallisuuden Seuran Toimituksia 1076, Helsinki: Suomaleisen Kirjallisuuden Seura, 2006.

Outakoski, A. (ed.) Rovaniemen historia i Rovaniemen seudun vaiheita vuotten 1631, Rovaniemi: 1965.

Palmgren, Nils and Herje Granberg, Helmer Osslund, 2nd Edition, Stockholm: 1952.

BIBLIOGRAPHY

Paulaharju, Samuli, *Kolttain mailta*, 2nd Edition, Helsinki: Suomalaisen Kirjallisuuden Seura, 2009.

Pelle, Larisa, 'Off to See Father Christmas', *Taleon Club Magazine*, St Petersburg, Jan. 2007.

Pennanen, Jukka, *Jos ei ole poropaimenia, kansa häviää, Kuolan poronhoitajen sosiokulttuurinen adaptaatio 20. vuosisadalla*, Suomalaisen Kirjallisuuden Seuran Toimituksia 779, Helsinki: Suomalaisen Kirjallisuuden Seura, 2000.

Priivin, M.M., *Vesna sveta. Izbrannoeyu*, Moscow: 1955.

Puisto, Tuula (ed.), *Sámi Dáidda*, Helsinki: Davviriikkaid Dáiddaguovddaš, 1981.

Pulkamo, Seija (ed.), *Rovaniemen seurakunta 350 vuotta*, Rovaniemi: 1982.

Qvigstad, J. and K.B. Wiklund, *Bibliographie der Lappischen Literatur von. Memoires de la Société Finno-Ougrienne XIII*, Helsinki: 1899.

Rae, Edward, FRGS, *The White Sea Peninsula: A Journey in Russian Lapland and Karelia*, London: 1881.

Ramqvist, Per H., 'Rock-Art and Settlement: Issues of Spatial Order in the Prehistoric Rock-Art of Fenno-Scandinavia', in George Nash and Christopher Chippindale (eds), *European Landscapes of Rock-Art*, London and New York: Routledge, 2002.

Rantala, Leif, *Articles and Books Concerning the Finnish Scientific Fieldwork on the Kola Peninsula from 1820 until 1917, Report in Educational Sciences, University of Lapland 5*, Rovaniemi: 2010.

—— (ed.) *Dokument om de ryska samerna och Kolahalvön, Lapplands universitets pedagogiska publikationer 15*, Rovaniemi: 2006.

—— *Kuolaan. Venäjän vallan aikana Kuolan niemimaalla käyneet suomalaiset tiedemiehet ja heidän kirjoituksensa*, Lapin yliopiston kasvatustieteellisiä raportteja 5, Rovaniemi: 2008.

Ruong, Israel, *The Lapps in Sweden*, Stockholm: 1967.

Rydving, Håkan, 'The Saami Drums at Religious Encounter in the 17th and 18th Centuries', in Tore Ahlbäck and Jan Bergman (eds), *The Saami Shaman Drum*, Scripta Instituti Donneriani Aboensis XIV, Stockholm: Donner Institute, Turku and Almqvist & Wiksell, 1991, pp. 28–51.

Sammallahti, Pekka, *The Saami Languages: An Introduction*, Kárášjohka/ Karasjok: 1998.

Sarri, Andreas and Margareta Sarri, *Welcome to Shittown. En fotodokumentär*, Kiruna: 2006.

Schanche, Audhild, *Graver i ur och berg. Samisk gravskikk og religion fra forhistorisk tid til nyere tid*, Karasjok: 2000.

Schefferus, Johannes, *Lapponia*, Frankfurt: 1674.

Seurujärvi-Kari, Irja (ed.) *Beaivvi Máná. Saamelaisten juuret ja nykyaika*, Suomalaisen Kirjallisuuden Seuran Tietolipas 164, Helsinki: Suomalaisen Kirjallisuuden Seura, 2000.

Siikala, Anna-Leena, Barbro Klein and Stein R. Mathisen (eds), *Creating Diversities: Folklore, Religion and the Politics of Heritage*, Finnish Literature

Society's Studia Fennica. Folklorista 14, Helsinki: Finnish Literature Society, 2004.

Simonsen, Povl, 'North Norwegian Rock Art', in Antero Kare (ed.), *Myanndash—Rock Art in the Ancient Arctic*, Rovaniemi: Arctic Centre Foundation, 2000.

Sjøvold, Thorleif, *The Iron Age Settlement of Arctic Norway: A Study of the Expansion of Iron Age Culture within the Arctic Circle. II. Late Iron Age*, Tromsø Museums Skrifter vol. X.2., Tromsø, Oslo and Bergen: Norwegian Universities Press, 1974.

Sköld, Peter, 'Saami and Smallpox in Eighteenth Century Sweden: Cultural Prevention of Epidemic Disease', in Robert P. Wheelersburg (ed.), *Northern People Southern States: Maintaining Ethnicities in the Circumpolar World*, Umeå: 1996.

—— *Samerna och deras Historia. Metodövningar i samisk 1600- och 1700-talshistoria*, Umeå: 1993.

—— *Samisk Bosätning i Gällivare 1550–1750*, Umeå: 1992.

—— 'The Saami Experience of Smallpox in Eighteenth-Century Sweden', unpublished document from 1995.

Slavyanski V., *Ocherki Severa*, V. pustynakh Laplandii Delo. god vozmoi, 1874 aprel'.

Solbakk, Aage, *'The Salmon Lords' Take Over Deatnu/the Tana River: English Angling, 1850–1900*, Karasjok: 2011.

—— *Sápmi Sameland. Samenes historie fram til 1751*, Karasjok: 2007.

Solovetskii Pyaterik, Moscow: 1991.

Sommier, Stephen, 'Sui Lapponi e sui Finlandesi Settentrionali', *Archivo per l'Antropologia e l'Etnologia*, XVI, I (1886).

—— *Viaggio in Norvegia ed in Lapponia*, Turin: 1881.

Sörlin, Sverker, 'Fransmans resor i det exotiska Lappland', in Pontius Grate (ed.), *Solen och nordstjärnan. Frankrike och Sverige på 1700-talet*, Stockholm: National Museum, 1993.

Storå, Nils, *Burial Customs of the Skolt Lapps*, Folk-lore Fellows Communications 210. Suomalainen Tiedeakatemia, Academic Scientiarum Fennica, Helsinki: 1971.

Svonni, Mikael, 'The Future of Saami: Minority Language Survival in Circumpolar Scandinavia', in Robert P. Wheelersburg (ed.), *Northern People Southern States. Maintaining Ethnicities in the Circumpolar World*, Umeå: 1996.

Tanner, Väinö, *Antropogeografiska studier inom Petsamo-området. 1. Skolt-lapparna*, Fennia 49, 4, Helsinki: 1929.

—— *Ihmismaantieteellisiä tutkimuksia Petsamon seudulta. I. Kolttalappalaiset*, Suomalaisen Kirjallisuuden Seuran Toimituksia 780, Susiluoto, Paulo (ed.), Helsinki: Suomalaisen Kirjallisuuden Seura, 2000.

Tegengren, H., *En utdöd lappkultur i Kemi Lappmark. Studier i Nordfinlands kolonisationshistoria*, Acta Academiae Aboensis, Humaniora 19, 4, Åbo: 1952.

BIBLIOGRAPHY

Tjarnoluskij, Vladimir, *Den vilda renen i myt och rit*, Jokkmokk: 1993.

Took, Roger, *Running with Reindeer: Encounters in Russian Lapland*, London: John Murray, 2003.

Tornæi, Johannis J., *Beskrifning ofver Tornå och Kemi Lappmarker* (written in 1672), Stockholm: 1772.

Turi, Johan, *Min bok om samene*, Karasjok: 2011.

—— *Muitalus sámiid birra (1910)*, Revised Edition, Karasjok: 2010.

Tuulentie, Seija, *Meidän vähemmistömme. Valtaväestön retoriikat saamelaisten oikeuksista käydyissä keskusteluissa*, Suomalaisen Kirjallisuuden Seuran Toimituksia 807, Helsinki: Suomalaisen Kirjallisuuden Seura, 2001.

Vahtola, Jouko, 'Spanska Sjukan i Enare Socken 1920', Presentation at the Nordic Sami History Symposium in Lövånger 13 to 14 February 1995, Umeå: 1995.

Valkeapää, Nils-Aslak, *Beaivi, Áhčážan*, Guovdageaidnu: 1988.

—— *Eanni, Eannážan*, Guovdageaidnu: 2001.

Vorren, K.D., E. Nilsen and B. Mørkved, 'Age and Agricultural History of the "-stadir" Farms of North and Central Norway', *Norsk Geografisk Tidsskrift*, 44 (1990), pp. 79–102.

Westerdahl, Christer, *'Et sätt som liknar them uti theras öfriga lefnadsart'. Om äldre samiskt båtbygge och samisk båthantering*, Skrifter utgivna av Johan Nordlander-sällskapet 11, Umeå: Johan Nordlander-sällskapet, 1987.

Whitaker, Ian, 'Ohthere's Account Reconsidered', *Arctic Anthropology*, 18 (1981), pp. 1–10.

—— 'Settler and Nomad in Northern Torne Lappmark', *Polar Record*, XXI (1983).

Ylikoski, J., 'Documents on the Russian Saami and the Kola Peninsula', Leif Rantala (ed.), *Polar Record* (2007).

—— 'Dokument om de ryska samerna och Kolahalvön', University of Lapland Publications in Education 15, Rovaniemi: 2006.

Yur'eva, P.A. *skazka o solntse*, Murmansk: 1978.

Zhilinskii, A.A., *Krainii sever Evropeiskoi Rossii*, Petrograd: 1919.

Zolotarev, D.A., *Loparskaya ekspeditsiya*, Leningrad: 1927.

INDEX

Åarjelhsaemien (South Sámi Theatre): productions staged by, 193

Abakumov, Commissar S.A.: military prison camp administered by, 115

Academy of Fine Arts: students of, 174

Acerbi, Giuseppe: observations of Sámi cultural practices, 4–5, 16, 26, 32–3, 45–6, 79–80, 97, 100–2, 104, 108, 121, 123–5, 129–30, 133–4, 152, 155–6, 168, 199, 208–9, 217, 222, 224–5, 237

Acta Lapponica (Lapp Journal): editorial staff of, 105

Adam of Bremen: *Gesta Hammaburgensis ecclesiae pontificum*, 10

agriculture: animal husbandry, 26, 29, 236–7; cattle, 238–9; development of, 236–8; horses, 238–9

Aikio, Inger-Mari: poetry of, 190–1, 197

Aikio, Jouni: 203

Aikio, Juhani: 236

Aikio, Marjut: 50

Aikio, Matti: *I dyreskind* (*In Deerskin*) (1906), 182

Aikio, Niilo: *Lieekejä pakoon: Saamelaiset evakossa 1944–1945* (Flight from the Flames: the Sámi evacuated 1944–1945), 63

Aikio, Samuli: *Olbmot ovdal min: Sámiid historjá 1700-logu rádjái* (People before us: the history of the Sami until the 18th century), 78

Aikio, Tiina: *Sámi váimmus* (*Lapland in my Heart*) (1995), 207

Ailekis Olmak: role in Sámi religious traditions, 82

Äimä, Frans: 183

Aira, Eva: 174

Ájtte: opening of (1989), 162

Akmeeli (shaman): 82–3

Alariesto, Andreas: background of, 171

Alariesto Museum: 171

alcoholism: 133–4; legal responses to, 134; suicide rates, 135; teetotalism, 134–5

Alexander II, Tsar: 42, 242

Alexander III, Tsar: reopening of Pechenga Monastery (1888), 115

Alexei II (Patriarch of All the Russias): 116

Alfred of Wessex: court of, 8–9

All-Russia Council for the National Economy: Northern Science Research Council, 250

Alstadius, Brita Kajsa: 110

d'Alviella, Albert Joseph: 153

d'Alviella, Count Goblet: 238; visit to Lapland (1868), 36, 124

INDEX

Pirak, Anta: *Jåhtte same viessom* (*A Reindeer Herdsman and his Life*) (1933), 186
Pirak, Lars: 172, 176; background of, 171; *Beive Niedia*, 172; *Doors Westward*, 176; *Reindeer Caravan Westward*, 176–7
Piras (Family, The): personnel of, 74
Pirtijäarvi, Ulla: 212
Pite Lappmark: 14; church construction in, 91
Piteå General Assembly: documents issued by, 12
Plakida, St Evstafii: patron saint of reindeer herding, 97
Pochesersky, M.: 145
Pohjantahti: 207
Polmak Church: first Sámi language radio broadcast (1936), 212
Ponoi Commune: Jokanga, 146, 232; Sosnovka, 146
Ponttoppidan, Erik: *Sandhed ti Gudfrygtighed* (Truth onto Godliness), 88; translation efforts of, 86
Porsanger, Biret-Ánde (Anders): death of, 90; dictionary compiled by, 90
Porsanger, Elena Sergeyevna: education of, 121–2
Pulsen, Anders: execution for sorcery (1692), 106
Prasnik Severa (Festival of the North): 74
Prokopios of Caesarea: 8
Putin, Vladimir: Russian President, 74

Quènes: cultural image of, 36
Qvigstad, Just Knud: *Bibliographie der Lappischen Literatur*, 179; writings of, 144

Radien-kidte (deity): role in Sámi religious pantheon, 82

Rae, Edward: 131, 135
Ramsay, Wilhelm: background of, 250
Rana-nieta (deity): role in Sámi religious pantheon, 8
Randulf, Johan: writings of, 143
Rangius, Lars: translation efforts of, 89
Rantala, Leif: 41, 60–1, 124, 129
Ranttila, Merja Aletta: 173; background of, 172; *Haavoittunut enkeli* (Wounded Angel, The), 172; *Sininen kettu* (Blue Fox), 172
Rasputin, Mikhail Ivanovich: 189; religious education of, 114
Rassy-aike (cult figure): 97
Ravila, Paavo Ilmari: co-editor of *Sabmelaš*, 184; studies of, 144
Rávgoš: productions staged by, 194
Reformation: 12–13, 106
reindeer: 6, 8, 31, 50, 52, 80, 83–4, 103–4, 125, 227, 255–6; association with Sámi in art, 14–16, 86, 165, 186; disease outbreaks amongst, 130–1; domestication of, 16, 216, 248; earmarks, 230; herding of, 4, 16, 19, 27, 30, 35, 37, 39, 41–5, 48, 51, 53, 59, 62, 64–7, 74, 76, 95, 97, 112, 130–1, 146, 153, 160–1, 168–9, 172, 184, 220, 223, 225, 227–35, 244, 248–9, 254, 256; hunting of, 5, 9–10, 22, 26, 139, 181, 189, 215–20, 225; in *kolkhoz*, 233–4; milking of, 13, 132, 230; pelts of, 9, 14; use in religious rituals, 80–1; *Vuopman*, 218
religious practices: 92, 152, 181; art associated with, 83–5; burial rituals, 120–1; church villages, 110; deities of, 80–3; depictions of, 172–3; *jápmináibmu*, 81; *Myanntasha* (ancestor cult), 103; *noaide/noaidi*, 103, 106, 108,

INDEX